Short-cut Demand Elasticities and Other Convenient Approaches to Consumer Demand

Kenneth W. Clements • Haiyan Liu
Marc Jim M. Mariano
Eliyathamby A. Selvanathan
Saroja Selvanathan • George Verikios

Short-cut Demand Elasticities and Other Convenient Approaches to Consumer Demand

Springer

Kenneth W. Clements
Department of Economics, Business School
University of Western Australia
Perth, WA, Australia

Haiyan Liu
Department of Economics, Business School
University of Western Australia
Perth, WA, Australia

Marc Jim M. Mariano
Commonwealth Scientific and Industrial Research Organisation
Dutton Park, QLD, Australia

Eliyathamby A. Selvanathan
Economics and Business Statistics Discipline, Department of Accounting Finance and Economics
Griffith University
Nathan, QLD, Australia

Saroja Selvanathan
Economics and Business Statistics Discipline, Department of Accounting Finance and Economics
Griffith University
Nathan, QLD, Australia

George Verikios
Department of Accounting, Finance and Economics
Griffith University
Nathan, QLD, Australia

ISBN 978-981-96-3587-0 ISBN 978-981-96-3588-7 (eBook)
https://doi.org/10.1007/978-981-96-3588-7

This Springer imprint is published by the registered company Springer Nature Singapore Pte Ltd.
The registered company address is: 152 Beach Road, #21-01/04 Gateway East, Singapore 189721, Singapore

Preface

This book is the culmination of a lengthy program of research collaboration among the co-authors on the application of the microeconomics of consumption theory to a number of applied problems. It soon became clear that our research necessitated the introduction of a number of simplifications, or amendments, to the theory to permit its use in many practical situations. We readily acknowledge we have drawn on the work of others in their earlier contributions to this area; in fact, in a number of instances we have been inspired by their work. Still, our work and its style provide a framework useful in guiding those wanting to learn about applied demand analysis, and a source for elasticities required by researchers for their own work.

In completing the book, we are greatly indebted to a large number of individuals and to our institutions. For their help and support, we thank Mohammad Farhad, Grace Gao, Kevin Hanslow, Izan, Yihui Lan, Garry Li, Andrew Luo, Chengcai Luo, Michael McLure, Ranjan Ray, Brendan Rynne, Jiawei Si, Tom Simpson, Lee Tate, Sebastian Tofts-Len, Long Vo, Vu Vuong, and Berwyn Wong. Ken Clements and Haiyan Liu thank the University of Western Australia for providing a conducive research environment. Clements also acknowledges the financial support of the ARC and BHP. Marc Mariano and George Verikios thank CSIRO, Griffith University, and KPMG for their support. Saroja Selvanathan and Selva Selvanathan acknowledge the support of Griffith University.

We have also benefitted from comments and suggestions received from participants at a number of seminars and conferences. Much of our work has also been "road-tested" on students and colleagues at Griffith University and the University of Western Australia, and we appreciate their interest and suggestions. Kym Anderson, Paul Burke, Peter Dixon, David Gruen and Thomas Hertel provided generous endorsements of the book, for which we are grateful.

Parts of the book draw on earlier renditions of our work published in the *American Journal of Agricultural Economics*, *Applied Economics*, *Economic Analysis and Policy*, *Economic Letters*, *Economic Modelling*, *Economic Record*, *European Economic Review*, and *Journal of Business*. We thank the editors and referees of these journals for their comments, assistance, and patience.

At Springer, Anushangi Weerakoon, Editor – Business, Economics, Law and Politics, and Ramya Prakash, Production Editor (Books), have been most helpful in dealing with our publisher.

Synopsis

Almost always at some point, analysts need to know about the determinants of consumption, the elasticities of demand. This book provides answers with a unique two-track approach. The first gives a self-contained, non-technical rendition, accessible to those with limited background. The second track contains the underlying theory, derivations, and some more advanced material. Subsequent chapters deal with the demand for food and other groups of goods, the system-wide approach to demand analysis, and the formulation of the demand side of equilibrium displacement and CGE models, including applications. This convenient source book, covering most major topics of this important part of the work of practitioners, will be valuable to students, consultants, business economists, and government policy analysts. Clarity of exposition and economic intuition is emphasised throughout.

Perth and Brisbane, Australia
January 2025

Kenneth W. Clements
Haiyan Liu
Marc Jim M. Mariano
Eliyathamby A. Selvanathan
Saroja Selvanathan
George Verikios

Competing Interests The authors have no competing interests to declare that are relevant to the content of this manuscript.

Testimonials

Understanding market demand and supply behaviour is fundamental for both business managers and government policymakers. This book is for empirical analysts seeking practical ways to estimate the likely responsiveness of buyers to changes in such things as prices and consumer incomes. Its illustrations range from individual food and beverage demands to product group demands and ultimately to economy-wide systemic approaches. No one is better placed than this set of authors to tackle these topics, as each of them has been pushing this intellectual frontier and testing it with their students for several decades. This masterful book allows the rest of us to also be beneficiaries of this collective endeavour.

Kym Anderson AC, Executive Director, Wine Economics Research Centre; CEPR Research Fellow; George Gollin Professor Emeritus, School of Economics and Public Policy, University of Adelaide; and Honorary Professor of Economics, Arndt-Corden Dept of Economics, Australian National University

There is an enormous wealth of information in this book about demand elasticities. The material is easily accessible and should appeal to readers who are interested in a quick overview of this by now voluminous field, to those who are interested in its intellectual history as well as to those who wish to delve more deeply.

David Gruen AO, Australian Statistician, Australian Bureau of Statistics

Contents

List of Figures

List of Tables

About the Authors

Kenneth Clements has been at the University of Western Australia since 1981 as Professor of Economics and Emeritus Professor. He has a PhD from the University of Chicago and has expertise in international finance, monetary economics, and applied microeconomics. His research has been supported by a series of grants from BHP and the Australian Research Council and has been published in the *American Journal of Agricultural Economics*, *Journal of Business*, *Marketing Science*, *Health Economics*, *European Economic Review*, *International Economic Review*, and *Journal of Business and Economic Statistics*, among others. Cambridge University Press published two of Ken's books *Economics and Marijuana* (with Xueyan Zhao) and *Currencies, Commodities and Consumption*. He is Distinguished Fellow of the Economic Society and Fellow of the Academy of Social Sciences in Australia; received the *Austin Holmes Award* from the WA Branch of the Economic Society of Australia; and was awarded a *Citation* for *Outstanding Contributions to Student Learning* from the Australian Learning and Teaching Council.

Haiyan Liu is Senior Economic Forecaster at the Department of Planning, Lands and Heritage (DPLH) in West Australia (WA). Her work involves modelling for land-use forecasting and the integration of land-use and transport models. Before joining DPLH, Haiyan held the positions of Analyst in the Energy Markets Division at the WA Economic Regulation Authority and Transport Modeller at the WA Department of Transport. She has experience in monitoring the wholesale electricity market and the economic evaluation of infrastructure projects. With a background in electrical engineering, Haiyan worked at the East China Architectural Design and Research Institute on major projects before moving to Australia. She graduated from the University of Western Australia (PhD and Master's) and Tongji University (Bachelors). Her research interest is the application of economic modelling to inform policy and other decision-making and has published in *Applied Economics*.

Marc Jim M. Mariano is Senior Research Scientist at the Commonwealth Scientific and Industrial Research Organisation (CSIRO, Australia). His work involves the development of state-of-the-art computable general equilibrium (CGE) models, and their application in economic impact assessment of industry projects and government policies at the regional, state, and national levels. Before joining CSIRO, Marc was Associate Director at KPMG where he provided advisory services to private and public clients based on advanced economic modelling. He has taught at the University of the Philippines and was a research economist at the Philippine Rice Research Institute. Marc has published a number of journal articles. His research interests include economy-wide modelling, climate change analysis, circular economy, energy transitions, consumer demand models, and household distributional analysis. Marc graduated from Monash University (PhD), the University of New England (Master's), and the University of the Philippines Los Banos (Bachelor's). He has received several scholarships including the *Australian Leadership Award* from AusAID, the *Dean's Postgraduate Research Excellence Award, Donald Cochrane Postgraduate Research Scholarship, and International Postgraduate Research Scholarship* from Monash University. Marc was awarded the *Best Master's Thesis Award* from the Australian Agricultural and Resource Economics Society and was recognised as an *Outstanding R&D Staff* at the Philippine Rice Research Institute.

Eliyathamby Antony Selvanathan is the Director of the Economics Policy Analysis Program (EPAP) and Professor of Econometrics at Griffith University, Queensland, Australia. He has also taught previously at the University of Jaffna (Sri Lanka), Murdoch University (Australia), and the University of Western Australia. Selva was educated at the University of Jaffna, the University of Bucharest (Romania), Murdoch University, and the University of Western Australia. He is one of the authors of the best-selling textbook in Australasia, *Business Statistics*, published by Cengage, currently in the eighth edition. His interests include applied econometrics, tourism economics, consumer demand models, and stochastic index numbers. He has published nine research monographs and well over 100 articles in journals such as *Review of Economic Studies*, *Journal of Econometrics*, *Journal of Business and Economic Statistics*, *Review of Economics and Statistics*, *Energy Economics*, *Journal of Travel Research*, and *Tourism Economics*. Selva has received several research and teaching awards, including the *Minister's Awards for Outstanding Contribution to Improving Literacy and/or Numeracy – Queensland state winner, Pro-Vice Chancellor's Excellence in Research Award (Research Supervision), Griffith Awards for Excellence in Teaching – Innovation Across the Institution, STARDS group*, and the *Inaugural University of Western Australia 75th Anniversary* Distinguished *Teaching Award.*

Saroja Selvanathan is Professor of Econometrics at Griffith University, Queensland, Australia, and Co-Editor-in-Chief of the *Journal of the Asia Pacific Economy.* She has also taught previously at the University of Jaffna (Sri Lanka), Murdoch University (Australia), and the University of Western Australia. Saroja was educated at the University of Jaffna, Murdoch University, and the University of Western Australia. Her research interests include consumer demand, time series analysis, tourism economics, and applied econometrics. She has published seven research monographs and over 100 journal articles plus book chapters. Saroja's publications have appeared in journals such as *Review of Economics and Statistics*, *Energy Economics*, *Resource Economics*, *Australian Journal of Agricultural Economics*, *Economic Modelling*, *Journal of Travel Research*, *Applied Economics*, *Tourism Analysis*, and *Tourism Economics*. She is a co-author of the Australian best-selling textbook, *Business Statistics*, published by Cengage, currently in the eighth edition. Saroja has received several university-wide research and *teaching* awards, including the *Vice Chancellor's Excellence in Research Award (Research Supervision)*, *Griffith Awards for Excellence in Teaching – Group Learning and Teaching Citation*, and *Griffith Awards for Excellence in Teaching – Innovation Across the Institution*, STARDS group.

George Verikios is Integrated Assessment Modelling Lead at the Commonwealth Scientific and Industrial Research Organisation (CSIRO, Australia) and Adjunct Professor of Economics at Griffith University. He is an expert in economic modelling and has built, overseen, and contributed to the development of many global and national economic models, and their application to the evaluation of diverse topics such as the economics of climate change, pandemic outbreaks, the circular economy, tax policy, trade liberalisation, and income distribution. George has consulting, research, and training experience in the university and public and private sectors. He has published over 30 articles in journals such as *Economic Modelling*, *The World Economy*, *Applied Economics*, *Australian Journal of Agricultural Economics*, *Journal of Asia Pacific Economy*, *Socio-Economic Planning Sciences*, *Journal of Cleaner Production*, and *Economic Record*.

Chapter 1
Introduction

1.1 User's Guide to Demand Elasticities

Suppose you are an analyst at a public-policy think tank tasked with investigating the effects of legalisation of marijuana. It is likely that the price would drop substantially, the consumption of substitutes such as alcohol and tobacco would fall, and marijuana would increase according to the law of demand. But by how much? What happens to the size of the industry? Could legalised marijuana be an attractive source of tax revenue to the government, or should it be taxed solely to curb overconsumption? What is needed is a measure of the sensitivity of consumption to variations in the price of the good, the price elasticity of demand, the percentage change in consumption following a 1% price change. There might be some information available on prices, but this could be of dubious quality, especially if it came from unreliable underground sources. Worse still, there is likely to be no information available on the quantity consumed, making estimation of the elasticity by econometric methods out of the question. There may be prior estimates from other jurisdictions, but you may have doubts about the transferability and/or reliability of those.

The approach we use starts with the quantity demanded of each good, dependent on the consumer's income and prices, the demand functions. These quantities represent the consumer's optimal choice, where "optimal" is given content by supposing the consumer maximises utility subject to a budget constraint. Utility is characterised by a function that satisfies certain mild economic properties. One important property is diminishing marginal utility—the consumer gains additional utility from an additional unit of each good, but the valuation declines with increasing consumption. This is nothing more than the conventional microeconomics of the utility-maximising consumer. But there is an important difference. We make it more immediately useful for the purpose of obtaining numerical values of demand elasticities by emphasising specificity and less generality.

K. W. Clements et al., *Short-cut Demand Elasticities and Other Convenient Approaches to Consumer Demand*, https://doi.org/10.1007/978-981-96-3588-7_1

This book helps answer the questions faced by the marijuana analyst by providing a number of possible ways to obtain plausible price elasticities when information is lacking. The first is the rule of one-half: For broad commodities with few substitutes, set the price elasticity to $-½$. This rule seems to hold for several major commodities including alcoholic beverages, cigarettes, water, petrol, and electricity. This is appropriate when the good forms an independent group in the consumer's utility function. There is, of course, a precise meaning to the term "independent group", which is set out in Chaps. 2 and 3. The rule has wide applicability as a rule of thumb and/or a quick, first-pass elasticity. Although the structure of the utility function is special, the rule of ½ is consistent with the analytic approach of utility maximisation.

Food warrants a prominent place in consumption economics. For a start, food is essential to sustain life. Moreover, it is mostly consumed several times a day and for many consumers, especially the poorer ones, food is the most important single item of expenditure. Chapters 4 and 5 deal with key elements of food demand, Engel's law (the share of income devoted to food falls with enhanced affluence), food demand elasticities, diet diversity, and the measurement of the quality of food consumption.

The book introduces the important topic of systems of demand equations as a practical way to implement utility-maximisation theory to deal with the simultaneous demand for all goods. Here, each good (and service) in the consumer's budget has its own demand equation, but these equations are related to one another. Cross-equation links derive from three sources, the first being the budget constraint. Since total expenditure is controlled for by taking it to be fixed, more spent on one good means less spent on at least one other. This is the adding-up constraint. Economic theory is the second source of interrelationships of the demand equations. As wine and beer are likely to be substitutes, a rise in wine prices will cause the consumer to economise on drinking wine by switching to beer. A prediction of the theory is that the impact of a one-dollar increase in the price of a bottle of wine on beer consumption is the same effect as a one-dollar rise in the cost of a bottle of beer on wine consumption, when the consumer's real income remains unchanged. In other words, the cross-price effects are symmetric. This interrelationship is known as symmetry of the substitution effects, or Slutsky symmetry, named after the Russian economist Eugene Slutsky (1915).

If alcoholic beverages (made up of beer, wine, and spirits) are treated as a group that at the margin the consumer values as being independent of, say, the meats group, then this structure of preferences leads to a further source of cross-equation constraints. To account for these constraints, the demand for the n goods in the budget needs to be treated as a whole, as a system of equations. This is known as the system-wide approach to demand analysis. Chapters 6 and 7 deal with this approach and highlights simplifications of the complex interrelationships among goods that are useful in practice. Several prominent demand systems are presented along with an assessment of their strengths and weaknesses. Index numbers are an efficient way of summarising considerable amounts of information. An example is the consumer price index (CPI), which is a popular gauge of inflation. The CPI involves the combination of a large number of prices of individual goods and services into one number, the value of the index. By aggregating the diverse prices into a single number, the CPI represents a valuable simplification, or short cut, to understanding the economy. The close link between index numbers and demand equations is also discussed in Chaps. 6 and 7.

Frequently, interest centres on a certain group of goods, rather than all those in the consumer's budget. An example is the group comprising the three alcoholic beverages mentioned above. We might be interested in the impact of alcohol taxes on drinking patterns and market shares of beer, wine, and spirits resulting from substituting away from higher-taxed beverages to lower-taxed ones. To quantify this effect we need values of the price elasticities. Further, we may wish to know the implications of extending the group by adding marijuana, a related good, to alcoholic beverages. Meat (beef, pork, lamb, and chicken) is another example of a group of goods that could be analysed in a similar manner.

The demand for a group of goods as a whole and the demands for goods belonging to the group constitute a manageable way of focusing attention on the group in question without the need to be concerned with goods outside the group. Hence, here again is a substantial simplification of demand theory that is valuable in practice. The book, in Chaps. 8 and 9, sets out this approach and illustrates with a specific case of the alcoholic beverages group.

Computable general equilibrium (CGE) models are widely used in academia as well as by economic consultants around the world. This vibrant area of research involves a comprehensive set of equations that encompass the whole economy. These models include the economic behaviour of consumers in purchasing goods and supplying labour, business in demanding intermediate and primary factors to produce final foods, and government in levying taxes and providing goods and services, as well as income support. Constructing these models is a major effort and should be considered a substantial achievement of applied economics. CGE models are an intensive user of demand elasticities for the consumer component of the models and other parts such as intermediate demands. Obviously, the implementation of large CGE models necessitates the underlying demand theory to be structured, that is, simplified. But the world-wide success of CGE models attests to such simplifications being worthwhile.

Equilibrium displacement models (EDMs) deal with a single sector (or industry) of the economy and treat the other parts as given. These models, which can be thought of partial-equilibrium CGE models, also need demand elasticities. Chapters 10 and 11 describe the use of demand elasticities in CGE models and EDM.

1.2 Nature of the Book

A key guiding principle of the book is simplification of the underlying demand theory, and related areas, in order to make things more immediately applicable in practice involving quantification. To analyse the impact of price changes on the demand for each good in an *n*-good budget requires the value of own- and across-price elasticities. These can be arranged in a matrix dimensioned $n \times n$, containing n^2 elements. For $n = 10$, for example, there are 100 elasticities to be determined. Without further structure on the problem, it would usually be impossible to obtain reliable econometric estimates of such a large number of parameters. The book shows how to usefully simplify matters to provide short-cut elasticities, making the problem at hand manageable. The underlying theory is used in specialised form, avoiding abstraction, generality, and complexity, thereby making the theory useful for practical applications.

The approach is consistent with Occam's razor, the principle of parsimony of trimming inconsequential matters, thereby keeping things simple but not simplistic. This is similar to what Zellner (2002) calls the KISS principle, not "keep it simple stupid" but "keep it *sophisticatedly* simple". Reflection on some of the big ideas in science (of which economics is part) reveals that this is not a contradiction in terms. In support of his approach, Zellner reports:

> …for many years, I have challenged many audiences to give me an example of a large, complex model in any field that works well in explaining past data and experience and in predicting new data. As yet, I have not heard of a single one.

Most of the material in the book is presented in a two-prong, or two-track, format. The first is non-technical, emphasising intuition, numerical examples, and applications. This self-contained exposition is designed for the reader wanting an introduction to the subject. For those wanting to delve deeper, the second prong gives details, including derivations, references to the prior literature and in some cases, additional results.

1.3 Previous Literature

There is a rich history of previous research dealing with the subject matter of the book and here we can only touch on those studies that are particularly prominent.

The law of demand, the negative relation between the price and quantity demanded of a good, has a long history going back at least as far as the late 1600s with the work of King and Davenant on the demand for wheat, as discussed by Evans (1967) and Stigler (1954). Stigler (1954) also contains a brief review of the subsequent history of the law of demand. Engel (1857) is a landmark paper on the relation between household expenditure patterns and income. A strong regularity is the fall in the share of expenditure devoted to food when the consumer's affluence rises, now known as Engel's law. The law has been verified so many times that it is one of the strongest of all economic laws. Houthakker (1957) is a widely cited source regarding the applicability of Engel's law.

Advances to make utility-maximising theory of consumer demand more operational for the econometric application of systems of demand functions include Stone (1954), Frisch (1959), Houthakker (1960), Barten (1964, 1967), and Theil (1965, 1967). There is a substantial literature in this area that has been reviewed by Brown and Deaton (1972), Powell (1974), Theil (1975/76, 1980), Barten (1977), Deaton and Muellbauer (1980), Bewley (1986), Deaton (1986), Goldberger (1987), Pollak and Wales (1992), and Wohlgenant (2021).

Comparing consumption patterns in different countries reveals substantial differences in going from the poorest African to the most affluent northern European countries. The dispersion of these data make it attractive for the application of demand systems. In-depth studies of international consumption patterns include Houthakker (1957), Goldberger and Gamaletsos (1970), Lluch and Powell (1975), Lluch et al. (1977), Theil et al. (1981), Theil and Clements (1987), Theil et al. (1989), Rimmer and Powell (1992), Selvanathan (1993), Chen (1999), Seale et al. (2003), Selvanathan and Selvanathan (2003), Seale and Regmi (2006), Regmi and Seale (2010), Muhammad et al. (2011), Gao (2012), and Liu (2018). The majority of these studies use the data from the International Comparisons Program (ICP) of the World Bank (n. d.). The ICP data are an invaluable research resource pertaining to the national accounts for a large number of countries, constructed on a consistent basis enabling direct comparisons across countries.

Important early work on the demand for groups of goods and within-group demands includes Leontief (1947a, b), Strotz (1957), Gorman (1959, 1968), Sono (1961), Barten and Turnovsky (1966), and Theil (1975/76). Pollak (1969) provides some related material, while Deaton and Muellbauer (1980) survey the area.

A popular application of demand elasticities is in CGE models. CGE models are a comprehensive representation of the whole economy, capturing the activity and behaviour of various economic agents such as households, firms, the government, and foreigners. One thing in common among these agents is that their behaviour is governed by price-responsive demand and supply functions. The strength of behavioural responses to relative prices is measured by the magnitude of price and income elasticities. The calibration of these elasticities, together with input-output coefficients, allows the models to be numerically solved, hence the name "computable" general equilibrium. CGE models answer questions like: How much demand for a commodity is affected by relative price changes? What is the change in quantity demanded for a one-dollar increase in income? How much more labour-hours are supplied when wages increase by 1%? In the CGE approach, these questions are addressed by taking into account the feedback effects on the rest of the economy. By contrast, the partial-equilibrium approach omits feedback and considers the direct effects only.

The parametrisation of the demand and supply functions has been a challenge among CGE modellers as this requires intensive econometric estimation. Availability of these parameters has been limited, especially for less developed countries, due to the lack of suitable data for econometric modelling. This obstacle is beginning to disappear as data are now published more frequently in many countries. In this book we illustrate in Chaps. 10 and 11 the use of microeconomic theory to estimate the required elasticities and how to incorporate them in an Australian CGE model. This includes the Armington (1969) price elasticities of import-domestic product substitution, the price and income elasticities of household demand, derived from the linear expenditure system, and the CES price elasticities of intermediate input substitution. Although the parameters are estimated using Australia data, our approach can be readily applied to other countries.

In economic impact assessments, CGE models are the successor of input-output (IO) models as established by Wassily Leontief (1936, 1941). Linear IO models were used extensively in the 1950s providing static multiplier coefficients to derive estimates of the total response of the economy as a result of some specified event, policy, or activity. IO models were then later extended to a social accounting matrix framework to include other economic agents such as households and government. In the 1960s, the increased efficiency of computing programs paved the way for solving linear programming (LP) models that introduced into the analysis optimisation theory and the allowance for price effects. The 1970s saw the development of more complex CGE models with early work on non-linearities of behavioural responses. CGE models are thus a natural outgrowth of the IO and LP models. In relation to IO models, CGE models are more general in that they capture not only inter-industry linkages, but also other linkages arising from economy-wide constraints (e.g. resource constraints, budget constraints, foreign exchange, etc.), substitution possibilities between commodities as driven by price changes, and ripple effects throughout the entire economy. Relative to LP models, CGE models incorporate neoclassical substitutability in production and demand, explicit specification of market prices, and detailed treatment of income flows in the economy. They also impose a Walrasian competitive equilibrium, where agents are price takers who maximise profits or utility and prices freely adjust to clear all markets.

The advances in solution techniques had led to the growth of CGE applications. Prominent computational approaches include the pioneering works of Scarf and co-authors (Scarf and Hansen 1973; Scarf and Shoven 1983), Adelman and Robinson (1978), and Johansen (1960). Scarf's approach involves a fixed-point algorithm where the model is solved by finding a fixed point in a mapping of prices through excess demand equations. Early applications of this approach were on tax policy experiments (Scarf and Hansen 1973; Scarf and Shoven 1983; Shoven and Whalley 1984). A second approach is the application of numerical solution techniques to solve a particular system of non-linear equations (Adelman and Robinson 1978). Another approach is the linearisation of the equations system and then approximating the solution through matrix inversion. This linear approximation technique was first applied by Johansen (1960) in his model of Norway and has been used extensively in Australia with the ORANI and MONASH models (Dixon et al. 1982; Dixon et al. 1992) and related developments. Other alternative programming techniques to solve CGE models are described in Ginsburgh and Waelbroeck (1981).

CGE modelling has become an established field with many applications around the world. It has evolved in various ways based on advances in geographical coverage, theoretical developments, database calibration and parametrisation, and cutting-edge applications. Many countries have their own single-country models; Dixon and Jorgenson (2013) provide references to these national models. There are also a number of multi-country CGE models used for the analysis of major global issues such as climate change, international trade, immigration, and food security, among others. Examples of these include the GTAP model of Purdue University (Hertel 2013), GTEM model of CSIRO (Cai and Arora 2015), and the ENVISAGE and LINKAGE models of the World Bank (van der Mensbrugghe 2011) and G-Cubed of McKibbin and Wilcoxen (2013).

References

Adelman I, Robinson S (1978) Income distribution policy in developing countries: a case study of Korea. Stanford University Press, Stanford, CA

Armington PS (1969) A theory of demand for products distinguished by place of production. IMF Staff Pap 16(1):159–178

Barten AP (1964) Consumer demand functions under conditions of almost additive preferences. Econometrica 32:1–38

Barten AP (1967) Evidence on the Slutsky conditions for demand equations. Review of Economic and Statistics 1:77–84

Barten AP (1977) The systems of consumer demand functions approach: a review. Econometrica 45:23–51

Barten AP, Turnovsky SJ (1966) Some aspects of the aggregation problem for composite demand equations. Int Econ Rev 7:231–259

Bewley RA (1986) Allocation models: specification, estimation and applications. Ballinger Publishing Co, Cambridge MA

Brown JAC, Deaton AS (1972) Models of consumer behaviour: a survey. Econ J 82:1145–1236

Cai Y, Arora V (2015) Disaggregating electricity generation technologies in CGE models: a revised technology bundle approach with an application to the U.S. clean power plan. Appl Energy 154: 543–555

Chen DL (1999) World consumption economics. World Scientific, Singapore

Deaton AS (1986) Demand analysis. In: Griliches Z, Intriligator MD (eds) Handbook of econometrics. Volume III. North-Holland, Amsterdam, pp 1768–1839

Deaton AS, Muellbauer J (1980) Economics and consumer behaviour. Cambridge University Press, Cambridge

Dixon PB, Jorgenson D (2013) Handbook of CGE modeling. Amsterdam: North Holland 1:995–1068

Dixon PB, Parmenter BR, Powell AA, Wilcoxen PJ (1992) Notes and problems in applied general equilibrium economics. North-Holland, Amsterdam

Dixon PB, Parmenter BR, Sutton J, Vincent DP (1982) ORANI: a multisectoral model of the Australian economy. North-Holland, Amsterdam

Engel E (1857) Die Produktions- und Consumptionsverhaltnisse des Konigreichs Sachsen. Reprinted in Engel's Die Lebenskosten belgischer Atbeiter-Familien. Dresden, 1895. ["The Production and Consumption Conditions of the Kingdom of Saxony"]

Evans GH (1967) The law of demand–the roles of gregory king and charles davenant. Q J Econ 81: 483–492

Frisch R (1959) A complete scheme for computing all direct and cross demand elasticities in a model with many sectors. Econometrica 27:177–196

Gao G (2012) World food demand. Am J Agric Econ 94:25–51

Ginsburgh V, Waelbroeck J (1981) Activity analysis and general equilibrium modelling. North-Holland, Amsterdam

Goldberger AS (1987) Functional form and utility: a review of consumer demand theory. Westview Press, Boulder and London

Goldberger AS, Gamaletsos T (1970) A cross-country comparison of consumer expenditure patterns. European Economic Review 1 1:357–400

Gorman WM (1959) Separability utility and aggregation. Econometrica 27:469–481
Gorman WM (1968) Conditions for additive Separability. Econometrica 36:605–609
Hertel T (2013) Global applied general equilibrium analysis using the global trade analysis project framework. In: Dixon PB, Jorgenson D (eds) Handbook of CGE modeling, vol 1. North Holland, Amsterdam, pp 815–876
Houthakker HS (1957) An international comparison of household expenditure patterns, commemorating the centenary of Engel's law. Econometrica 25:532–551
Houthakker HS (1960) Additive preferences. Econometrica 28:244–257
Johansen L (1960) A multisectoral study of economic growth. North-Holland, Amsterdam
Leontief WW (1936) Quantitative input-output relations in the economic system of the United States. Rev Econ Stat 18:105–125
Leontief WW (1941) The structure of the American economy 1919–1929. Harvard University Press, Cambridge, MA
Leontief WW (1947a) A note on the interrelationship of subsets of independent variables of a continuous function with continuous first derivatives. Bull Am Math Soc 53:343–350
Leontief WW (1947b) Introduction to a theory of the internal structure of functional relationships. Econometrica 15:361–373
Liu H (2018) Cross-country food consumption patterns: theory and measurement. PhD thesis,. The University of Western Australia
Lluch C, Powell AA (1975) International comparisons of expenditure patterns. Eur Econ Rev 6: 375–403
Lluch C, Powell AA, Williams RA (1977) Patterns in household demand and savings. Oxford University Press, Oxford
McKibbin WJ, Wilcoxen PJ (2013) A global approach to energy and the environment: the G-cubed model. In: Dixon PB, Jorgenson D (eds) Handbook of CGE modeling, vol 1. North Holland, Amsterdam, pp 995–1068
Muhammad A, Seale JL Jr, Meade B, Regmi A (2011) International evidence on food consumption patterns: an update using 2005 international comparison program data. In: Technical bulletin 1929. Economic research service. United States Department of Agriculture. Revised 2013
Pollak RA (1969) Conditional demand functions and consumption theory. Q J Econ 83:60–78
Pollak RA, Wales TJ (1992) Demand system specification and estimation. Oxford University Press, New York and Oxford
Powell AA (1974) Empirical analytics of demand systems. DC Heath, Lexington MA
Regmi A, Seale JL (2010) Cross-price elasticities of demand across 114 countries. Technical Bulletin No. 1925, Economic Research Service, United States Department of Agriculture
Rimmer MT, Powell AA (1992) Demand patterns across the development Spectrum: estimates for the AIDADS system. In: Preliminary working paper no. OP–75, Centre of Policy Studies and Impact Project. Monash University
Scarf HE, Hansen T (1973) The computation of economic equilibria. Yale University Press, New Haven, CT
Scarf HE, Shoven JB (1983) Applied general equilibrium analysis. Cambridge University Press, New York
Seale JL, Regmi A (2006) Modelling international consumption patterns. Rev Income Wealth 52: 603–624
Seale JL, Regmi A, Bernstein J (2003) International evidence on food consumption patterns. In: Technical bulletin 1904. Economic Research Service. United States Department of Agriculture, Washington, D.C.
Selvanathan S (1993) A system-wide analysis of international consumption patterns. Kluwer, Boston
Selvanathan S, Selvanathan EA (2003) International consumption patterns: OECD versus LDC. World Scientific, Singapore
Shoven JB, Whalley J (1984) Applied general-equilibrium models of taxation and international trade: an introduction and survey. J Econ Lit 22:1007–1051

Slutsky E (1915) Sulla Teoria del Bilancio del Consumatore. Giornale degli Economisti 51:1–26. ["On the Theory of the Consumer's Budget"]

Sono M (1961) The effect of price changes on the demand and supply of separable goods. Int Econ Rev 2:239–271

Stigler GJ (1954) The early history of empirical studies in consumer behavior. J Polit Econ 62:95–113

Stone R (1954) Linear expenditure systems and demand analysis: an application to the pattern of British demand. Econ J 64:511–527

Strotz RH (1957) The empirical implications of a utility tree. Econometrica 27:269–280

Theil H (1965) The information approach to demand analysis. Econometrica 33:67–87

Theil H (1967) Economics and information theory. North-Holland and Rand McNally, Amsterdam and Chicago

Theil H (1975/76) Theory and measurement of consumer demand. Two volumes. North-Holland, Amsterdam

Theil H (1980) The system-wide approach to microeconomics. The University of Chicago Press, Chicago

Theil H, Chung C-F, Seale JL (1989) International evidence on consumption patterns. JAI Press, Greenwich, Connecticut

Theil H, Clements KW (1987) Applied demand analysis: results from system-wide approaches. Ballinger, Cambridge, MA

Theil H, Suhm FE, Meisner JF (1981) International consumption comparisons: a system-wide approach. North-Holland, Amsterdam

van der Mensbrugghe D (2011) LINKAGE technical reference document: version 7.1. The World Bank, Washington, DC

Wohlgenant MK (2021) Market interrelationships and applied demand analysis. Springer International Publishing

World Bank (n.d.) International comparison program. https://www.worldbank.org/en/programs/icp

Zellner A (2002) Keep it sophisticatedly simple. In: Zellner A, Keuzenkamp HA, McAleer M (eds) Simplicity, Inference and modelling. Cambridge University Press, Cambridge, pp 242–262

Chapter 2
Demand Elasticities Simplified I: Main Results

This chapter suggests the rule of thumb that price elasticities are $-½$. The presentation is self-contained, covering motivations for the rule, key aspects of the underlying theory, interpretations, and evidence. There are minimal formalities and few, if any, references to the literature. The subsequent chapter is for readers who require full details, formalities, justifications, and references, as well as the sources of material covered by the two chapters.

2.1 The Importance of Price Elasticities

It is no exaggeration to say that the price sensitivity of demand for a good is at the heart of many, perhaps most, issues in applied microeconomics. To take a stylised example, consider the world market for cereals. Suppose the income elasticity of cereal demand is 0.5 and income grows at 6% per annum, implying growth in consumption of $0.5 \times \log \frac{106}{100} = 0.029$, or about 3% on account of income. Allowing for changes in the price, growth is $0.5 \times \log \frac{106}{100} + \eta \Delta \log p$, where $\eta < 0$ is the price elasticity and $\Delta \log p$ is the growth in the relative price. If, for simplicity, the supply of the good is fixed and the market clears each year, the change in the price, for various values of the price elasticity, is:

$$\Delta \log p = -\frac{0.5 \times \log\frac{106}{100}}{\eta} = -\frac{0.029}{\eta} = \begin{cases} 0.039, \text{if } \eta = -0.75 \\ 0.058, \text{if } \eta = -0.50 \\ 0.117, \text{if } \eta = -0.25. \end{cases}$$

The price change is inversely proportional to the value of $-\eta$, so that when the elasticity is -0.75, income growth causes the price to rise by about 4%, but when demand is more inelastic and $\eta = -0.25$, the price rises by three times more to a bit

K. W. Clements et al., *Short-cut Demand Elasticities and Other Convenient Approaches to Consumer Demand*, https://doi.org/10.1007/978-981-96-3588-7_2

over 12%. The more inelastic the demand, the more the price has to rise to compensate for the income growth. The value of the price elasticity is key.

When we cannot place sufficient confidence in the available elasticity estimates, what value should be used? Or what if there are no data and it is simply impossible to estimate the elasticity, as in the case of the demand for an illegal good such as marijuana in many jurisdictions? A popular approach is to use a Cobb-Douglas utility function, which implies price elasticities of -1. For many broad aggregates (such as food, clothing, and housing) this is likely to overstate the degree of substitution. As the price elasticity reflects the availability of substitutes, it would seem likely for goods that are not too finely defined substitution is limited and the elasticity low. For these goods, a case can be made to set the price elasticity to $-½$, which we call the rule of ½. This case rests on the evidence from prior estimates and analytical considerations.

Relatedly, in a widely cited survey, Dawkins et al. (2001, p. 3690) discuss "calibrated" computable general equilibrium models, where the elasticities come from a number of sources external to the model, and they reveal one such source is the:

> "idiot's law of elasticities" where all elasticities are one until someone shows them to be otherwise, or "coffee-table elasticities" where informal discussions and opinions around the coffee table determine whether a value of, say, 0.5 or 2.0 is chosen.

In this chapter we show the choice of 0.5 for price elasticities of demand has more than a mere coffee-table pedigree.

2.2 Demand Equations

Consumption theory deals with the determinants of the demand for n goods. Let $q_1, \cdots, q_n$ denote the quantities consumed of each of these goods and $p_1, \cdots, p_n$ be the corresponding prices. Then, $p_i q_i$ is expenditure on good i and $\sum_{i=1}^{n} p_i q_i$ is total expenditure, to be denoted by M and referred to as "income" for short. Taking prices and income as given, the consumer chooses the bundle of goods $q_1, \cdots, q_n$ to maximise utility subject to the available resources as measured by M. The objective function to be maximised is the consumer's utility function $u(q_1, \cdots, q_n)$, in which the marginal utility of each good, $\frac{\partial u}{\partial q_i}, i = 1, \cdots, n,$ is positive. This constrained maximisation problem leads to the demand functions

$$q_i = q_i(M, p_1, \cdots, p_n), \quad i = 1, \cdots, n.$$

Hence, consumption of good i is a function of income and prices.

A key property of the demand equations is the income and price sensitivity of consumption of each good. The income sensitivity of good i is measured by its income elasticity, defined as $\eta_i = \frac{\partial \log q_i}{\partial \log M}$. Bearing in mind that for $x > 0$, $d \log x = \frac{dx}{x}$, this η_i is the percentage change in the quantity demanded of good i following a 1-per cent change in income. Similarly, the own-price sensitivity is $\eta_{ii} = \frac{\partial \log q_i}{\partial \log p_i}$, the percentage change in q_i per unit percentage change in the price of the good p_i. The cross-price sensitivity is η_{ij}, $i \neq j$. Elasticities are unit free and can be compared across goods with different units of measurement such as beer (measured in terms of litres) and rice (grams).

The logarithmic differential of the demand equations is

$$d\log q_i = \eta_i d\log M + \sum_{j=1}^{n} \eta_{ij} d\log p_j, \quad i = 1, \cdots, n. \tag{2.1}$$

Here, the (logarithmic) change in demand for good i is a weighted sum of the change in income and the prices, where the weights are the corresponding elasticities η_i and η_{ij}. The weight attached to the jth price change in the ith equation is η_{ij}, and can be referred to as the $(i,j)^{th}$ price elasticity for $i, j = 1, \cdots, n$. Goods with an income elasticity $\eta_i > 1$ grow faster than income and are known as "luxuries", and those with $\eta_i < 1$ are "necessities". Not all goods can be luxuries, nor can they all be necessities: A weighted average of the income elasticities is unity. Usually, the main concern regarding price elasticities is with the value of own-price elasticity η_{ii}. The law of demand says $\eta_{ii} < 0$, so consumption of the good falls when its price rises. Frequently, the cross-price elasticity $\eta_{ij} > 0$ and in such a case, an increase in the price of j shifts consumption away from good j (as $\eta_{jj} < 0$) to good i. Goods i and j then satisfy the same want, at least to a certain extent; they compete with one another and are said to be "substitutes". The two goods are "complements" when $\eta_{ij} < 0$.

2.3 A Simplification

The demand Eqs. (2.1) are general, but generality comes with a cost, the substantial number of price elasticities, whose values are unknown in most applications. For $n = 10$ goods, for example, there are $10^2 = 100$ price elasticities. Simplifications are called for.

It may be argued that the good's own price is likely to have a more substantial impact on the quantity demanded than the prices of other goods. One simplification of the demand equations might be to ignore the role of all prices other than the own. This could be achieved as follows:

1. Express the demands in real terms. Replace the change in nominal income $d \log M$ by the change in real income, defined as $d\log \frac{M}{P^\dagger}$. Here, income is deflated by a weighted average of the price changes, $d\log P^\dagger = \sum_{j=1}^{n} \alpha_j d\log p_j$, where the $\alpha_j' s$ are positive weights with a unit sum.
2. Similarly, replace nominal prices by relative prices, $d\log \frac{p_j}{P^{\dagger\dagger}}$, where $d\log P^{\dagger\dagger} = \sum_{j=1}^{n} \beta_j d\log p_j$, with $0 < \beta_j < 1$, $\sum_{j=1}^{n} \beta_j = 1$.

The ith demand equation in (2.1) then becomes $d\log q_i = \eta_i d\log \frac{M}{P^\dagger} + \sum_{j=1}^{n} \eta_{ij} d\log \frac{p_j}{P^{\dagger\dagger}}$. Ignoring cross-price effects means $\eta_{ij} = 0$, $i \neq j$, so that only the own-price term remains and

$$d\log q_i = \eta_i d\log \frac{M}{P^\dagger} + \eta_{ii} d\log \frac{p_i}{P^{\dagger\dagger}}.$$

A pragmatic specification of the two deflators might be to set both sets of weights equal to the observed expenditure shares, $\alpha_j = \beta_j = \frac{p_j q_j}{M}$. Such an approach does simplify matters considerably, but there are two problems. First, the value of the own-price elasticity η_{ii} is still unknown. Second, setting the weights of the price indexes equal to the expenditure shares is ad hoc without firm analytical foundation.

A better approach that still focuses attention on the own-price elasticities is to start with the following specific form of the utility function:

$$u(q_1, \cdots, q_n) = \sum_{i=1}^{n} u_i(q_i), \tag{2.2}$$

where $u_i(\cdot)$ is the ith sub-utility function which only depends on consumption of good i. This additive structure means that the marginal utility of the ith good, $\frac{\partial u}{\partial q_i}$, depends only on the consumption of that good, not on any of the others. Formally, (2.2) means that all second-order cross derivatives vanish, $\frac{\partial^2 u}{\partial q_i \partial q_j} = 0, i \neq j; i, j = 1, \cdots, n$. If the commodities are fairly broad groups, such as food, housing, clothing, and so on, it is not too difficult to imagine utility as being derived from the consumption of food *and* clothing *and* housing *and* so on, where the underscoring of the word "and" emphasises the additive nature of the manner in which goods are combined. These broad commodity groups might be interpreted as representing the "basic wants" of the consumer such as the desire for energy, shelter, and warmth. These wants might be sufficiently distinct to be separate from each other that they exhibit little interactions in the utility function. Admittedly, this description of preferences cannot be literally true in many situations. Nonetheless, in view of the simplicity of (2.2), it seems natural to postulate that broad groups are independent in generating utility, at least as a starting point. The utility function (2.2) is described as being of the preference independence form.

The attraction of preference independence is that it leads to a major simplification of the own-price elasticities. As an approximation, each own-price elasticity η_{ii} is a common multiple ϕ of the good's income elasticity η_i. That is,

$$\eta_{ii} \approx \phi\eta_i, \quad i = 1, \cdots, n. \tag{2.3}$$

The multiplier $\phi < 0$ is the inverse of the income elasticity of the marginal utility of income; for short, ϕ is called the "income flexibility".

The value of the price elasticity reflects the availability of substitutes—it is low when there are few alternatives and high when there are many. On the other hand, the income elasticity is a measure of the good's luxuriousness. Engel's law states that food is a necessity, that is, it is an essential, not a luxury, and its income elasticity is less than unity. High-fashion handbags are a strong luxury and so their $\eta_i > 1$. As the price and income elasticity would seem to reflect distinct properties of the good, it might come as a surprise that Eq. (2.3) links them so tightly together. But there is really no contradiction as the proportionality relationship agrees with common usage of the terms "essential" and "luxury". Take salt as an example. This is an "essential" (or a necessity) that humans cannot do without—that is, consumption cannot be postponed or replaced with something else, so it has few substitutes and a low price elasticity. The reverse is true of, say, a foreign vacation, which is likely to have a high income elasticity, as usually it is discretionary and can be cancelled or delayed. This is a luxury with a high price elasticity. The same applies for handbags. It is almost as if a low own-price elasticity is synonymous with a low income elasticity, and similarly for high price and income elasticities.

An additional implication of preference independence (2.2) is that as an approximation, cross-price elasticities vanish, that is, $\eta_{ij} \approx 0,\ i \neq j$. Again, this is not implausible for broad aggregates which are unlikely to substantially interact in generating utility.

2.4 The Rule of ½

The values of income elasticities tend to be easier to obtain than price elasticities. There are more reliable econometric estimates of income elasticities from studies that use household survey data as well as aggregate time-series data. Even when these values are not available, in some cases a rough idea of the luxuriousness or otherwise of a good can be gauged from its nature. For example, food is a clear necessity, while foreign vacations are likely to be a luxury. If this approach is not applicable and almost nothing is known about the likely nature of the good, a sensible default value for the income elasticity is unity. As a weighted average of income elasticities is unity, setting $\eta_i = 1$ means that the good is treated as an "average" one with a representative value.

Equation (2.3), $\eta_{ii} \approx \phi\eta_i$, can be used to estimate price elasticities on the basis of income elasticities and the single value of the income flexibility. If we set $\eta_i = 1$, the average value, the question then becomes, what value to use for ϕ? As discussed in detail in Chap. 3, $\phi = -½$ is a centre-of-gravity value of a number of estimates. Thus, the values $\eta_i = 1$ and $\phi = -½$ lead to the rule of (minus) one-half:

$$\eta_{ii} \approx -\frac{1}{2}. \tag{2.4}$$

In words, price elasticities are approximately minus one-half, a rule suggested by Clements (2008).

Goods that are more finely defined than the broad aggregates are likely to be more interdependent in the utility function and not exhibit preference independence. Under certain conditions, set out in Chap. 3, such goods can be aggregated into groups of goods with the groups more likely to be preference independent. In such cases, the rule of ½ applies to the groups. In other words, the above approach is not limited to broad aggregates of goods, but is also applicable in a wider context where finely defined goods can interact in generating utility in an unrestrictive fashion.

To summarise, (2.4) is a valuable relationship as it allows price elasticities to be estimated on the basis of minimal information, the value of a single parameter ϕ, the income flexibility. While there is obviously dispersion among the individual estimates found in prior studies, the evidence points to $\phi = -\frac{1}{2}$ as a centre-of-gravity value. This is also the value of the own-price elasticities according to the rule of ½. Here is a more-detailed recap of the theory lying behind (2.4):

1. The starting point is preference independence, whereby the marginal utility of each good is unaffected by variations in the consumption of all others.
2. Preference independence implies price elasticities are approximately proportional to the corresponding income elasticities. The factor of proportionality (ϕ) is the inverse of the income elasticity of the marginal utility of income, the "income flexibility".
3. Setting the income elasticity at its average value of unity, the proportionality relationship means that as an approximation, the average commodity has a price elasticity equal to the income flexibility ϕ.
4. As a number of prior estimates point to $\phi = -\frac{1}{2}$, it follows that price elasticities are approximately $-\frac{1}{2}$.

Broadly defined commodities such as food, clothing, housing, etc. are consumed in one way or another by all consumers. Such hugely diverse goods are so distinct that in all probability, there would be limited scope for substituting one for another. This can be taken to mean each marginal utility is more or less independent of the consumption of the other goods, consistent with the additive form of the utility function under preference independence. These considerations are consistent with the rule $\eta_{ii} \approx -\frac{1}{2}$ for broad aggregates.

The rule of ½ is a rule of substantial practical use. However, as should be clear from the above discussion, the rule is not a "law", but a broad guideline for elasticity of demand for certain types of goods.

2.5 Evidence on Price Elasticities

This section reports on surveys and meta-studies of estimates of the price elasticities of demand that have been carried out for a handful of commodities. While not overwhelming, the evidence seems not entirely at variance with the rule of ½.

The price sensitivity of alcoholic beverages has important implications for several reasons. What is the efficient rate of taxation of each beverage? How much government revenue can be raised? How much would consumer prices rise if alcohol taxes were increased? What taxes are needed to control abuse of alcohol, limit damage to health from excess consumption, and, more generally, deal with the negative externalities? Addressing these issues requires knowledge of the price elasticity. In view of its role, it is unsurprising that there are a number of econometric estimates available in the literature of this elasticity. Table 2.1 contains a summary of several surveys and meta-studies. It is to be noted that a substantial number of observations lie behind the figures in the table. For example from the first row of panel A, Nelson (2014) analysed 191 estimated own-price elasticities of beer and found the mean to be −0.20. Panel A also shows that the mean of the means for beer over six studies is −0.47, while the mean of the medians reported in three studies is −0.37. The conclusion is clear: The prior literature finds beer to be price inelastic. This is corroborated by Penm (1988) who analyses the Australian demand for beer by package type (cans and bottles, and bulk) and finds the own-price elasticity of beer as a group to be about −0.50. Panels B and C reveal wine and spirits to be a bit more elastic on average, but still price inelastic.

The means of the medians of the elasticities in Table 2.1 are −0.37 (beer), −0.56 (wine), and −0.66 (spirits). Interestingly, these values are not greatly at variance with the rule of ½. Note that based on the means, Gallet (2007) finds wine and spirits to be price elastic (panels B and C). But as in both cases the median of the elasticities is below 1, it seems Gallet's high means are skewed by outliers and should be downplayed.

The price elasticity of certain other goods has also been studied extensively and meta-studies are summarised in Table 2.2. For convenience, this table reproduces from Table 2.1 the means and medians for the three alcoholic beverages. Cigarettes, for example, are highly addictive with few other goods that are directly competing, and so smoking is unlikely to be highly responsive to higher prices. The first row panel 4 of the table confirms prior expectation as the mean of more than 500 estimates of the elasticity is −0.48. The other panels of the table, with the exception of the final one, reveal a similar result for other goods: The demand for beer, wine, spirits, water, petrol, and electricity is also price inelastic, at least on average. Where there is a distinction between the long- and the short-run elasticity, the means of the former are higher, which makes good economic sense as consumers can take some time to adjust to price changes.

Not only is consumption of these goods price inelastic but as Fig. 2.1 clearly shows, the elasticities are clustered around −½. This figure uses the medians of the elasticities of the first seven goods of Table 2.2. The major exception is for the last

Table 2.1 Alcohol price elasticities

Source	Mean	Median	Number of underlying estimates/ studies
A. Beer			
Nelson (2014)	−0.20		191
Sornpaisarn et al. (2013)	−0.50		7
Nelson (2013b)		−0.29	
Fogarty (2010)	−0.45	−0.33	154
Elder et al. (2010)		−0.50	18
Wagenaar et al. (2009)	−0.46		105
Gallet (2007)	−0.83	−0.36	315
Selvanathan and Selvanathan (2005)	−0.37		10
Mean	**−0.47**	**−0.37**	**114**
B. Wine			
Nelson (2013a)	−0.65	−0.45	197
Nelson (2013b)		−0.46	
Fogarty (2010)	−0.65	−0.55	155
Elder et al. (2010)		−0.64	22
Wagenaar et al. (2009)	−0.69		93
Gallet (2007)	−1.11	−0.70	300
Selvanathan and Selvanathan (2005)	−0.46		10
Mean	**−0.71**	**−0.56**	**130**
C. Spirits			
Nelson (2013a)	−0.70	−0.55	202
Nelson (2013b)		−0.54	89
Fogarty (2010)	−0.73	−0.76	162
Elder et al. (2010)		−0.79	21
Wagenaar et al. (2009)	−0.80		103
Gallet (2007)	−1.09	−0.68	294
Selvanathan and Selvanathan (2005)	−0.57		10
Mean	**−0.78**	**−0.66**	**126**

Source: Clements et al. (2022).

good of Table 2.2, branded products, where the mean elasticity is −1.76, meaning demand is highly elastic. The reason is that a good of a certain brand would usually face substantial competition from other brands of the same good. In other words, there are many substitutes available for branded goods, leading to elastic demand.

What are the common features of the first seven goods? Take beer as an example: Some beer drinkers might be induced to switch to wine following a rise of the price of beer. But the popular and realistic idea of many "hard-core" beer drinkers means that the price rise would most likely need to be large in order to bring about a substantial conversion of beer drinkers to wine. For this reason, beer is likely to have only limited

Table 2.2 Price elasticities of demand for selected products

Product (1)		Mean (2)	Median (3)	Number of observations (4)	Length of run (5)	Source (6)
1.	Beer	−0.47	−0.37	114		Table 2.1
2.	Wine	−0.71	−0.56	130		Table 2.1
3.	Spirits	−0.78	−0.66	126		Table 2.1
4.	Cigarettes	−0.48		523		Gallet and List (2003)
			−0.40	368	Short run	Gallet and List (2003)
			−0.44	155	Long run	Gallet and List (2003)
	Mean	**−0.48**	**−0.42**			
5.	Residential water	−0.41	−0.35	314		Dalhuisen et al. (2003)
		−0.51		124		Espey et al. (1997)
			−0.38		Short run	Espey et al. (1997)
			−0.64		Long run	Espey et al. (1997)
	Mean	**−0.46**	**−0.46**			
6.	Petrol	−0.26	−0.23	363	Short run	Espey (1998)
		−0.25		46	Short run	Goodwin et al. (2004)
		−0.25	−0.21	387	Short run	Graham and Glaister (2002, p. 48)
		−0.58	−0.43	277	Long run	Espey (1998)
		−0.64		51	Long run	Goodwin et al. (2004)
		−0.53		70		Espey (1996)
		−0.77	−0.55	213	Long run	Graham and Glaister (2002, p. 48)
		−0.35	−0.35	52	Intermediate	Graham and Glaister (2002, p. 54)
	Mean	**−0.45**	**−0.35**			
7.	Residential electricity	−0.35	−0.28	123	Short run	Espey and Espey (2004)
		−0.85	−0.81	125	Long run	Espey and Espey (2004)
	Mean	**−0.60**	**−0.55**			
8.	Branded products	−1.76		337		Tellis (1988)

Source: Adapted from Clements (2008).

substitutes and a low elasticity. On the other hand, different brands of beer are good substitutes for one another and price discounting of one brand would be likely to cause some to switch from one brand to another, so the inter-brand elasticities would be large. This outcome would be consistent with the elasticity of −1.76 for branded

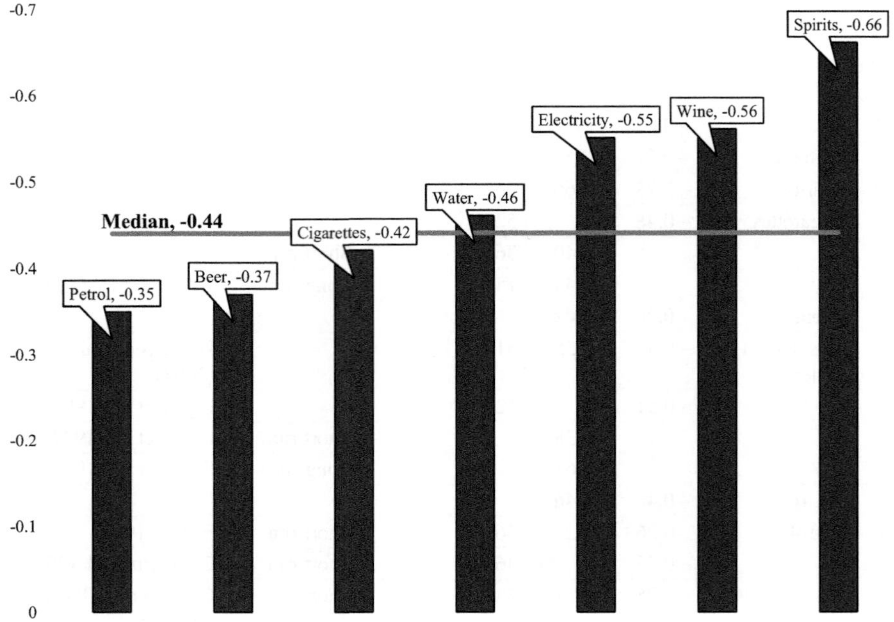

Fig. 2.1 Price elasticities of demand (Medians). Source: Table 2.2

goods. By contrast, the goods in the first seven panels of Table 2.2 are all fairly broad aggregates with few substitutes. As for beer, most of the substitution that does take place is likely to be vis-à-vis members of the same group, and so confined to within the aggregated good. Generally speaking, broad aggregates tend to have few substitutes. The demand for these goods seems to be consistent with the rule of ½.

Although labour demand is not the subject of consumption theory, its elasticity is nonetheless interesting. The meta-analysis by Lichter et al. (2015) analyses the wage elasticity of demand for labour with than 1300 estimates from 151 studies. They find a mean elasticity of -0.55 and a median of -0.42.

2.6 Two Further Appearances of ½

Another form of the consumer's utility function is the constant elasticity of substitution (CES). This is:

$$u(q_1, \cdots, q_n) = \left(\sum_{i=1}^{n} \alpha_i q_i^{-\rho} \right)^{-\frac{1}{\rho}}, \quad \alpha_i > 0, \sum_{i=1}^{n} \alpha_i = 1, \rho \geq -1, \rho \neq 0. \tag{2.5}$$

Here, q_i is the quantity demanded of good i, as before, while α_i $(i = 1, \cdots, n)$ and ρ are constant parameters. The elasticity of substitution is $\sigma = \frac{1}{1+\rho} > 0$, which is also a constant, as implied by the CES name given to (2.5).

The CES contrasts with utility function (2.2) in two respects. First, it is in explicit algebraic form, while (2.2) is not. The second difference relates to the marginal utilities implied by (2.5), which are

$$\frac{\partial u}{\partial q_i} = \left(\sum_{j=1}^{n} \alpha_j q_j^{\frac{\sigma-1}{\sigma}}\right)^{\frac{1}{\sigma-1}} \alpha_i q_i^{-\frac{1}{\sigma}}, \quad i = 1, \cdots, n.$$

As $\frac{\partial^2 u}{\partial q_i \partial q_j} \neq 0, i \neq j; i, j = 1, \cdots, n,$ goods interact in a marginal utility sense. That is, the CES is not additive, or not of the preference independence form, unlike (2.2).

Defining a price index as $P^* = \left(\sum_{j=1}^{n} \alpha_j^{\sigma} p_j^{1-\sigma}\right)^{\frac{1}{1-\sigma}}$ and M as income, as before, the demand equation for good i implied by CES utility is

$$q_i = \alpha_i^{\sigma} \frac{M}{P^*} \left(\frac{p_i}{P^*}\right)^{-\sigma}.$$

As shown in Chap. 3, the ith own-price elasticity is $\eta_{ii} = -\sigma(1 - w_i)$, where $w_i = \frac{p_i q_i}{M}$ is the share of income devoted to the good (known as the budget share). A budget-share weighted average of the elasticities lies in the range $\left[-\sigma\left(1 - \frac{1}{n}\right), 0\right]$ and the average of the upper and lower limits is $-½\sigma\left(1 - \frac{1}{n}\right) \approx -½\sigma$, where approximation ignores the term $½\sigma\frac{1}{n}$. This is different to rule (2.4) although there is a link with the role played by the value $-½$. Of course, if the elasticity of substitution $\sigma = 1$, we get back to (2.4). While $\sigma = 1$ is a frequent choice, strictly speaking it is inadmissible in the CES as it corresponds to $\rho = 0$.

A second manifestation of $-½$ is in money demand. Money is assumed to pay no interest and the demand for real money balances (m) depends positively on real income (y), on account of transactions demand, and negatively on the opportunity cost, the interest rate: $m = f(y, i)$. The popular Baumol (1952)-Tobin (1956) model derives optimal money holdings on the basis of cost-minimisation. Cost is the sum of (i) the transaction costs of switching from an interest-bearing asset into money and (ii) the opportunity cost of foregone interest associated with holding money. This yields a money demand function of the specific form:

$$m = \sqrt{\frac{cy}{2i}}, \tag{2.6}$$

where $c > 0$ reflects the fixed transaction cost of switching assets. The interest elasticity is

$$\frac{\partial(\log m)}{\partial(\log i)} = -½.$$

This elasticity is completely analogous to the price elasticity of demand, which means this is a monetary-economics version of the rule of ½.

An additional property of demand Eq. (2.6) is that the income elasticity is ½, which is interpreted as economies of scale—a doubling of income leads to a 50-per cent increase in money holdings. This model is highly unusual in economics as it provides specific numerical values of the elasticities just from the theory itself.

2.7 Summary

In dealing with a new environment—new products, new data, new consumers, etc.—often a good's price sensitivity is unknown. Even when econometric estimates are available, doubts about reliability can make them not as useful as they might seem. This issue arises in many applications of price theory. When there is little or nothing known with confidence, what value should be used for the own-price elasticity of demand for a good? As a useful rule, the elasticity is −½. This applies to broad aggregates with few good substitutes.

The theory underlying the rule is based on three assumptions. First, goods are additive in generating utility of the consumer, in the sense that the marginal utility of each good is independent of the consumption of the others. This form of utility is known as preference independence, which links the price elasticity to the income elasticity of the good. The second assumption is that the value of the income elasticity of the marginal utility is −2, for which there is some empirical support, as set out in Chap. 3. Finally, the good's income sensitivity is taken to be average, making its income elasticity unity. The rule of ½ is a guideline not a law, and might be used as a reasonable benchmark or starting value for subsequent research.

Prescribing a specific numerical value for the elasticity is a bold move. But there is some evidence in favour of the rule of ½. Chap. 3 discusses evidence supporting the assumption of preference independence for broad groups of goods. This research overturns previous findings against preference independence. That chapter also shows estimates of the income elasticity of the marginal utility tend to cluster around the value −2. Additionally, meta-studies of the price elasticity for a number of commodities—beer, wine, spirits, cigarettes, water, petrol, and electricity—tend to point towards the value of −½.

The rule of ½ has theoretical and empirical support.

References

Baumol WJ (1952) The transactions demand for cash: an inventory theoretic approach. Q J Econ 66:545–556

Clements KW (2008) Price elasticities of demand are minus one-half. Econ Lett 99:490–493
Clements KW, Mariano MJM, Verkios G, Wong B (2022) How elastic is alcohol consumption? Econ Anal Policy 76:568–581
Dalhuisen JM, Florax RJGM, de Groot HLF, Nijkamp P (2003) Price and income elasticities of residential water demand: a meta-analysis. Land Econ 79:292–308
Dawkins C, Srinivasan T, Whalley J (2001) Calibration. In: Heckman JJ, Leamer E (eds) Handbook of econometrics, vol 5. Elsevier
Elder RW, Lawrence B, Ferguson A, Naimi TS, Brewer RD, Chattopadhyay SK, Toomey TL, Fielding JE (2010) The effectiveness of tax policy interventions for reducing excessive alcohol consumption and related harms. Am J Prev Med 38:217–229
Espey M (1996) Explaining the variation in elasticity estimates of gasoline demand in the United States: a meta-analysis. Energy J 17:49–60
Espey M (1998) Gasoline demand revisited: an international meta-analysis of elasticities. Energy Econ 20:273–295
Espey JA, Espey M (2004) Turning on the lights: a meta-analysis of residential electricity demand elasticities. J Agric Appl Econ 36:65–81
Espey M, Espey JA, Shaw WD (1997) Price elasticity of residential demand for water: a meta-analysis. Water Resour Res 33:1369–1374
Fogarty J (2010) The demand for beer, wine and spirits: a survey of the literature. J Econ Surv 24: 428–478
Gallet CA (2007) The demand for alcohol: a meta-analysis of elasticities. Aust J Agric Resour Econ 51:121–135
Gallet CA, List JA (2003) Cigarette demand: a meta-analysis of elasticities. Health Econ 12:821–835
Goodwin P, Dargay J, Hanly M (2004) Elasticities of road traffic and fuel consumption with respect to price and income: a review. Transp Rev 24:275–292
Graham D, Glaister S (2002) Review of income and price elasticities of demand for road traffic. Working Paper. Center for Transport Studies, Imperial College of Science, Technology and Medicine
Lichter A, Peichl A, Siegloch S (2015) The own-wage elasticity of labour demand: a meta-regression analysis. Eur Econ Rev 80:94–119
Nelson JP (2013a) Robust demand elasticities for wine and distilled spirits: meta-analysis with corrections for outliers and publication bias. J Wine Econ 8:294–317
Nelson JP (2013b) Meta-analysis of alcohol price and income elasticities—with corrections for publication bias. Heal Econ Rev 3:1–10
Nelson JP (2014) Estimating the price elasticity of beer: meta-analysis of data with heterogeneity, dependence, and publication bias. J Health Econ 33:180–187
Penm JH (1988) An econometric study of the demand for bottled, canned and bulk beer. Econ Record 64:268–274
Selvanathan S, Selvanathan EA (2005) The demand for alcohol, tobacco and marijuana: international evidence. Ashgate, Aldershot
Sornpaisarn B, Shield K, Cohen J, Schwartz R, Rehm J (2013) Elasticity of alcohol consumption, alcohol-related harms, and drinking initiation in low- and middle-income countries: a systematic review and meta-analysis. Int J Alcohol Drug Res 2:45–58
Tellis GJ (1988) The price elasticity of selected demand: a meta-analysis of econometric models of sales. J Mark Res 25:331–341
Tobin J (1956) The interest elasticity of the transactions demand for cash. Rev Econ Stat 38:241–247
Wagenaar AC, Salois MJ, Komro KA (2009) Effects of beverage alcohol price and tax levels on drinking: a meta-analysis of 1003 estimates from 112 studies. Addiction 104:179–190

Chapter 3
Demand Elasticities Simplified II: Further Results and Details

This chapter builds on Chap. 2's material by giving detailed derivations of the results and references to the related literature. A couple of other topics are also discussed that are complementary to the theme of the previous chapter but not covered there. This chapter is for those wishing to delve further into foundational matters. But since Chap. 2 is more or less self-contained, this chapter is not a prerequisite for its predecessor.

3.1 Uses and Sources of Price Elasticities

Chapter 2 started by discussing the uses of price elasticities to predict price changes. Two other major uses should be mentioned. First, computable general equilibrium (CGE) models involve the numerical modelling of the economy with considerable detail, with maybe more than 100 sectors. These models make extensive use of systems of demand equations with the values of the corresponding elasticities drawn from a number of sources. For a survey of CGE models, see Dixon and Jorgenson (2012).

A second major use of price elasticities is in the design of policy, from optimal taxation to those seeking to offset externalities and other distortions with commodity taxes. This optimal tax formulation originated from Ramsey (1927), who studied how goods should be taxed in order to raise a given amount of revenue while minimising the distortionary effects as measured by the deadweight loss. The solution involves an equiproportional reduction in the consumption of each good, which, in the simplest case, is achieved by setting tax rates in inverse proportion to price elasticities. Stiglitz (2015) gives an account of developments in the theory of optimal taxation following Ramsey.

Tobacco taxes to reduce smoking and fat taxes to reduce obesity are examples of policies designed to deal with external effects/distortions. If taxation is to be used to reduce consumption of a particular good by $\alpha > 0\%$, the rate needs to be set such that

K. W. Clements et al., *Short-cut Demand Elasticities and Other Convenient Approaches to Consumer Demand*, https://doi.org/10.1007/978-981-96-3588-7_3

the price rises by $-\frac{\alpha}{\eta} > 0\%$, where $\eta < 0$ is the price elasticity, as before. If the elasticity is −½, the price needs to rise by 20% to achieve a 10-per cent reduction in consumption. For examples of this research, see Powell et al. (2013) and Zhen et al. (2013).

There have been many attempts to estimate demand equations that depend primarily on income and prices. Despite substantial progress, there are still issues that remain unresolved. A partial listing of major studies on the income and price sensitivity of demand, each dealing with a large number of countries includes Chen (1999), Gao (2012a), Goldberger and Gamaletsos (1970), Houthakker (1957), Liu (2018), Lluch and Powell (1975), Lluch et al. (1977), Muhammad et al. (2011), Regmi and Seale (2010), Rimmer and Powell (1992), Seale and Regmi (2006), Seale et al. (2003), Selvanathan (1993), Selvanathan and Selvanathan (2003), Theil and Clements (1987), and Theil et al. (1989).

There are a number of different demand models that can be used to estimated elasticities. Popular models include the linear expenditure system (LES, Stone 1954), the Rotterdam model (Barten 1964; Theil 1965), the almost ideal demand system (AIDS) and its quadratic extension (Deaton and Muellbauer 1980a; Banks et al. 1997), and the translog (Christensen et al. 1975). For major reviews, see Bewley (1986), Deaton (1986), Deaton and Muellbauer (1980b), Goldberger (1987), Pollak and Wales (1992), Powell (1974), and Theil (1975/76, 1980). Relatedly, Boysen (2019) compares the impact of different demand systems on CGE results. Chapter 6 of the book contains details of the major demand systems and an assessment of their strengths and weaknesses.

3.2 Utility Function and Budget Constraint

Denote by q_i the quantity consumed of good i ($i = 1, \cdots, n$) and the utility function by $u(q_1, \cdots, q_n)$. Goods are assumed to be good, so additional consumption of each good adds to utility with each marginal utility, $\frac{\partial u}{\partial q_i}$, positive. Marginal utility is assumed to fall with an additional unit of consumption of the good. That is, there is diminishing marginal utility, $\frac{\partial^2 u}{\partial q_i \partial q_i} < 0, i = 1, \cdots, n$. Let $\boldsymbol{q}$ denote the column vector of the quantities of the n goods, $\boldsymbol{q} = [q_1, \cdots, q_n]'$. As a sufficient condition for what follows, it is assumed that the $n \times n$ Hessian matrix of the utility function, $\frac{\partial^2 u}{\partial \boldsymbol{q} \partial \boldsymbol{q}'}$, is negative definite. This represents generalised diminishing marginal utility.

The consumer has a fixed amount of money to spend on n goods, which is expressed in the form of the budget constraint:

$$\sum_{i=1}^{n} p_i q_i = M, \tag{3.1}$$

where p_i is the price of good i and M is total expenditure (to be referred to as "income" for short). There are two implications of the budget constraint. The first is obtained by differentiating both sides of Eq. (3.1) with respect to M to give $\sum_{i=1}^{n} \partial(p_i q_i)/\partial M = 1$, or

$$\sum_{i=1}^{n} w_i \eta_i = 1, \tag{3.2}$$

where $w_i = \frac{p_i q_i}{M}$ is the fraction of income spent on good i, which is known as the budget share, and $\eta_i = \frac{\partial(p_i q_i)/\partial M}{w_i} = \frac{\partial \log q_i}{\partial \log M}$ is the corresponding income elasticity. A good is labelled a necessity (luxury) if its $\eta_i < 1$ ($\eta_i > 1$). According to Eq. (3.2), a budget-share weighted average of the income elasticities is unity, so not all goods can be necessities, nor can they all be luxuries. For the second implication, we differentiate (3.1) with respect to the price of good j to give $q_j + \sum_{i=1}^{n} \frac{p_i \partial q_i}{\partial p_j} = 0$, or multiplying through by p_j/M,

$$w_j + \sum_{i=1}^{n} w_i \eta_{ij} = 0, \quad j = 1, \cdots, n, \tag{3.3}$$

where $\eta_{ij} = \frac{\partial q_i}{\partial p_j} \frac{p_j}{q_i} = \frac{\partial \log q_i}{\partial \log p_j}$ is price elasticity of consumption of good i with respect to the price of j, known as the $(i, j)^{th}$ price elasticity.

As the consumer is constrained to spend only the fixed amount M, additional expenditure on one good necessitates reduced spending on at least one other. This is an allocation problem and Eqs. (3.2) and (3.3) are aggregation constraints reflecting the reshuffling of income among goods following changes in income and prices.

3.3 Constrained Maximisation

The problems faced by the consumer is to choose the quantities demanded to maximise utility subject to the budget constraint. To do this, form the Lagrangian $L(q_1, \cdots, q_n; \lambda) = u(q_1, \cdots, q_n) - \lambda\left(\sum_{i=1}^{n} p_i q_i - M\right)$, where $\lambda > 0$ is a Lagrange multiplier. The first-order conditions for a utility maximum are

$$\frac{\partial u}{\partial q_i} = \lambda p_i, \quad i = 1, \cdots, n, \tag{3.4}$$

and the budget constraint (3.1). Condition (3.4) mean that the utility value of the last dollar spent is equalised across goods, $\frac{\partial u}{\partial (p_i q_i)} = \lambda$. There are n + 1 equations in the first-order conditions (3.1) and (3.4) which can in principle can be solved for $q_1, \cdots,$ q_n and λ. The solution values of the quantities are functions of income and prices, so we can write

$$q_i = q_i(M, p_1, \cdots, p_n), \quad i = 1, \cdots, n.$$

These are the demand functions describing how the quantities vary with changes in income and prices. Similarly, the solution value of the multiplier can be expressed as $\lambda = \lambda(M, p_1, \cdots, p_n)$.

Denote the vector of prices by $\boldsymbol{p} = [p_1, \cdots, p_n]'$ and write the demand functions in vector form as $\boldsymbol{q} = \boldsymbol{q}(M, \boldsymbol{p})$. Substitute the demands into the utility function to give $u(\boldsymbol{q}(M, \boldsymbol{p})) = u_I(M, \boldsymbol{p})$, which is the indirect utility function. Then

$$\frac{\partial u_I}{\partial M} = \sum_{i=1}^{n} \frac{\partial u}{\partial q_i} \frac{\partial q_i}{\partial M} = \lambda \sum_{i=1}^{n} p_i \frac{\partial q_i}{\partial M} = \lambda,$$

where the second last step follows from Eq. (3.4) and the last from (3.2). This establishes that the multiplier λ is interpreted as the marginal utility of income, the utility-value of an increment in income.

The previously introduced $(i,j)^{th}$ price elasticity is $\eta_{ij} = \frac{\partial \log q_i}{\partial \log p_j}$. As this holds constant the consumer's money income M, real income falls when p_j rises. Thus, η_{ij} is called the uncompensated price elasticity, also known as the Marshallian elasticity. There is another version of the elasticity that gives the quantity response when real income is held unchanged. The Slutsky equation decomposes η_{ij} into a real-income-constant component and the impact of changed real income:

$$\eta_{ij} = \eta_{ij}^* - w_j \eta_i.$$

Take the last term on the right-hand side, $-w_j\eta_i$. Here, η_i is the income elasticity of good i, the good whose quantity changes, and $w_j = \frac{p_j q_j}{M}$ is the budget share of j, the good whose price changes; and the minus sign reflects the fall in real income when the price rises. This term is known as the income effect of the price change. When the income effect is purged, what is left is the substitution effect of the price change, $\eta_{ij} + w_j \eta_i = \eta_{ij}^*$, the other term on the right-hand side of the Slutsky equation. Accordingly, η_{ij}^* is called the compensated price elasticity, in contrast to η_{ij}, the uncompensated version. A term also used for η_{ij}^* is the Slutsky elasticity.

3.4 Changes in Marginal Utilities

Consider the marginal utility of consumption of good i, $\frac{\partial u}{\partial q_i}$. Diminishing marginal utility means that additional consumption of the good causes its marginal utility to fall. But what about the impact of other goods on $\frac{\partial u}{\partial q_i}$? These effects can be summarised by the sign of second-order cross derivatives $\frac{\partial^2 u}{\partial q_i \partial q_j}, i \neq j; i, j = 1, \cdots, n$.

The sign of $\frac{\partial^2 u}{\partial q_i \partial q_j}$ is the same as that of $\frac{\partial \log\left(\frac{\partial u}{\partial q_i}\right)}{\partial \log q_j}$, which is a convenient formulation for what follows.

The effect of a change in the jth price on q_k ($k = 1, \cdots, n$) is, in logarithmic terms, η_{kj} ($k = 1, \cdots, n$), the price elasticities. Accordingly, the impact on the marginal utility of i is $\sum_{k=1}^{n} \frac{\partial \log\left(\frac{\partial u}{\partial q_i}\right)}{\partial \log q_k} \eta_{kj}$. If all cross effects were to vanish, only the ith term in the summation remains: $\sum_{k=1}^{n} \frac{\partial \log\left(\frac{\partial u}{\partial q_i}\right)}{\partial \log q_k} \eta_{kj} = \frac{\partial \log\left(\frac{\partial u}{\partial q_i}\right)}{\partial \log q_i} \eta_{ij}$. From the first-order condition (3.4),

$$\log \frac{\partial u}{\partial q_i} = \log \lambda + \log p_i. \tag{3.5}$$

With no cross effects, the derivative of this equation with respect to $\log p_j$ is

$$\frac{\partial \log\left(\frac{\partial u}{\partial q_i}\right)}{\partial \log q_i} \eta_{ij} = \frac{\partial \log \lambda}{\partial \log p_j} + \delta_{ij}, \tag{3.6}$$

where δ_{ij} is the Kronecker delta ($\delta_{ij} = 1$ if $i = j, 0$ otherwise).

Again in logarithms, the effect of a change in income on q_i is $d \log q_i = \eta_i d \log M$, where η_i is the income elasticity. Thus, differentiating Eq. (3.5) with respect to $\log M$ gives

$$\frac{\partial \log\left(\frac{\partial u}{\partial q_i}\right)}{\partial \log q_i} \eta_i = \frac{1}{\phi},$$

where $\frac{1}{\phi} = \frac{\partial \log \lambda}{\partial \log M} < 0$ is the income elasticity of the marginal utility of income. The reciprocal of this elasticity, ϕ, is known as the income flexibility. Write the above equation as

$$\frac{\partial \log\left(\frac{\partial u}{\partial q_i}\right)}{\partial \log q_i} = \frac{1}{\phi\eta_i}. \tag{3.7}$$

Substituting the right-hand side of Eq. (3.7) for $\frac{\partial \log\left(\frac{\partial u}{\partial q_i}\right)}{\partial \log q_i}$ in (3.6) yields $\frac{1}{\phi\eta_i}\eta_{ij} = \frac{\partial \log \lambda}{\partial \log p_j} + \delta_{ij}$, or, multiplying through by $\phi\eta_i$,

$$\eta_{ij} = \phi\frac{\partial \log \lambda}{\partial \log p_j}\eta_i + \phi\delta_{ij}\eta_i. \tag{3.8}$$

Multiply both sides of this equation by w_i and summing over $i = 1, \cdots, n$ gives

$$\sum_{i=1}^{n} w_i\eta_{ij} = \phi\left(\frac{\partial \log \lambda}{\partial \log p_j} + w_j\eta_j\right), \tag{3.9}$$

which follows from constraint (3.2) and $\sum_{i=1}^{n} w_i\delta_{ij}\eta_i = w_j\eta_j$.

As from (3.3) the left-hand side of Eq. (3.9) is $-w_j$, we have $\frac{-w_j}{\phi} = \frac{\partial \log \lambda}{\partial \log p_j} + w_j\eta_j$, or

$$\frac{\partial \log \lambda}{\partial \log p_j} = -w_j\left(\eta_j + \phi^{-1}\right).$$

Substitute this back into Eq. (3.8) to give $\eta_{ij} = -\phi w_j(\eta_j + \phi^{-1})\eta_i + \phi\delta_{ij}\eta_i$. Collecting terms, this is

$$\eta_{ij} = \phi\eta_i(\delta_{ij} - w_j\eta_j) - \eta_i w_j, \quad i,j = 1, \cdots, n. \tag{3.10}$$

3.5 The Key Proportionality

In the above, the price elasticities η_{ij} are uncompensated and so include both income and substitution effects. The last term on the right of Eq. (3.10), $-\eta_i w_j$, is the income effect of the price change and the term immediately to the right of the equals sign, $\phi\eta_i(\delta_{ij} - w_j\eta_j)$, is the compensated price elasticity η_{ij}^*. The term $\phi\eta_i w_j\eta_j$ is approximately zero as

(i) The income flexibility ϕ tends to lie in the range $[-1, 0]$, as discussed below.
(ii) The income elasticity η_i has an average of unity.
(iii) w_j is a positive fraction on average equal to $\frac{1}{n}$.

Thus, as the product of two fractions is a small number, $\phi\eta_i w_j \eta_j \approx 0$ and the compensated elasticity is $\eta^*_{ij} = \phi\eta_i(\delta_{ij} - w_j\eta_j) \approx \phi\eta_i\delta_{ij}$. For $i = j$, the compensated own-price elasticities are

$$\eta^*_{ii} \approx \phi\eta_i, \quad i = 1, \cdots, n. \tag{3.11}$$

According to this equation the (compensated own-) price elasticities are proportional to income elasticities, so luxuries are more price elastic than necessities, a result known as Pigou's (1910) law (Deaton 1974). The (negative) factor of proportionality is the income flexibility, ϕ. Under the above conditions, as an approximation cross-price elasticities vanish, $\eta^*_{ij} \approx 0, i \neq j$. This is not implausible for broad aggregates that could be expected to have little or no interactions in generating utility.

As noted previously, the income flexibility is the inverse of the income elasticity of the marginal utility of income, that is, $\phi = \left(\frac{\partial \log \lambda}{\partial \log M}\right)^{-1}$. There is another interpretation of ϕ. Multiplying both sides of the ith equation in (3.11) by w_i and then summing gives $\sum_{i=1}^n w_i\eta^*_{ii} \approx \phi\sum_{i=1}^n w_i\eta_i = \phi$, where the second step is based on Eq. (3.2). This shows that under the above conditions, the income flexibility is approximately a budget-share weighted average of the price elasticities. Relatedly, Powell (1992) shows that when there are no cross-utility effects, $-\phi$ coincides with the average elasticity of substitution.

Equation (3.8) refers to the effect on consumption of good i from a change in the price of j. A price increase $dp_j > 0$ makes the consumer worse off, so in view of diminishing marginal utility, we would expect the marginal utility of income λ to increase. If the consumer were compensated for the price increase such that λ remains unchanged, the first term on the right-hand side of (3.8) involving $\frac{\partial \log \lambda}{\partial \log p_j}$ vanishes and the proportionality relation becomes exact, $\eta^*_{ii} = \phi\eta_i$, and now η^*_{ii} is interpreted as the marginal-utility-constant or Frisch (1932) price elasticity. A further implication is that all Frisch cross-price elasticities are zero.

To simplify the exposition in Chap. 2, there was no distinction between the compensated and uncompensated price elasticities. However, as the above discussion makes clear, the proportionality between price and income elasticities refers to the compensated elasticities $\eta^*_{ii}, i = 1, \cdots, n$.

Milton Friedman's (1935) first publication was an early contribution to this topic in the form of a comment on Pigou (1910). Snow and Warren Jr. (2015) introduce a generalisation of Pigou's law.

3.6 Preference Independence

The above material is based on the condition that the marginal utility of each good i depends only on the quantity consumed of that good, not that of any others. This means that tastes can be characterised by an additive utility function, that is

$$u(q_1,\cdots,q_n)=\sum_{i=1}^{n}u_i(q_i), \tag{3.12}$$

where $u_i(\cdot)$ is the ith sub-utility function which only depends on consumption of good i. Accordingly, $\frac{\partial u}{\partial q_i}=\frac{du_i}{dq_i}$. The utility function (3.12) is described as being of the preference independence form. As discussed in Chap. 2, this additive structure could be reasonable for broadly aggregated goods, at least as a starting point. Additivity shares a certain symmetry with the budget constraint [Eq. (3.1)] where expenditures on the goods are added together.

Under preference independence $\frac{\partial^2 u}{\partial q_i \partial q_j}=0, i\neq j$. But observed consumption implied by the utility function $u(q_1,\cdots,q_n)=\sum_{i=1}^{n}u_i(q_i)$ is also consistent with the monotonic transformation $f(u)$, with $f^{'}>0$. Now

$$\frac{\partial^2 f}{\partial q_i \partial q_j}=f'\frac{\partial^2 u}{\partial q_i \partial q_j}+f''\frac{\partial u}{\partial q_i}\frac{\partial u}{\partial q_j},$$

which is non-zero even when $\frac{\partial^2 u}{\partial q_i \partial q_j}=0$. Thus, we need to confine ourselves to the quasi-cardinal world in which utility is additive up to a positive *linear* transformation so that $f^{''}=0$. Cardinality means utility can be measured on some form of linear scale, making interpersonal comparisons possible. Once thought to be too strong, cardinal utility has recently become more palatable to economists. One possible reason is the growing use of surveys that ask individuals how happy they are, with the responses recorded on a numerical scale. Importantly, the responses are compared across individuals, which can be interpreted as utility comparisons of the sort permitted by cardinality. Tella and MacCulloch (2006) survey the use of happiness data in economics. A related reason for support of cardinality is that in financial economics, risk-return preferences are routinely compared across individuals or groups of individuals; for example, with comparisons of the values of the Arrow-Pratt coefficients of risk aversion. A final reason could well be that preference independence leads to simplifications for demand analysis that promise so much [Eq. (3.11)], simplifications that now seems not inconsistent with the evidence, as discussed in the next section.

3.7 Can Preference Independence be Relied upon?

Frisch (1959, p. 186) argues preference independence is not likely to be appropriate for narrowly defined goods, but satisfactory for broadly defined goods:

> If the goods are specified in all concrete detail (say, margarine with one technical specification as distinguished from margarine with another technical specification), it will hardly ever be realistic to assume [preference] independence for any of the goods. But if the goods are aggregated in a reasonable way ... one will in practice get goods about which we can say a priori with considerable confidence that they are [preference] independent.

While preference independence would seem to be reasonable for broad aggregates, it is still a strong assumption. For example, it rules out complementarity and inferior goods. Therefore, it is perhaps not surprising that the hypothesis has been subject to considerable empirical testing, some of which has resulted in the applicability of preference independence being severely questioned.

In an influential paper, Deaton (1974) tests preference independence indirectly by investigating whether luxuries are more price elastic than necessities, the proportionality relationship between price and income elasticities [Eq. (3.11)]. Using UK data, he finds a lack of proportionality and concludes in unequivocal terms: "*[T]he assumption of additive preferences* [preference independence] *is almost certain to be invalid in practice and the use of demand models based on such an assumption will lead to severe distortion of measurement*" (his emphasis). However, such a strong conclusion needs to be tempered by the work of Selvanathan (1993), who uses elasticities from 18 Organisation for Economic Cooperation and Development (OECD) countries and finds the evidence not inconsistent with the proportionality relationship. We shall return to this evidence in Chap. 7 of the book.

Direct tests of preference independence involve examining the validity of the implied parametric restrictions on demand equations. For example, the preference-independent version of the Rotterdam model, due to Barten (1964) and Theil (1965), is

$$\bar{w}_{it} Dq_{it} = \theta_i DQ_t + \phi\theta_i \left(Dp_{it} - \sum_{j=1}^{n} \theta_j Dp_{jt} \right) + \varepsilon_{it}, \quad i = 1, \cdots, n. \tag{3.13}$$

Here $\overline{w}_{it} = ½(w_{it} + w_{i,t-1})$ is the arithmetic average of the ith budget share in periods t and $t - 1$; $Dq_{it} = \log q_{it} - \log q_{i,t-1}$ is the ith quantity log-change; $\theta_i = \partial(p_i q_i)/\partial M$ is the ith marginal share; $DQ_t = \sum_{i=1}^{n} \overline{w}_{it} Dq_{it}$ is the Divisia (1926) quantity index, a measure of the change in real income; $\phi < 0$ is the income flexibility, as before; $Dp_{it} = \log p_{it} - \log p_{i,t-1}$ is the log-change in the price of good i; and ε_{it} is a disturbance term. The parameters of this model are $\theta_1, \cdots, \theta_n$ and ϕ. Eq. (3.13) expresses the share-weighted change in the demand for good i in terms of changes in income and the good's relative price, $Dp_{it} - \sum_{j=1}^{n} \theta_j Dp_{jt}$. This is a constrained system as it contains only the own-relative price on the right-hand side; and for $i = 1, \cdots, n$, the price coefficients of the relative price terms, $\phi\theta_i$ are constrained to be proportional to the corresponding marginal shares.

The appropriateness of the preference independence hypothesis can be tested by comparing the fit of Eq. (3.13) with that of its unconstrained counterpart containing all n relative prices:

$$\bar{w}_{it}Dq_{it} = \theta_i DQ_t + \sum_{j=1}^{n} \nu_{ij}\left(Dp_{jt} - \sum_{k=1}^{n}\theta_k Dp_{kt}\right) + \varepsilon_{it}, \quad i = 1, \cdots, n,$$

where ν_{ij} is a new price coefficient. In a review of earlier econometric evidence, Barten (1977) concludes that the restrictions of preference independence tend to be rejected. But caution is needed here as the tests employed in many of the earlier studies are subject to small-sample biases (Laitinen 1978). When this issue is avoided using a resampling approach, preference independence is rejected less frequently (Selvanathan 1987, 1993; Selvanathan and Selvanathan 2005b). Again, we return to this evidence in Chap. 7. In another test of preference independence, Clements et al. (1985) use four sets of estimated elasticities to examine the validity of Eq. (3.11). In each case, the hypothesis of proportionality of price and income elasticities does not seem to be grossly violated.

In summary, while it is not possible to give iron-clad guarantees, it now seems preference independence is not an unreasonable hypothesis for broad aggregates of goods.

3.8 The Marginal Utility of Income

This section simplifies some of the previous derivations by imposing more structure on the problem to obtain almost the same result of proportionality between price and income elasticities. To enhance readability, we start with a brief recap of some of the previous material; when an equation from before is reproduced, a prime is added to the original equation number.

Table 3.1 contains a summary of the main concepts to be used. The marginal utility of good i is $\frac{\partial u}{\partial q_i}$ and if cross effects in utility are ignored, the impact of logarithmic change in the price of j on this marginal utility is $\frac{\partial \log\left(\frac{\partial u}{\partial q_i}\right)}{\partial \log q_i}\eta_{ij}$, where η_{ij} is the elasticity of q_i with respect to p_j. The first-order condition for a maximum, $\frac{\partial u}{\partial q_i} = \lambda p_i$, in logarithmic form is

$$\log \frac{\partial u}{\partial q_i} = \log \lambda + \log p_i. \qquad ((3.5)')$$

With no cross effects, the derivative of this equation with respect to $\log p_j$ is

Table 3.1 Glossary of symbols and results

Symbol	Meaning
q_i	Quantity consumed of good i, $i = 1, \ldots, n$
p_i	Price of good i
$u(q_1, \cdots, q_n)$	Utility function
$\frac{\partial u}{\partial q_i}$	Marginal utility of good i
$\sum_{i=1}^{n} p_i q_i = M$	Budget constraint where M is income
$w_i = \frac{p_i q_i}{M}$	Budget share of i
$\eta_i = \frac{\partial \log q_i}{\partial \log M}$	Income elasticity of i
$\eta_{ij} = \frac{\partial \log q_i}{\partial \log p_j}$	Uncompensated elasticity of demand for i with respect to price of j, $i, j = 1, \ldots, n$. Money income held constant
$\eta^*_{ij} = \eta_{ij} + w_j \eta_i$	Compensated elasticity of demand for i with respect to price of j, i, $j = 1, \ldots, n$. Real income held constant
$\lambda = \frac{\partial u_I}{\partial M}$	Marginal utility of income with $u_I(M, \mathbf{p})$ indirect utility function
$q_i = q_i(M, p_1, \cdots, p_n)$	Demand function for i
$\phi = \left(\frac{\partial \log \lambda}{\partial \log M}\right)^{-1} < 0$	Income flexibility, the reciprocal of the income elasticity of the marginal utility of income
$\eta_{ij} = \phi \eta_i (\delta_{ij} - w_j \eta_j) - \eta_i w_j$	Uncompensated elasticity of demand for i with respect to price of j. Holds under independent marginal utilities, $\frac{\partial(\partial u/\partial q_i)}{\partial q_j} = 0, i \neq j$
$\eta^*_{ii} \approx \phi \eta_i$	As an approximation, compensated own-price elasticity (η^*_{ii}) a multiple ϕ of corresponding income elasticity. Holds under independent marginal utilities
$u(q_1, \cdots, q_n) = \sum_{i=1}^{n} u_i(q_i)$	Preference-independent utility function with $u_i(\cdot)$ the ith sub-utility function depending on consumption of good only

$$\frac{\partial \log\left(\frac{\partial u}{\partial q_i}\right)}{\partial \log q_i} \eta_{ij} = \frac{\partial \log \lambda}{\partial \log p_j} + \delta_{ij}, \qquad ((3.6)')$$

where δ_{ij} is the Kronecker delta.

Denote the income elasticity of i by η_i and the income elasticity of the marginal utility of income, $\frac{\partial \log \lambda}{\partial \log M}$, by $\frac{1}{\phi}$, where ϕ is the income flexibility. The effect of a logarithmic change in income on $\log \frac{\partial u}{\partial q_i}$ is, from Eq. (3.5)$'$, $\frac{\partial \log\left(\frac{\partial u}{\partial q_i}\right)}{\partial \log q_i} \eta_i = \frac{1}{\phi}$. Write this as.

$$\frac{\partial \log\left(\frac{\partial u}{\partial q_i}\right)}{\partial \log q_i} = \frac{1}{\eta_i \phi}. \qquad ((3.7)')$$

Combining Eqs. (3.6)$'$ and (3.7)$'$ gives $\frac{1}{\phi \eta_i} \eta_{ij} = \frac{\partial \log \lambda}{\partial \log p_j} + \delta_{ij}$, or

$$\eta_{ij} = \phi\eta_i\left(\frac{\partial \log \lambda}{\partial \log p_j} + \delta_{ij}\right).$$

Accordingly, for $i = j$,the own-price elasticity is

$$\eta_{ii} = \phi\eta_i\left(\frac{\partial \log \lambda}{\partial \log p_i} + 1\right). \tag{3.14}$$

This is a rearrangement of Eq. (3.8) for $i = j$.

The dependence of the marginal utility on income is measured by the income flexibility ϕ. More will be said subsequently regarding the likely value of ϕ, but for the present all we need is that $\phi < 0$. With cardinal utility, a poor person valuing an extra dollar of income more than Elon Musk values such an increment comes as a natural assumption, making $\phi < 0$. How might λ depend on the price of an individual good? If the good dominates the budget, a change in its price could have a substantial impact; and conversely, a good absorbing a tiny amount of income could have a near-zero impact. The impact of the price of a good in between the two extremes is unclear. Take the "average good", one whose budget share is $\frac{1}{n}$, where n is the number of goods. The dependence λ on the price of such a good is much less clear than the case of income. In the absence of information to the contrary, we could set $\frac{\partial \log \lambda}{\partial \log p_i} = 0$ as the expected value, while appreciating the considerable uncertainty. Interestingly, the assumption of a constant marginal utility of income has a long history starting with Marshall (1920, Note VI), as discussed by Silberberg (2008).

When $\frac{\partial \log \lambda}{\partial \log p_i} = 0$, Eq. (3.14) becomes

$$\eta_{ii} = \phi\eta_i, \quad i = 1, \cdots, n. \tag{3.15}$$

This states that own-price elasticities are proportional to income elasticities. This is almost the same as before, that is, $\eta^*_{ii} \approx \phi\eta_i$, the only difference is that the approximation proportionality is now exact. Result (3.15) is also identical to that involving Frisch elasticities which hold the marginal utility of income constant by varying the consumer's income, as discussed above.

3.9 Groups of Goods

What exactly are the n goods demanded? A literal interpretation is they are the individual products bought by the consumers such as bread, rice, beef, chicken, etc. But this begs the question, what constitutes a product? Should white bread be distinguished from wholemeal, or basmati from jasmine rice? What of different brands of almost-identical cans of tuna? While any definition of goods is unavoidably arbitrary, some progress is possible with groups of goods interpreted as aggregates of the underlying products. Thus, the food group, comprising all types of bread, rice, and other edibles, could be one of the n goods. This has the advantage of reducing the dimension of the problem to something more manageable while still remaining within the utility-maximisation approach. Assuming preference independence at the group level would be consistent with this assumption being more palatable when referring to broad groups, rather than more finely defined products, as mentioned previously. With this structure of the utility function, the previous proportionality result [Eq. (3.11)] can be interpreted as referring to groups of goods. This section, mostly based on Clements (1987) and Theil (1975/76, 1980), provides an introduction to approach, while Chaps. 8 and 9 contain a comprehensive treatment.

Let the n goods be divided into $G < n$ groups, denoted by $\boldsymbol{S}_1,\cdots,\ \boldsymbol{S}_G$, such that each good belongs to only one group. To give an economic interpretation to them, each group could contain goods that are reasonably close substitutes, while there is no/limited substitution between goods belonging to different groups. That is, within each group, goods can interact fully while in a marginal utility sense, there are no between-group effects. In such a case, the utility function can be represented as the preference-independent form with respect to groups:

$$u(q_1,\cdots,q_n) = \sum_{g=1}^{G} u_g(\boldsymbol{q}_g), \tag{3.16}$$

where $u_g(\cdot)$ is the sub-utility function of group g and $\boldsymbol{q}_g$ is the vector of $q_i's$ belonging to group g. When gods are ordered appropriately, the Hessian matrix of Eq. (3.16) is block-diagonal, with the gth block containing $\frac{\partial^2 u}{\partial q_i \partial q_j}, i,j \in \boldsymbol{S}_g$. This is known as block independence, a generalisation of preference independence as represented by Eq. (3.12). When each group contains only one of the n goods and $G = n$, utility function (3.16) coincides with (3.12). The budget share of group $\boldsymbol{S}_g$ is $W_g = \sum_{i \in \boldsymbol{S}_g} w_i$ and the within-group budget share of $i \in \boldsymbol{S}_g$ is $\frac{w_i}{W_g}$, with $\sum_{i \in \boldsymbol{S}_g} \frac{w_i}{W_g} = 1$.

Preference independence leads to the (approximate) proportionality of price and income elasticities, as indicated by Eq. (3.11):

$$\eta_{ii}^* \approx \phi \eta_i, \quad i = 1,\cdots,n.$$

Here, all cross-price elasticities vanish. Under block independence, the within-group cross elasticities $\left(\eta_{ij}^*, i,j \in \boldsymbol{S}_g\right)$ are non-zero and the above equation becomes

$$\sum_{j \in \boldsymbol{S}_g} \eta_{ij}^* \approx \phi \eta_i, \quad i \in \boldsymbol{S}_g, g = 1,\cdots,G. \tag{3.17}$$

In words, for a given good i, the sum of the own- and within-group cross-price elasticities are approximately proportional to the income elasticity of the good, with the income flexibility the proportionality factor.

Averaging both sides of Eq. (3.17) over $i \in S_g$, using the within-group budget shares as weights, gives

$$\sum_{i \in S_g} \frac{w_i}{W_g} \sum_{j \in S_g} \eta_{ij}^* \approx \phi \sum_{i \in S_g} \frac{w_i}{W_g} \eta_i, \quad g = 1, \cdots, G.$$

This can be written as

$$\mathrm{N}_{gg}^* \approx \phi \mathrm{N}_g, \quad g = 1, \cdots, G. \tag{3.18}$$

Here, $\mathrm{N}_{gg}^* = \sum_{i \in S_g} \frac{w_i}{W_g} \sum_{j \in S_g} \eta_{ij}^*$ is the own-price elasticity of group g and $\mathrm{N}_g = \sum_{i \in S_g} \frac{w_i}{W_g} \eta_i$ is the income elasticity of this group with $\sum_{g=1}^{G} W_g \mathrm{N}_g = \sum_{i=1}^{n} w_i \eta_i = 1$, that is, the weighted-average of the group income elasticities is unity. Result (3.18) reveals that under block independence, group price and income elasticities are approximately proportional with the income flexibility as the proportionality factor. This is the groupwise version of Eq. (3.11).

To summarise, block independence amounts to preference independence with respect to the groups of goods. While preference independence of finely distinguished goods is likely to be too strong a condition, preference independence of groups of goods is likely to be more appropriate. Accordingly, the previous material on preference independence and the associated proportionality is best interpreted as referring to groups of goods, not the individual goods themselves.

3.10 Estimates of the Income Flexibility

Clements and Si (2017, 2018) and Clements et al. (2020b) estimate the income flexibility ϕ using the preference-independent version of the Rotterdam model [Eq. (3.13)]. As the marginal share θ_i appears three times on the right-hand side of that equation, it clearly plays an important role. Treating this as a constant parameter implies a linear Engel curve which seems implausible and can lead to unattractive implications of the behaviour of the income elasticities, as will be discussed in Sect. 3.21. An alternative approach is to set $\theta_i = \overline{w}_{it} + \beta_i$, with β_i a constant satisfying $\sum_{i=1}^{n} \beta_i = 0$. This form of the marginal share is implied by Working's (1943) model. After rearrangements, Eq. (3.13) then becomes

$$\bar{w}_{it}(Dq_{it} - DQ_t) = \beta_i DQ_t + \phi(\bar{w}_{it} + \beta_i)(Dp_{it} - DP_t') + \varepsilon_{it}, \quad i = 1, \cdots, n, \tag{3.19}$$

where $DP_t' = \sum_{i=1}^{n} (\overline{w}_{it} + \beta_i) Dp_{it}$ is a marginal-share weighted price index.

Clements et al. (2020b) estimate system (3.19) for $n = 9$ with annual data for each of the 37 OECD countries separately. The income elasticities, of the form $1 + \frac{\beta_i}{\overline{w}_{it}}$, differ across countries, but they can summarised by averaging over countries, as in

Table 3.2 Income elasticities: Means, 37 OECD countries

Commodity	Income elasticity
1. Food and alcohol	0.57
2. Clothing and footwear	1.01
3. Housing and utilities	0.60
4. Furnishings, equipment	1.30
5. Health	0.98
6. Recreation and culture	1.38
7. Education	1.41
8. Restaurants and hotels	1.06
9. Misc goods and services	1.48

Source: Clements et al. (2020b)

Table 3.3 First set of income flexibilities: Time-series estimates for each OECD country (Standard errors in parentheses)

1. Australia	−0.414 (0.054)	21. Lithuania	−0.394 (0.089)
2. Austria	−0.463 (0.062)	22. Luxembourg	−0.848 (0.143)
3. Belgium	−0.050 (0.047)	23. Mexico	−0.830 (0.000)
4. Canada	−0.350 (0.048)	24. Netherlands	−0.282 (0.066)
5. Colombia	−0.082 (0.045)	25. New Zealand	−0.624 (0.067)
6. Czech rep.	−0.438 (0.067)	26. Norway	−0.906 (0.082)
7. Denmark	−0.530 (0.087)	27. Poland	−0.606 (0.071)
8. Estonia	−0.321 (0.055)	28. Portugal	−0.612 (0.083)
9. Finland	−0.486 (0.059)	29. Slovak rep.	−0.477 (0.058)
10. France	−0.444 (0.046)	30. Slovenia	−0.336 (0.084)
11. Germany	−0.300 (0.051)	31. South Africa	−0.376 (0.046)
12. Greece	−0.148 (0.134)	32. Spain	−0.219 (0.062)
13. Hungary	−0.524 (0.052)	33. Sweden	−0.515 (0.068)
14. Iceland	−0.806 (0.095)	34. Switzerland	−1.706 (0.031)
15. Ireland	−2.459 (0.053)	35. Turkey	−0.183 (0.039)
16. Israel	−0.017 (0.059)	36. UK	−0.812 (0.078)
17. Italy	−0.526 (0.048)	37. United States	−0.601 (0.047)
18. Japan	−0.605 (0.160)		
19. Korea	−0.209 (0.046)	Mean	−0.538 (0.067)
20. Latvia	−0.423 (0.106)		

Source: Clements et al. (2020b)

Table 3.2. As can be seen, food with an elasticity of 0.57 is a clear necessity, in agreement with Engel's law, while education and miscellaneous goods and services are both strong luxuries. Table 3.3 contains the 37 ϕ-estimates, which seem to be more or less scattered randomly around the mean of −0.54. Using several tests,

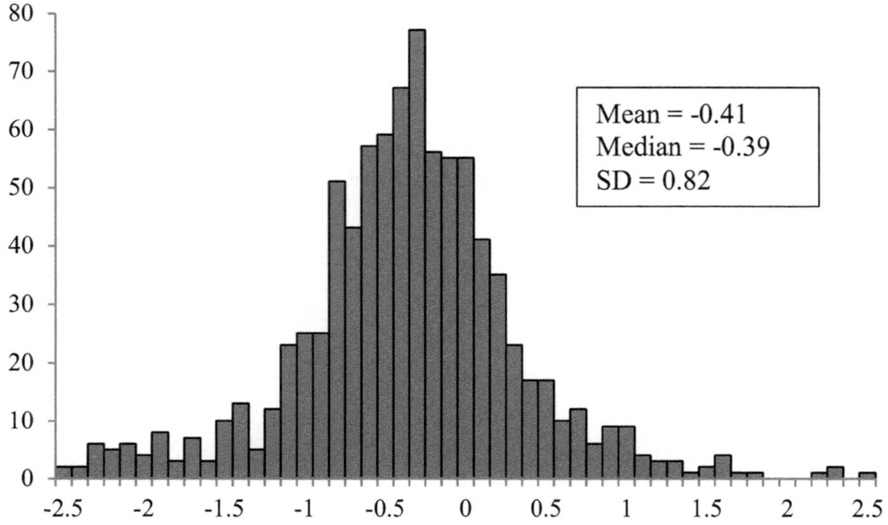

Fig. 3.1 Second set of income flexibilities: Estimates for each year and each OECD country. *Note*: Values are truncated to [−2.5, 2.5]. *Source*: Clements and Si (2017, 2018)

Clements and Si (2017) find that these income flexibility estimates are indeed unrelated to income.

As ϕ appears as a common coefficient in each of the n equations of (3.19), if β_i is known, ϕ can be estimated for each year and country with a cross-commodity regression by regressing $\overline{w}_{it}(Dq_{it} - DQ_t) - \beta_i DQ_t$ on $(\overline{w}_{it} + \beta_i)(Dp_{it} - DP'_t)$ for $i = 1, \cdots, 9$. Using the OECD data, Clements and Si (2018) apply this procedure with the $\beta_i' s$ set at their previously estimated values. The ϕ-estimates are given in Fig. 3.1 in the form of a frequency distribution. There is a fairly well-defined centre-of-gravity to this distribution and the mean is −0.41, which is not too far away from the previous mean of −0.54.

Clements and Si (2018) also apply the approach described in the previous paragraph to the 2011 round of the International Comparison Program (World Bank 2015). Rather than comparing changes from 1 year with the next, this cross-country application involves a comparison of each of the 176 countries with each of the others, a total of ${}^{176}C_2$=15,400 pairwise comparisons. Figure 3.2 shows the average over all countries of the estimates of ϕ is −0.52.

The centre of gravity of each of the three sets of income flexibility estimates seems not too far from −½. This value is also in broad agreement with earlier estimates as reviewed by Clements and Zhao (2009, p. 228–29), as well as being consistent with a survey of older studies by Brown and Deaton (1972, p. 1206), who state "there would seem to be fair agreement on the use of a value for ϕ around minus one half".

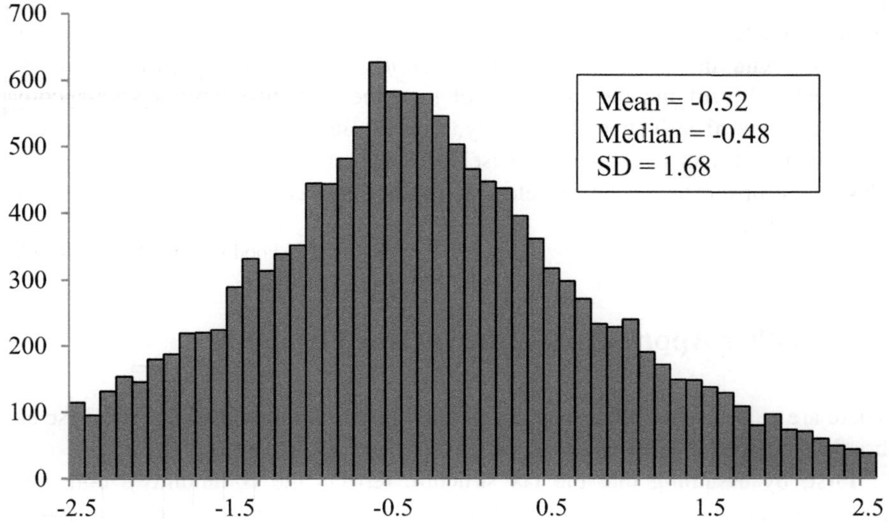

Fig. 3.2 Third set of income flexibilities: Estimates for each pair of 176 ICP countries, 2011. *Note*: Values are truncated to [−2.5, 2.5]. *Source*: Clements and Si (2018)

3.11 Frisch's Conjecture

In a prominent paper, Frisch (1959) discusses the dependence on income of the income elasticity of the marginal utility of income, among other things. He denotes the marginal utility of income by ω and its income elasticity by $\breve{\omega}$, which he calls the "money flexibility". This elasticity is the inverse of the income flexibility ϕ. Clearly, care is needed not to confuse these similarly named concepts. Frisch conjectures that the absolute value of $\breve{\omega}$ decreases with income, which means $|\phi|$ increases with income, or that the marginal utility of income decreases more rapidly for the rich relative to the poor. While the basis for this conjecture is not entirely clear, Frisch (1959, p. 189) refers to three values of $\breve{\omega}$ obtained by Johansen with Norwegian data from the 1950s: Converting to the income flexibility ϕ by taking reciprocals, these values are $\frac{1}{-1.94} = -0.52$ (derived from the demand elasticities for agricultural products), $\frac{1}{-2.13} = -0.47$ (industrial foods and beverages) and $\frac{1}{-1.85} = -0.54$ (land and air transport). He comments, "It is truly remarkable that data taken from such different sources and giving such different budget proportions and Engel elasticities, give such consistent values of [$\breve{\omega}$]. A compromise value of about −2 for the money flexibility $\breve{\omega}$ ought to be a reasonable estimate." This compromise value implies $\phi = -\frac{1}{2}$.

As mentioned, Clements and Si (2017) find the income flexibility to be unrelated to income, which does not support Frisch's conjecture. The conjecture has also been tested in several other studies as summarised by Clements and Zhao (2009, p. 228). The majority of the evidence is not strongly supportive of the conjecture, but there are some exceptions including DeJanvry et al. (1972), Gao (2012b, p. 106), and

Lluch et al. (1977). Accordingly, the empirical status of the Frisch conjecture has not been completely resolved. It should be acknowledged that there is a fundamental difficulty with the precise measurement of ϕ. As the income elasticity of the marginal utility of income, the issue of how the elasticity evolves with income involves the third derivative of the utility function. Because such higher-order effects are usually difficult to estimate precisely, the uncertainty around the value of this elasticity is unsurprising. Nevertheless, for the above reasons, setting ϕ to −½ seems a reasonable choice.

3.12 Other Approaches to the Income Flexibility

There are at least three other ways of estimating the income flexibility ϕ. These are briefly discussed in what follows.

First, by assuming that the tax structure reflects the community's collective attitude to the "fair" distribution of income, ϕ can be estimated from the country's income-tax schedule with the equal sacrifice model. Using this approach, Evans (2005) finds the average estimate of $-\frac{1}{\phi}$ from 20 OECD countries to be about 1.4, so ϕ is about −0.71. An open issue is the underlying basis for the tax schedule: Can it really be interpreted as an explicit statement of the people's collective values, or is the schedule set politically/administratively, or some other equally opaque process.

Secondly, using survey data on self-reported happiness as a type of direct measure of utility, Layard et al. (2008) estimate $-\frac{1}{\phi}$ to range over 1.19–1.34, with a combined estimate of 1.26, implying $\phi \in [-0.75, -0.84]$, and $\phi = -0.79$ corresponding to the combined estimate. Following Layard et al., Gandelman and Hernández-Murillo (2015) estimate the coefficient of relative risk aversion for 75 countries by regressing happiness on income and find that it varies between 0 and 3 and tends to be closely scattered around 1. Although they do not note it, in principle this coefficient is equivalent to $-\frac{1}{\phi}$. When $-\frac{1}{\phi} = 1$, $\phi = -1$, and utility is inversely proportional to income. The values of the income flexibility found by these studies differ from −½, although it seems questionable whether reported subjective happiness is strictly synonymous with utility of the utility-maximising consumer.

The life-cycle model and choice under uncertainty is the third way of estimating ϕ. Related to Evans (2005), Groom and Maddison (2019) present five ways of estimating ϕ: (i) the equal sacrifice model; (ii) the Euler-equation approach for the life-cycle model (Hansen and Singleton 1982) to estimate $-\frac{1}{\phi}$ by regressing the growth in consumption on the real interest rate; (iii) the Rotterdam model for food and non-food under preference independence, Eq. (3.13) for $n = 2$; (iv) the coefficient of relative risk aversion with insurance data; and (v) the subjective happiness approach of Layard et al. (2008). These five approaches yield a combined estimate of $\frac{1}{\phi}$ of about −1.5, or $\phi \approx -0.67$, which is unlikely to be significantly different from −0.5.

Stern (1977) provides an earlier review of alternative approaches to the measurement of ϕ, including saving behaviour.

3.13 Distributional Weights

Acland and Greenberg (2023) derive distributional weights for benefit-cost analysis. Suppose the indirect utility function for consumer c with income M_c is isoelastic:

$$u(M_c) = \left(\frac{1}{1+\frac{1}{\phi}}\right) M_c^{1+\frac{1}{\phi}}, \quad \text{with } u'_{M_c} = M_c^{\frac{1}{\phi}}.$$

As can be seen, $\frac{1}{\phi}$ is the elasticity of the marginal utility of income $\left(u'_{M_c}\right)$. Acland and Greenberg (2023) propose the weight for consumer c, relative to someone with mean income $\overline{M}$, to be $w_{M_c} = \frac{u'_{M_c}}{u'_{\overline{M}}}$. With diminishing marginal utility, $w_{M_c} > 1$ for $M_c < \overline{M}$. The above utility function means that $w_{M_c} = \left(\frac{M_c}{\overline{M}}\right)^{\frac{1}{\phi}}$. For example, if c has income 25% below the mean, the weight for this individual is $w_{M_c} = \left(\frac{1-0.25}{1}\right)^{\frac{1}{\phi}} = 1.8$ for $\frac{1}{\phi} = -2$, or $\phi = -\frac{1}{2}$. As the weight for average income recipient is $w_{\overline{M}} = \left(\frac{\overline{M}}{\overline{M}}\right)^{\frac{1}{\phi}} = 1$, the weight accorded to c in this case is 80% higher than the mean. The plot below illustrates this relation. Views will differ regarding the "reasonableness" of such an implication and the whole idea of distribution weighting; Harberger (1978) provides a valuable discussion of the issue. Even so, the above approach generates some insight and is of considerable interest.

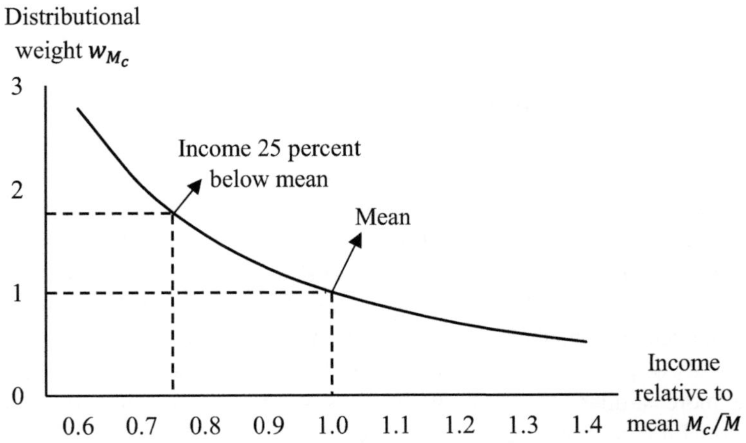

Acland and Greenberg (2023) also survey a number of approaches to estimating $-\frac{1}{\phi}$ and locate 158 studies that use data for the USA and UK. From these studies, they present a weighted-average estimate of $-\frac{1}{\phi}$ of 1.6 with a standard error of 0.22. In view of this standard error, using $-\frac{1}{\phi}=2$ or $\phi=-\frac{1}{2}$ is unlikely to be seriously misguided.

3.14 The Rule of ½

According to Eq. (3.11), price and income elasticities are proportional with the income flexibility the factor of proportionality, $\eta_{ii}^{*}\approx\phi\eta_i, i=1,\cdots,n$. With $\phi=-\frac{1}{2}$ and the income elasticity set at its average of unity, the rule of ½ emerges:

$$\eta_{ii}^{*}\approx-\frac{1}{2},\quad i=1,\cdots,n.$$

This rule involves the compensated price elasticities, although, as stated before, Chap. 2 did not distinguish between compensated and uncompensated elasticities.

The rule of ½ is based on three assumptions: (i) the utility function is of the preference independence form, with broad aggregates with limited substitutes likely to be in that category; (ii) the income flexibility equals −½; and (iii) the income elasticity of the good is unity—although a weighted average of income elasticities is unity, this assumption is just an approximation used in the absence of further information.

The rule of ½ is not universal and only applies to some goods. While the rule should not be oversold, it is nevertheless a useful rule of thumb when nothing is known about the price elasticity.

3.15 Alcohol Elasticities

Table 3.4 is a more extensive version of Table 2.1.

There is a literature comparing alcohol consumption patterns across countries, including Aizenman and Brooks (2008), Anderson et al. (2018), Clements et al. (2020a), Colen and Swinnen (2016), Eriksson et al. (2001), Holmes and Anderson (2017), Mills (2018), Nelson (2010), Selvanathan (1991), Selvanathan (2006), Selvanathan and Selvanathan (2007), and Smith and Solgaard (2000). As discussed by Clements et al. (2020a), one finding is the tendency for drinking patterns to become more similar across countries, possibly because of globalisation, more international travel, rapid communication of cultural trends, etc.

Table 3.4 Details of alcohol price elasticities

Source	Mean	Median	Number of underlying estimates/ studies	Comments
A. Beer				
Nelson (2014)	−0.20		191	Sample of 191 estimates from 114 primary studies. Australia, Canada, Ireland, New Zealand, the UK, and the USA account for 143 estimates. Median publication date 1997; median sample year 1977. "Overall, the analysis indicates the average price elasticity of beer is about −0.20" (Nelson 2014, p. 186).
Sornpaisarn et al. (2013)	−0.50		7	Based on 7 primary studies of consumption in low- and middle-income countries.
Nelson (2013b)		−0.29		Based on 86 primary studies in mostly high-income countries. Corrected for outliers, dependence, heterogeneity and publication bias.
Fogarty (2010)	−0.45	−0.33	154	Based on 141 primary studies in mostly high-income countries. Higher elasticities obtained with higher-frequency data. Elasticities tend to rise over time.
Elder et al. (2010)		−0.50	18	Based on 18 primary studies in high-income countries. Time-series/panel data.
Wagenaar et al. (2009)	−0.46		105	Based on 112 primary studies in high-income countries.
Gallet (2007)	−0.83	−0.36	315	Based on 132 primary studies in 24 mostly high-income countries. Mostly time-series data.
Selvanathan and Selvanathan (2005a, p. 232)	−0.37		10	Based on estimates for 10 high-income countries with varying sample periods ranging from 1950 to 2002.
Mean	**−0.47**	**−0.37**		
B. Wine				
Nelson (2013a)	−0.65	−0.45	197	Based on 104 primary studies in mostly high-income countries. Median publication date 1997, median sample year 1977. Mostly annual time-series data at country level. Median is 50th percentile of cumulative random-effect averages.

(continued)

Table 3.4 (continued)

Source	Mean	Median	Number of underlying estimates/ studies	Comments
Nelson (2013b)		−0.46		See Nelson (2013b), panel A above.
Fogarty (2010)	−0.65	−0.55	155	See Fogarty (2010), panel A above.
Elder et al. (2010)		−0.64	22	See Elder et al. (2010), panel A above.
Wagenaar et al. (2009)	−0.69		93	See Wagenaar et al. (2009), panel A above.
Gallet (2007)	−1.11	−0.70	300	See Gallet (2007), panel A above.
Selvanathan and Selvanathan (2005a, p. 232)	−0.46		10	See Selvanathan and Selvanathan (2005a), panel A above.
Mean	**−0.71**	**−0.56**		
C. Spirits				
Nelson (2013a)	−0.70	−0.55	202	See Nelson (2013a), panel B above.
Nelson (2013b)		−0.54	89	See Nelson (2013b), panel A above.
Fogarty (2010)	−0.73	−0.76	162	See Fogarty (2010), panel A above.
Elder et al. (2010)		−0.79	21	See Elder et al. (2010), panel A above.
Wagenaar et al. (2009)	−0.80		103	See Wagenaar et al. (2009), panel A above.
Gallet (2007)	−1.09	−0.68	294	See Gallet (2007), panel A above.
Selvanathan and Selvanathan (2005a, p. 232)	−0.57		10	See Selvanathan and Selvanathan (2005a), panel A above.
Mean	**−0.78**	**−0.66**		

Source: Clements et al. (2022a)

3.16 Constant Elasticity of Substitution Utility

A popular choice of the form of utility function is one with a constant elasticity of substitution (CES). This takes the form

$$u(q_1, \cdots, q_n) = \left(\sum_{i=1}^{n} \alpha_i q_i^{-\rho} \right)^{-\frac{1}{\rho}}, \quad \alpha_i > 0, \sum_{i=1}^{n} \alpha_i = 1, \rho \geq -1, \rho \neq 0. \qquad (3.20)$$

Here, q_i is the quantity demanded of good i, while α_i $(i = 1, \cdots, n)$ and ρ are constant parameters. The elasticity of substitution is $\sigma = \frac{1}{1+\rho} > 0$, which is also a constant, as implied by the name "CES" given to (3.20). The plot below illustrates the relation between the value of ρ, which governs curvature of the utility function, and the elasticity of substitution σ:

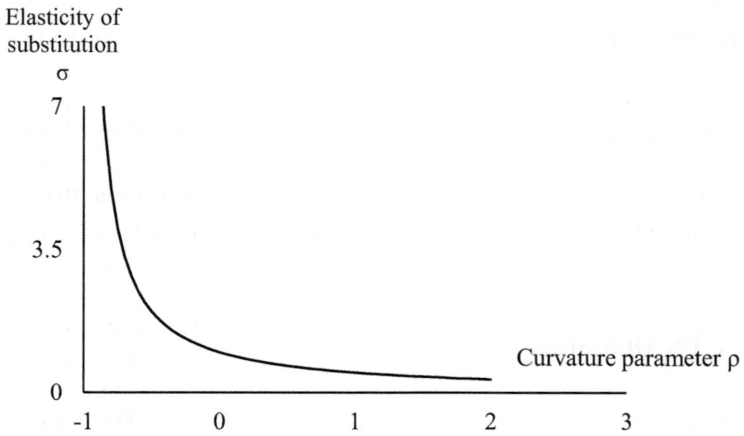

The CES can accommodate a wide range of behaviour, from approaching no substitution ($\sigma \to 0$, the Leontief case), to Cobb-Douglas ($\sigma \to 1$), to perfect substitution ($\sigma \to \infty$, linear utility).

Formally, the CES is a mean of order r of the n quantities with $r = -\rho$. Since $x^{-\beta} = \frac{1}{x^\beta}, x > 0$, utility function (3.20) can be expressed as

$$u(q_1, \cdots, q_n) = \frac{1}{\left\{\sum_{i=1}^{n} \alpha_i \left(\frac{1}{q_i}\right)^\rho\right\}^{\frac{1}{\rho}}}.$$

As the α_i are all positive and have a unit sum, the term $\sum_{i=1}^{n} \alpha_i \left(\frac{1}{q_i}\right)^\rho$ is interpreted as a proper weighted average of $\left(\frac{1}{q_1}\right)^\rho, \cdots, \left(\frac{1}{q_n}\right)^\rho$. Thus, when $\rho = 1$, this is a proper weighted average of the reciprocals, $\sum_{i=1}^{n} \alpha_i \left(\frac{1}{q_i}\right)$, and utility is the reciprocal of this weighted average:

$$u(q_1, \cdots, q_n) = \frac{1}{\sum_{i=1}^{n} \alpha_i \left(\frac{1}{q_i}\right)}.$$

This is a weighted harmonic mean of the q_i. The harmonic mean is never greater than the arithmetic mean and emphasises smaller values at the expense of larger ones. For example, when x is lognormal with arithmetic mean μ and variance θ^2, the harmonic mean is $\exp\left(\mu - \frac{1}{2}\theta^2\right)$, which shows greater dispersion lowers the harmonic relative to the arithmetic mean. This property carries over directly to the weighted harmonic case. Note also that when $\rho = 1$, the elasticity of substitution $\sigma = \frac{1}{1+\rho} = \frac{1}{2}$.

The CES function was introduced by Arrow et al. (1961) and Biddle (2020) gives a fascinating history of its development. The CES is now the workhorse model in a number of areas such as the Armington (1969) approach to the foreign/domestic split of expenditures used in many CGE models (Hilberry and Hummels 2013; Lloyd and Zhang 2006), industrial organisation (Dixit and Stiglitz 1977), economic geography (Krugman 1991; Krugman and Venables 1996), economic growth (De La Grandville 2008), and international trade theory (Costinot and Rodríguez-Clare 2014). A special issue of the *Journal of Macroeconomics* edited by Klump and Papageorgiour (2008) was devoted to reviews of the theory and measurement of the CES. Chirinko (2008) surveys estimates of the elasticity of substitution obtained from the CES, while Knoblach et al. (2020) provide a meta-study of US estimates of that elasticity. The CES and some alternatives are reviewed in Matsuyama (2023).

3.17 CES Demands

To derive the demand equations associated with CES utility (3.20), it is convenient to replace the weight α_i with $\beta_i^{\frac{1}{\sigma}}$ and ρ with $\frac{1-\sigma}{\sigma}$, so that

$$u(q_1, \cdots, q_n) = \left(\sum_{i=1}^{n} \alpha_i q_i^{-\rho}\right)^{-\frac{1}{\rho}} = \left(\sum_{i=1}^{n} \beta_i^{\frac{1}{\sigma}} q_i^{\frac{\sigma-1}{\sigma}}\right)^{\frac{\sigma}{\sigma-1}}.$$

The ith marginal utility is

$$\frac{\partial u}{\partial q_i} = \left\{\frac{\sigma}{\sigma-1}\left(\sum_{i=1}^{n} \beta_i^{\frac{1}{\sigma}} q_i^{\frac{\sigma-1}{\sigma}}\right)^{\frac{\sigma}{\sigma-1}-1}\right\}\left\{\frac{\sigma-1}{\sigma} \beta_i^{\frac{1}{\sigma}} q_i^{\left(\frac{\sigma-1}{\sigma}-1\right)}\right\}$$

$$= \left\{\left(\sum_{i=1}^{n} \beta_i^{\frac{1}{\sigma}} q_i^{\frac{\sigma-1}{\sigma}}\right)^{\frac{1}{\sigma-1}}\right\}\left\{\beta_i^{\frac{1}{\sigma}} q_i^{\frac{-1}{\sigma}}\right\} = \left(\sum_{i=1}^{n} \beta_i^{\frac{1}{\sigma}} q_i^{\frac{\sigma-1}{\sigma}}\right)^{\frac{1}{\sigma-1}} \left(\frac{\beta_i}{q_i}\right)^{\frac{1}{\sigma}}.$$

For a budget-constrained utility maximum, each marginal utility must be proportional to the price of the good:

$$\left(\sum_{i=1}^{n} \beta_i^{\frac{1}{\sigma}} q_i^{\frac{\sigma-1}{\sigma}}\right)^{\frac{1}{\sigma-1}} \left(\frac{\beta_i}{q_i}\right)^{\frac{1}{\sigma}} = \lambda p_i. \tag{3.21}$$

Here, $\lambda > 0$ is the Lagrange multiplier.

Taking the ratio of Eq. (3.21) for good i to that for j, the first term, $\left(\sum_{i=1}^{n} \beta_i^{\frac{1}{\sigma}} q_i^{\frac{\sigma-1}{\sigma}}\right)^{\frac{1}{\sigma-1}}$, cancels, as does λ, and we obtain $(\beta_i/q_i)^{\frac{1}{\sigma}}/(\beta_j/q_j)^{\frac{1}{\sigma}} = p_i/p_j$.

This is equivalent to $\left(\frac{p_i}{p_j}\right)^{\sigma} = \frac{\beta_i q_j}{\beta_j q_i}$, so that

$$q_j = \left(\frac{p_j}{p_i}\right)^{-\sigma} \frac{\beta_j q_i}{\beta_i}. \tag{3.22}$$

Using (3.22),

$$\begin{aligned} \sum_{j=1}^{n} p_j q_j &= p_i q_i + \sum_{j \neq i}^{n} p_j q_j = p_i q_i + \sum_{j \neq i}^{n} p_j \left(\frac{p_j}{p_i}\right)^{-\sigma} \frac{\beta_j q_i}{\beta_i} \\ &= p_i q_i + \sum_{j \neq i}^{n} p_j^{1-\sigma} p_i^{\sigma} \frac{\beta_j q_i}{\beta_i} = q_i \sum_{j=1}^{n} p_j^{1-\sigma} p_i^{\sigma} \frac{\beta_j}{\beta_i}. \end{aligned}$$

It follows from the budget constraint that $q_i \sum_{j=1}^{n} p_j^{1-\sigma} p_i^{\sigma} \frac{\beta_j}{\beta_i} = M$, so that $q_i = \frac{M}{\sum_{j=1}^{n} p_j^{1-\sigma} p_i^{\sigma} \frac{\beta_j}{\beta_i}}$. Substituting α_i^{σ} for β_i, we obtain the demand equation for good i:

$$q_i = \frac{M \alpha_i^{\sigma} p_i^{-\sigma}}{\sum_{j=1}^{n} \alpha_j^{\sigma} p_j^{1-\sigma}}. \tag{3.23}$$

The budget share, defined as $w_i = \frac{p_i q_i}{M}$, corresponding to (3.23) is

$$w_i = \frac{\alpha_i^{\sigma} p_i^{1-\sigma}}{\sum_{j=1}^{n} \alpha_j^{\sigma} p_j^{1-\sigma}}. \tag{3.24}$$

Define the CES price index as

$$P^* = \left(\sum_{j=1}^{n} \alpha_j^{\sigma} p_j^{1-\sigma}\right)^{\frac{1}{1-\sigma}}. \tag{3.25}$$

The denominator in (3.23) can be replaced with $(P^*)^{1-\sigma}$ to give $q_i = \frac{M \alpha_i^{\sigma} p_i^{-\sigma}}{(P^*)^{1-\sigma}}$, or

$$q_i = \alpha_i^{\sigma} \frac{M}{P^*} \left(\frac{p_i}{P^*}\right)^{-\sigma}. \tag{3.26}$$

This is just (3.23) in more compact form.

As stated above, in the CES σ is a constant parameter. To verify this, recall the elasticity of substitution is the elasticity of the ratio of the quantities of a pair of goods, $\frac{q_j}{q_i}$, with respect to the corresponding marginal rate of substitution, which is the ratio of the two marginal utilities. Let X denote the marginal rate of substitution. From above, the ith marginal utility is $\left(\sum_{i=1}^{n}\beta_i^{\frac{1}{\sigma}}q_i^{\frac{\sigma-1}{\sigma}}\right)^{\frac{1}{\sigma-1}}\left(\frac{\beta_i}{q_i}\right)^{\frac{1}{\sigma}}$, so that

$$X = \frac{(\beta_i/q_i)^{\frac{1}{\sigma}}}{(\beta_j/q_j)^{\frac{1}{\sigma}}} = \left(\frac{\beta_i q_j}{\beta_j q_i}\right)^{\frac{1}{\sigma}},$$

or $\frac{q_j}{q_i} = \frac{\beta_j}{\beta_i}X^{\sigma}$. Thus,

$$\log\frac{q_j}{q_i} = \log\frac{\beta_j}{\beta_i} + \sigma\log X.$$

As $\partial\left(\log\frac{q_j}{q_i}\right)/\partial(\log X) = \sigma$, this confirms that σ is the constant elasticity of substitution. This elasticity is the same for all pairs of goods.

3.18 CES Price Elasticities

Demand Eq. (3.26) is homogeneous of degree zero, with an income elasticity of unity and price elasticity $-\sigma$. Clearly, the CES would not be appropriate for food demand as the unity income elasticity would violate Engel's law. The price elasticity of $-\sigma$ is the elasticity with respect to the relative price $\frac{p_i}{P^*}$, with real income, as measured by $\frac{M}{P^*}$, held constant. This does not coincide with either the uncompensated or the compensated elasticity as defined previously.

To derive the more familiar price elasticities, we shall use the logarithmic differential of price index (3.25):

$$d\log P^* = \frac{1}{1-\sigma}d\log\left(\sum_{j=1}^{n}\alpha_j^{\sigma}p_j^{1-\sigma}\right) = \sum_{j=1}^{n}\left(\frac{\alpha_j^{\sigma}p_j^{1-\sigma}}{\sum\limits_{k=1}^{n}\alpha_k^{\sigma}p_k^{1-\sigma}}\right)d\log p_j.$$

From Eq. (3.24), this simplifies to

$$d\log P^* = \sum_{j=1}^{n} w_j d\log p_j. \tag{3.27}$$

The log-differential of Eq. (3.26) is $d\log q_i = d\log M - (1-\sigma)d\log P^* - \sigma d\log p_i$, which, using (3.27), becomes

$$d\log q_i = d\log M - \sum_{j=1}^{n} \{\sigma\delta_{ij} + (1-\sigma)w_j\} d\log p_j,$$

where δ_{ij} is the Kronecker delta, as before. The own- and cross-price uncompensated elasticities are the price coefficients in the above equation, viz.,

$$\eta_{ii} = -\{\sigma + (1-\sigma)w_i\}, \quad i=1,\cdots,n; \quad \eta_{ij} = -(1-\sigma)w_j, \quad i \neq j; i,j=1,\cdots,n. \tag{3.28}$$

Key properties of the uncompensated elasticities are:

1. An equivalent expression for the own-price elasticity is $\eta_{ii} = -[(1-w_i)\sigma + w_i]$. Thus, $|\eta_{ii}|$ is a weighted average of σ and unity and therefore must lie somewhere between these two values.
2. For $i \neq j$, the cross-price elasticity $\eta_{ij} < 0$ when $\sigma < 1$, making i and j gross complements. When $\sigma > 1$, $\eta_{ij} > 0$, so i and j are gross substitutes.
3. Since $\sum_{j=1}^{n} \eta_{ij} + \eta_i = 0$, $i = 1, \cdots, n$, an equiproportional change in all prices and income leaves consumption of each good unchanged, reflecting the homogeneity of degree zero of the demand eqs.
4. A budget-share weighted average of the own-price elasticities is

$$\sum_{i=1}^{n} w_i\eta_{ii} = -\left\{\sigma + (1-\sigma)\sum_{i=1}^{n} w_i^2\right\}.$$

Since $\sum_{i=1}^{n} w_i^2 \in \left[\frac{1}{n}, 1\right]$, it follows that

$$\sum_{i=1}^{n} w_i\eta_{ii} \in -\left\{\sigma + (1-\sigma)\frac{1}{n}, 1\right\}.$$

There are two interesting special cases of the lower limit of this weighted sum, $-\left\{\sigma + (1-\sigma)\frac{1}{n}\right\}$. (i) When $\sigma > 1$, but not "too large", $(1-\sigma)\frac{1}{n} \rightarrow 0$ as n get larger and $\sum_{i=1}^{n} w_i\eta_{ii} \rightarrow -\sigma$. (ii) When $\sigma < 1$, then whatever the size of n, $(1-\sigma)\frac{1}{n}$ is the product of two positive fractions, which will be small and can be approximated by zero. Thus, $\sum_{i=1}^{n} w_i\eta_{ii} \approx -\sigma$. In these cases, the lower limit of the average price elasticity can be approximated $-\sigma$, the elasticity of substitution with the sign changed. Interestingly, this $-\sigma$ coincides with the elasticity of demand Eq. (3.26) with respect to the relative price $\frac{p_i}{P^*}$.

5. The average of the above two limits is

$$-\frac{1}{2}\left\{\sigma+(1-\sigma)\frac{1}{n}+1\right\}\approx-\frac{1}{2}\{\sigma+1\}.$$

This may be useful to use if the shares are unknown, all possible values of the price elasticity are equally likely and σ is known. For example, the average elasticity is then $-\frac{1}{2}\{\sigma+1\}=-\frac{3}{4}$ when $\sigma=\frac{1}{2}$.

The compensated price elasticity can be derived from the uncompensated counterpart simply adding back the income effect of a price change. When the price of good j increases by $d\log p_j>0$ with M remaining unchanged, the consumer's real income falls by $-w_jd\log p_j<0$. This is the income effect of the price change that needs to be added back to money income in order to hold real income constant. As income elasticities are unity in the CES, consumption of good i increases by this amount, $w_jd\log p_j$. Thus, for a unit percentage increase in the price, we need to add the corresponding budget share to the uncompensated elasticity to obtain the compensated version:

$$\eta_{ii}^{*}=-\sigma(1-w_i),\quad i=1,\cdots,n;\quad \eta_{ij}^{*}=\sigma w_j,\quad i\neq j;i,j=1,\cdots,n. \tag{3.29}$$

Five features of the compensated elasticities can be noted:

1. $\left|\eta_{ii}^{*}\right|<\sigma$ as the budget share is a positive fraction.
2. For $i\neq j,\eta_{ij}^{*}>0$, making all pairs of goods net substitutes.
3. $\sum_{j=1}^{n}\eta_{ij}^{*}=0,i=1,\cdots,n,$ which reflects demand homogeneity. That is, when real income is constant, an equiproportional change in all prices leaves consumption of each good unchanged.
4. A budget-share weighted average of the own-price elasticities is

$$\sum_{i=1}^{n}w_i\eta_{ii}^{*}=-\sigma\left(1-\sum_{i=1}^{n}w_i^2\right)\in-\left[\sigma\left(1-\frac{1}{n}\right),0\right].$$

For reasons discussed above for the uncompensated case, when $w_i=\frac{1}{n}\forall i$, $\sum_{i=1}^{n}w_i\eta_{ij}^{*}\approx-\sigma$.

5. The average of the above two limits is $-\frac{1}{2}\sigma\left(1-\frac{1}{n}\right)\approx-\frac{1}{2}\sigma$.

When presenting the CES results in Chap. 2, to simplify matters there was no distinction between the compensated and uncompensated elasticities.

3.19 CES and ½

Consider the special case in which $\sigma = \frac{1}{2}$ corresponding to $\rho = \frac{1-\sigma}{\sigma} = 1$. The value of ρ reflects the nature of the commodities and their degree of substitutability; the range of this parameter is $\rho > -1, \neq 0$, with lower values meaning greater substitutability (higher σ). If $\rho = 1$ can be considered a "central", "representative", or "reasonable" value for goods with limited substitutability, it may be worthwhile to consider the implications of this specific value.

From demand Eq. (3.26), the own-price elasticity is $-\sigma$, as mentioned previously. As the elasticity is with respect to the deflated own price $\frac{p_i}{P^*}$, this is a special type of elasticity. The deflator employed in the relative price, P^*, is the CES index defined by Eq. (3.25), $P^* = \left(\sum_{j=1}^{n} \alpha_j^{\sigma} p_j^{1-\sigma}\right)^{\frac{1}{1-\sigma}}$; when $\sigma = \frac{1}{2}$, the index becomes $P^* = \left(\sum_{j=1}^{n} \sqrt{\alpha_j p_j}\right)^2$. This squared-square-root expression is an unfamiliar price index, making the $-\sigma$ elasticity a less straightforward concept than either the uncompensated or the compensated versions. Consequently, we shall consider the implications of $\sigma = \frac{1}{2}$ for the uncompensated and compensated price elasticities. Column 2 of the table below gives the values of these two elasticities. Thus, in absolute value, the uncompensated elasticity is above ½ by ½ · w_i, while the compensated one is below ½ by exactly the same amount, so the average of the two is ½:

$$\left.\frac{\eta_{ii} + \eta_{ii}^*}{2}\right]_{\sigma = \frac{1}{2}} = \frac{-\frac{1}{2}(1 + w_i) - \frac{1}{2}(1 - w_i)}{2} = -\frac{1}{2}. \tag{3.30}$$

Column 3 of the table gives the two elasticities with σ unrestricted. The average of these is

$$\left.\frac{\eta_{ii} + \eta_{ii}^*}{2}\right]_{\sigma \text{ free}} = \frac{-[\sigma + (1 - \sigma)w_i] - \sigma(1 - w_i)}{2} = -\frac{1}{2} w_i - \sigma(1 - w_i). \tag{3.31}$$

This is a weighted average of $-\frac{1}{2}$ and $-\sigma$, where the weights are the budget share and its complement. Accordingly,

$$\left.\frac{\eta_{ii} + \eta_{ii}^*}{2}\right]_{\sigma \text{ free}} \to \begin{cases} -\sigma, & as\ w_i \to 0 \\ -\dfrac{1}{2}, & as\ w_i \to 1. \end{cases}$$

Type of own-price elasticity (1)	Special case $\rho = 1, \sigma = \frac{1}{2}$ (2)	Generic case $\sigma = \frac{1}{1+\rho} > 0$ (3)
Uncompensated η_{ii}	$-\frac{1}{2}(1 + w_i)$	$-[\sigma + (1 - \sigma)w_i]$
Compensated η_{ii}^*	$-\frac{1}{2}(1 - w_i)$	$-\sigma(1 - w_i)$

In other words, the average falls in the range $\left[-\frac{1}{2}, -\sigma\right]$, so the more prominent the good in the budget, the closer the average will be to $-\frac{1}{2}$. For less prominent goods, the average is closer to $-\sigma$. Result (3.31) is stronger than (3.30) as it holds for any value of σ. But in another sense it is weaker as it only determines the range in which the average falls, not the specific value. Nonetheless, it is of considerable interest that the value ½ still plays a prominent role.

Next, consider the completely general case, one without CES utility. From the Slutsky equation, $\eta_{ii} = \eta_{ii}^* - w_i\eta_i$, where η_i is the income elasticity, the average price elasticity is $\frac{\eta_{ii}+\eta_{ii}^*}{2} = -\frac{1}{2}w_i\eta_i + \eta_{ii}^*$. Clearly, this equals $-\frac{1}{2}w_i\eta_i$ when there is no substitution $\left(\eta_{ii}^* = 0\right)$; and $-\frac{1}{2}w_i$ under a unitary income elasticity and $\eta_{ii}^* = 0$.

Why is the average elasticity of any interest? There are two possibilities:

1. The analyst may be uncertain whether to use the uncompensated or compensated elasticity, or may suspect the choice to be unimportant for the question at hand, as it might be when the good occupies a small budget share. Using the average of the two elasticities may be a useful way of proceeding in such situations.
2. As discussed above, $\rho = 1$ might be considered a central value of the substitution parameter for broad aggregates, implying an elasticity of substitution of $\sigma = \frac{1}{2}$. In this case, the average of the two types of the elasticity is $-\frac{1}{2}$, as indicated by Eq. (3.30). This result could also be useful.

3.20 Assessing CES

The CES function, $\left(\sum_{i=1}^{n}\alpha_i q_i^{-\rho}\right)^{-\frac{1}{\rho}}$, has $n + 1$ parameters, where n is the number of goods. This is a parsimonious parameterisation that still allows for a wide range of substitutability. Additionally, corresponding demands have a simple log-linear form:

$$\log q_i = k_i + \log\frac{M}{P} - \sigma\log\frac{p_i}{P}. \tag{3.32}$$

In short, the CES approach is popular because it is an attractively simple way to reduce a large-scale problem to something more manageable. Another feature of the CES is its relationship to the rule of ½.

But there are restrictions built into the CES that need to be appreciated. First, the CES is separable (but not additive). Second, the elasticity of substitution between each pair of goods is constrained to be identical and is taken to be a constant, independent of income and relative prices. A third restriction is homotheticity, that is, each income elasticity is unity, as is clear from Eq. (3.32). Accordingly, when income increases by $x > 0\%$ and other factors are unchanged, consumption of each good also increases by x. For example, when the approach is applied conditionally to wine demand in Australia, the consumption of imported French and Australian-produced wines increases equiproportionately with total wine consumption. The luxuriousness of the two types of wine is then taken to be the same, which may be reasonable. However, in the view of Engel's law, the unit income elasticity also means the CES is unsuitable to apply to the demand for food as a single aggregate. Consequently, although the CES has a number of attractions, it will not be applicable in all circumstances.

3.21 Changes in Income Elasticities

When the economy experiences sustained economic growth over the longer term, real income grows, as does aggregate consumption. Luxuries ($\eta_i > 1$) grow faster than average, while necessities ($\eta_i < 1$) grow slower, so the pattern of consumption is in large part determined by the magnitude of the income elasticities. With consumption such a large component of most modern economies, the pattern of consumption can also determine industry structure of the whole economy. Because there is no compelling reason for the income elasticities to be constant over a long period of time, the question arises: How might these elasticities change when there is substantial income growth? We shall consider some important cases.

Consider the Rotterdam model under preference independence, Eq. (3.13), and its generalisation, the unnumbered system following (3.13). When prices are held constant, both systems become $\overline{w}_{it}Dq_{it} = \theta_i DQ_t$, where disturbances have been set at their expected values of zero. Dividing both sides by $\overline{w}_{it}$ shows that the income elasticity of good i is $\eta_i = \frac{\theta_i}{\overline{w}_{it}}$. When $\theta_i =$ constant, as it is in Rotterdam, the elasticity is inversely proportional to the budget share, that is, $\frac{d\eta_i}{\eta_i} = -\frac{d\overline{w}_{it}}{\overline{w}_{it}}$. Thus, when income growth causes the budget share of food to fall according to Engel's law, the corresponding income elasticity rises. The movement of the share and elasticity in opposite directions violates economic intuition as it means greater affluence makes food less of a necessity, or more of a luxury. More generally, with constant marginal shares, the income elasticities of all necessities rise with income growth while those of luxuries fall. This weakness of the Rotterdam model is shared by the linear expenditure system (LES) as it also has constant marginal shares. As mentioned previously, constant marginal shares imply linear Engel curves. This problem could be of practical importance for those CGE models that use the LES, especially for simulations with major income changes.

According to Working's (1943) model, the budget share of good i is a linear function of the logarithm of income:

$$w_i = \alpha_i + \beta_i \log M. \tag{3.33}$$

The implied marginal share is $\theta_i = w_i + \beta_i$, which is not constant. By definition, the income elasticity is $\eta_i = \frac{\theta_i}{w_i}$, which in the case of model (3.33) takes the form:

$$\eta_i = 1 + \frac{\beta_i}{w_i}. \tag{3.34}$$

As β_i is a constant coefficient, when $\beta_i < 0$ the good is always a necessity ($\eta_i < 1$). The good is normal, or not inferior while remaining a necessity, when $w_i > -\beta_i > 0$, a condition that will be assumed, as is reasonable. When $\beta_i > 0$ the good is a luxury ($\eta_i > 1$). A good cannot change from being a luxury to a necessity, nor vice versa.

It follows from (3.34) that $\frac{d\eta_i}{\eta_i} = -\frac{\beta_i/w_i}{\eta_i}\frac{dw_i}{w_i}$, or

$$\frac{d\eta_i}{\eta_i} = \left(\frac{1-\eta_i}{\eta_i}\right)\frac{dw_i}{w_i}. \tag{3.35}$$

This reveals that for a necessity, the income elasticity moves in the same direction as the share, while the reverse is true for luxuries. Thus, for food ($\eta_i < 1$), as income rises, the share falls as does the elasticity. This direction of change is plausible, so Working's model is one solution to the constant-marginal-share problem.

Equation (3.35) indicates the dependence of the elasticity on the budget share. We can go further by analysing its dependence on income. Use (3.33) in the form $dw_i = \beta_i d\log M = \beta_i \frac{dM}{M}$ and divide by w_i to give $\frac{dw_i}{w_i} = \frac{\beta_i}{w_i}\frac{dM}{M}$ or

$$\frac{dw_i}{w_i} = (\eta_i - 1)\frac{dM}{M}.$$

Combining the above equation with (3.35) gives

$$\frac{d\eta_i}{\eta_i} = -\frac{(\eta_i - 1)^2}{\eta_i}\frac{dM}{M}.$$

This reveals that when income grows, the income elasticities of both luxuries and necessities fall.

3.22 More on Income Elasticities

Working's model (3.33) is the income part of the almost ideal demand system (AIDS) of Deaton and Muellbauer (1980a). *The Economist* (October 17, 2015, https://www.economist.com/finance-and-economics/2015/10/17/reality-cheque) describes the income part of the AIDS this way:

> The new approach allowed for different responses according to the level of income, so that a 1% pay boost might raise porridge demand by 2% for a pauper, but only 0.1% for a prince.

This information is tabulated below.

Individual	Pay boost (Per cent)	Porridge demand (Per cent change)	Implied income elasticity
Pauper	1	2	$\frac{2}{1}=2$
Prince	1	0.1	$\frac{0.1}{1}=0.1$

The last column shows that the income elasticity of porridge declines as income rises, which is plausible and, as shown above, follows from Working's model. But the example is problematic. First, with an income elasticity of 2, porridge is a strong luxury for the pauper. For a basic foodstuff to have such a large elasticity is not impossible but stretches credibility. A more serious issue is the fall in the elasticity from 2 to 0.1, meaning that porridge switches from being a luxury (for the pauper) to a necessity (the prince). As mentioned above, according to Working's model, a good cannot change category, that is, if a good is initially a luxury (or a necessity), it stays that way—it cannot switch. Accordingly, as the AIDS incorporates Working's model, the example from *The Economist* is impossible—it is not permitted by the AIDS.

Suppose the system of demand equations takes the specific form.

$$\log q_i = \eta_i \log M + \text{price term},\ i = 1, \cdots, n.$$

This is log-linear in income with each income elasticity taken to be a constant. There is a major problem with this formulation. When good i is a luxury ($\eta_i > 1$) and prices remain unchanged, expenditure on the good grows faster than income. With sufficient income growth, expenditure on the good would eventually exceeds income, violating the budget constraint. Thus, luxuries must be ruled out, but as $\sum_{i=1}^{n} w_i \eta_i = 1$, necessities cannot exist also in this approach. This implies that when each $\eta_i =$ constant, they all must take the value of unity, in contradiction to Engel's law and other interesting aspects of the luxury-necessity distinction.

An example of when income elasticities are constant is the Cobb-Douglas utility function:

$$u(q_1, \cdots, q_n) = A \prod_{i=1}^{n} q_i^{\alpha_i}, \quad \sum_{i=1}^{n} \alpha_i = 1.$$

The constant parameters are $A > 0$ and the $0 < \alpha_i < 1$. The corresponding demands are $q_i = \alpha_i \frac{M}{p_i}, i = 1 \cdots, n$, or

$$\log q_i = \alpha_i' + \log M - \log p_i, \quad i = 1 \cdots, n.$$

All income elasticities here are constant and unity. Additionally, the uncompensated own-price elasticities are -1, cross-price elasticities 0, and the budget shares are $\frac{p_i q_i}{M} = \alpha_i, i = 1, \cdots, n,$ which are also constants.

The constant elasticity system is not commonly used. An exception to this statement is the CES demand system, which in log form is

$$\log q_i = \log M + \log \left(\frac{\alpha_i^{\sigma} p_i^{-\sigma}}{\sum_{j=1}^{n} \alpha_j^{\sigma} p_j^{1-\sigma}} \right), \quad i = 1, \cdots, n.$$

Here, income elasticities are also all constant and unity. As mentioned above, the CES is used extensively in international trade, industrial organisation, and other areas, where the emphasis tends to be on the demand for different varieties of the same basic good and the luxury-necessity distinction is not paramount. Note the link between the CES and Cobb-Douglas: The Cobb-Douglas is a special case of CES when the elasticity of substitution $\sigma \to 1$.

3.23 Sources

Parts of Chap. 2 draw freely on Clements (2008, 2019). That chapter also includes material from Clements et al. (2022a).

The source of much of this chapter is the online appendices of Clements (2019) and Clements et al. (2020b). It is also based in part on the text of Clements (2019), as well as Clements (1987), Clements et al. (2022a, 2022b), and Selvanathan et al. (2024).

References

Acland D, Greenberg DH (2023) The elasticity of marginal utility of income for distributional weighting and social discounting: a meta-analysis. J Benefit-Cost Anal 14:386–405

Aizenman J, Brooks E (2008) Globalization and taste convergence: the cases of wine and beer. Rev Int Econ 16:217–233

Anderson K, Meloni G, Swinnen J (2018) Global alcohol markets: evolving consumption patterns, regulations, and industrial organizations. Ann Rev Resour Econ 10:105–132

Armington PS (1969) A theory of demand for products distinguished by place of production. IMF Staff Pap 16:159–178

Arrow KJ, Chenery HB, Minhas BS, Solow RM (1961) Capital-labor substitution and economic efficiency. Rev Econ Stat 43:225–250

Banks J, Blundell R, Lewbel A (1997) Quadratic Engel curves and consumer demand. Rev Econ Stat 79:527–539

Barten AP (1964) Consumer demand functions under conditions of almost additive preferences. Econometrica 32:1–38

Barten AP (1977) The Systems of Consumer Demand Functions Approach: a review. Econometrica 45:33–51

Bewley RA (1986) Allocation models: specification, estimation and applications. Ballinger Publishing Co, Cambridge, MA

Biddle J (2020) The origins of the CES production function. History of Political Economy 52:621–652

Boysen O (2019) When does specification or aggregation across consumers matter for economic impact analysis models? An investigation into demand systems. Empir Econ 56:137–172

Brown A, Deaton A (1972) Surveys in applied economics: models of consumer behaviour. Econ J 82:1145–1236

Chen DL (1999) World consumption economics. World Scientific, Singapore

Chirinko RS (2008) σ: the long and short of it. J Macroecon 30:671–686

Christensen LR, Jorgenson DW, Lau LJ (1975) Transcendental logarithmic utility functions. Am Econ Rev 65:367–383

Clements KW (1987) The demand for groups of goods and conditional demand. In: Theil H, Clements KW (eds) Applied demand analysis: results from system-wide approaches. Ballinger, Cambridge, MA, pp 163–184

Clements KW (2008) Price elasticities are minus one-half. Econ Lett 99:490–493

Clements KW (2019) Four Laws of consumption. Econ Rec 95:358–385

Clements KW, Kappelle S, Roberts EJ (1985) Are luxuries more price elastic than necessities? UWA Econ Discussion Paper 85:05

Clements KW, Lan Y, Liu H (2020a) Understanding alcohol consumption across countries. Appl Econ 52(40):4421–4439

Clements KW, Si J, Selvanathan EA, Selvanathan S (2020b) Demand elasticities for 9 goods in 37 countries. Appl Econ 52:2636–2655

Clements KW, Mariano MJM, Verkios G, Wong B (2022a) How elastic is alcohol consumption? Econ Anal Policy 76:568–581

Clements KW, Mariano MJ, Verikios G (2022b) Expenditure patterns, heterogeneity and long-term structural change. Econ Model 113:105888

Clements KW, Si J (2017) Notes on the pattern of OECD consumption." Unpublished working paper,. UWA Business School

Clements KW, Si J (2018) "Divisia and Frisch are friends." UWA Economics Discussion Paper 18–05

Clements KW, Zhao X (2009) Economics and marijuana: consumption, pricing and legalisation. Cambridge University Press, Cambridge

Colen L, Swinnen J (2016) Economic growth, globalisation and beer consumption. J Agric Econ 67:186–207

Costinot A, Rodríguez-Clare A (2014) Trade theory with numbers: quantifying the consequences of globalization. In: Handbook of international economics, vol 4. Elsevier, pp 197–261

De La Grandville O (2008) Economic growth: a unified approach. Cambridge University Press, Cambridge

Deaton AS (1974) A reconsideration of the empirical implications of additive preferences. Econ J 84:338–348

Deaton AS (1986) Demand analysis. In: Griliches Z, Intriligator MD (eds) Handbook of econometrics. Volume III. North-Holland Publishing Company, Amsterdam, pp 1768–1839
Deaton AS, Muellbauer J (1980a) An almost ideal demand system. Am Econ Rev 70:312–326
Deaton AS, Muellbauer J (1980b) Economics and consumer behaviour. Cambridge University Press, Cambridge
DeJanvry A, Bieri J, Nunez A (1972) Estimation of demand parameters under consumer budgeting: an application to Argentina. Am J Agric Econ 54:422–430
Divisia F (1926) L'indice Monétaire et la Théorie de la Monnaie. Revue d'Économie Politique 40: 49–81
Dixit AK, Stiglitz JE (1977) Monopolistic competition and optimum product diversity. Am Econ Rev 67:297–308
Dixon PB, Jorgenson DW (eds) (2012) Handbook of computable general equilibrium modeling. North-Holland, Amsterdam
Elder RW, Lawrence B, Ferguson A, Naimi TS, Brewer RD, Chattopadhyay SK, Toomey TL, Fielding JE (2010) The effectiveness of tax policy interventions for reducing excessive alcohol consumption and related harms. Am J Prev Med 38:217–229
Eriksson TV, Bentzen JB, Smith V (2001) Convergence in alcohol consumption: time series based tests of bivariate convergence in European countries. Cahiers D'economie Et Sociologie Rurales 60:59–74
Evans DJ (2005) The elasticity of marginal utility of consumption: estimates for 20 OECD countries. Fisc Stud 26:197–224
Fogarty J (2010) The demand for beer, wine and spirits: a survey of the literature. J Econ Surv 24: 428–478
Friedman M (1935) Professor Pigou's method for measuring elasticities of demand from budgetary data. Q J Econ 50:151–163
Frisch R (1932) New methods of measuring marginal utility. J. C. B. Mohr, Tubingen
Frisch R (1959) A complete scheme for computing all direct and cross demand elasticities in a model with many sectors. Econometrica 27:177–196
Gallet CA (2007) The demand for alcohol: a meta-analysis of elasticities. Aust J Agric Resour Econ 51:121–135
Gandelman N, Hernández-Murillo R (2015) Risk aversion at the country level. Federal Reserve Bank of St. Louis Review 97:53–66
Gao G (2012a) World food demand. Am J Agric Econ 94:25–51
Gao X (2012b) The economic behaviour of seven billion consumers: food, functional form and quality. PhD thesis. The University of Western Australia
Goldberger AS (1987) Functional form and utility: a review of consumer demand theory. Westview Press, Boulder and London
Goldberger AS, Gamaletsos T (1970) A cross-country comparison of consumer expenditure patterns. European Econ Rev 1:357–400
Groom B, Maddison D (2019) New estimates of the elasticity of marginal utility for the UK. Environ Resour Econ 72:1155–1182
Hansen L, Singleton K (1982) Generalized instrumental variables estimation of nonlinear rational expectations models. Econometrica 50:1269–1286
Harberger AC (1978) On the use of distributional weights in social cost-benefit analysis. J Polit Econ 86(2):87–120
Hilberry R, Hummels D (2013) Trade elasticity parameters for a computable general equilibrium model. In: Dixon PB, Jorgenson DW (eds) Handbook of Computable General Equilibrium Modelling, vol 1. Elsevier, pp 1213–1269
Holmes AJ, Anderson K (2017) Convergence in national alcohol consumption patterns: new global indicators. J Wine Econ 12:117–148
Houthakker HS (1957) An international comparison of household expenditure patterns, commemorating the centenary of Engel's law. Econometrica 25:532–551

Klump R, Papageorgiour C (eds) (2008) The CES production function in the theory and empirics of economic growth. J Macroecon 30:599–800

Knoblach M, Roessler M, Zwerschke P (2020) The elasticity of substitution between capital and labour in the US economy: a meta-regression analysis. Oxf Bull Econ Stat 82:62–82

Krugman P (1991) Increasing returns and economic geography. J Polit Econ 99:483–499

Krugman P, Venables AJ (1996) Integration, specialization and adjustment. Eur Econ Rev 40:959–967

Laitinen K (1978) Why is demand homogeneity so often rejected? Econ Lett 1:187–191

Layard R, Mayraz G, Nickell S (2008) The marginal utility of income. J Public Econ 92:1846–1857

Liu H (2018) Cross-country food consumption patterns: theory and measurement. PhD thesis. The University of Western Australia

Lloyd PJ, Zhang XG (2006) The Armington model. Productivity Commission, Staff Working Paper, Melbourne

Lluch C, Powell AA (1975) International comparisons of expenditure patterns. Eur Econ Rev 6: 375–403

Lluch C, Powell AA, Williams RA (1977) Patterns in household demand and savings. Oxford University Press, Oxford

Matsuyama K (2023) Non-CES aggregators: a guided tour. Ann Rev Econ 15:235–265

Marshall A (1920) Principles of economics, 8th edn. Macmillan, London

Mills TC (2018) Is there convergence in national alcohol consumption patterns? Evidence from a compositional time series approach. J Wine Econ 13:92–98

Muhammad A, Seale JL Jr, Meade B, Regmi A (2011) International evidence on food consumption patterns: an update using 2005 international comparison program data. In: Technical bulletin 1929. Economic research service. United States Department of Agriculture. Revised 2013

Nelson JP (2010) Alcohol advertising bans, consumption and control policies in seventeen OECD countries, 1975–2000. Appl Econ 42:803–823

Nelson JP (2013a) Robust demand elasticities for wine and distilled spirits: meta-analysis with corrections for outliers and publication bias. J Wine Econ 8:294–317

Nelson JP (2013b) Meta-analysis of alcohol price and income elasticities–with corrections for publication bias. Heal Econ Rev 3:1–10

Nelson JP (2014) Estimating the price elasticity of beer: meta-analysis of data with heterogeneity, dependence, and publication bias. J Health Econ 33:180–187

Pigou AC (1910) A method of determining the numerical value of demand elasticities. Econ J 20: 636–640

Pollak RA, Wales TJ (1992) Demand system specification and estimation. Oxford University Press, New York and Oxford

Powell AA (1974) Empirical analytics of demand systems. DC Heath and Company, Lexington, MA

Powell AA (1992) Sato's insight on the relation between the Frisch 'parameter' and the average elasticity of substitution. Econ Lett 40:173–175

Powell LM, Chriqui JF, Khan T, Wada R, Chaloupka FJ (2013) Assessing the potential effectiveness of food and beverage taxes and subsidies for improving public health: a systematic review of prices, demand and body weight outcomes. Obes Rev 14:110–128

Ramsey FP (1927) A contribution to the theory of taxation. Econ J 37:47–61

Regmi A, Seale JL (2010) Cross-price elasticities of demand across 114 countries. In: Technical Bulletin No. 1925, Economic Research Service. United States Department of Agriculture

Rimmer MT, Powell AA (1992) Demand patterns across the development spectrum: estimates for the AIDADS system. In: Preliminary Working paper no. OP-75, Centre of Policy Studies and Impact Project. Monash University

Seale JL, Regmi A (2006) Modelling international consumption patterns. Rev Income Wealth 52: 603–624

Seale JL, Regmi A, Bernstein J (2003) International evidence on food consumption patterns. In: Technical Bulletin 1904. Economic Research Service. United States Department of Agriculture, Washington, D.C.
Selvanathan EA (1991) Cross-country alcohol consumption comparison: an application of the Rotterdam demand system. Appl Econ 23:1613–1622
Selvanathan EA, Clements KW, Selvanathan S (2024) Estimating the elasticity of substitution: an index-number approach. J Int Trade & Econ Dev:1
Selvanathan S (1987) A Monte Carlo test of preference Independence. Econ Lett 25:259–261
Selvanathan S (1993) A system-wide analysis of international consumption patterns. Kluwer, Boston
Selvanathan S (2006) How similar are alcohol drinkers? International evidence. Appl Econ 38: 1353–1362
Selvanathan S, Selvanathan EA (2003) International consumption patterns: OECD versus LDC. World Scientific, Singapore
Selvanathan S, Selvanathan EA (2005a) The demand for alcohol, tobacco and marijuana: international evidence. Ashgate, Aldershot
Selvanathan S, Selvanathan EA (2005b) Is utility additive? Further evidence. Appl Econ 37:83–86
Selvanathan S, Selvanathan EA (2007) Another look at the identical tastes hypothesis on the analysis of cross-country alcohol data. Empir Econ 32:185–215
Silberberg E (2008) Marginal utility of money. In: Durlauf SN, Blum LE (eds) The new Palgrave dictionary of economics, 2nd edn. Palgrave Macmillan
Smith DE, Solgaard HS (2000) The dynamics of shifts in European alcoholic drinks consumption. J Int Consum Mark 12:85–109
Snow A, Warren RS Jr (2015) Pigou's law and the proportionality of income and Price elasticities of demand. Econ Lett 132:136–138
Sornpaisarn B, Shield K, Cohen J, Schwartz R, Rehm J (2013) Elasticity of alcohol consumption, alcohol-related harms, and drinking initiation in low- and middle-income countries: a systematic review and meta-analysis. Int J Alcohol Drug Res 2:45–58
Stern N (1977) The marginal valuation of income. In: Artis M, Norbay R (eds) Studies in modern economic analysis: proceedings of the association of university teachers of economics Edinburgh, 1976. Blackwell, Oxford, pp 209–254
Stiglitz JE (2015) In praise of Fank Ramsey's contribution to the theory of taxation. Econ J 125: 235–268
Stone R (1954) Linear expenditure systems and demand analysis: an application to the pattern of British demand. Econ J 64:511–527
Tella RD, MacCulloch R (2006) Some uses of happiness data in economics. J Econ Perspect 20:25–46
Theil H (1965) The information approach to demand analysis. Econometrica 33:67–87
Theil H (1975/76) Theory and measurement of consumer demand. Two volumes. North-Holland Publishing Company, Amsterdam
Theil H (1980) The system-wide approach to microeconomics. The University of Chicago Press, Chicago
Theil H, Chung C-F, Seale JL (1989) International evidence on consumption patterns. JAI Press, Inc, Greenwich, Connecticut
Theil H, Clements KW (1987) Applied demand analysis: results from system-wide approaches. Ballinger Publishing Co, Cambridge, MA
Wagenaar AC, Salois MJ, Komro KA (2009) Effects of beverage alcohol price and tax levels on drinking: a meta-analysis of 1003 estimates from 112 studies. Addiction 104:179–190
Working H (1943) Statistical laws of family expenditure. J Am Stat Assoc 38:43–56

World Bank (2015) 2011 international comparison program results. http://siteresources.worldbank.org/ICPEXT/Resources/ICP_2011.html

Zhen C, Finkelstein EA, Nonnemaker JM, Karns SA, Todd JE (2013) Predicting the effects of sugar-sweetened beverage taxes on food and beverage demand in a large demand system. Am J Agric Econ 96:1–25

Chapter 4
Food Demand I: Main Results

4.1 Introduction

Food is essential to sustain life, yet there is substantial inequality in the distribution of food across consumers. Some people are so poor they have barely enough to eat and subsequently suffer from malnutrition. Other people over-consume and suffer from obesity which can lead to cardiovascular disease, diabetes, etc. There is also great diversity in food consumption across the distribution of income. Poor countries in the world devote a major fraction of their income to food, in some cases more than 50%, while the richest can spend 10% or less. The composition of diets also differs noticeably for different types of consumers, especially between the rich and poor.

This chapter deals with a number of the key aspects of the economics of food consumption including Engel's law, the income and price elasticities of food, the diversity of the composition of food consumed across countries, and the quality of food. As will be shown, many of the differences in food consumption patterns can be explained by economic factors. As before, the chapter is self-contained while the next chapter provides additional details, including references to the previous literature, as well as touching on some related material.

4.2 Engel's Law and the Food Share

Figure 4.1 shows the weekly food consumption of two families of roughly the same size in Chad and Norway, a poor and rich country, respectively. There is an extreme contrast in terms of volume, variety, and overall appeal of the food "basket". Although there is less food in Chad, its cost as a proportion of total consumption spending (51%) is much higher than that in Norway (11%). This illustrates Engel's (1857) law at the country level: While higher income leads to more expensive food

K. W. Clements et al., *Short-cut Demand Elasticities and Other Convenient Approaches to Consumer Demand*, https://doi.org/10.1007/978-981-96-3588-7_4

Fig. 4.1 Food consumption in Chad and Norway. *Note*: GDP p.c. is in US dollars using market exchange rates. *Sources*: World Bank (2015); Hungry Planet (http://world.time.com/2013/09/20/hungry-planet-what-the-world-eats)

of superior quality, the food share is still lower in the more affluent country. Engel's law is possibly one of the strongest laws of economics.

A decline in the food share means spending rises at a slower rate than income, or the food income elasticity, η, is less than unity (the good is a necessity). Accordingly, another way of expressing Engel's law is that $\eta < 1$. Table 4.1 provides information on incomes and food in a large number of countries in 2005, from Gao (2012). The substantial variation in income across countries is notable, with the ratio of the fourth quartile to the first more than 20. As per capita income falls (as we go down the table) the food share has a strong tendency to rise in agreement with Engel's law, and in the vast majority of cases, the food income elasticity is substantially less than unity. Numerous other studies have found $\eta < 1$. Figure 4.2 shows a similar result with more recent data from the 2011 round of the International Comparison Program (ICP) of the World Bank (2015): In the poorest countries the food share is 50% or more, while in the richest it falls to around 10%.

Some insight into Engel's law is given by the simple linear case. Suppose food expenditure, e, depends solely on income, M, that is, $e = e(M)$. Denote the food share by $w = \frac{e}{M}$ and the income elasticity by $\eta = \frac{\partial \log e}{\partial \log M}$. The change in the share is $dw = (\eta - 1)w\frac{dM}{M}$, so that w falls with income growth when the elasticity $\eta < 1$. In the simplest possible case of proportionality, $e = \beta M$, $\beta > 0$, Engel's law is not satisfied as $\eta = 1$, the food share is constant and equal to β. When some part of food expenditure is independent of income the elasticity is less than unity:

$$e = \alpha + \beta M, \quad \alpha, \beta > 0; \quad \eta = \frac{\beta}{\frac{\alpha}{M} + \beta}, \quad 0 < \eta < 1.$$

As income rises, so does spending on food but because of the constant α, it rises at a lower rate causing the food share to fall. The α-part of food expenditure might be interpreted as the cost of "subsistence" consumption, such as the cost of 2500

Table 4.1 Income and food consumption in 138 countries, 2005

Country	Income	Food		Country		Food	
	(US = 100)	Budget share (%)	Income elasticity		Income (US = 100)	Budget share (%)	Income elasticity
(1)	(2)	(3)	(4)	(5)	(6)	(7)	(8)
A. Fourth quartile				**B. Third quartile**			
1. USA	100.0	6.2	0.23	36. Bahrain	41.6	19.0	0.42
2. Luxembourg	92.2	6.9	0.25	37. Korea	40.4	13.7	0.43
3. Iceland	80.7	8.9	0.27	38. Estonia	39.4	15.4	0.43
4. Norway	77.7	9.7	0.28	39. Slovak	38.8	15.7	0.44
5. UK	76.9	7.1	0.28	40. Lithuania	38.3	22.9	0.44
6. Austria	76.4	8.7	0.28	41. Poland	36.7	17.8	0.45
7. Switzerland	74.6	9.3	0.29	42. Croatia	36.1	19.3	0.46
8. Canada	74.4	7.7	0.29	43. Macao	36.1	13.3	0.46
9. Netherlands	72.4	8.2	0.29	44. Latvia	33.4	19.2	0.48
10. Sweden	72.0	8.3	0.30	45. Lebanon	32.0	27.8	0.49
11. France	71.5	10.6	0.30	46. Mexico	28.7	22.0	0.51
12. Australia	70.6	8.5	0.30	47. Belarus	27.3	34.7	0.53
13. Denmark	69.8	8.1	0.30	48. Kazakhstan	26.5	18.6	0.53
14. Belgium	68.4	10.3	0.31	49. Mauritius	26.3	23.4	0.54
15. Germany	67.5	9.1	0.31	50. Russia	26.3	25.5	0.54
16. Hong Kong	66.3	8.9	0.31	51. Bulgaria	26.1	19.5	0.54
17. Ireland	66.2	4.6	0.31	52. Iran	25.2	23.4	0.55
18. Japan	66.0	12.3	0.31	53. Romania	24.4	25.0	0.55
19. Taiwan	64.5	14.8	0.32	54. Oman	24.2	22.1	0.56
20. Cyprus	63.4	13.7	0.32	55. Argentina	24.0	22.5	0.56
21. Finland	63.0	9.3	0.32	56. Serbia	23.7	25.6	0.56
22. Spain	61.9	11.8	0.33	57. Saudi Arabia	23.6	18.5	0.56

(continued)

Table 4.1 (continued)

Country	Income	Food		Country		Food	
	(US = 100)	Budget share (%)	Income elasticity		Income (US = 100)	Budget share (%)	Income elasticity
(1)	(2)	(3)	(4)	(5)	(6)	(7)	(8)
23. Italy	61.6	12.3	0.33	58. Chile	23.3	16.2	0.56
24. Greece	59.4	13.8	0.34	59. Uruguay	22.1	19.0	0.58
25. N.Z.	57.7	11.5	0.34	60. Bosnia Herz.	21.9	28.5	0.58
26. Israel	54.7	12.9	0.36	61. Macedonia	20.5	30.9	0.60
27. Malta	54.3	13.9	0.36	62. Ukraine	19.8	32.1	0.60
28. Singapore	53.6	8.2	0.36	63. South Africa	19.3	17.6	0.61
29. Qatar	50.5	13.6	0.37	64. Malaysia	19.3	17.3	0.61
30. Slovenia	50.0	11.9	0.38	65. Turkey	18.9	23.1	0.62
31. Portugal	49.0	13.1	0.38	66. Montenegro	18.7	32.2	0.62
32. Brunei	48.7	18.4	0.38	67. Brazil	18.7	15.5	0.62
33. Kuwait	47.0	14.8	0.39	68. Venezuela	17.1	26.1	0.64
34. Czech	46.3	13.1	0.40	69. Thailand	16.1	15.9	0.65
35. Hungary	42.6	13.3	0.42	70. Albania	14.6	24.6	0.67
Mean	64.9	10.7	0.3	Mean	26.6	21.8	0.5
Median	66.0	10.3	0.3	Median	24.4	22.0	0.6
SD	12.7	2.9	0.043	SD	7.6	5.5	0.069
C. Second quartile				**D. First quartile**			
71. Colombia	14.5	24.3	0.68	105. India	5.5	33.7	0.85
72. Ecuador	13.7	25.9	0.69	106. Cambodia	5.3	47.2	0.85
73. Jordan	13.7	28.9	0.69	107. Yemen	5.2	41.1	0.85
74. Tunisia	13.7	24.8	0.69	108. Sudan	4.5	55.6	0.87
75. Peru	13.6	29.2	0.69	109. Lao P.D.R.	4.4	47.3	0.87
76. Egypt	13.5	41.6	0.69	110. Djibouti	4.4	33.6	0.87
77. Armenia	13.1	65.1	0.70	111. Kenya	4.3	33.3	0.88

78. Moldova	13.0	24.2	0.70	112. Sao Tome P.	4.3	53.7	0.88
79. Maldives	12.9	22.9	0.70	113. Congo, R.	4.1	37.5	0.88
80. Gabon	12.7	36.3	0.70	114. Cameroon	4.0	43.4	0.88
81. Fiji	12.6	26.3	0.71	115. Nigeria	4.0	56.7	0.88
82. Georgia	12.1	36.7	0.71	116. Senegal	3.9	48.9	0.89
83. Botswana	11.9	21.9	0.72	117. Chad	3.5	55.0	0.90
84. Namibia	10.9	26.0	0.74	118. Mauritania	3.4	63.6	0.90
85. Swaziland	10.8	41.9	0.74	119. Nepal	3.4	48.7	0.90
86. Azerbaijan	10.5	57.9	0.74	120. Bangladesh	3.3	49.9	0.90
87. Syrian Arab	10.5	41.7	0.74	121. Benin	3.3	43.6	0.90
88. Bolivia	10.2	27.8	0.75	122. Ghana	3.3	49.2	0.90
89. Equat. Guinea	10.1	39.5	0.75	123. Coted 'Ivoire	3.1	43.3	0.91
90. Paraguay	9.9	32.3	0.75	124. S. Leone	3.1	42.4	0.91
91. Cape Verde	8.8	28.8	0.77	125. M'gascar	3.0	57.0	0.91
92. Bhutan	8.0	34.5	0.79	126. Togo	2.7	48.6	0.92
93. Kyrgyz	8.0	40.8	0.79	127. Burkina Faso	2.5	42.0	0.93
94. Sri Lanka	7.9	36.4	0.79	128. Guinea	2.4	44.0	0.93
95. Iraq	7.8	32.1	0.80	129. Mali	2.3	46.7	0.93
96. Mongolia	7.7	35.9	0.80	130. Angola	2.3	40.7	0.93
97. Tajikistan	7.7	55.0	0.80	131. Malawi	2.1	23.3	0.93
98. Philippines	7.5	43.9	0.80	132. Rwanda	2.1	42.7	0.94
99. Indonesia	7.4	41.6	0.80	133. C. Africa	1.9	56.8	0.94
100. Pakistan	7.3	48.8	0.81	134. M'bique	1.7	60.1	0.95
101. Morocco	7.2	31.1	0.81	135. Liberia	1.3	25.8	0.96
102. Lesotho	7.1	35.5	0.81	136. Niger	1.3	46.4	0.96
103. China	7.0	24.1	0.81	137. G-Bissau	1.2	52.3	0.96
104. Vietnam	6.8	31.3	0.82	138. Congo, D. R.	0.4	62.2	0.99

(continued)

Table 4.1 (continued)

Country (1)	Income (US = 100) (2)	Food: Budget share (%) (3)	Food: Income elasticity (4)	Country (5)	Income (US = 100) (6)	Food: Budget share (%) (7)	Food: Income elasticity (8)
Mean	10.3	35.1	0.7	Mean	3.2	46.4	0.9
Median	10.4	33.4	0.7	Median	3.3	47.0	0.9
SD	2.5	10.2	0.047	SD	1.2	9.4	0.034

Note: Income is real total consumption per capita with US = 100
Source: Gao (2012) with quartiles added

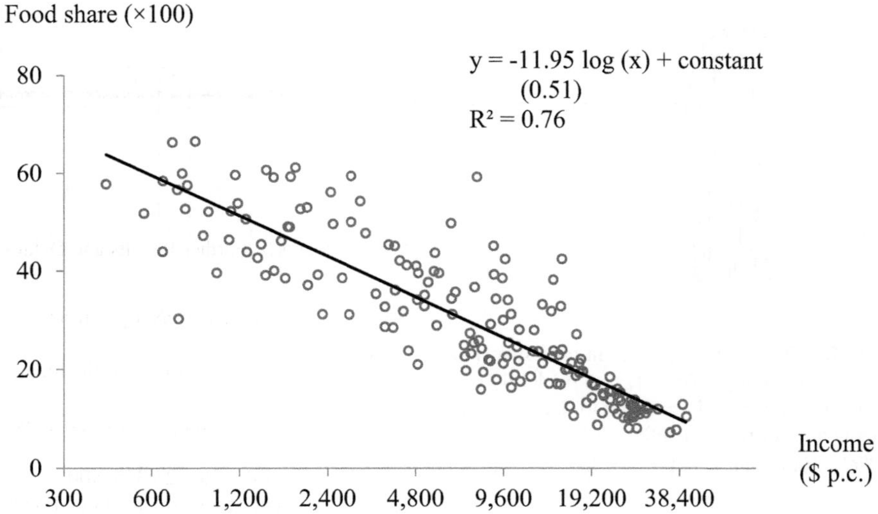

Fig. 4.2 Food and income, 176 countries, 2011. *Note*: Income is real total consumption per capita in $US, using PPP exchange rates. Food is the combination of two categories from the World Bank's (2015) International Comparison Program (ICP): (i) food and non-alcoholic beverages and (ii) alcoholic beverages, tobacco, and narcotics. Of the 182 ICP countries, we use 176. We omit (i) the duplicate entries for Russia, Sudan, and Egypt; (ii) Cuba and Bonaire as they have incomplete data; and (iii) Algeria as there are issues with its data

calories per day needed to sustain life, or the $1.90-per-day poverty line of the World Bank. At the heart of Engel's law is a subsistence food requirement more or less independent of income.

4.3 The Strong Version of Engel's Law

Returning to the Chad-Norway comparison, the food share and income in the two countries are:

	Food share (Percentage)	Income ($US per capita)
Chad	51	2000
Norway	11	62,000
Difference	−40	60,000
Ratio $= \frac{\text{share difference}}{\text{log difference of income}}$	$\frac{-40}{\log 62{,}000 - \log 2{,}000} = -11.7$	

The difference in the share, relative to the logarithmic income difference, is −11.7. This figure is not far from the mean of this ratio for all possible pairs of the 176 countries of −11.9, as revealed in Fig. 4.3. Figure 4.2 shows the food share declining arithmetically as income rises geometrically, that is

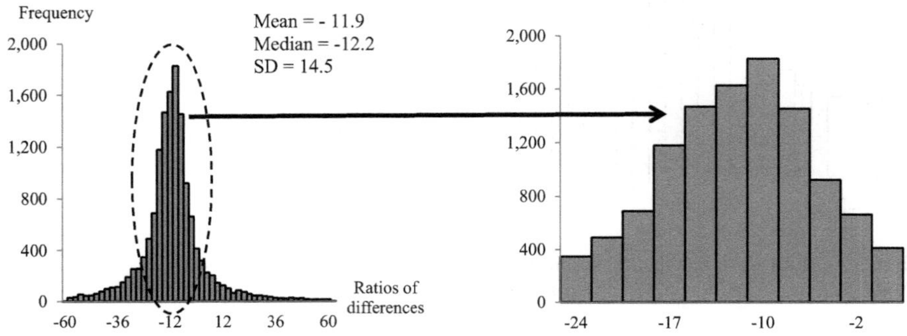

Fig. 4.3 Ratios of differences in food shares to income differences, pairs of 176 countries, 2011. *Note*: For country c ($c = 1, \cdots, 176$) let w_c be the food share and M_c be real income per capita. Countries are ranked according to decreasing income, so country c is richer than d for $d > c$. This frequency distribution refers to the ratios $100 \times \frac{w_c - w_d}{\log M_c - \log M_d}$, $c,d = 1,\cdots,176, d > c$. There are ${}^{176}C_2 = ½176 \cdot (176 - 1) = 15{,}400$ such ratios, but values are truncated to $[-60, 60]$

$$w = \alpha + \beta \log M, \quad \beta < 0. \tag{4.1}$$

This is Working's (1943) model. Suppose country c is twice as affluent as country d so that according to Eq. (4.1) the difference in the shares is

$$w_c - w_d = \beta(\log M_c - \log M_d) = \beta(\log 2M_d - \log M_d) = \beta \log 2.$$

With the slope coefficient $\beta = -15$, a value not too different from the mean of Fig. 4.3, when income doubles, $w_c - w_d = -15 \times 0.69 \approx -10$, since $\log 2 = 0.69$. In words, a doubling of income leads to a 10-percentage-point decline in the food share. This is the strong version of Engel's law (Theil et al., 1989).

The strong law can be used to infer differences in incomes from food shares, an idea going back to Engel (1857). This can be realistic when there is fairly reliable data on food consumption—such as that from a household survey—but lower-quality (or no) information on income. As the food share is unit free and dimensionless, tricky problems with inflation adjustments and currency conversions can be avoided.

The fall in Norway's share relative to Chad's is 40 percentage points. If the strong law applies for each doubling of income, the implication is that Norway's true income is double Chad's four times over, or a multiple $2^4 = 16$. Contrast this with the income multiple based on market exchange rates of $\frac{62{,}000}{2{,}000} = 31$. This situation is illustrated in Fig. 4.4, where for countries other than Norway, food expenditure is governed by eq. (4.1), as represented by the solid line. The point C represents the observed food share and income of Chad, while N is that of Norway. Bringing Norway onto the Engel curve by moving it from the point N to N$'$ entails an almost 50% reduction in its measured income from \$62,000 to \$2,000 × 16 = \$32,000 per capita. For Norway, the share is $\varepsilon > 0$ larger than predicted by Eq. (4.1), that is,

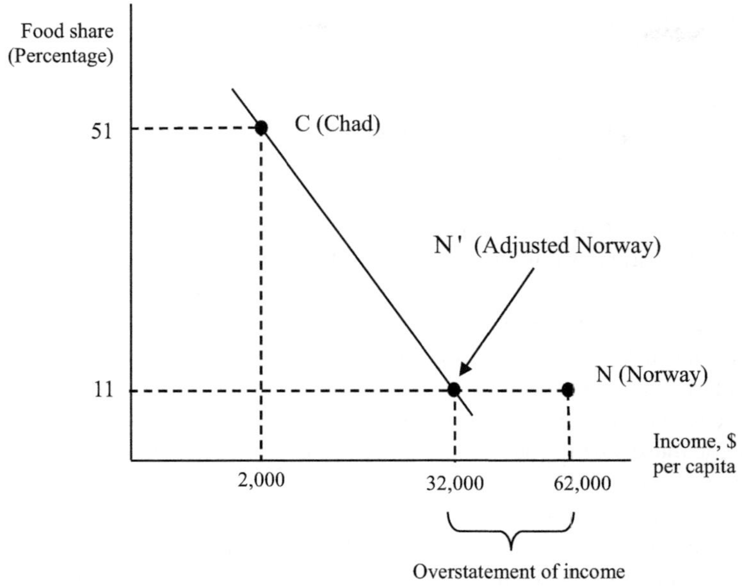

Fig. 4.4 Food and income measurement

$w = \alpha + \beta \log M + \varepsilon$, so that relative to the Engel curve, Norway's income is overstated by a multiple $\exp\left(-\frac{\varepsilon}{\beta}\right) = \exp\left\{\log\left(\frac{62{,}000}{32{,}000}\right)\right\} = 1.94$, or by 94%. Although this is only an illustrative example, the difference between Engel-adjusted and measured income reflects the well-known characteristic of the currencies of rich countries like Norway to be overvalued, while those of poor countries tend to be undervalued (Balassa, 1964, Harrod, 1939, Samuelson, 1964).

This shows that Engel's law can be used as a benchmark for the relationship between the food share and income. A substantial departure from the Engel curve can be interpreted as saying something other than measured income is playing a role. The approach described above identifies that "something" as an overstatement of income caused by the use of market exchange rates to convert incomes in the two countries into a common currency. This is based on the reasonable assumption of no (or only modest) mismeasurement of the food share relative to that of income. This approach can be extended to account for the influence of relative prices on the food share and the composition of the consumption basket, as in Clements and Chen (2010). In other research, the departure from the Engel curve has been ascribed to an overstatement of the price level when using the consumer price index (CPI) as the income deflator.

A qualification to Working's model with $\beta < 0$ is when income is sufficiently high the share becomes negative, which is inadmissible. Thus, the model is applicable for income less than $\bar{M} = \exp\left(-\frac{\alpha}{\beta}\right)$. Similarly, for $w < 1$, income must exceed $\bar{M} = \exp\left(\frac{1-\alpha}{\beta}\right) = \left\{\exp\left(\frac{1}{\beta}\right)\right\}\bar{M}$.

4.4 The Income Elasticity of Food

Returning to Table 4.1, countries are ranked in terms of decreasing income per capita. In the richest quartile, the income elasticities of food are low and equal to 0.3 on average. As income falls, the income average elasticity rises to 0.5 for the third quartile, 0.7 for the second quartile, and 0.9 for the poorest. This rise in the elasticity as income falls is entirely plausible.

Table 4.1 elasticities refer to incomes in 2005. These can be updated to allow for subsequent growth quite easily as follows: (i) Take the country's income in 2005 from Table 4.1 and inflate it by the subsequent growth; (ii) identify the country further up the list with the resulting higher income; and (iii) select that country's income elasticity to be the elasticity for the new country in the more recent year. This procedure is likely to work satisfactorily for countries in the third quartile and below, but not for those in the fourth quartile with an insufficient number of higher-up countries that are richer.

There are other situations in which the above approach is not applicable. Two such cases can be highlighted. When a country is not among the 138 of Table 4.1, a simple procedure to estimate its elasticity is as follows. Take the country's per capita income (relative to the USA), deflate it to 2005, and then select the elasticity of a Table 4.1 country with a similar affluence. A second case requiring special treatment is for a country (or for a specific group of consumers) not included in Table 4.1 and with unknown income. If the food budget share is known, this could be matched to a country included in the table, and then extrapolate income with the above procedure. Alternatively, Working's model (4.1), $w = \alpha + \beta \log M$, could be employed. As the implied income elasticity is $1 + \frac{\beta}{w}$, when, for example, 30% of income is spent on food and $\beta = -0.15$, the income elasticity is $1 + \frac{-0.15}{0.30} = \frac{1}{2}$. A property of this model is that when income grows, the share and the income elasticity fall, aligning with intuition and the above discussion.

4.5 The Food Price Elasticity

To discuss the price elasticity, we start with a brief review of some foundational material. The impact of a price change on the consumption of any good can be decomposed into income and substitution effects. Suppose the price of good j rises by $dp_j > 0$, with money income and the other prices unchanged. Real income falls in proportion to pre-existing consumption of good j, q_j, that is, by $q_j dp_j$. The change in consumption of good i is then

$$dq_i = \frac{\partial q_i}{\partial p_j} dp_j = \left(\frac{\partial q_i^*}{\partial p_j} - q_j \frac{\partial q_i}{\partial M} \right) dp_j.$$

Here, $\frac{\partial q_i^*}{\partial p_j} dp_j$ is the substitution effect of the price change reflecting the response when real income is held constant, and $-q_j \frac{\partial q_i}{\partial M} dp_j$ is the income effect reflecting the reduction in real income. Writing the above in terms of slopes, $\frac{\partial q_i}{\partial p_j} = \frac{\partial q_i^*}{\partial p_j} - q_j \frac{\partial q_i}{\partial M}$, and then multiplying both sides by $\frac{p_j}{q_i}$, gives the Slutsky equation in elasticity form:

$$\eta_{ij} = \eta_{ij}^* - w_j \eta_i. \tag{4.2}$$

On the left-hand side η_{ij} is the $(i,j)^{th}$ uncompensated price elasticity. On the right, we have the corresponding compensated elasticity η_{ij}^*; the term $w_j = \frac{p_j q_j}{M}$ is the proportion of income spent on j (the "budget share"); and $\eta_i = \frac{\partial q_i / q_i}{\partial M / M} = \frac{\partial \log q_i}{\partial \log M}$ is the ith income elasticity. The uncompensated elasticity η_{ij} is also known as the Marshallian price elasticity, while η_{ij}^* is also called the Slutsky elasticity.

Next, use Eq. (4.2) to write the own-price elasticity of food as

$$\eta_{FF} = \eta_{FF}^* - w_F \eta_F. \tag{4.3}$$

As food is essential to sustain life, it could reasonably be argued that for very poor people with low food consumption, there are few, if any, substitutes available. In the extreme, the compensated elasticity η_{FF}^* might approach zero. Consequently, for the poor, it might not be unreasonable to approximate η_{FF}^* by zero, so that Eq. (4.3) becomes

$$\eta_{FF} \approx -w_F \eta_F. \tag{4.4}$$

In words, the price elasticity is approximated by the income effect of the price change. For example, if the consumer spends one-half of their income on food and the income elasticity is 0.8, the approximate price elasticity is $-\frac{1}{2} \times 0.8 = -0.4$.

While this approximation is motivated by an intuitively plausible argument for a poor consumer, is it completely implausible to apply the same argument to those with medium to high incomes? That is, following an increase in food prices and holding real income unchanged, would more affluent consumers be likely to substantially economise on food consumption. Perhaps not. Accordingly, to explore what sort of results might follow, in the table below, we apply approximation (4.4) to the quartile means from Table 4.1:

Quartile	Income (US = 100)	Food: Budget share $w_F \times 100$	Income elasticity η_F	Product $-w_F \eta_F$
4	64.9	10.7	0.3	−0.04
3	26.6	21.8	0.5	−0.12
2	10.3	35.1	0.7	−0.26
1	3.2	46.4	0.9	−0.42

The last column gives the approximate food price elasticities. Thus, for the poorest countries (quartile 1) the price elasticity is approximated by -0.4, while for the second quartile this falls absolutely to -0.3, then -0.1 for quartile 3, and almost zero for the richest group. These values appear fairly reasonable.

Finally, there is another interpretation of the product of the share and the income elasticity, $w_F\eta_F$ in (4.4). Using the definitions $w_F = \frac{p_F q_F}{M}$ and $\eta_F = \frac{\partial q_F/q_F}{\partial M/M}$, the term $w_F\eta_F$ simplifies to $\frac{p_F \partial q_F}{\partial M}$, or when the price of food is constant, $w_F\eta_F = \frac{\partial(p_F q_F)}{\partial M}$. This is the slope of the Engel curve or the share of a one-dollar increase in income that is spent on food, which is known as the marginal share. An equivalent way of expressing the income elasticity is, therefore, the ratio of the marginal share to the budget share, $\eta_F = \frac{\partial(p_F q_F)/\partial M}{w_F}$.

4.6 Individual Food Items

The analysis of food consumption as an aggregate has several valuable uses, including the measurement of nutrition, affluence, and well-being. There is also the identification of fundamental empirical regularities such as Engel's law. What of the individual items of food consumption? This section shows they also exhibit interesting patterns related to Engel's law. Nutritionists emphasise a healthy diet means a diversified one, such as eating several vegetables per day. In this section and the next we discuss the measurement of diet diversification, the degree to which food consumption is spread across a range of items.

Figure 4.5 gives an overview of disaggregated food consumption in 2011 for 155 countries; this information comes from unpublished disaggregated data of the International Comparison Program (World Bank, n.d.). The figure shows that on average over all countries, food absorbs 27% of total consumption and that is split into seven broad groups. Bread and cereals account for 19% of food. Within that broad group there are five items, with 22% going to rice, 24% to other cereals, etc. In total, there are 31 items of food of all types.

The figures in Fig. 4.5 are averages over 155 countries. As there is great dispersion of income and consumption among countries, Table 4.2 provides a disaggregation of the items by income quartile (income is measured by real total consumption per capita). Columns 2–5 contain the budget shares for each income quartile and for many items there is considerable disparity across the income distribution. For example, rice accounts for only 0.2% of the budget for countries in the fourth quartile, while that proportion increases by a factor well over 20 to be 5.4% for those in the first quartile. For the poorest countries (quartile 1), it can be seen from column 5 that the important items in the budget are rice and other cereals, with each accounting for more than 5%. Fresh or chilled vegetables, as well as potatoes, are other prominent items for the poorest. For the richest countries (quartile 4), there seems to be a more uniform expenditure pattern with no single item representing more than 1% of the total. The largest items for these countries are

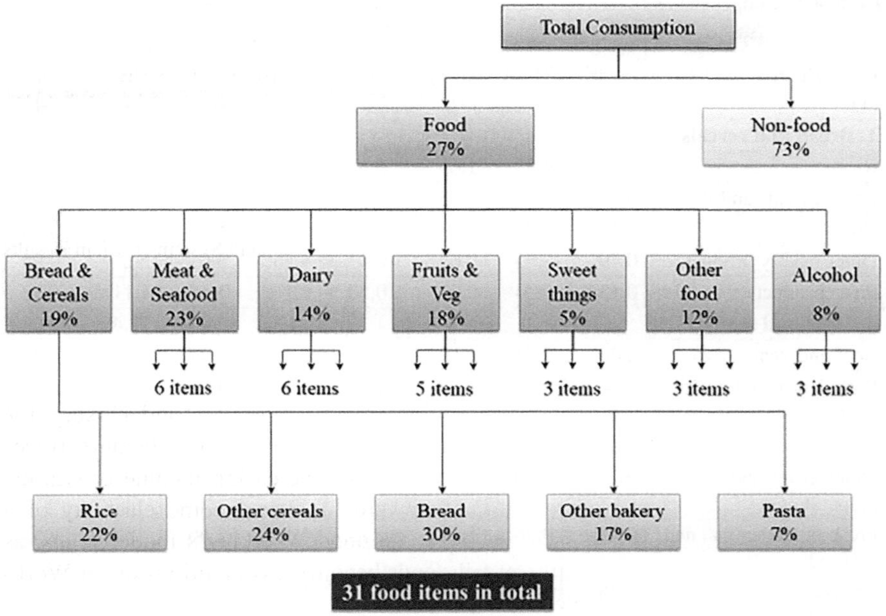

Fig. 4.5 Structure of food consumption, 155 countries, 2011 (Percentage budget shares, averages over countries)

(i) other meats and preparation and (ii) mineral water, soft drinks, etc. (0.74 and 0.75%, respectively). The last entries of columns 2–5 are the budget shares for food: For the top quartile counties, food accounts for 11%, while this increases to 46% for those in the bottom quartile, reflecting Engel's law.

The emboldened figures of columns 6–9 of Table 4.2 are the shares of food expenditure devoted to each of the seven food groups. The most dramatic difference across the income distribution is for bread and cereals. For the richest-quartile countries, 14% of the food budget is devoted to this group, less than one-half that of the poorest (29%). This is a type of Engel effect at the micro-commodity level. This disparity is also related to Bennett's (1941) law, which states that the share of cereals in calories rises with decreasing affluence, or higher-quality foods become more prominent in the diet and staples less prominent as income rises. For the group "other food", the pattern is the opposite to bread and cereals: On average, the richest countries allocate 16% to other food, while for the poorest this share falls to 9%. Interestingly, the share for alcohol for the richest countries is more than twice that of the poorest (10% versus 4%).

Table 4.2 Budget shares of 31 food items by income quartile, 155 countries in 2011

Group/Item (1)	Budget shares Fourth (2)	Third (3)	Second (4)	First (5)	Conditional budget shares Fourth (6)	Third (7)	Second (8)	First (9)
1. Bread and cereals					**14.28**	**14.81**	**18.76**	**29.47**
Rice	0.16	0.58	1.65	5.41	1.42	2.50	5.09	11.64
Other cereals and flour	0.21	0.53	1.63	5.79	1.91	2.52	5.14	12.06
Bread	0.61	1.24	1.73	1.72	5.42	5.65	5.19	3.70
Other bakery products	0.49	0.65	0.66	0.43	4.35	3.01	2.23	0.95
Pasta products	0.13	0.24	0.33	0.50	1.17	1.13	1.11	1.12
2. Meat and seafood					**24.36**	**24.53**	**22.41**	**21.10**
Beef and veal	0.40	0.75	1.50	2.32	3.55	3.47	4.73	4.96
Pork, lamb, mutton, and goat	0.44	0.90	1.07	1.67	3.90	4.07	3.56	3.73
Poultry	0.41	1.27	1.62	1.25	3.75	5.99	5.33	2.74
Other meats and preparations	0.74	1.30	0.94	0.84	6.72	5.72	3.01	1.76
Fresh or frozen fish and seafood	0.47	0.76	1.46	2.15	4.13	3.66	4.58	4.54
Preserved fish and seafood	0.26	0.33	0.38	1.52	2.32	1.60	1.21	3.37
3. Dairy					**13.16**	**15.89**	**15.76**	**11.64**
Fresh milk	0.30	0.56	0.91	1.08	2.59	2.54	2.86	2.42
Preserved milk and milk products	0.40	1.05	1.26	0.87	3.61	4.86	4.06	2.04
Cheese	0.41	0.66	0.76	0.21	3.60	2.96	2.37	0.46
Eggs and egg-based products	0.11	0.37	0.69	0.54	0.98	1.71	2.11	1.23
Butter and margarine	0.12	0.27	0.39	0.60	1.05	1.27	1.21	1.29
Other edible oils and fats	0.16	0.56	1.00	1.93	1.32	2.54	3.15	4.19
4. Fruit and vegetables					**16.25**	**17.25**	**19.12**	**20.56**
Fresh or chilled fruit	0.66	1.16	1.59	1.64	5.90	5.30	5.24	3.77
Frozen, preserved or processed fruits	0.13	0.20	0.22	0.44	1.23	0.99	0.71	0.97
Fresh or chilled vegetables	0.60	1.52	2.73	3.14	5.47	6.83	8.59	7.28
Fresh or chilled potatoes	0.14	0.47	0.82	2.95	1.27	1.97	2.51	6.43
Frozen or preserved vegetables	0.26	0.44	0.67	1.03	2.38	2.16	2.08	2.11

(continued)

Table 4.2 (continued)

Group/Item (1)	Budget shares Fourth (2)	Third (3)	Second (4)	First (5)	Conditional budget shares Fourth (6)	Third (7)	Second (8)	First (9)
5. Sweet things					**5.95**	**5.16**	**4.93**	**4.06**
Sugar	0.06	0.42	0.76	1.36	0.52	1.92	2.42	3.02
Jams, marmalades, and honey	0.06	0.12	0.19	0.12	0.57	0.59	0.63	0.25
Confectionery, choc, and ice cream	0.53	0.58	0.59	0.35	4.86	2.65	1.88	0.79
6. Other food					**15.51**	**12.78**	**12.06**	**8.83**
Food products n.e.c.	0.66	0.85	1.55	2.18	6.19	4.06	5.45	4.91
Coffee, tea and cocoa	0.25	0.52	0.54	0.50	2.26	2.31	1.68	1.11
Min. Waters, soft drinks, etc.	0.75	1.29	1.44	1.19	7.06	6.41	4.93	2.82
7. Alcohol					**10.48**	**9.59**	**6.96**	**4.34**
Spirits	0.28	0.78	0.55	0.42	2.58	3.52	1.81	0.96
Wine	0.43	0.46	0.31	0.37	3.98	2.08	1.01	0.79
Beer	0.41	0.86	1.11	1.15	3.92	3.99	4.14	2.60
Total	11.05	21.71	31.07	45.66	100	100	100	100

Notes

1. *Columns 2–5*: Budget shares are the proportions of total consumption expenditure devoted to each food item.
2. *Columns 6–9:* Conditional budget shares are the proportions of total food expenditure devoted to each food items. Food group conditional budget shares are **emboldened** and are sums of the conditional shares in the corresponding group.
3. All values are averaged over countries in the relevant quartile.
4. All entries are ×100.
5. Mean incomes (in $US per capita) by quartile are
Q4 = 25,974, Q3 = 12,341, Q2 = 6,010, Q1 = 1,525.

4.7 Diet Diversity

Diet diversity can be measured with the data on individual food items. It is convenient to introduce some notation that in part redefines some of the previous concepts. Let p_{ic} be the price of item i in country c and q_{ic} the corresponding quantity consumed per capita. Thus, $p_{ic}q_{ic}$ is expenditure per capita on the item and $w_{ic} = \frac{p_{ic}q_{ic}}{M_c}$ is the share of the item in total food expenditure per capita (M_c). Previously M was used to denote total expenditure or income, while now it will be used for food expenditure. We shall now refer to w_{ic} as the ith budget share, although strictly speaking, this is the "conditional" share, conditional on food, but no confusion will arise with this nomenclature. A measure of the cross-item dispersion of the food basket is

$$\Pi_{wc} = \sum_{i=1}^{31} w_{ic}\left(\log w_{ic} - \log \bar{W}_c\right)^2, \quad \log \bar{W}_c = \sum_{i=1}^{31} w_{ic} \log w_{ic}. \tag{4.5}$$

This takes the logarithms of the shares, squares the deviations from their weighted mean, $\log \overline{W}_c$, and then takes the weighted sum over the 31 items, where the weights are the shares themselves. That is, Π_{wc} is a weighted logarithmic variance of the budget shares. The weighting pattern reflects the economic importance of items in the budget as measured by the budget shares. The variance is lower when food expenditure is more uniformly distributed to the individual items, so Π_{wc} is an *inverse* measure of diet diversity.

Parallel to (4.5) are analogous price and quantity variances:

$$\begin{cases} \Pi_{pc} = \sum_{i=1}^{31} w_{ic}(\log p_{ic} - \log P_c)^2, & \log P_c = \sum_{i=1}^{31} w_{ic} \log p_{ic} \\ \Pi_{qc} = \sum_{i=1}^{31} w_{ic}(\log q_{ic} - \log Q_c)^2, & \log Q_c = \sum_{i=1}^{31} w_{ic} \log q_{ic}. \end{cases} \tag{4.6}$$

These are weighted measures of dispersion of prices and quantities among the 31 items. There is also the corresponding price-quantity covariance and correlation:

$$\Pi_{pq,c} = \sum_{i=1}^{31} w_{ic}(\log p_{ic} - \log P_c)(\log q_{ic} - \log Q_c), \quad \rho_c = \frac{\Pi_{pq,c}}{\sqrt{\Pi_{pc}\Pi_{qc}}}.$$

As substitution among the individual items is likely, there would be a tendency for consumers to move away from relatively more expensive items towards cheaper ones; thus, the covariance $\Pi_{pq,\,c}$ is expected to be negative. Since $\log w_{ic} = \log p_{ic} + \log q_{ic} - \log M_c$, the variances and covariance satisfy $\Pi_{wc} = \Pi_{pc} + \Pi_{qc} + 2\Pi_{pq,\,c}$.

The food volume index in (4.6), $\log Q$, averaged over countries in each income quartile, is contained in column 2 of Table 4.3. For example, the log-difference in food consumption per capita between countries in the third and fourth quartiles is 4.39–4.68 $= -0.29$, or $100 \times (e^{-0.29} - 1) = -25\%$, so that the volume of food consumption is 25% lower in the third quartile, on average. There is a much bigger drop in going from the second to the first quartile countries, where the log-difference is 3.23–4.08 $= -0.85$, or almost 60%. According to Eq. (4.5), a more specialised diet implies a larger variance of the shares and is less diversified. As can be seen from column 3 of Table 4.3, this variance rises noticeably as income falls, which confirms the greater diversity of diets of the rich and the lower diversity of those of the poor. For the richest quartile, the standard deviation (SD) is $\sqrt{\Pi_w} = \sqrt{50.86 \times 10^{-2}} \approx 71\%$, while this is about 100% for the poorest quartile. The lack of a diversified diet of the poor in large part reflects their tendency to be more intensive in the consumption of bread and cereals, referred to previously as a micro-commodity Engel effect.

Table 4.3 Food index numbers

Income quartile (1)	Food volume index $\log Q$ (2)	Variances ×100: Budget shares Π_w (3)	Prices Π_p (4)	Quantities Π_q (5)	Price quantity ×100: Covariance Π_{pq} (6)	Correlation ρ (7)
4	4.68	50.86	7.95	64.58	−10.84	−42.29
3	4.39	50.42	10.86	70.50	−15.47	−52.95
2	4.08	66.28	15.38	98.12	−23.61	−58.38
1	3.23	99.55	25.12	149.85	−37.71	−57.27

Note: Values are averaged over countries

The budget-share variance comprises price, quantity, and covariance terms, that is, $\Pi_{wc} = \Pi_{pc} + \Pi_{qc} + 2\Pi_{pq,\ c}$, as above. Since nutrition is associated with the quantities consumed, the quantity variance Π_q is the relevant measure as it strips out the influence of prices. Columns 4 and 5 of Table 4.3 reveal that quantities contribute a reasonably large part to the budget-share variance. The effect of prices is more modest for the richer countries but becomes increasingly important as income falls. For the first income quartile, prices account for 25.12/99.55 = 25% of the budget-share variance. On average, quantities are more than six times more variable than prices on the basis of the variances, or more than twice as large if the SDs are used. The lower dispersion of prices (relative to quantities) agrees with other findings based on time-series data, where it has been interpreted as reflecting the role of sticky prices, causing quantities to do most of the adjusting to shocks to the markets. The negative price-quantity correlations of column 7 of Table 4.3 show that, on average, consumers economise on the relatively more expensive items in favour of cheaper items, as expected.

4.8 The Inequality of Diversity

Further insight into the structure of food consumption can be obtained by splitting the dispersion measures into components involving the seven food groups. Denote the groups by $S_1, \cdots, S_7$, and the weighted average of the (logarithmic) budget shares belonging to group g by $\log \overline{W}_{gc} = \sum_{i \in S_g} \frac{w_{ic}}{W_{gc}} \log w_{ic}$, where $W_{gc} = \sum_{i \in S_g} w_{ic}$ is the budget share of g. The group indexes are consistent in aggregation as they satisfy $\sum_{g=1}^{7} W_{gc} \log \overline{W}_{gc} = \log \overline{W}_c$, where $\log \overline{W}_c$ is as defined in eq. (4.5). The budget share variance for country c can then be expressed as

$$\Pi_{wc} = \sum_{i=1}^{31} w_{ic}(\log w_{ic} - \log \bar{W}_c)^2 = \sum_{g=1}^{7} W_{gc}(\log \bar{W}_{gc} - \log \bar{W}_c)^2 + \sum_{g=1}^{7} W_{gc}\left[\sum_{i \in S_g} \frac{w_{ic}}{W_{gc}}(\log w_{ic} - \log \bar{W}_{gc})^2\right].$$

Table 4.4 Components of dispersion of food consumption

Income quartile	Total variance (×100)	Component (Percentages) Between group	Within group
	A. *Budget shares*		
4	50.86	33.23	66.77
3	50.42	30.21	69.79
2	66.28	36.15	63.85
1	99.55	47.85	52.15
	B. *Prices*		
4	7.95	40.75	59.37
3	10.86	37.29	62.71
2	15.38	40.64	59.36
1	25.12	43.71	56.29
	C. *Quantities*		
4	64.58	34.17	65.83
3	70.50	32.44	67.55
2	98.12	37.36	62.64
1	149.85	50.24	49.76

Note: Total variances are from Table 4.3. Values are averaged over countries

The first term after the second equals sign is a weighted logarithmic variance of the group shares, the between-group component of the total. The second term is the within-group component, a weighted average of the variances, $\sum_{i \in S_g} \frac{w_{ic}}{W_{gc}} (\log w_{ic} - \log \overline{W}_{gc})^2, g = 1, \cdots, 7$. Panel A of Table 4.4 shows that the between effect ranges from one-third to one-half of the total variance of the budget shares. The other two panels in the table apply the same decomposition to prices and quantities, with the relative contributions remaining broadly the same as for the budget shares. From the last row of panel C (referring to quantities), it is noteworthy that diet diversity of the poorest countries is about evenly split between the consumption of different groups of food items and within-group consumption. For the other countries, on average, the source of diet diversity is tilted more towards to the within-group effect.

The between-group component of the quantity variance is an inverse measure of diet diversity—the spread of food consumption across bread and cereals, meat and seafood, dairy, fruit, etc. Arguably, this is what brings more nutritional value. Based on the information in panel C of Table 4.4, the between-group quantity variances are:

Income quartile	Between-group quantity variance (×100)
4	64.58 × 0.3417 = 22.07
3	70.50 × 0.3244 = 22.87
2	98.12 × 0.3736 = 36.66
1	149.85 × 0.5024 = 75.28

There are huge differences in this component across the income distribution: The ratio of the richest to the poorest countries is $\frac{22.07}{75.28}$, so that the diversity of the diets of the rich, relative to that of the poor, is $\frac{1/22.07}{1/75.28} = 3.4$. That is, the diets of the rich are almost 3.5 times more diverse than the poor's. Contrast this with the total variance (second column of panel C of Table 4.4) for which the diversity ratio is $\frac{149.85}{64.58} = 2.3$, considerably less than the between-group measure. The conclusion is clear: Ignoring the between-within distinction for the broader food groups and just focusing on the total variance masks a substantial part of the inequality of diet diversity.

What if instead of the quantity variance, we were to use the variance of the budget shares to measure diet diversity? At least part of the inequality would be missed: From panel A of Table 4.4, the rich-poor diversity ratio for the between-measure is $\frac{99.55 \times 0.4785}{50.86 \times 0.3323} = \frac{47.63}{16.90} = 2.8$, while the corresponding ratio for the total is $\frac{99.55}{50.86} = 2.0$. The between-ratio is again higher than that for the total, so the conclusion remains the same, viz., inequality is underestimated by the total. But now there are two differences: (i) The gap between the two ratios is smaller, so the under-estimation of inequality appears to be less severe. (ii) The between ratio is now noticeably smaller than before (2.8 versus 3.4), again leading to a reduction in apparent inequality. For these reasons, it seems preferable to exclude the impact of prices from diet diversity and use quantities rather than budget shares to obtain a reliable measure of diet inequality.

4.9 Disaggregated Food Elasticities

Income elasticities of the 31 food items are provided in Table 4.5. The majority of elasticities are less than unity (classified as necessities). Moreover, these have a tendency to rise as we move from the richest countries to the poorest; this tendency mirrors that for the elasticity of food as a whole, discussed earlier. However, about one-third of the elasticities exceed unity and tend to move in the opposite direction—they tend to fall as income falls. An interesting group of items is beverages—items 27–31. Except for beer (item 31), beverages have elasticities exceeding unity for all quartiles, and these fall with income. For spirits (item 29) for example, in the fourth-quartile countries the elasticity is 2.0, making it a strong luxury, while in the first quartile, the elasticity falls to 1.4, still a luxury but less so. Taken literally, these beverages are a luxury for everyone, but are less of a luxury for the less affluent. In other words, spirits are closer to a necessity for the poor and more of a luxury for the rich. While this might not be completely implausible and reflect the type/brand choice within spirits, such a literal interpretation should not be taken too seriously.

Table 4.6 contains the income elasticities for the food groups. These groups are somewhat different to those of Table 4.2, but the differences are minor and can be disregarded for our purposes. With the exception of beverages for the top three quartiles and other food for the first quartile, the elasticities are less than unity, some substantially less so. For example, the elasticities for cereals are of the order of 0.5,

Table 4.5 Income elasticities of food

	Income quartile			
Food item	Fourth	Third	Second	First
1. Rice	0.18	0.15	0.04	0.90
2. Other cereals and flour	0.18	0.15	0.14	0.82
3. Bread	0.99	1.16	1.21	1.08
4. Other bakery products	1.94	1.57	1.52	1.39
5. Pasta products	0.24	0.77	0.94	0.99
6. Beef and veal	0.18	0.19	0.81	0.92
7. Pork, lamb, mutton, and goat	0.49	0.96	1.01	1.04
8. Poultry	0.91	1.25	1.26	1.07
9. Other meats and preparations	1.85	1.51	1.47	1.31
10. Fresh or frozen fish and seafood	0.45	0.80	1.09	1.07
11. Preserved fish and seafood	0.18	0.15	0.14	0.96
12. Fresh milk	0.21	0.79	1.02	0.97
13. Preserved milk and milk products	1.30	1.33	1.31	1.12
14. Cheese	2.09	1.63	1.56	1.68
15. Eggs and egg-based products	0.06	1.08	1.22	1.04
16. Butter and margarine	0.18	0.64	0.86	0.95
17. Other edible oils and fats	0.18	0.15	0.58	0.89
18. Fresh or chilled fruit	1.45	1.32	1.32	1.18
19. Frozen, preserved, or processed fruits	0.36	0.70	0.74	0.98
20. Fresh or chilled vegetables	0.01	0.90	1.13	1.04
21. Fresh or chilled potatoes	0.18	0.15	0.23	0.98
22. Frozen or preserved vegetables	0.18	0.51	0.82	0.92
23. Sugar	1.45	1.32	1.32	1.18
24. Jams, marmalades, and honey	0.36	0.70	0.74	0.98
25. Confectionery, chocolate, and ice cream	0.01	0.90	1.13	1.04
26. Food products n.e.c.	0.36	0.56	0.95	0.97
27. Coffee, tea, and cocoa	1.24	1.27	1.24	1.08
28. Min. Water, soft drink, fruit, and veg juice	1.60	1.39	1.36	1.19
29. Spirits	2.00	1.55	1.52	1.37
30. Wine	1.83	1.51	1.46	1.30
31. Beer	0.87	1.12	1.17	1.05

Note: Elasticities are conditional on real total food expenditure held constant and are averaged over countries

making the group a clear necessity, which is easily understood. Similarly, fish and oils and fats have low elasticities for some countries. For beverages, the elasticities are around unity, on the luxury-necessity borderline.

Next, consider the price elasticities. For the groups of food, we shall approximate the price elasticities as follows:

Table 4.6 Income elasticities of food groups

	Income quartile			
Commodity groups	Fourth	Third	Second	First
1. Cereals	0.560	0.486	0.428	0.683
2. Meat	0.724	0.855	0.916	0.895
3. Fish	0.278	0.332	0.653	0.820
4. Dairy	0.665	0.854	0.899	0.891
5. Oils and fats	0.085	0.209	0.659	0.758
6. Fruits and vegetables	0.436	0.548	0.760	0.820
7. Other food	0.665	0.749	0.909	1.030
8. Beverages	1.077	1.318	1.138	0.916

Note: These are unconditional elasticities that allow total food to vary

1. Suppose food as a whole is "sufficiently distinct" that its consumption can be considered by itself. As discussed in Chaps. 2 and 3, the precise meaning of food being "sufficiently distinct" is that its marginal utility is unaffected by the consumption of other goods. Such an assumption might be consistent with food being essential to sustain life.
2. Suppose the groups within food are sufficiently broad that each is also distinct, that is, the marginal utility of each food group is independent of consumption of items in other food groups.
3. Under these two conditions, price elasticities are proportional to income elasticities, as set out in Chap. 3. Denoting the own-price elasticity of group i ($i = 1, \cdots, 8$ groups) by η_{ii} and the corresponding income elasticity by η_i, the relationship is

$$\eta_{ii} = \phi\eta_i, \quad i = 1, \cdots, 8. \tag{4.7}$$

   The factor of proportionality $\phi < 0$ is the inverse of the income elasticity of the marginal utility of income, known as the income flexibility. Equation (4.7) is known as Pigou's (1910) law.

Equation (4.7) implies that groups with lower income elasticities—stronger necessities—have lower absolute price elasticities. This is not inconsistent with the intuitive notion that a price increase of an essential ($\eta_i < 1$) is unlikely to induce a reduction of consumption to any substantial degree. On the other hand, luxuries ($\eta_i > 1$) are more likely to be deferrable, so a price rise might be expected to result in a substantial reduction in consumption.

According to a number of studies, the income flexibility is clustered around −½ (as discussed in Chap. 3). Thus, using $\phi = -½$ in Eq. (4.7), the price elasticity of a food group in Table 4.6 is one-half of its income elasticity. For example, on average the price elasticity for cereals for countries in the fourth income quartile is $-½ \times 0.56 = -0.28$. This is a reasonable value for such a group.

Applying the same approach to the individual food items would be a mistake as these are unlikely to exhibit independence of marginal utilities. For example, it would be unlikely for the marginal utility of pork to be unaffected by the consumption of poultry. Typically, the consumer would choose pork or poultry, not both, so the marginal utility of one would fall when the other is chosen, making the items substitutes.

To conclude this section, it should be noted that condition (4.7) is a simplification of reality. But it may well be a useful simplification when applied to broad groups of commodities as it enables the approximation of price elasticities from minimal information—the income elasticities and the income flexibility. The simplification is particularly useful when reliable information on the value of a price elasticity is not available, as can frequently be the case.

4.10 A Behavioural Approach to Quality

As affluence rises, the budget share of food falls dramatically. In other words, the intensity of spending moves away from the dominant necessity of life to goods with a less-of-a-necessity status. In a fundamental sense, the nature of the consumption basket improves if the dominant necessity accounts for a smaller fraction, and consumption could reasonably be described as of higher "quality". Here, quality is based on the revealed preference of the consumer—the composition of the budget—not on any outside judgements as to what constitutes quality. This notion of quality differs from the usual hedonic approach that deals with the physical characteristics of the good where the quality of a car, for example, is related to its fuel efficiency, emissions, acceleration, etc.

To explain this measure of quality further, write the budget constraint, $M=\sum_{i=1}^{n}p_iq_i$, in change form as $d(\log M) = d(\log P) + d(\log Q)$, where $(\log P)=\sum_{i=1}^{n}w_i d(\log p_i)$ and $d(\log Q)=\sum_{i=1}^{n}w_i d(\log q_i)$ are Divisia (1926) price and volume indexes, with $w_i=\frac{p_iq_i}{M}$ the budget share of good i. Define the ith income elasticity as $\eta_i=\frac{\partial \log q_i}{\partial \log M}$. The relative importance of the growth in consumption of good i can be measured by its deviation from average, $d(\log q_i) - d(\log Q)$. Luxuries are preferred to necessities by the consumer as when income rises, and spending on the former rises proportionately more than the latter. Suppose we observe for a certain good i that $d(\log q_i) - d(\log Q) > 0$; if the good is a luxury ($\eta_i > 1$), its above-average growth then contributes to the desirability, or quality, of the basket. Alternatively, if the good is a necessity ($\eta_i < 1$), its above-average growth diminishes quality. The general proposition is that faster (slower) growth of a luxury (necessity) enhances quality, while slower (faster) growth of a luxury (necessity) detracts from quality. The direction of change in quality consequently involves the sign of the product $(\eta_i - 1) \times [\, d(\log q_i) - d(\log Q)]$. Application to all n goods simultaneously involves a budget-share weighted average of these products:

$$y_q = \sum_{i=1}^{n} w_i(\eta_i - 1)[\, d(\log q_i) - d(\log Q)]. \tag{4.8}$$

Equation (4.8) is an index of the change in quality of the consumption basket. As $\sum_{i=1}^{n} w_i \eta_i = 1$, the term $\eta_i - 1$ is the deviation of the income elasticity from the weighted mean of the elasticities of the n goods, while $d(\log q_i) - d(\log Q)$ is the deviation of consumption of the good from the weighted mean $d(\log Q) = \sum_{i=1}^{n} w_i d(\log q_i)$. Thus, Eq. (4.8) defines the weighted covariance between the income elasticities and the quantities consumed. When this covariance is positive, on average the consumption of luxuries grows faster than necessities and the quality of the basket improves.

The price and spending quality indexes, y_p and y_{pq}, are defined analogously to (4.8) and satisfy $y_{pq} = y_q + y_p$, which is a type of factor reversal property. As $y_q = y_{pq} - y_p$, the index y_p acts as a deflator that transforms the quality of spending, y_{pq}, a nominal concept, into the quality of consumption, y_q, a real concept. This means that y_p can be interpreted as an index of the price of quality.

4.11 Food Quality

To apply the quality index (4.8) to food, w_i is now interpreted as the proportion of total food expenditure devoted to the ith food item (from columns 6–9 of Table 4.2) and η_i as the good's income elasticity within food (Table 4.5). Strictly speaking, this share and the elasticity are now conditional (conditional on the value of total food). However, in order not to overburden the discussion, this distinction will not be made as the meaning will be clear from the context. With cross-country data, it is natural to compare one country with another, so that for countries c and d, the relative difference in consumption of good i is $\log q_i^{cd} = \log\left(q_i^c / q_i^d\right)$ and the corresponding budget share is $w_i^{cd} = \left(w_i^c + w_i^d\right)/2$. Defining the two-country income elasticity as $\eta_i^{cd} = \left[w_i^c / \left(w_i^c + w_i^d\right)\right] \cdot \eta_i^d + \left[w_i^d / \left(w_i^c + w_i^d\right)\right] \cdot \eta_i^d$, the index of the quality of consumption in country c relative to d is thus:

$$y_q^{cd} = \sum_{i=1}^{31} w_i^{cd} \left(\eta_i^{cd} - 1\right)\left(\log q_i^{cd} - \log Q^{cd}\right), \tag{4.9}$$

where $\log Q^{cd} = \sum_{i=1}^{31} w_i^{cd} \log q_i^{cd}$ is the Divisia volume index in c relative to d.

Index (4.9) compares the quality of consumption in country c to country d, so with 155 countries, there are a large number of these pairs to be considered. To compress the results, we convert the pairwise indexes to ones for which each country has a single value only by averaging over all its pairwise comparisons:

Table 4.7 Food quality indexes

Income quartile (1)	Index (2)	Interquartile differences: Fourth (3)	Third (4)	Second (5)	First (6)
A. *Quality of consumption*					
Fourth	17.88		11.84	24.13	36.00
Third	6.04			12.30	24.17
Second	−6.26				11.87
First	−18.13				
B. *Price of quality*					
Fourth	−1.68		−1.59	−2.27	−2.91
Third	−0.10			−0.69	−1.32
Second	0.59				−0.64
First	1.23				
C. *Quality of spending*					
Fourth	16.19		10.25	21.86	33.10
Third	5.94			11.61	22.84
Second	−5.67				11.23
First	−16.90				

Note: All entries are ×100

$$y_q^c = \frac{1}{155}\sum_{d=1}^{155} y_q^{cd}, \quad c = 1, \cdots, 155, \tag{4.10}$$

and similarly for prices and spending, y_p^c, y_{pq}^c. Index (4.10) converts the bilateral measure y_q^{cd}, involving the two countries c and d, into a single-dimension one for c. Table 4.7 gives the results. From columns 4–6 of the first row of panel A, the quality of consumption for countries in the fourth quartile is, on average, about 12, 24, and 36% greater than that of countries in the third, second, and first quartiles, respectively. The price of quality falls modestly as income rises (panel B) and due to the small price differences, the pattern of the quality of spending (panel C) is similar to that for consumption (panel A). In short, the quality of food consumption is lower for poorer consumers, as is to be expected. As there is substantially less dispersion among countries in the first quartile (not shown here), if you are poor the quality of your consumption is not only lower than that of the more affluent, but also quite similar to that of most of your immediate neighbours.

Panel A of Fig. 4.6 plots the index of the quality of consumption $\left(y_q^c\right)$ against income. On average, higher-quality food is associated with higher income. This positive relationship is even more compelling when quartile means are used (the diamonds in the figure). The coefficient of log income in the regression is 12.06, which is 100 times the elasticity (only the dependent variable is ×100). With an income elasticity of 12.06/100 = 0.12 when we move from one country to another that is 50% richer, the quality of the food basket improves by about 6%. While the

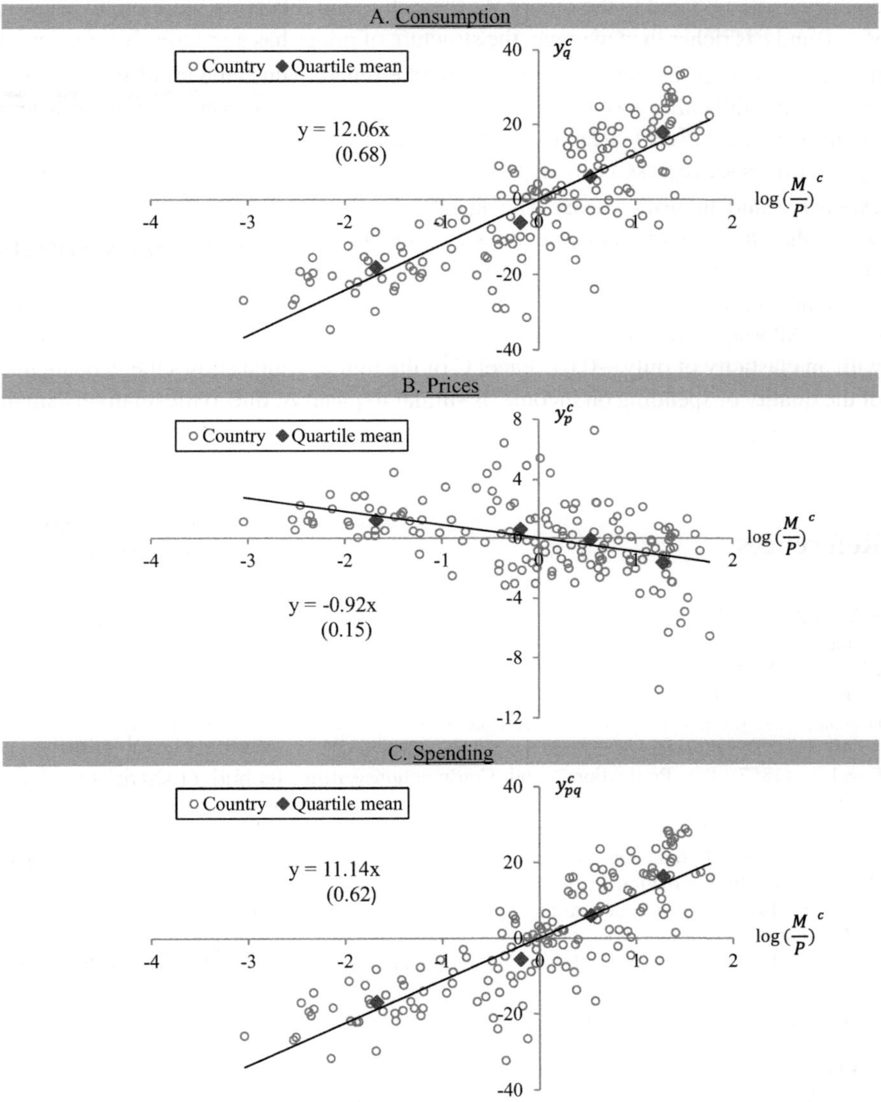

Fig. 4.6 Food quality and income. *Notes*: Panel A is a scatter plot of the multilateral index of the quality of consumption of the 31 goods in the food baskets in 155 countries against income measured as a deviation from its mean. Panels B and C are analogous plots for the quality indexes of prices and spending. Indexes are × 100

income sensitivity is low, it can be interpreted as simply saying that it is not easy to increase the quality of the food basket.

Panel B of Fig. 4.6 is a similar scatter for the index of the price of quality, y_p^c. A positive value of the index means the prices of luxuries are higher, on average, in country c as compared to the others. As the rich spend relatively more on luxuries, if $y_p^c > 0$ and c is richer than average, the structure of prices has a progressive impact on the distribution of income: If nominal income remains unchanged, a rich person's real income falls after moving from the rest of the world to country c, from where luxuries were relatively cheap to where they are more expensive. Conversely, when $y_p^c < 0$, prices are regressive in the rich country c since necessities are relatively more expensive and luxuries cheap. The negatively sloped regression line in panel B shows that the price of quality declines with income, meaning luxuries are relatively cheaper and necessities more expensive in rich countries on average. Taken literally, the richer the country, the more regressive (or less progressive) is the structure of prices. Although the coefficient of log income is significant, this tendency is small with an elasticity of only -0.01. Panel C of the figure, which shows the dependence of the quality of spending on income, is similar to panel A, due to the relatively small role for the price of quality.

References

Balassa B (1964) The purchasing-power parity doctrine: a reappraisal. J Polit Econ 72:584–596

Bennett MK (1941) Wheat in National Diets. Wheat Studies 18:37–76

Clements KW, Chen DL (2010) Affluence and food: a simple way to infer incomes. Am J Agric Econ 92:909–926

Divisia F (1926) L'indice Monétaire et la Théorie de la Monnaie. Revue d'Économie Politique 40: 49–81. ["The Monetary Index and the Theory of Money"]

Engel E (1857) Die Produktions- und Consumptionsverhaltnisse des Konigreichs Sachsen. Reprinted in Engel's Die Lebenskosten belgischer Atbeiter-Familien. Dresden, 1895. ["The Production and Consumption Conditions of the Kingdom of Saxony"]

Gao G (2012) World food demand. Am J Agric Econ 94:25–51

Harrod RF (1939) International economics. Nisbet, Cambridge

Pigou AC (1910) A method of determining the numerical value of demand elasticities. Econ J 20: 636–640

Samuelson PA (1964) Theoretical notes on trade problems. Review of Economics and Statistics May 1:145–154

Theil H, Chung C-F, Seale JL (1989) International evidence on consumption patterns. JAI Press, Inc, Greenwich, Connecticut

Working H (1943) Statistical laws of family expenditure. J Am Stat Assoc 38:43–56

World Bank (2015) 2011 international comparison program results. http://siteresources.worldbank.org/ICPEXT/Resources/ICP_2011.html

World Bank (n.d.) 2011 International comparison program data for researchers. World Bank, Washington, DC

Chapter 5
Food Demand II: Further Results and Details

This chapter provides further information on, sources and elaboration of Chap. 4's material.

5.1 Engel's Law and the Food Share

Section 4.2 on Engel's law is from Clements (2019).

In the *Wealth of Nations*, Adam Smith (1776) comments, "the desire of food is limited in every man by the narrow capacity of the human stomach" while "conveniences and ornaments of building, dress, equipage, and household furniture seems to have no limit." This points to the low income elasticity of food. A widely cited source on empirical support for Engel's law is Houthakker (1957). For further research related to Engel's law, see Chai and Moneta (2010), Chakrabarty and Hildenbrand (2011), Clements and Si (2018), Gao (2012), Houthakker (1987), and Ogaki (1992). Stigler (1954) discusses the history of Engel's law.

5.2 The Strong Version of Engel's Law

Section 4.3, dealing with the strong version of Engel's law, is mostly from Clements (2019). Part of this section is also from that source. The strong version of Engel originates from Theil et al. (1989).

Working's (1943) model expresses the food budget share (w) as a linear function of the logarithm of income (M), $w = \alpha + \beta \log M$. This is also referred to as the Working-Leser (1963) model. Pritchett and Spivack (2013) apply this model to food consumption and note the "striking empirical stability of the …coefficient [β] across time and space and widely available estimates of … food shares". Using a slope coefficient of -12.5, which aligns with the evidence in Figs. 4.2 and 4.3, Pritchett

K. W. Clements et al., *Short-cut Demand Elasticities and Other Convenient Approaches to Consumer Demand*, https://doi.org/10.1007/978-981-96-3588-7_5

and Spivack (2013) also estimate income by inverting the model. Clements and Chen (2010) use a similar approach but also allow for differences in relative prices. Chen (1999, Sect. 5.8) gives a detailed survey of estimates of β and shows they are centred around -14.0 when derived from cross-sectional data and -11.0 for time-series data. The similarity in the slope coefficients using different data provides reassuring evidence for the robustness of Working's model for food.

It is reasonable for the food income elasticity to fall as the consumer becomes richer—for the rich, a given proportionate increase in income has a lower impact on food consumption than for the poor. But it is likely that the elasticity falls to some positive value and does not become negative, so food does not become an inferior good. The income elasticity of Working's model is $1+\frac{\beta}{w}$, which is positive when $w > -\beta$. This implies income must be less than $\overline{\overline{M}}$, where $\alpha+\beta\log\overline{\overline{M}} = -\beta$, or $\overline{\overline{M}} = \exp\left(-1-\frac{\alpha}{\beta}\right)$. As for $w > 0$, the upper bound for income is $\bar{M} = \exp\left(-\frac{\alpha}{\beta}\right)$. Thus, the new upper bound ensuring that the elasticity remains positive is $\overline{\overline{M}} = \exp(-1)\bar{M}$. Since $\exp(-1) = 0.37$, the new upper bound $\overline{\overline{M}}$ is 63% less than $\bar{M}$, the income value when the share turns negative. For a thorough assessment of the admissible income ranges and the likelihood of the violation of the bounds, see Chen (1999, Chap. 5).

As mentioned in Sect. 4.3, a departure from the Engel curve can be ascribed to mismeasurement of income. Prior research has attributed this to problems with the price index used to deflate money income. Usually the price index is the CPI, which is subject to substitution and quality biases that inflate the index. See Costa (2001), Hamilton (2001), and Nakamura (1996). In related work, Almås (2012) uses Engel curves to analyse the bias in the estimates of income of the Penn World Table; see also Barnett (2024) and Nakamura et al. (2016). In earlier work, the food share itself has been used as an inverse measure of welfare; for example, see Orshansky (1965, 1969), Rao (1981), and Van Praag et al. (1982).

The forerunner to the above methods is the so-called Engel (1895) approach to measuring the cost of a child. To briefly explain the approach, let N_h be the number of children in household h and suppose the share of income devoted to food rises by $\gamma > 0$ percentage points when a child is added to the household. Thus, an extended version of Working's model is

$$w_h = \alpha + \beta \log M_h + \gamma N_h.$$

The cost of a child answers the question: What increase in income would be required to offset the higher spending on food by holding the share unchanged? This is $\Delta \log M_h = -\frac{\gamma}{\beta}$. For example, if the share rises by $\gamma = 1.5$ percentage points with an additional child and $\beta = -0.15$, then $\Delta \log M_h = \frac{0.015}{0.15} = 0.1$. Thus, the cost of the child is about 10% of income, which seems reasonable. Jayasinghe (2022) contains a recent treatment of this procedure.

While simple and still widely employed, the Engel approach to the cost of a child is subject to some limitations, including the uncritical identification of the food share with welfare, the assumption that the coefficient of income, β, is the same for all households, and the assumed identical cost for each additional child (no hand-me-downs). For references to the Engel approach, criticisms and alternatives, including the influential Barten (1964) model, see Deaton (2016) and Deaton and Muellbauer (1986). Ray (2018, Chap. 2) also reviews alternative approaches. As noted by Deaton and Muellbauer (1980, p. 205), a general formulation of the cost of a child is via the cost function that allows for complete scope of substitution among goods: If $C(u_0, \boldsymbol{p}_0, N_0)$ is the cost function for some reference utility u_0, given the price vector $\boldsymbol{p}_0$ and number of children N_0, then a constant-utility index of the cost of an additional child is $\frac{C(u_0, \boldsymbol{p}_0, N_0+1)}{C(u_0, \boldsymbol{p}_0, N_0)}$. For example, if this index takes the value 1.075 the cost of the $(N_0 + 1)^{th}$ child is 7.5% of income.

5.3 Food Elasticities

Cornelsen et al. (2015) and Green et al. (2013) summarise a large number of food demand studies with a meta-regression approach; Clements and Si (2016) extend that work. Other studies of income and price elasticities of food include Chen (1999, Chap. 5), Edgerton et al. (1996), Gao (2012), Liu (2018), Meade et al. (2014), Muhammad et al. (2011), Okrent and Alston (2011), Seale et al. (2014), Seale et al. (2003), and Wohlgenant (2021, Chap. 5). Most of these sources provide further references to the literature.

5.4 Engel's Law and Prices

In view of the relative importance of the food sector in a number of countries, Engel's law is likely to have economy-wide implications. As highlighted by Podkaminer (2011), Engel's law can lead to substantial changes in the structure of prices. This will be demonstrated with material from Clements et al. (2022).

Consider a simple stylised economy with two goods, food (F) and non-food (N). For $i = F, N$, denote by q_i the quantity of good i, η_i the income elasticity, $\eta_{ii} < 0$ the price elasticity, and p_i the price. The demand for food and non-food can be expressed as

$$d(\log q_F) = \eta_F d(\log Q) + \eta_{FF} d\left(\log \frac{p_F}{p_N}\right),$$

$$d(\log q_N) = \eta_N d(\log Q) + \eta_{NN} d\left(\log \frac{p_N}{p_F}\right),$$

where $d(\log Q)$ is the change in real income. By Engel's law, the food income elasticity is less than unity, while that of non-food exceeds unity since a budget-share weighted average of the two is unity. That is, $\eta_F < 1 < \eta_N$.

On the supply side, suppose the production possibility frontier shifts out in an unbiased manner due to factor accumulation and neutral technical change. This means that the production of each good is proportional to real income:

$$d(\log q_F) = d(\log Q), \quad d(\log q_N) = d(\log Q).$$

This specification neutralises supply conditions so as to isolate the Engel effect. As from the supply side $d(\log q_F) = d(\log q_N)$, market clearing requires that $\eta_F d(\log Q) + \eta_{FF} d\left(\log \frac{p_F}{p_N}\right) = \eta_N d(\log Q) + \eta_{NN} d\left(\log \frac{p_N}{p_F}\right)$, or

$$d\left(\log \frac{p_F}{p_N}\right) = \theta(\eta_F - \eta_N) d(\log Q),$$

where $\theta = -\frac{1}{\eta_{FF}+\eta_{NN}} > 0$. When income grows, $d(\log Q) > 0$ and the relative price of food falls as $(\eta_F - \eta_N) < 0$. The larger the difference between the income elasticities, the cheaper food becomes. This is known as the Engel effect. The coefficient θ measures the substitutability between the two goods—when they are poor substitutes, the greater θ is and the larger the Engel effect.

To illustrate the implication of the above, suppose $\eta_{FF} = \eta_{NN} = -\frac{1}{2}$, so that $\theta = 1$, and $\eta_F = 0.6$ and $\eta_N = 1.3$. Then, the change in the food relative price is a multiple $0.6 - 1.3 = -0.7$ of the growth in income; if income grows by 2%, food prices fall by about 1.5%. The Harrod (1939)-Balassa (1964)-Samuelson (1964) (HBS) effect means that because of its slower productivity growth, the relative price of the service sector rises over time. Identifying non-food as services, the combined impact of the HBS and Engel effects is an amplified fall in the relative food price that accompanies economic growth. As consumption of the poor is intensive in the necessity (food), economic growth that leads to cheaper food is beneficial for them.

5.5 Individual Food Items and Diet Diversity

The majority of Sects. 4.6–4.8 on the diversity of food budgets is from Clements and Si (2018) including the online appendices. This section contains additional material on the measurement of diversity.

A popular measure of diversity is a simple count of the number of individual items of food consumed by a household. Clearly, this index is increasing in the number of items consumed. While Ruel (2003) argued this gives an indication of the nutritional value of the diet, one problem with this approach is the mixing of units: How does one interpret an index that adds vegetables to meat? Another issue is that counting disregards the volume consumed of each item; that is, as long as the composition of the meal (as measured by the number of items) is the same, the index remains unchanged whatever the magnitude of each unit and/or the overall size of the meal.

The Berry index is another popular measure of diversity. This takes the form

$$\text{Berry} = 1 - \sum_{i=1}^{n} w_i^2, \quad \text{with range } \left[0, 1 - \frac{1}{n}\right].$$

Here, n is the number of goods in the basket and w_i is the fraction of income spent on good i (the budget share). This index is 1 minus a weighted average of the shares, where the weights are the shares themselves, and is increasing in n, meaning more diversity. The sum of the squared shares is known as the Herfindahl-Hirschman index used in industrial organisation to measure market concentration. As the shares are pure numbers, the Berry index has the advantage of being unit free. A related diversity index is the entropy, defined as

$$\sum_{i=1}^{n} w_i \log \frac{1}{w_i}, \quad \text{with range } [0, \log n].$$

This is also unit free and increasing in n. Here the shares are weighted by $\log \frac{1}{w_i}$. There is no convenient algebraic relation between the Berry and entropy, but they would be positively correlated.

An interesting result emerges for the Berry index when the Engel curves are of Working's form, $w_i = \alpha_i + \beta_i \log M$, $i = 1, \cdots, n$. Berry then becomes

$$\begin{gathered} \text{Berry} = A + B \log M + C(\log M)^2, \\ A = 1 - \sum_{i=1}^{n} \alpha_i^2, \quad B = -2 \sum_{i=1}^{n} \alpha_i \beta_i, \quad C = -\sum_{i=1}^{n} \beta_i^2. \end{gathered} \tag{5.1}$$

The index is quadratic in log$M$; a 1-per cent change in income causes the index to change by B + 2C log M. Since $\sum_{i=1}^{n} \alpha_i \beta_i$ is mostly likely to be negative, the coefficient B is expected to be positive, while C is definitely negative. As a result, the income sensitivity of the index declines with income, which is a type of diminishing returns. Recalling that the ith income elasticity associated with Working's model is $\eta_i = 1 + \frac{\beta_i}{w_i}$, when these elasticities become closer to unity, the β_i's are closer to zero, as are the coefficients B and C. In such a case, the index tends to $A = 1 - \sum_{i=1}^{n} \alpha_i^2$, a constant independent of income. This is exactly as it should be since if each $\beta_i = 0$, then Working's model reduces to $\alpha_i = w_i$ and $A = 1 - \sum_{i=1}^{n} w_i^2$, the original Berry index. Further, $B = -2\sum_{i=1}^{n} \alpha_i w_i(\eta_i - 1)$, and $C = -\sum_{i=1}^{n} w_i^2(\eta_i - 1)^2$. Thus, a lower dispersion among the income elasticities makes Berry less sensitive to income. Although depending on Working's model, this would seem to be a property that should hold for all reasonable measures of diversity.

As the quadratic (5.1) has a maximum at $\log M^* = -\frac{B}{2C}$, it can be expressed as

$$\text{Berry} = A' + C(\log M - \log M^*)^2, \quad A' = A - \frac{B^2}{4\,C}.$$

Since $C < 0$, this form makes explicit that the index gets closer to its maximum value of $A' = A - \frac{B^2}{4\,C}$ as the deviation, $\log M - \log M^*$, becomes smaller. As the deviations rise, the index declines more than proportionally. In terms of the parameters of Working's model, the maximum value of Berry is $A' = A - \frac{B^2}{4\,C} = 1 - \sum_{i=1}^{n} \alpha_i^2 + \left(\sum_{i=1}^{n} \alpha_i \beta_i\right)^2 / \sum_{i=1}^{n} \beta_i^2$. Previous research on the diversity of consumption patterns and its relation to income includes Chai and Moneta (2012), Drescher et al. (2008), Falkinger and Zweimüller (1996), Jackson (1984), Li (2021), Shonkwiler et al. (1987), Theil and Finke (1983), Thiele and Weiss (2003), and Weiss (2011); for a survey, see Chai et al. (2015). Somewhat relatedly, Khoury et al. (2014) examine food supplies in a number of countries and find increasing diversity in consumption over a 50-year period.

The relation between the dispersion of prices and the dispersion of quantities has been studied with time-series data. Quantities are usually found to be more dispersed than prices. This research includes Chen (1999), Clements (1982), Finke (1985), Meisner (1979), Selvanathan (1993), Theil (1967), and Wong et al. (2017), among others.

The Australian Guide to Healthy Eating is an example of a source pointing to the benefits of diet diversity (https://www.eatforhealth.gov.au/guidelines/australian-guide-healthy-eating). The beneficial role of diversity is also enshrined in popular aphorisms such as "variety is the spice of life", "don't put all your eggs in one basket", and "a change is as good as a holiday".

5.6 Measuring Quality

The first part of Sect. 4.9 on the disaggregated income elasticities of food is from the online appendix of Clements and Si (2018). Sections 4.10 and 4.11 on food quality are from Clements and Si (2018), as are parts of this section.

There are two conventional approaches to measuring quality. The first approach is hedonic analysis of the prices of varieties of a generic type of good that differ only in their physical form ("quality"). The prices are regressed on selected characteristics of the goods to obtain their shadow prices; constant-quality prices are then obtained by stripping out the effects of different characteristics of the goods (Griliches 1961).

Adam Smith (1776) states, "the rich man consumes no more food than his poor neighbour. In quality it may be very different… but in quantity it is very nearly the same". This is closely related to Houthakker's law that states with increasing income, the growth in food spending exceeds that of the volume of food consumed (Timmer et al. 1983, p. 58). This excess can be interpreted as a certain form of growth in food quality. Accordingly, the second approach uses prices themselves as a measure of quality. On the understanding that prices are approximately constant in a cross section of consumers, the income elasticity of food can be measured by the elasticity of expenditure, $\eta = \frac{\partial \log\,(p \times q)}{\partial \log M} = \frac{\partial \log q}{\partial \log M}$. On the other hand when prices vary, η can be decomposed into quantity and quality elasticities, $\eta = \frac{\partial \log\,(p \times q)}{\partial \log M} = \frac{\partial \log\,q}{\partial \log M} + \frac{\partial \log\,p}{\partial \log M}$. In Houthakker's (1987) words, "agriculture produces quantity, while food processing and trade produce quality". This approach to measuring quality is now usually attributed to Prais and Houthakker (1955) and Theil (1953). For related research, see Bils and Klenow (2021), Cox and Wohlgenant (1986), Cramer (1973), Deaton (1988), Gale and Hang (2007), Hicks and Johnson (1968), Wohlgenant (2021, Chap. 6), and Yu and Abler (2009).

A problem with hedonic analysis that only a limited number of commodities possess easily identifiable physical characteristics. Since many services (such as education and medicine) have little or no physicality and as services comprise such a large part of the budget of many consumers, especially those in high-income countries, hedonics would struggle with measuring the quality of the budget as a whole. Theil (1975/76) introduced a new way of measuring quality that avoids this problem: Denoting the budget share of good i by w_i, its income elasticity by η_i, and the change in relative consumption by $d(\log q_i) - d(\log Q)$, this approach is based on the weighted covariance between the n income elasticities and their relative consumption, that is,

$$y_q = \sum_{i=1}^{n} w_i(\eta_i - 1)[\, d(\log q_i) - d(\log Q)]. \tag{5.2}$$

This is the quality index of the budget as a whole. The index is positive when the consumption pattern moves in the direction of luxuries, or away from necessities, so quality improves when $y_q > 0$. This is based on the idea that luxuries are of superior quality while necessities are not. In contrast to the above second approach, index (5.3) does not rely on price differences to measure quality. Index (5.2) was extended by Clements and Gao (2012) to the quality of spending and the price of quality.

Two examples give insights into the workings of the quality index (5.2). First, suppose the demands are log-linear in income and prices are constant:

$$d(\log q_i) = \alpha_i + \eta_i d(\log Q), \quad i = 1, \cdots, n. \tag{5.3}$$

As the equations are formulated in terms of changes, the intercept α_i is the autonomous trend in consumption of good i, η_i is its income elasticity, and $d(\log Q)$ is the change in income. Index (5.2) implied by (5.3) takes the simple form

$$y_q = A + V \cdot d(\log Q), \quad \text{with } A = \sum_{i=1}^{n} w_i(\eta_i - 1)\alpha_i, \quad V = \sum_{i=1}^{n} w_i(\eta_i - 1)^2. \quad (5.4)$$

Quality is now log-linear also, with the coefficient V the income elasticity of quality. This V is a budget-share weighted variance of the income elasticities of the n goods. When all income elasticities are unity, $V = 0$ and the elasticity of quality is zero. In this case, each good is on the luxury/necessity border, meaning that a change in the pattern of consumption brought about by an increase in income amounts to changes in neutral goods offsetting changes in other neutrals, leaving the quality of the basket unchanged. In contrast, when some income elasticities are not unity, $V > 0$ and quality increases with income as luxuries become consumed more intensively than necessities. In general, the more dispersion among the elasticities, the greater is the income sensitivity of quality. This is similar to the previous discussion of the Berry index of diversity of consumption [Eq. (5.1)].

As $\sum_{i=1}^{n} w_i\eta_i = 1$, the intercept A in the quality Eq. (5.4) can be expressed as

$$A = \sum_{i=1}^{n} w_i(\eta_i - 1)(\alpha_i - \bar{\alpha}), \quad \bar{\alpha} = \sum_{i=1}^{n} w_i\alpha_i.$$

This is a weighted covariance of the income elasticities and the trend terms of the demand functions (5.3), the α_i's. Thus, when the two variables are positively correlated, on average luxuries (necessities) grow faster (slower) than necessities (luxuries) on account of trends and $A > 0$.

As a second example, suppose, as before, the Engel curves take the form of Working's model, $w_i = \alpha_i + \beta_i \log M, i = 1, \cdots, n, \sum_{i=1}^{n} \beta_i = 0$. The income elasticity of i is $\eta_i = 1 + \beta_i/w_i$, implying $\beta_i > 0$ (<0) codes a luxury (necessity). Then, the index of quality is $y_q = \sum_{i=1}^{n} \beta_i \log q_i$, where q_i is the quantity consumed of i, or

$$e^{y_q} = \prod_{i=1}^{n} q_i^{\beta_i}. \quad (5.5)$$

The weights in the index are now fixed and (5.5) is of the Cobb-Douglas form. The sum of the exponents is zero, not unity as in the constant-returns-to-scale version of the Cobb-Douglas production function. This is an attractively simple form that shows that higher consumption of luxuries ($\beta_i > 0$) enhances quality, and vice versa for necessities ($\beta_i < 0$). Suppose each good grows from period $t - 1$ to t at the same rate $k \times 100\%$, so that $q_{it} = q_{i,t-1}(1 + k)$, $i = 1, \cdots, n$. Then quality in t is

$$y_{qt} = y_{q,t-1} + \sum_{i=1}^{n} \beta_i(1 + k) = y_{q,t-1}.$$

Quality is unchanged as the pattern of consumption is constant. Result (5.5) can also be written as $e^{y_q} = \prod_{i=1}^{n} q_i^{w_i(\eta_i - 1)}$, where the exponents are weighted deviations of income elasticities from their weighted mean. This again emphasises how non-unity income elasticities drive the quality index.

In recent research that seems consistent with the luxury-necessity approach, Caron et al. (2020) report a positive correlation between income elasticities and the skill-intensity of goods. They also refer to papers on trade and quality, and the link between quality and skilled labour (Feenstra and Romalis 2014; Fieler et al. 2018; Hallak 2010). Using the luxury-necessity approach, Sect. 4.11 briefly mentioned the impact of the structure of food prices on the distribution of income. Other approaches to this topic have been employed by Broda and Romalis (2009), Muellbauer (1974), Nicholas et al. (2010), and Pendakur (2002).

References

Almås I (2012) International income inequality: measuring PPP bias by estimating Engel curves for food. Am Econ Rev 102:1093–1117

Balassa B (1964) The purchasing-power parity doctrine: a reappraisal. J Polit Econ 72:584–596

Barnett E (2024) More than money: improving welfare measurement. Honours dissertation, The University of Western Australia

Barten AP (1964) Family composition, prices and expenditure patterns. In: Hart P, Mills G (eds) Econometric analysis for national economic planning. Butterworth, London

Bils M, Klenow PJ (2021) Quantifying quality growth. Am Econ Rev 91:1006–1030

Broda C, Romalis J (2009) The welfare implications of rising price dispersion." Working Paper,. Booth School of Business, The University of Chicago

Caron J, Fally T, Markusen J (2020) Per capita income and the demand for skills. J Int Econ 123: 103306

Chai A, Moneta A (2010) Engel Curves. J Econ Perspect 24:225–240

Chai A, Moneta A (2012) Back to Engel? Some evidence for the hierarchy of needs. J Evol Econ 22:649–676

Chai A, Rohde N, Silber J (2015) Measuring the diversity of household spending patterns. J Econ Surv 29:423–440

Chakrabarty M, Hildenbrand W (2011) Engel's law reconsidered. J Math Econ 47:289–299

Chen DL (1999) World consumption economics. World Scientific, Singapore

Clements KW (1982) Divisia moments of Australian consumption. Econ Lett 9:43–48

Clements KW (2019) Four laws of consumption. Economic Record 95:358–385

Clements KW, Chen DL (2010) Affluence and food: a simple way to infer incomes. Am J Agric Econ 92:909–926

Clements KW, Gao G (2012) Quality, quantity, spending and prices. Eur Econ Rev 56:1376–1391

Clements KW, Lan Y, Liu H, Vo L (2022) The ICP, PPP and household expenditure patterns. UWA Economics Discussion Paper 22:18

Clements KW, Si J (2016) Price elasticities of food demand: compensated vs uncompensated. Health Econ 25:1403–1408

Clements KW, Si J (2018) Engel's law, diet diversity and the quality of food consumption. Am J Agric Econ 100:1–22

Cornelsen L, Green R, Turner R, Dangour AD, Shankar B, Mazzocchi M, Smith RD (2015) What happens to patterns of food consumption when food prices change? Evidence from a systematic review and meta-analysis of food price elasticities globally. Health Econ 24:1548–1559

Costa DL (2001) Estimating real income in the United States from 1888 to 1994: correcting CPI bias using Engel curves. J Polit Econ 109:1288–1310
Cox TL, Wohlgenant MK (1986) Prices and quality effects in cross-section demand analysis. Am J Agric Econ 68:908–919
Cramer JS (1973) Interaction of income and price in consumer demand. Int Econ Rev 14:351–363
Deaton AS (1988) Quality, quantity and spatial variation of price. Am Econ Rev 78:418–430
Deaton AS (2016) Measuring and understanding behavior, welfare, and poverty. Am Econ Rev 106:1221–1243
Deaton AS, Muellbauer J (1980) Economics and consumer behaviour. Cambridge University Press, Cambridge
Deaton AS, Muellbauer J (1986) On measuring child costs: with applications to poor countries. J Polit Econ 94:720–744
Drescher L, Thiele S, Weiss CR (2008) The taste for variety: a hedonic analysis. Econ Lett 101:66–68
Edgerton DL, Assarsson B, Hummelmose A, Laurila IP, Rickertsen K, Vale PH (1996) The econometrics of demand systems with applications to food demand in the Nordic countries. Springer Science and Business Media
Engel E (1895) Die Lebenskosten belgischer Arbeiter-Familien Fruher und Jetzt. International Statistical Institute Bulletin 9:1–124. ["The Cost of Living of Belgian Working-Class Families Then and Now"]
Falkinger J, Zweimüller J (1996) The cross-country Engel curve for product diversification. Struct Chang Econ Dyn 7:79–97
Feenstra RC, Romalis J (2014) International prices and endogenous quality. Q J Econ 129:477–527
Fieler AC, Eslava M, Xu DY (2018) Trade, quality upgrading and input linkages: theory and evidence from Colombia. Am Econ Rev 108:109–146
Finke R (1985) Divisia moments of US consumption, 1929–1982. Econ Lett 17:223–226
Gale F, Hang K (2007) Demand for food quantity and quality in China, Economic research report no. 32. Economic Research Service, United States Department of Agriculture
Gao G (2012) World food demand. Am J Agric Econ 94:25–51
Green R, Cornelsen L, Dangour AD, Shankar B, Mazzocchi M, Smith RD (2013) The effect of rising food prices on food consumption: systematic review with meta-regression. Br Med J 346: 3703
Griliches Z (1961) Hedonic Price indexes for automobiles: an econometric analysis of quality change. In: The Price statistics of the federal government. General series, vol No. 73. Columbia University Press, New York, NY, pp 137–196
Hallak JC (2010) A product-quality view of the Linder hypothesis. Rev Econ Stat 92:453–466
Hamilton BW (2001) Using Engel's law to estimate CPI bias. Am Econ Rev 91:619–630
Harrod RF (1939) International economics. Nisbet, Cambridge
Hicks WW, Johnson SR (1968) Quantity and quality components for income elasticities of demand for food. Am J Agric Econ 50:1512–1517
Houthakker HS (1957) An international comparison of household expenditure patterns, commemorating the centenary of Engel's law. Econometrica 25:532–551
Houthakker HS (1987) Engel's Law. In: Eatwell J, Milgate M, Newman P (eds) The new Palgrave: a dictionary of economics, vol 2. Macmillan, London, pp 143–144
Jackson LF (1984) Hierarchic demand and the Engel curve for variety. Rev Econ Stat 66:8–15
Jayasinghe M (2022) Poverty, food consumption and economic development. Springer Nature, Singapore
Khoury CK, Bjorkman AD, Dempewolf H, Ramirez-Villegas J, Guarino L, Jarvis A, Rieseberg LH, Struik PC (2014) Increasing homogeneity in global food supplies and the implications for food security. PNAS 111:4001–4006
Leser C (1963) Forms of Engel functions. Econometrica 31:694–703
Li N (2021) An Engel Curve for Variety. Rev Econ Stat 103:72–87

Liu H (2018) Cross-country food consumption patterns: theory and measurement. PhD thesis, The University of Western Australia
Meade B, Regmi A, Seale JL Jr, Muhammad A (2014) New international evidence on food consumption patterns: a focus on cross-price effects based on 2005 international comparisons, Technical bulletin 1937. Economic Research Service, United States Department of Agriculture
Meisner JF (1979) Divisia moments of US industry, 1947-1978. Econ Lett 4:239–242
Muellbauer J (1974) Prices and inequality: the United Kingdom experience. Econ J 84:32–55
Muhammad A, Seale JL Jr, Meade B, Regmi A (2011) International evidence on food consumption patterns: an update using 2005 international comparison program data. In: Technical Bulletin 1929. Economic Research Service. United States Department of Agriculture. Revised 2013
Nakamura E, Steinsson J, Liu M (2016) Are Chinese growth and inflation too smooth? Evidence from Engel curves. Am Econ J Macroecon 8:113–144
Nakamura L (1996) Is US economic performance really that bad? Working Paper 95, Federal Reserve Bank of Philadelphia
Nicholas A, Ray R, Valenzuela R (2010) Evaluating the distributional implications of price movements: methodology, application and Australian evidence. Economic Record 86:352–366
Ogaki M (1992) Engel's law and cointegration. J Polit Econ 100:1027–1046
Okrent AM, Alston JM (2011) Demand for food in the United States: a review of literature, evaluation of previous estimates and presentation of new estimates of demand, Giannini Foundation monograph 48. University of California, Agriculture and Natural Resources
Orshansky M (1965) Counting the poor: another look at the poverty profile. Soc Secur Bull 28:3–29
Orshansky M (1969) How poverty is measured. Mon Labor Rev 92:37–41
Pendakur K (2002) Taking prices seriously in the measurement of inequality. J Public Econ 86:47–69
Podkaminer L (2011) Why are goods cheaper in rich European countries? Beyond the Balassa–Samuelson effect. Metroeconomica 62:712–728
Prais SJ, Houthakker HS (1955) The analysis of family budgets. Cambridge University Press, Cambridge
Pritchett L, Spivack M (2013) Estimating income/expenditure differences across populations: new fun with old Engel's law. CGD Working Paper 339. Center for Global Development, Washington, DC
Rao VVB (1981) Measurement of deprivation and poverty based on the proportion spent on food: an exploratory exercise. World Dev 9:337–353
Ray R (2018) Household behaviour, prices and welfare. Springer Nature, Singapore
Ruel MT (2003) Operationalizing dietary diversity: a review of measurement issues and research priorities. J Nutr 133:3911–3926
Samuelson PA (1964) Theoretical notes on trade problems. Rev Econ Stat May 1:145–154
Seale JL, Dahl CP, Moss CR, Regmi A (2014) International evidence on cross-price effects of food and other goods. In: Sickles RC, Horrace WC (eds) Festschrift in honor of Peter Schmidt: econometric methods and applications. Springer Science + Business Media, New York, pp 125–218
Seale JL, Regmi A, Bernstein J (2003) International evidence on food consumption patterns. In: Technical bulletin 1904. Economic research service. United States Department of Agriculture, Washington, D.C.
Selvanathan S (1993) A system-wide analysis of international consumption patterns. Kluwer, Boston
Shonkwiler JS, Lee J-Y, Taylor TG (1987) An empirical model of demand for a varied diet. Appl Econ 19:1403–1410
Smith A (1776) An inquiry into the nature and causes of the wealth of nations. Version edited by E. Cannan, reprinted by the University of Chicago Press, 1976
Stigler GJ (1954) The early history of empirical studies in consumer behavior. J Polit Econ 62:95–113
Theil H (1953) Qualities, prices and budget inquiries. Rev Econ Stud 19:129–147

Theil H (1967) Economics and information theory. North-Holland and Rand McNally, Amsterdam and Chicago

Theil H (1975/76) Theory and measurement of consumer demand. Two volumes. North-Holland Publishing Company, Amsterdam

Theil H, Chung C-F, Seale JL (1989) International evidence on consumption patterns. JAI Press, Inc, Greenwich, Connecticut

Theil H, Finke R (1983) The consumer's demand for diversity. Eur Econ Rev 23:395–400

Thiele S, Weiss C (2003) Consumer demand for food diversity: evidence for Germany. Food Policy 28:99–115

Timmer CP, Falcon WP, Pearson SR (1983) Food policy analysis. Johns Hopkins, Baltimore and London

Van Praag BM, Spit JS, Van de Stadt H (1982) A comparison between the food ratio poverty line and the Leyden poverty line. Rev Econ Stat 64:691–694

Weiss CR (2011) Consumer demand for food variety. In: Roosen J, Lusk JL, Shogren JF (eds) The Oxford handbook of the economics of food consumption and policy. Oxford University Press, Oxford

Wohlgenant MK (2021) Market interrelationships and applied demand analysis. Springer International Publishing

Wong L, Selvanathan EA, Selvanathan S (2017) Empirical analysis of Australian consumption patterns. Empir Econ 52:799–823

Working H (1943) Statistical laws of family expenditure. J Am Stat Assoc 38:43–56

Yu X, Abler D (2009) The demand for food quality in rural and urban China. Am J Agric Econ 91: 57–69

Chapter 6
Demand Systems I: Main Results

This chapter presents the theoretical foundations of demand systems and several specific models, highlighting links with microeconomics, interpretations, and their strengths and weaknesses. Index numbers as summary measures of prices and volumes, and their relation to consumer demand, are also briefly discussed. Details and further material are contained in the next chapter.

6.1 The Nature of a Demand System

To analyse the demand for a single commodity i in isolation of the consumption of all other commodities, one can use a demand function of the form

$$q_i = q_i(M, P, p_i) = f\left(\frac{M}{P}, \frac{p_i}{P}\right), \tag{6.1}$$

where q_i is the quantity consumed of commodity (or service) i, p_i is the price of i, M is consumer income, and P is a general price index.

For simplicity, if we assume a log-linear functional form among the three variables q_i, $\frac{p_i}{P}$, and $\frac{M}{P}$, then demand function (6.1) can be written as

$$\log(q_i) = \alpha + \beta \log\left(\frac{M}{P}\right) + \gamma \log\left(\frac{p_i}{P}\right).$$

This equation can be estimated using time-series data to obtain estimates of the parameters α, β, and γ. The income and own-price elasticities are

K. W. Clements et al., *Short-cut Demand Elasticities and Other Convenient Approaches to Consumer Demand*, https://doi.org/10.1007/978-981-96-3588-7_6

$$\eta_i = \frac{\partial(\log q_i)}{\partial\left(\log \frac{M}{P}\right)} = \beta, \qquad \eta_{ii}^* = \frac{\partial(\log q_i)}{\partial\left(\log \frac{p_i}{P}\right)} = \gamma.$$

The income variable in the above demand equation, $\frac{M}{P}$, is real income, money income (M) deflated by a general price index (P). When real income is held constant, if the relative price $\left(\frac{p_i}{P}\right)$ changes, then the response of consumption reflects the pure substitution effect. As the γ coefficient measures this response, it is known as the "income-compensated" price elasticity. Since demand curves slope downwards, $\eta_{ii}^* < 0$. The size of η_{ii}^* reflects the availability of substitutes. When there are many substitutes available for a good, it is price elastic (that is, $|\eta_{ii}^*| > 1$).

The income and price variables in Eq. (6.1) are expressed in real terms as they are deflated by a general price index. Therefore, if we change M, P, and p_i by a scalar multiple λ to λM, λP, and λp_i (also known as an equiproportionate change), then such change is expected to have no effect on consumption. That is, from (6.1),

$$q_i(\lambda M, \lambda P, \lambda p_i) = f\left(\frac{\lambda M}{\lambda P}, \frac{\lambda p_i}{\lambda P}\right) = f\left(\frac{M}{P}, \frac{p_i}{P}\right) = q_i(M, P, p_i).$$

This property is known as the absence of money illusion of the consumer or for short, demand homogeneity. In other words, demand functions are homogeneous of degree zero.

During the initial days of applied demand analysis, when computers were not in use, log-linear demand equations were commonly used due to their simplicity and ease of estimation. However, these demand equations suffer from several deficiencies. The first is that such demand equations are not built from consumer preferences (utility). Secondly, such demand equations consider only the demand for a commodity in isolation from all other goods as the cross-price elasticities are zero:

$$\eta_{ij}^* = \frac{d(\log q_i)}{d\left(\log \frac{p_j}{P}\right)} = 0, \qquad i \neq j.$$

As a solution, the above demand equation can be extended by including the prices of all n goods, and by including an equation for each good:

$$\log(q_i) = \alpha_i + \beta_i \log\left(\frac{M}{P}\right) + \sum_{j=1}^{n} \gamma_{ij} \log\left(\frac{p_j}{P}\right), \qquad i = 1, \ldots, n.$$

The income elasticity is still β_i, and the compensated own ($i = j$) and cross-price ($i \neq j$) elasticities are

$$\eta_{ii}^{*}=\frac{\partial(\log q_i)}{\partial\left(\log \frac{p_i}{P}\right)}=\gamma_{ii} \quad \text{and} \quad \eta_{ij}^{*}=\frac{\partial(\log q_i)}{\partial\left(\log \frac{p_j}{P}\right)}=\gamma_{ij}, \qquad i\neq j.$$

The above model consists of n equations which describe the demand for the n goods simultaneously. Accordingly, this is known as a "system-wide" demand model (Theil 1980). The above demand equations are a directly specified system without reference to any consumer utility function. Under the system-wide framework, we derive the demand equations based on utility maximisation, where the consumer chooses the consumption basket $(q_1, \cdots, q_n)$ to maximise utility subject to a budget constraint. Here, the demand for each of the n goods is treated as part of the simultaneous-maximisation problem. This approach is useful for testing demand theory hypotheses such as demand homogeneity and Slutsky symmetry which shall be discussed in the subsequent chapter.

Now we revisit the consumer's utility-maximisation problem discussed in Chap. 3 that led to a system of demand equations. Let the consumer purchase $q_1, \cdots, q_n$ quantities of n commodities at prices $p_1, \cdots, p_n$, and let M be income available to make these purchases. We propose the consumer has stable preferences which can be described by means of a utility function given by

$$u=u(q_1,\cdots,q_n).$$

The consumer maximises utility subject to the budget constraint:

$$\sum_{i=1}^{n} p_i q_i = M. \tag{6.2}$$

To solve this maximisation problem, we use the Lagrangian function:

$$u^*(q_1,\cdots,q_n,\lambda)=u(q_1,\cdots,q_n)+\lambda\left(M-\sum_{i=1}^{n} p_i q_i\right),$$

where λ is a Lagrange multiplier. The first-order conditions are the budget constraint (6.2) and

$$\frac{\partial u}{\partial q_i}=\lambda p_i, \; i=1,\ldots,n. \tag{6.3}$$

The demand equations are solutions to the $(n + 1)$ Eqs. (6.2) and (6.3). These take the form

$$q_i=q_i(M,p_1,\cdots,p_n), \qquad i=1,\ldots,n. \tag{6.4}$$

There are a number of constraints that system (6.4) should satisfy. The first constraint is that the demand equations must satisfy the budget constraint (6.2) for all values of income and prices. The second is demand homogeneity. If we apply Euler's theorem to (6.4) and using the fact the demand functions are homogeneous of degree zero, we get

$$M\frac{\partial q_i}{\partial M}+\sum_{j=1}^{n}p_j\frac{\partial q_i}{\partial p_j}=0, \qquad i=1,\ldots,n.$$

Dividing both sides by q_i and rearranging, we have

$$\left(\frac{\partial q_i/q_i}{\partial M/M}\right)+\sum_{j=1}^{n}\left(\frac{\partial q_i/q_i}{\partial p_j/p_j}\right)=0.$$

That is,

$$\frac{\partial(\log q_i)}{\partial(\log M)}+\sum_{j=1}^{n}\frac{\partial(\log q_i)}{\partial(\log p_j)}=0, \quad \text{or} \quad \eta_i+\sum_{j=1}^{n}\eta_{ij}=0, \qquad i=1,\ldots,n.$$

This is demand homogeneity in elasticity form.

The third constraint is Slutsky symmetry, which states that when real income is held constant, the effect of an increase in the price of commodity j on the demand for i is equal to the reciprocal effect of an increase in the price of commodity i on the demand for j. That is,

$$\frac{\partial q_i^*}{\partial p_j}=\frac{\partial q_j^*}{\partial p_i}, \qquad i,j=1,\ldots,n, \qquad \text{with } \frac{\partial q_i^*}{\partial p_j}=\left.\frac{\partial q_i}{\partial p_j}\right|_{du=0}.$$

As holding utility constant is equivalent to keeping real income unchanged, $\partial q_i^*/\partial p_j$ is known as the substitution effect. In elasticity form, symmetry can be written as

$$w_i\eta_{ij}^*=w_j\eta_{ji}^*,$$

where $\eta_{ij}^*=\frac{\partial\left(\log q_i^*\right)}{\partial\left(\log p_j\right)}=\eta_{ij}+w_j\eta_i$ is the compensated price elasticity of commodity i with respect to the price of j; $\eta_{ij}=\frac{\partial(\log q_i)}{\partial\left(\log p_j\right)}$ is the corresponding uncompensated elasticity, which includes the effect of real income changing as a result of the price change; and $w_i=p_iq_i/M$ is the budget share of i.

6.2 Engel Curves

An Engel curve expresses expenditure on a certain commodity as a function of income with prices remaining constant. A set of n Engel curves can be considered as a demand system without prices, or where prices are unchanged. In household survey data each household may face more or less the same set of prices; in such a situation, Engel curves can be used to understand the income responses of consumers. An important characteristic of the Engel curve for good i is its marginal share and the associated income elasticity:

$$\theta_i = \frac{\partial(p_i q_i)}{\partial M}, \qquad \eta_i = \frac{\theta_i}{w_i}. \tag{6.5}$$

The marginal share θ_i is the fraction of a one-dollar increase in income spent on the good; and as the increment to income is spent on something, $\sum_{i=1}^{n}\theta_i = 1$. The income elasticity η_i is a measure of luxuriousness or otherwise of the good, with the convention that $\eta_i < 1$ denotes a necessity and $\eta_i > 1$ a luxury.

An example of a simple Engel curve system is the linear case:

$$p_i q_i = \alpha_i + \beta_i M, \qquad i = 1, \ldots, n. \tag{6.6}$$

Here, the intercept α_i and slope coefficient β_i are parameters satisfying $\sum_{i=1}^{n}\alpha_i = 0$ and $\sum_{i=1}^{n}\beta_i = 1$, reflecting the budget constraint. The coefficient β_i is the marginal share and in the linear case a constant. This Engel system was mentioned before in Chap. 4.

Another functional form is the popular and widely applicable Working's (1943) model. This model, previously discussed in Chap. 3, expresses the budget shares as linear functions of the logarithm of income:

$$w_i = \alpha_i + \beta_i \log M, \qquad i = 1, \ldots, n. \tag{6.7}$$

As the budget shares sum to unity, it follows that the coefficients satisfy $\sum_{i=1}^{n}\alpha_i = 1$ and $\sum_{i=1}^{n}\beta_i = 0$. When $M = 1$, the above reduces to $w_i = \alpha_i$, so α_i, can be interpreted as the budget share of the consumer whose income equals 1, which amounts to a choice of units for income. As $dw_i = \beta_i d(\log M)$, the slope coefficient β_i can be interpreted as 100 times the change in w_i resulting from a 1-per cent increase in income.

Multiplying both sides of Working's model by M, and then differentiating with respect to M gives the marginal share:

$$\theta_i = w_i + \beta_i.$$

Dividing by w_i, we obtain the income elasticity of commodity i as

$$\eta_i = 1 + \frac{\beta_i}{w_i}.$$

This shows that a commodity is a necessity if β_i is negative ($\eta_i < 1$) and a luxury if β_i is positive ($\eta_i > 1$). As the budget share of a luxury increases with income, prices remaining constant, the above formula implies that increasing income causes the income elasticity of such a good to fall towards 1. The income elasticity of a necessity also declines with increasing income under Working's model. Thus, as the consumer becomes more affluent, all goods become less luxurious under Working's model, which is plausible.

A generalised version of Working's model was proposed by Laitinen et al. (1983) in the form

$$w_i = \alpha_i M^\lambda + \beta_i \frac{(M^\lambda - 1)}{\lambda}, \qquad i = 1, \ldots, n,$$

where $\sum_{i=1}^n \alpha_i = 1$ and $\sum_{i=1}^n \beta_i = -\lambda$. Using L'Hopital's rule, when $\lambda \to 0$ we have $(M^\lambda - 1)/\lambda \to \log M$. Therefore, when $\lambda \to 0$, the generalised model reduces to the original version (6.7), Working's model. The marginal share of good i is

$$\theta_i = (1 + \lambda) w_i + \beta_i.$$

Under Working's model, the marginal share is a linear function of the corresponding budget share w_i. Under the generalised version, a similar linear relationship exists between θ_i and w_i. The corresponding income elasticity is

$$\eta_i = (1 + \lambda) + \frac{\beta_i}{w_i}.$$

These expressions clearly reduce to those of Working's model when $\lambda \to 0$. van Hoa (1983) and van Hoa et al. (1983) contain more on the generalised model.

6.3 Linear Expenditure System

While in a cross-sectional context prices might be roughly constant, this is not the case for a time series. Prices need to be added to demand equations. For example, to allow for varying prices the obvious extension of the system of linear Engel curves (6.6) is

$$p_i q_i = \alpha_i + \beta_i M + \sum_{j=1}^{n} \rho_{ij} p_j, \qquad i = 1, \dots, n.$$

Stone's (1954) linear expenditure system (LES) is a particular version of the above. LES can be derived from the Stone-Geary utility function:

$$u(q_1, \dots, q_n) = \sum_{i=1}^{n} \beta_i \log(q_i - \gamma_i), \tag{6.8}$$

where $\sum_{i=1}^{n} \beta_i = 1$; $0 < \beta_i < 1$; and $q_i > \gamma_i > 0$, $i = 1, \cdots, n$. As it is additive in the individual goods, this utility function is of the preference-independence form discussed in Chap. 3.

Using the first-order conditions (6.3) and the budget constraint (6.2) gives the following demand equation for good i in expenditure form:

$$p_i q_i = p_i \gamma_i + \beta_i \left(M - \sum_{j=1}^{n} p_j \gamma_j \right). \tag{6.9}$$

Thus, expenditure on commodity i is a linear function of income and the n prices. LES has the following simple interpretation: The consumer initially buys γ_i units of commodity i at price p_i, spending $p_i \gamma_i$, known as "subsistence expenditure" on that commodity. This first stage process leads to total subsistence expenditure $\sum_{j=1}^{n} p_j \gamma_j$ and leaves a balance of $M - \sum_{j=1}^{n} p_j \gamma_j$, "supernumerary income". In the second stage, the consumer allocates a proportion β_i of supernumerary income, $\beta_i \left(M - \sum_{j=1}^{n} p_j \gamma_j \right)$, to commodity i.

The marginal share of i in (6.9) is $\beta_i > 0$, which means LES rules out inferior goods. The income elasticity of commodity i is

$$\eta_i = \frac{\beta_i}{w_i}.$$

The uncompensated price elasticities are

$$\eta_{ij} = \delta_{ij} \left(\frac{s_i}{w_i} - 1 \right) - s_j \eta_i.$$

Here, δ_{ij} is Kronecker's delta ($\delta_{ij} = 1$ for $i = j, 0$ otherwise) and $s_i = \frac{p_i \gamma_i}{M}$. Since $0 < \beta_i < 1$ and $q_i > \gamma_i$, the own-price elasticity lies in the range -1 to 0. In other words, the demand for each good is price inelastic. In addition, $\eta_{ij} < 0$, so all pairs of goods are gross complements.

Lluch (1973) introduced a sophisticated extension of LES involving savings, known as the extended linear expenditure system (ELES). He embeds the Stone-

Geary utility function (6.8) in an intertemporal utility maximisation problem, subject to an expected wealth constraint to yield

$$p_i q_i = p_i \gamma_i + \mu \beta_i \left(Y - \sum_{j=1}^{n} p_j \gamma_j \right), \qquad i = 1, \ldots, n. \tag{6.10}$$

As before, $\sum_{i=1}^{n} \beta_i = 1, 0 < \beta_i < 1$; and $q_i > \gamma_i > 0$, $i = 1, \ldots, n$. The new variable is Y, which is income defined as $Y = M +$ savings, with $M = \sum_{i=1}^{n} p_i q_i$, total expenditure on the n commodities, as before. Previously, when savings did not entry the picture, M was referred to as "income", but that was merely shorthand for "total expenditure"; with ELES, however, there is a distinction between income Y and total expenditure M.

Summing both sides of Eq. (6.10), we get the aggregate consumption function:

$$M = (1 - \mu) \sum_{j=1}^{n} p_j \gamma_j + \mu\, Y, \tag{6.11}$$

This is a Keynesian consumption function with the intercept a linear function of prices and the income-slope coefficient μ, the marginal propensity to consume. Thus, consumption is a weighted average of subsistence expenditure $\sum_{j=1}^{n} p_j \gamma_j$ and income, with weights the marginal propensity to save, $1 - \mu$, and the marginal propensity to consume, m.

From Eq. (6.11), $Y = \left\{ M - (1 - \mu) \sum_{j=1}^{n} p_j \gamma_j \right\} / \mu$, which when substituted back into (6.10) gives

$$p_i q_i = p_i \gamma_i + \beta_i \left(M - \sum_{j=1}^{n} p_j \gamma_j \right), \qquad i = 1, \ldots, n.$$

Since this is LES (6.9), ELES can be decomposed into the conventional LES and an aggregate consumption function. Hence, ELES extends LES by endogenously determining total expenditure. Hence, the expressions for LES expenditure and price elasticities are also applicable to ELES.

An alternative derivation of (6.10) was suggested by Betancourt (1973) and Howe (1975) by augmenting Stone-Geary utility (6.8) with savings (s) with no subsistence requirement: $u(q_1, \ldots, q_n, s) = \sum_{i=1}^{n} \beta_i \log(q_i - \gamma_i) + \beta_{n+1} \log s$. Maximising this function subject to $M + s = Y$ then yields ELES.

6.4 Quadratic Expenditure System

The Engel system (6.6) and LES (6.9) both have linear Engel curves. As Allen and Bowley (1935) pointed out, a linear Engel curve was "only a first approximation to a regular curve", and it has been found that linearity does not adequately represent expenditure patterns for all commodities. Nicholson (1949) estimated quadratic Engel curves, but did not investigate the form of the associated demand functions. This task was taken up by Howe (1974) and Pollak and Wales (1978) who introduced a further extension to LES in the form of the quadratic expenditure system (QES).

Stone-Geary utility (6.8) is an example of a direct utility function, written $u(\boldsymbol{q})$, where $\boldsymbol{q} = [q_1, \cdots, q_n]'$. Constrained utility maximisation leads to demand functions of the form (6.4), which can be written in vector form as $\boldsymbol{q} = \boldsymbol{q}(M, \boldsymbol{p})$, with $\boldsymbol{p}$ a vector of the n prices. As discussed in Chap. 3, substituting $\boldsymbol{q}(M, \boldsymbol{p})$ for $\boldsymbol{q}$ in $u(\boldsymbol{q})$ gives $u(\boldsymbol{q}(M, \boldsymbol{p})) = u_I(M, \boldsymbol{p})$, the indirect utility function whereby utility depends on income and prices. As the direct and indirect functions contain exactly the same information regarding preferences, the original demand functions can be recovered from $u_I(M, \boldsymbol{p})$. According to Roy's identity, $q_i = -\frac{\partial u_I/\partial p_i}{\partial u_I/\partial M}$. QES is based on the following indirect utility function:

$$u_I(M, \boldsymbol{p}) = -\frac{\prod_{k=1}^{n} p_k^{\beta_k}}{\left(M - \sum_{j=1}^{n} p_j \gamma_j\right)} + \mu \frac{\prod_{k=1}^{n} p_k^{\beta_k}}{\prod_{k=1}^{n} p_k^{c_k}}.$$

Roy's identity then yields the demand function for commodity i:

$$q_i = \left[\frac{\beta_i}{p_i}\left(M - \sum_{j=1}^{n} p_j \gamma_j\right) + \gamma_i\right] - \mu \frac{(\beta_i - c_i)\left(M - \sum_{j=1}^{n} p_j \gamma_j\right)^2}{p_i\left(\prod_{k=1}^{n} p_k^{c_k}\right)},$$

or by multiplying both sides by p_i, the demand equation in expenditure form:

$$p_i q_i = p_i \gamma_i + \beta_i \left(M - \sum_{j=1}^{n} p_j \gamma_j\right) + a_i \left(M - \sum_{j=1}^{n} p_j \gamma_j\right)^2, \tag{6.12}$$

where $a_i = \mu(c_i - \beta_i)\left(\prod_{k=1}^{n} p_k^{-c_k}\right)$ and the coefficients satisfy $\sum_{i=1}^{n} \beta_i = 1$, $\sum_{i=1}^{n} c_i = 1$ and $\sum_{i=1}^{n} a_i = 0$.

Equation (6.12) is QES for the ith commodity. Obviously, QES is an augmented version of LES with a quadratic income term added. The corresponding marginal share is

$$\theta_i = \frac{\partial(p_i q_i)}{\partial M} = \beta_i + \rho_i,$$

where $\rho_i = 2a_i\left(M - \sum_{j=1}^{n} p_j \gamma_j\right)$. The income and uncompensated price elasticities are

$$\eta_i = \frac{(\beta_i + \rho_i)}{w_i}, \qquad \eta_{ij} = \delta_{ij}\left(\frac{s_i}{w_i} - 1\right) - s_j \eta_i - \frac{\rho_i}{2w_i}\left(\frac{c_j}{M}\right),$$

where $w_i = p_i q_i / M$ is the budget share of commodity of i; δ_{ij} is Kronecker's delta; and $s_i = p_i \gamma_i / M$ is the fraction of income devoted to the subsistence consumption of i. When $c_i = \beta_i$,we have $a_i = \rho_i = 0$, and QES collapses to LES.

6.5 Rotterdam Model

LES and QES are based on algebraic specifications of the direct and indirect utility functions. Barten (1964) and Theil (1965) approached this from another angle, resulting in the Rotterdam demand model. Rather than using a particular utility function, it is based on a general form of preferences that allows for goods to interact fully but can be used to test for various restrictions such as preference independence. Chapter 3 introduced the preference-independent version of the Rotterdam model. The more general form of the model is:

$$w_i d(\log q_i) = \theta_i d(\log Q) + \sum_{j=1}^{n} \nu_{ij} d\left(\log \frac{p_j}{P'}\right), \qquad i = 1, \dots, n, \tag{6.13}$$

where θ_i is the marginal share of i; $d(\log Q) = \sum_{i=1}^{n} w_i d(\log q_i)$ is the Divisia (1926) quantity index; and $d\left(\log \frac{p_j}{P'}\right) = d(\log p_j) - d(\log P')$ is the change in the relative price of j with deflator $d(\log P') = \sum_{i=1}^{n} \theta_i d(\log p_i)$, the Frisch (1932) price index.

The price coefficients in (6.13) are

$$\nu_{ij} = \frac{\lambda}{M} p_i p_j u^{ij}, \qquad i, j = 1, \cdots, n.$$

Here, λ is the marginal utility of income (the Lagrange multiplier) and u^{ij} is the $(i,j)^{th}$ element of the inverse of the Hessian matrix of the utility function. There are n^2

values of u^{ij} which can be expressed as the $n \times n$ matrix $[u^{ij}] = \left[\frac{\partial^2 u}{\partial q_i \partial q_j}\right]^{-1}$. The $\nu_{ij}'s$ are subject to the constraints

$$\sum_{j=1}^{n} \nu_{ij} = \phi\theta_i, \qquad i = 1, \cdots, n, \tag{6.14}$$

where $\phi = \left(\frac{\partial \log \lambda}{\partial \log M}\right)^{-1} < 0$ is the income flexibility, the reciprocal of the income elasticity of the marginal utility of income, introduced in Chap. 3.

An equivalent formulation of (6.13) is in terms of absolute rather than relative prices:

$$w_i d(\log q_i) = \theta_i d(\log Q) + \sum_{j=1}^{n} \pi_{ij} d(\log p_j), \qquad i = 1, \ldots, n. \tag{6.15}$$

The new coefficients are the $\pi_{ij}'s$. These are known as Slutsky price coefficients, defined as $\pi_{ij} = \nu_{ij} - \phi\theta_i\theta_j$ and are subject to homogeneity and symmetry constraints:

$$\sum_{j=1}^{n} \pi_{ij} = 0, \qquad i = 1, \ldots, n; \qquad \pi_{ij} = \pi_{ji}, \qquad i, j = 1, \ldots, n.$$

Dividing both sides of (6.15) by w_i, the income and compensated price elasticities are:

$$\eta_i = \frac{\theta_i}{w_i}, \qquad i = 1, \ldots, n; \qquad \eta_{ij}^* = \frac{\pi_{ij}}{w_i}, \qquad i, j = 1, \ldots, n.$$

Since Eqs. (6.13) and (6.15) are formulated in infinitesimal changes, applications require some adjustments. The Rotterdam approach is as follows: For any variable $x_t > 0$, let $Dx_t = \log x_t - \log x_{t-1}$ be the log-change operator from period $t-1$ to t, and define $\overline{w}_{it} = \frac{1}{2}(w_{it} + w_{it-1})$ as the average of the budget share in $t-1$ and t. Then, the finite-change version of the relative price system (6.13) is

$$\overline{w}_{it} Dq_{it} = \theta_i DQ_t + \sum_{j=1}^{n} \nu_{ij}\left(Dp_{jt} - DP_t'\right), \qquad i = 1, \ldots, n,$$

where $DQ_t = \sum_{i=1}^{n} \overline{w}_{it} Dq_{it}$ and $DP_t' = \sum_{i=1}^{n} \theta_i Dp_{it}$ and where the coefficients θ_i and ν_{ij} are treated as constants. Under preference independence, $\nu_{ij} = 0$, $i \neq j$, and in view of constraint (6.14), $\nu_{ii} = \phi\theta_i$. This gives the simpler form which contains income and only the own price:

$$\overline{w}_{it}Dq_{it} = \theta_i DQ_t + \phi\theta_i\left(Dp_{it} - DP_t'\right), \qquad i = 1, \ldots, n.$$

Similar adjustments apply to the finite-change version of the absolute price system (6.15):

$$\overline{w}_{it}Dq_{it} = \theta_i DQ_t + \sum_{j=1}^{n} \pi_{ij} Dp_{jt}, \qquad i = 1, \ldots, n.$$

Should the relative or absolute price version be used? For testing the homogeneity and symmetry constraints, the absolute price version can be used. For further structuring the form of the utility function, such as preference independence, the relative price version is used. Imposing restrictions on preferences that limit the degree of interaction among goods reduces the number of unknown coefficients to be estimated, which can be especially valuable for systems involving a large number of goods. These issues are discussed further in the next chapter.

If prices are unchanged, the ith equation of the Rotterdam model is $w_i d(\log q_i) = \theta_i d(\log Q)$ or in finite changes, $\overline{w}_{it}Dq_{it} = \theta_i DQ_t$, which implies a linear Engel curve. This is a weakness of the model that is shared with LES (6.9). One way to deal with the problem is to use a polynomial, such as QES (6.12). Another approach is to continue to use differentials and reparametrise with the non-linear Engel curves of Working's model (6.7), $w_i = \alpha_i + \beta_i \log M$. As discussed above, Working's marginal share takes the form $\theta_i = w_i + \beta_i$, which varies with the budget share, in contrast to the Rotterdam parametrisation. Using this expression and replacing w_i with $\overline{w}_{it}$, the two reparametrised versions of Rotterdam are

$$\overline{w}_{it}\left(Dq_{it} - DQ_t\right) = \beta_i DQ_t + \sum_{j=1}^{n} \nu_{ij}\left(Dp_{jt} - DP_t'\right), \qquad i = 1, \ldots, n,$$

and

$$\overline{w}_{it}\left(Dq_{it} - DQ_t\right) = \beta_i DQ_t + \sum_{j=1}^{n} \pi_{ij} Dp_{jt}, \qquad i = 1, \ldots, n.$$

These have exactly the same right-hand side variables as the original Rotterdam systems, the changes in income and prices. The only difference is the quantity changes on the left are now deviated from their weighted means. The marginal share of i takes the form $\theta_i = \overline{w}_{it} + \beta_i$ and income elasticity $\eta_i = 1 + \frac{\beta_i}{\overline{w}_{it}}$. These reparametrisations are known as the CBS demand system (Keller and van Driel 1985).

6.6 Simpler Systems

In the absolute price version of Rotterdam (6.15), $w_i d(\log q_i) = \theta_i d(\log Q) + \sum_{j=1}^{n} \pi_{ij} d(\log p_j), i = 1, \ldots, n$, the number of Slutsky coefficients π_{ij} is of the order of n^2, which increases rapidly as the system contains more and more commodities. As mentioned, placing restrictions on preferences is a way to limit the number of coefficients.

Keller (1984) proposed a useful alternative approach to limit the growth in coefficients by introducing the new parameters λ (not the marginal utility of income, as it was previously) and ψ_i, $i = 1, \cdots, n$, with $\sum_{i=1}^{n} \psi_i = 1$, and redefining the $\pi_{ij}'s$ as

$$\pi_{ij} = \lambda(\psi_i \delta_{ij} - \psi_i \psi_j), \qquad i, j = 1, \cdots, n,$$

where δ_{ij} is Kronecker's delta. These coefficients, which satisfy the homogeneity and symmetry constraints, are used in the reparametrised Rotterdam system of the previous section, $\overline{w}_{it}(Dq_{it} - DQ_t) = \beta_i DQ_t + \sum_{j=1}^{n} \pi_{ij} Dp_{jt}, i = 1, \cdots, n$. The price substitution part of that model consequently becomes

$$\sum_{j=1}^{n} \pi_{ij} Dp_{jt} = \lambda \psi_i (Dp_{it} - DP_{\psi t}), \qquad \text{with } DP_{\psi t} = \sum_{i=1}^{n} \psi_i Dp_{it}.$$

Thus, the new system is

$$\overline{w}_{it}(Dq_{it} - DQ_t) = \beta_i DQ_t + \lambda \psi_i (Dp_{it} - DP_{\psi t}), \qquad i = 1, \cdots, n. \tag{6.16}$$

Keller (1984) refers to this as the CBS substitution independence model. There are only $2n - 1$ free parameters here, viz., $(n-1)\ \beta_i's + (n-1)\ \psi_i's +$ one λ.

There are two interesting special cases of system (6.16):

1. When ψ_i is set equal to $\overline{w}_{it} + \beta_i$ and $\lambda = \phi$, the income flexibility, system (6.16) then takes the form

$$\overline{w}_{it}(Dq_{it} - DQ_t) = \beta_i DQ_t + \phi(\overline{w}_{it} + \beta_i)(Dp_{it} - DP_t'), \qquad i = 1, \cdots, n.$$

   The price deflator here is the Frisch index $DP_t' = \sum_{i=1}^{n} (\overline{w}_{it} + \beta_i) Dp_{it}$, as before. This is the preference-independent version of the reparametrised Rotterdam model in relative prices.

2. When $\psi_i = \overline{w}_{it}$ the Frisch index becomes Divisia $DP_t = \sum_{i=1}^{n} \overline{w}_{it} Dp_{it}$, and (6.16) becomes

$$\overline{w}_{it}(Dq_{it} - DQ_t) = \beta_i DQ_t + \lambda\, \overline{w}_{it}(Dp_{it} - DP_t), \qquad i = 1, \cdots, n.$$

This model was proposed by Selvanathan (1985) and is referred to as an even simpler demand system. This system contains only n parameters, $(n-1)\ \beta_i' s +$ one λ.

These simpler demand systems have only two explanatory variables, namely, income and the own relative price. They have at least three advantages: First, the systems are straightforward to interpret. Second, there is an economy of parametrisation such that the models can be used even when n is large. Third, they can be estimated using OLS (either iterated or non-iterated). It seems likely these systems have a substantial degree of robustness, including being insensitive to data problems such as measurement error.

6.7 Almost Ideal Demand System

Three ways of characterising consumer preferences have been discussed above: The algebraic specification of the direct utility function $u(\boldsymbol{q})$; the indirect utility function $u_I(M,\boldsymbol{p})$; and the Rotterdam approach based on a general utility function consistent with a variety of forms. A fourth way to proceed is with the cost function which, roughly speaking, can be described as solving indirect utility to express income in terms of utility and prices. Income is then the minimum cost of obtaining the optimal consumption basket at the prevailing prices. The cost function, written as $C(u,\boldsymbol{p})$, contains the same information on preferences as $u(\boldsymbol{q})$ and $u_I(M,\boldsymbol{p})$. The budget share is given by logarithmic differentiation of the cost function with respect to the price: $w_i = \frac{\partial(\log C)}{\partial(\log p_i)}$, a result known as Shephard's lemma.

The almost ideal demand system (AIDS) of Deaton and Muellbauer (1980) starts with a cost function of the form

$$\log\{C(u,\boldsymbol{p})\} = (1-u)\log\{a(\boldsymbol{p})\} + u\log\{b(\boldsymbol{p})\},$$

where

$$\log\{a(\boldsymbol{p})\} = \alpha_0 + \sum_{k=1}^{n} \alpha_k \log\, p_k + \frac{1}{2}\sum_{k=1}^{n}\sum_{j=1}^{n} \gamma_{kj}^{*} \log p_k \log p_j,$$

$$\log\{b(\boldsymbol{p})\} = \log\{a(\boldsymbol{p})\} + \beta_0 \prod_{k=1}^{n} p_k^{\beta_k}.$$

These are price indexes with the $\alpha_k' s, \beta_k' s$, and $\gamma_{kj}^{*\prime} s$ all constants. Application of Shephard's lemma gives for good i:

$$w_i = \alpha_i + \beta_i \log\left(\frac{M}{P^*}\right) + \sum_{j=1}^{n} \gamma_{ij} \log p_j, \tag{6.17}$$

where

$$\log\left(\frac{M}{P^*}\right) = \log M - \log P^*, \quad \log P^* = \log\{a(\boldsymbol{p})\} \quad \text{and} \quad \gamma_{kj} = \frac{1}{2}\left(\gamma_{kj}^* + \gamma_{jk}^*\right).$$

Equation (6.17) is AIDS for good i.

A common practice is to replace the non-linear price index P^* in (6.17) with Stone's linear index $\log P = \sum_{k=1}^{n} \mathrm{w}_k \log \mathrm{p}_k$. The model then becomes the linear almost ideal demand system (LI-AIDS). The income and uncompensated price elasticities are

$$\eta_i = 1 + \frac{\beta_i}{w_i}, \quad i = 1, \ldots, \quad n;$$

$$\eta_{ij} = -\delta_{ij} + \left(\frac{1}{w_i}\right)\left[\gamma_{ij} - \beta_i\left(w_j - \beta_j \log\left(\frac{M}{P}\right)\right)\right], \quad i, j = 1, \ldots, n.$$

There are two links between AIDS and the material presented in earlier sections of the chapter. First, the income elasticity $\eta_i = 1 + \frac{\beta_i}{w_i}$ has the same form as that from Working's model; equivalently, the income part of (6.17) is just Working's model (6.7).

A second link is with the Rotterdam demand model. To show this, take the differential of the budget share, $w_i = p_i q_i / M$, and the budget constraint, $M = \sum_{i=1}^{n} p_i q_i$:

$$dw_i = w_i d(\log p_i) + w_i \mathrm{d}(\log q_i) - w_i d(\log M), \quad d(\log M) = d(\log P) + d(\log Q).$$

Here, $d(\log P) = \sum_{i=1}^{n} w_i d(\log p_i)$ is the Divisia price index and $d(\log Q) = \sum_{i=1}^{n} w_i d(\log q_i)$, as before. Substituting for $w_i \mathrm{d}(\log q_i)$ from Eq. (6.15), using $\mathrm{d}(\log M) = d(\log P) + d(\log Q)$ and then collecting terms, gives

$$\mathrm{d}w_i = (\theta_i - w_i) d(\log Q) + \sum_{j=1}^{n} \left(\pi_{ij} + w_i \delta_{ij} - w_i w_j\right) d\left(\log p_j\right),$$

where δ_{ij} is Kronecker's delta, as before. Now, the 'coefficient' of the price change of j, $\pi_{ij} + w_i \delta_{ij} - w_i w_j$, is the same as γ_{ij} in eq (6.17). Also, using Working's marginal share, $\theta_i = w_i + \beta_i$, $\gamma_{ij} = \pi_{ij} + w_i \delta_{ij} - w_i w_j$, the above equation becomes

$$\mathrm{d}w_i = \beta_i d(\log Q) + \sum_{j=1}^{n} \gamma_{ij} d\left(\log p_j\right).$$

For $i = 1, \cdots, n$, this is the differential version of LI-AIDS.

6.8 Quadratic Almost Ideal System

In AIDS, the budget share is a linear function of log M, so the share always either increases or decreases with income. As income rises, a good cannot switch from being a luxury (whose share rises with income) to a necessity (decreasing share) or vice versa. Furthermore, the ranking of goods according to income elasticities is invariant to income changes (Clements 1987). The quadratic AIDS (QAIDS), introduced by Banks et al. (1997), allows for more flexibility.

QAIDS is based on the following indirect utility function

$$u_I(M, \boldsymbol{p}) = \left[\left(\frac{\log M - \log a(\boldsymbol{p})}{b(\boldsymbol{p})}\right)^{-1} + \lambda(\boldsymbol{p})\right]^{-1},$$

where $a(\boldsymbol{p})$ and $b(\boldsymbol{p})$ are the same price indices of AIDS, while $\lambda(\boldsymbol{p}) = \sum_{i=1}^{n} \lambda_i \log \mathrm{p}_i$ is a new index with $\sum_{i=1}^{n} \lambda_i = 0$. The term $\left(\frac{\log M - \log a(\boldsymbol{p})}{b(\boldsymbol{p})}\right)$ is the indirect utility function corresponding to the above cost function of AIDS. Application of Roy's identity gives QAIDS:

$$w_i = \alpha_i + \beta_i \left[\log\left(\frac{M}{a(\boldsymbol{p})}\right)\right] + \mu_i \left[\log\left(\frac{M}{a(\boldsymbol{p})}\right)\right]^2 + \sum_{j=1}^{n} \gamma_{ij} \log p_j, \qquad i = 1, \ldots, n,$$

where $\mu_i = \lambda_i / b(\boldsymbol{p})$. The implied income and uncompensated price elasticities are

$$\eta_i = 1 + \frac{\beta_i}{w_i} + \frac{2\mu_i}{w_i}\left[\log\left(\frac{M}{a(\boldsymbol{p})}\right)\right], \qquad i = 1 \ldots, n,$$

and

$$\eta_{ij} = -\delta_{ij} + \left(\frac{1}{w_i}\right)\left[\gamma_{ij} - \beta_i\left(w_j - \beta_j \log\left(\frac{M}{P}\right)\right)\right] + \frac{\mu_i \beta_j}{w_i}\left[\log\left(\frac{M}{a(\boldsymbol{p})}\right)\right]^2, \qquad i,j = 1, \cdots, n.$$

6.9 Other Systems

Following the introduction of AIDS, two major issues have been identified in the estimation of demand systems. One is that several studies using large consumer expenditure data sets have found Engel curves with significant curvature and variation across goods, such as linear, quadratic, or S-shaped (for example, Blundell et al. 2007). The second issue is that the error terms in models cannot be interpreted as random utility parameters representing unobserved heterogeneity (for example, Lewbel 2001; Beckert and Blundell 2004). Even though these issues exist with AIDS, that model remains popular as proposed alternatives are non-linear and can be difficult to estimate.

Lewbel and Pendakur (2009) developed the exact affine Stone index (EASI) implicit Marshallian demand system to address the two issues. Like AIDS, EASI expresses budget shares as linear in parameters. In contrast to AIDS, EASI allows for flexible interactions between prices and expenditures, permits almost any functional form for Engel curves, and allows error terms in the model to correspond to unobserved preference heterogeneity random utility parameters. EASI is derived from a cost function and takes the form

$$w_i = \sum_{r=0}^{5} b_{ri} y^r + \sum_{l=1}^{L} (C_{li} z_l + D_{li} z_l y) + \sum_{l=0}^{L} \sum_{k=1}^{J} A_{lki} z_l p_k + \sum_{k=1}^{J} B_{ki} p_k y + \varepsilon_i, \quad i = 1, \ldots, n,$$

where y^r is the rth-order polynomial ($r = 0, \ldots, 5$) in real total expenditure; p_k is now the log-price of commodity k ($=1, \ldots, J$); z_l is the lth demographic characteristic ($l = 1, \ldots, L$); and ε_i is an error term. The terms $z_l y$, $z_l p_k$, and $p_k y$ are interactions between the variables; and b_{ri}, C_{li}, D_{li}, A_{lki}, and B_{ki} are parameters to be estimated.

According to EASI, the compensated price effects on the budget shares are governed by the parameters A_{lki}, B_{ki}, C_{li}, D_{li}. The income coefficients b_{ri}, $r = 0, \ldots, 5$, specify the budget shares as fifth-order polynomials that allow the Engle curves to have complicated shapes. The general form of EASI can be estimated using generalised method of moments (GMM) or three stage least squares. However, a simplification is to express real total expenditure y in terms of the nominal expenditure, M, deflated by the Stone index, $\sum_{k=1}^{J} w_k p_k$. EASI can then be estimated as a linear system, as is the case with LI-AIDS.

Another popular system is the translog, introduced by Christensen et al. (1975). This is based on the indirect utility function of the form

$$u_I(M, \boldsymbol{p}) = \sum_{i=1}^{n} \beta_i \log\left(\frac{p_i}{M}\right) + \frac{1}{2} \sum_{i=1}^{n} \sum_{j=1}^{n} \beta_{ij} \log\left(\frac{p_i}{M}\right) \log\left(\frac{p_j}{M}\right),$$

where the $\beta_i's$ and the $\beta_{ij}'s$ are constants. Application of Roy's identity gives the demand system in share form:

$$w_i = \frac{\left[\beta_i + \sum_{j=1}^{n} \beta_{ij} \log\left(\frac{p_j}{M}\right)\right]}{\left[\sum_{k=1}^{n} \beta_k + \sum_{k=1}^{n} \sum_{j=1}^{n} \beta_{kj} \log\left(\frac{p_j}{M}\right)\right]}, \qquad i = 1, \ldots, n.$$

The final system to be discussed is the one derived from the constant-elasticity-of-substitution (CES) utility function, previously introduced in Chap. 3. The CES is

$$u(\boldsymbol{q}) = \left(\sum_{i=1}^{n} \alpha_i q_i^{-\rho}\right)^{-\frac{1}{\rho}},$$

where $\alpha_i > 0, \sum_{i=1}^{n} \alpha_i = 1,\ \rho \geq -1$ and $\rho \neq 0$. The elasticity of substitution is $\sigma = \frac{1}{1+\rho} > 0$. The corresponding demand for good i and its budget share are

$$q_i = \alpha_i^{\sigma} \frac{M}{P^*} \left(\frac{p_i}{P^*}\right)^{-\sigma}, \qquad w_i = \alpha_i^{\sigma} \left(\frac{p_i}{P^*}\right)^{1-\sigma}, \tag{6.18}$$

where P^* is a price index defined as $P^* = \left(\sum_{j=1}^{n} \alpha_j^{\sigma} p_j^{1-\sigma}\right)^{\frac{1}{1-\sigma}}$. The income elasticity of i is unity and the own-price elasticity $\frac{\partial(\log q_i)}{\partial(\log p_i)}$ is $-\{\sigma + (1 - \sigma)w_i\}$.

In differential form, the first member of (6.18) is

$$d(\log q_i) = d(\log M) + \sum_{j=1}^{n} \eta_{ij} d(\log p_j),$$

where $\eta_{ij} = -\{\sigma\delta_{ij} + (1 - \sigma)w_i\}$ is the $(i,j)^{th}$ uncompensated price elasticity. In the Cobb-Douglas case, $\sigma = 1$ and (6.18) becomes

$$q_i = \alpha_i \frac{M}{p_i}, \qquad w_i = \alpha_i,$$

with $\eta_{ii} = -1$, $i = 1, \ldots, n$, and $\eta_{ij} = 0$, $i, j = 1, \ldots, n$, $i \neq j$.

6.10 Strengths and Weaknesses

No single demand system dominates all others, with each having its own strengths and weaknesses. LES was popular in early days of demand analysis as at that time it was the only system that adequately described the consumption of the n goods simultaneously in a manner consistent with basic economic principles. The popularity of LES was also due to several other attractive features. Firstly, it is linear in variables income and the prices. Secondly, it has a clear interpretation that the total expenditure is first allocated to meet subsistence requirements and then to supernumerary consumption. Thirdly, LES satisfies the basic properties of microeconomic theory, viz., budget constraint, homogeneity of degree zero and symmetry of the substitution effects, as well as being consistent with Engel's law (the income elasticity of food demand is less than unity). Fourthly, the number of free parameters to be estimated is modest at $2n - 1$.

There are number of the major drawbacks with LES as well. First, it is based on an additive utility function, or preference independence, which is probably suited more to broad aggregates such as food, clothing, housing, etc., rather than finely distinguished goods. Second, inferior goods are ruled out. Third, own-price elasticities are usually constrained to lie between -1 and 0, making goods price inelastic, and all pairs of goods gross complements. Fourth, LES has linear Engel curves which is a restrictive property when the range of income is substantial.

As with LES, AIDS also has its own strengths and weaknesses. It can be considered as an arbitrary second-order approximation to any demand system, that is, it is a flexible functional form. It has non-linear Engel curves and when the price index P^* is replaced with the Stone index, the system is easy to estimate. Further, homogeneity and symmetry can be tested as linear constraints on parameters of AIDS. A major issue with the estimation of linearised AIDS is that it has a potential simultaneity bias problem, because the budget share appears on both sides of each equation. AIDS in its full-blown form [Eq. (6.17)] and the translog are both non-linear in the parameters which can mean special challenges for estimation.

Since the Rotterdam model also has linear Engel curves, it is subject the same limitations as LES in this regard. The Rotterdam permits testing homogeneity and symmetry in a simple way, like AIDS, but has the additional advantage that hypotheses about the nature of preferences (such as preference independence) can also be tested. The Rotterdam is not derived from a specific form of the utility function, direct or indirect, or a specific cost function, making it consistent with variety of forms of preferences. Demand equations derived from a specific form might seriously mislead if the assumed form of preferences is wrong. As a consequence, the Rotterdam is arguably more robust in applications than models based on specific preferences.

The Rotterdam has been strongly criticised on theoretical grounds because its parameters can only be strictly constant when all income elasticities are unity, own-price elasticities equal minus one, and cross-price elasticities zero. Taken at face value, these restrictions cast grave doubts on the usefulness of the model, verging on condemning it to be near useless. As discussed in detail the next chapter, there have been substantial responses to this criticism that place the Rotterdam in a more favourable light. These criticisms may not be too serious in practice as long as the Rotterdam parameters are close to being constant.

The elasticity of substitution, σ in the CES system (6.18) can take any positive value and thus capture a wide degree of substitution between goods. However, as the system implies unity income elasticities, its use tends to be limited to the demand for different varieties of the same good—varieties that are close substitutes. Chapters 10 and 11 discuss the use of CES in the demand for foreign and domestic varieties.

6.11 Index Numbers

Index numbers are a convenient way of summarising the movements of prices and quantities. They also play a major role in demand systems: Deflating nominal income by a broad price index yields the real income variable used in demand equations, and a price index acts as deflator for relative prices. This section gives a brief introduction to index numbers.

As before, the differential of the budget constraint, $M=\sum_{i=1}^{n} p_i q_i$, is

$$d(\log M)=\sum_{i=1}^{n} w_i d(\log p_i)+\sum_{i=1}^{n} w_i d(\log q_i)=d(\log P)+d(\log Q).$$

Here, $w_i = p_i q_i / M$ is the budget share of good i and

$$d(\log P)=\sum_{i=1}^{n} w_i d(\log p_i), \qquad d(\log Q)=\sum_{i=1}^{n} w_i d(\log q_i). \tag{6.19}$$

These are Divisia price and quantity indexes. This establishes the change in income can be cleanly split into distinct price and volume components. The index $d(\log P)$ is a weighted average of the n price changes, the weights being the budget shares reflecting the relative economic importance of each good as measured by the expenditure pattern. The quantity index $d(\log Q)$ has an analogous interpretation. Note that since $d(\log M)-d(\log P)=\sum_{i=1}^{n} w_i d(\log q_i)=d(\log Q)$, nominal income deflated by the price index is equal to the quantity index. This means that the quantity index $d(\log Q)$ can also be identified as an index of the change in real income.

The indexes in (6.19) can also be considered as weighted first-order moments of the distributions of price and quantity changes. The corresponding second-order moments are the Divisia price and quantity variances:

$$\Pi=\sum_{i=1}^{n} w_i[d(\log p_i)-d(\log P)]^2, \qquad \mathrm{K}=\sum_{i=1}^{n} w_i[d(\log q_i)-d(\log Q)]^2.$$

These measure the degree to which the prices and quantities of the individual commodities move disproportionately. When all prices change proportionately, $\Pi = 0$ and is positive otherwise; and similarly for the quantity variance K. Studies such as Selvanathan et al. (2022) and Rathnayaka et al. (2024) have found that the quantity variance systematically exceeds the price variance, a result that can be interpreted as reflecting the price stickiness of consumer goods. There is also the Divisia price-quantity covariance and correlation:

$$\Gamma = \sum_{i=1}^{n} w_i[d(\log p_i) - d(\log P)][d(\log q_i) - d(\log Q)], \qquad \rho = \frac{\Gamma}{\sqrt{\Pi \cdot \mathrm{K}}}.$$

These measure the co-movement of prices and quantities and are expected to be negative to reflect the tendency of the consumer to move away from those commodities having above-average price increases. These moments are related according to

$$\sum_{i=1}^{n} w_i \left[d(\log w_i) - \sum_{j=1}^{n} w_j d(\log w_j) \right]^2 = \Pi + \mathrm{K} + 2\Gamma.$$

The left-hand side is the Divisia variance of the changes in the budget shares.

As shown by Selvanathan et al. (2024), combining Divisia indexes with the CES leads to a new way to estimate elasticity of substitution σ. In the demand equation associated with CES utility, (6.18), $q_i = \alpha_i^\sigma \frac{M}{P^*} \left(\frac{p_i}{P^*}\right)^{-\sigma}$, the price index is $P^* = \left(\sum_{j=1}^{n} \alpha_j^\sigma p_j^{1-\sigma}\right)^{\frac{1}{1-\sigma}}$. Using the second member of (6.18), the change in this index is

$$d(\log P^*) = \frac{1}{1-\sigma} d\left[\log\left(\sum_{i=1}^{n} \alpha_i^\sigma p_i^{1-\sigma}\right)\right] = \sum_{i=1}^{n} \frac{\alpha_i^\sigma p_i^{1-\sigma}}{\sum_{j=1}^{n} \alpha_j^\sigma p_j^{1-\sigma}} d(\log p_i)$$

$$= \sum_{i=1}^{n} w_i d(\log p_i).$$

Thus, in differential form, P^* coincides with the Divisia price index of (6.19).

In logarithmic-changes, the demand equation in (6.18) is

$$d(\log q_i) = [d(\log M) - d(\log P^*)] - \sigma[d(\log p_i) - d(\log P^*)].$$

Using $d(\log P^*) = d(\log P)$ and $(\log M) - d(\log P) = d(\log Q)$, the above becomes

$$d(\log q_i) - d(\log Q) = -\sigma[d(\log p_i) - d(\log P)].$$

Multiplying both sides by $d(\log p_i) - d(\log P)$ and then taking a budget-share weighted average, we obtain a relationship between price-quantity covariance and price variance, $\Gamma = -\sigma\Pi$, so that

$$\sigma = -\frac{\Gamma}{\Pi} = -\rho\sqrt{\frac{\mathrm{K}}{\mathrm{P}}}.$$

In words, the elasticity of substitution σ is the product of the (i) negative of the price-quantity correlation $(-\rho)$; and (ii) the ratio of the standard deviation of quantities to that of prices $\left(\sqrt{\mathrm{K}}/\sqrt{\Pi}\right)$. As mentioned, quantities are usually more volatile than prices, which means $\left(\sqrt{\mathrm{K}}/\sqrt{\Pi}\right) > 1$. Thus, $\sigma < 1$ (>1) when $-\rho < \sqrt{\Pi/\mathrm{K}}$ $\left(> \sqrt{\Pi/\mathrm{K}}\right)$.

Many countries measure inflation by the consumer price index (CPI) which refers to the cost of a fixed basket of goods and services in one period compared to that in some base period. The two major assumptions with this approach are (1) consumers do not substitute between commodities as the same basket is used in both periods and (2) the focus is only on the "price changes", ignoring consumers' utility. Since the weights of the CPI are typically based on the base-period basket in the form as a Laspeyres index, there is a possibility of an in-built inflationary bias. An alternative is the cost-of-living index, based on the economic approach of constrained utility maximisation. Formally, the cost-of-living index measures the change in the cost of purchasing a basket of goods and services in two different periods, while achieving the same level of utility. Thus, consumers are allowed to substitute between commodities in response to relative price changes. The parameters of demand systems are used as inputs into the cost-of-living index.

An example of a cost-of-living index is that associated with the CES utility. This involves the unit cost function that compares prices at time t, $p_{1t}, \cdots, p_{nt}$, with those at some base period 0 using base-period budget shares as weights, $w_{10}, \cdots, w_{n0}$, where $w_{i0} = p_{i0}q_{i0}/\sum_{j=1}^{n} p_{j0}q_{j0}$, $i = 1, \cdots, n$. The CES unit cost function is a cost-of-living index and takes the form

$$\left[\sum_{i=1}^{n} w_{i0}\left(\frac{p_{it}}{p_{i0}}\right)^{1-\sigma}\right]^{\frac{1}{1-\sigma}}.$$

This is known as the Lloyd (1975), Moulton (1996) (LM) index. When $\sigma = 0$, the index takes the form $\sum_{i=1}^{n} w_{i0}\left(\frac{p_{i1}}{p_{i0}}\right)$, which is the Laspeyres index, while when $\sigma \to 1$, it becomes Cobb-Douglas, $\sum_{i=1}^{n} w_{i0} \log\left(\frac{p_{i1}}{p_{i0}}\right)$. In practice, prices usually become available earlier than expenditures or equivalently, the budget shares are observed only with a lag. Consequently, the LM index is attractive as it involves information usually available at time t (or soon thereafter), the base-period shares and price ratios p_{it}/p_{i0}. For more on this index, see Ivancic et al. (2009).

As established above, the Divisia index $d(\log P)$ is also consistent with the CES. But $d(\log P)$ differs from the LM index in two essential characteristics. First, it involves the unknown parameter, the elasticity of substitution σ, whereas as Divisia involves observables only, the n budget shares and prices. A second difference is that the LM index is formulated in levels, not changes, whereby constants drop out (including the influence of arbitrary base-periods).

References

Allen RGD, Bowley AL (1935) Family expenditure: a study of its variation. P. S. King, London

Banks J, Blundell R, Lewbel A (1997) Quadratic Engel curves and consumer demand. Rev Econ Stat 79:527–539

Barten AP (1964) Consumer demand functions under conditions of almost additive preferences. Econometrica 32:1–38

Beckert W, Blundell RW (2004) Invertibility of nonparametric stochastic demand functions. Birkbeck Working Papers in Economics and Finance 0406, Department of Economics, Mathematics & Statistics, Birkbeck

Betancourt RR (1973) The analysis of patterns of consumption in underdeveloped countries. Paper presented to the ECIEL conference on consumption, prices, and economic development, Hamburg, Germany

Blundell RW, Chen X, Kristensen D (2007) Semi-nonparametric IV estimation of shape-invariant Engle curves. Econometrica 75:1613–1669

Christensen LR, Jorgenson DW, Lau LJ (1975) Transcendental logarithmic utility functions. Am Econ Rev 65:367–383

Clements KW (1987) Alternative approaches to consumption theory." Chapter 1. In: Theil H, Clements KW (eds) Applied demand analysis: results from system-wide approaches. Ballinger, Cambridge, MA, pp 1–36

Deaton AS, Muellbauer J (1980) An almost ideal demand system. Am Econ Rev 70:312–326

Divisia F (1926) L'indice Monétaire et la Théorie de la Monnaie. Revue d'Économie Politique 40: 49–81. The Monetary Index and the Theory of Money

Frisch R (1932) New methods of measuring marginal utility. J. C. B. Mohr, Tubingen

Howe H (1974) Estimation of the quadratic expenditure system: a cross-section case. Am Econ 18: 13–38

Howe H (1975) Development of the extended linear expenditure system from simple saving assumptions. Eur Econ Rev 6:305–310

Ivancic L, Diewert E, Fox KJ (2009) Using a constant elasticity of substitution index to estimate a cost-of-living index: from theory to practice. Discussion Papers 2010-15, School of Economics, The University of New South Wales

Keller WJ (1984) Some simple but flexible differential consumer demand systems. Econ Lett 16: 77–82

Keller WJ, van Driel J (1985) Differential consumer demand systems. Eur Econ Rev 27:375–390

Laitinen K, Theil H, Raparla T (1983) A generalization of working's model. Econ Lett 13:97–100

Lewbel A (2001) Demand systems with and without errors. Am Econ Rev 91:611–618

Lewbel A, Pendakur K (2009) Tricks with Hicks: the EASI demand system. Am Econ Rev 99:827–863

Lloyd PJ (1975) Substitution effects and biases in nontrue price indices. Am Econ Rev 65:301–313

Lluch C (1973) The extended linear expenditure system. Eur Econ Rev 4:21–32

Moulton BR (1996) Constant elasticity cost-of-living index in share relative form. Bureau of Labour Statistics, Washington, DC

Nicholson JL (1949) Variations in working class family expenditure. J R Stat Soc Ser A (General) 112:359–418

Pollak RA, Wales TJ (1978) Estimation of complete demand systems from household budget data: the linear and quadratic expenditure systems. Am Econ Rev 68:348–359

Rathnayaka SD, Selvanathan S, Selvanathan EA (2024) Economic development and consumption patterns in Asian countries. Springer, Singapore

Selvanathan EA (1985) An even simpler differential demand system. Econ Lett 19:343–347

Selvanathan EA, Clements KW, Selvanathan S (2024) Estimating the elasticity of substitution: an index-number approach. J Int Trade Econ Dev. https://doi.org/10.1080/09638199.2024.2382290

Selvanathan EA, Selvanathan S, Jayasinghe M (2022) Household demand for consumer goods in developing countries: a comparative perspective with developed countries. Routledge, London

Stone R (1954) Linear expenditure systems and demand analysis: an application to the pattern of British demand. Econ J 64:511–527

Theil H (1965) The information approach to demand analysis. Econometrica 33:67–87

Theil H (1980) The system-wide approach to microeconomics. The University of Chicago Press, Chicago

van Hoa T (1983) The integrability of generalised working models. Econ Lett 13:101–104

van Hoa T, Ironmonger DS, Manning I (1983) Energy consumption in Australia: evidence from a generalised working model. Econ Lett 12:383–389

Working H (1943) Statistical law of family expenditure. J Am Stat Assoc 38:43–56

Chapter 7
Demand Systems II: Further Results and Details

7.1 Introduction

As estimating a large system of unrestricted demand equations involves an impossibly large number of coefficients, imposing a priori restrictions is a key way of reducing the number of estimated coefficients. This chapter deals with the testing of the restrictions implied by demand homogeneity, symmetry, and preference independence. One problem is that when the test procedures are based on the asymptotic distribution of the test statistic without correction for small-sample bias, the results are more biased towards rejecting the null hypothesis. We discuss this and related econometric issues that come with estimating demand systems.

Although the theory of the utility-maximising consumer refers to the individual, it is frequently applied in aggregate to all consumers at the national level. The chapter details that under reasonable circumstances, this practice can be justified. This chapter also discusses the similarity of consumption patterns across countries and sources of values of the income elasticity of the marginal utility of income—an important parameter of a demand system that reflects overall price substitutability.

7.2 Matrix Formulation

For T periods, the absolute price version of the Rotterdam model from Chap. 6 with an error term ε_{it} added is

$$\overline{w}_{it} Dq_{it} = \theta_i DQ_t + \sum_{j=1}^{n} \pi_{ij} Dp_{jt} + \varepsilon_{it}, \qquad i = 1, \ldots, n; t = 1, \ldots, T, \tag{7.1}$$

where θ_i is the ith marginal share satisfying $\sum_{i=1}^{n} \theta_i = 1$; π_{ij} is the $(i,j)^{th}$ Slutsky coefficient satisfying $\sum_{j=1}^{n} \pi_{ij} = 0$; and all other notations are as defined in Chap. 6.

K. W. Clements et al., *Short-cut Demand Elasticities and Other Convenient Approaches to Consumer Demand*, https://doi.org/10.1007/978-981-96-3588-7_7

The error terms are assumed to be normally distributed, independent over time, and have zero means.

Summing both sides of (7.1) over $i = 1, \ldots, n$ gives $\sum_{i=1}^{n} \varepsilon_{it} = 0$ for $t = 1, \ldots, T$. As the ε_{it}'s are linearly dependent and one of the equations is redundant, it can be deleted (Barten 1969). The best linear unbiased estimators of the parameters are the same as those obtained by estimating each equation separately by least squares (LS). Let $\boldsymbol{\Sigma}$ be the $(n - 1) \times (n - 1)$ contemporaneous covariance matrix of the disturbance term ε_{it} of (7.1) for $i = 1, \ldots, n - 1$. In general, $\boldsymbol{\Sigma}$ is unknown. For estimation and hypothesis testing, it is common practice to approximate this matrix by its unbiased estimator $\boldsymbol{S}$, the matrix of mean squares and cross products of the LS residuals.

Denoting $y_{it} = \overline{w}_{it} Dq_{it}$, $\boldsymbol{\gamma}_i = [\theta_i, \pi_{i1} \ldots \pi_{in}]'$, and $\boldsymbol{x}_t = [DQ_t, Dp_{1t} \ldots Dp_{nt}]'$, and deleting the nth equation (7.1) can be written for $t = 1, \cdots, T$ as

$$\boldsymbol{y}_i = \boldsymbol{X}\boldsymbol{\gamma}_i + \boldsymbol{\varepsilon}_i, \qquad i = 1, \cdots, n-1,$$

where $\boldsymbol{y}_i = [y_{it}]$ is a T-vector; $\boldsymbol{X}$ is a $T \times (n + 1)$ matrix whose t^{th} row is $\boldsymbol{x}_t'$; and $\boldsymbol{\varepsilon}_i = [\varepsilon_{it}]$ is a T-vector. Write the above equation system compactly as

$$\boldsymbol{y} = (\boldsymbol{I}_{n-1} \otimes \boldsymbol{X})\boldsymbol{\gamma} + \varepsilon,$$

where $\boldsymbol{I}_{n-1}$ is the identity matrix of order $(n - 1)$; $\boldsymbol{y} = [\boldsymbol{y}_i]$, $\boldsymbol{\gamma} = [\boldsymbol{\gamma}_i]$ and $\boldsymbol{\varepsilon} = [\boldsymbol{\varepsilon}_i]$ are vectors consisting of the corresponding $(n - 1)$ sub-vectors; and $\otimes$ is the Kronecker product.

7.3 Testing Homogeneity and Symmetry

The restriction for demand homogeneity is

$$\sum_{j=1}^{n} \pi_{ij} = 0, \qquad i = 1, \cdots, n.$$

Let $\boldsymbol{a} = [0, 1 \ldots 1]'$ be an $(n + 1)$-vector. Then, the restriction can be written in vector form as

$$\boldsymbol{a}'\boldsymbol{\gamma}_i = 0, \qquad i = 1, \cdots, n.$$

For $i = 1, \cdots, n - 1$, this can be expressed as $\boldsymbol{R}\boldsymbol{\gamma} = \boldsymbol{0}$, where $\boldsymbol{R} = \boldsymbol{I}_{n-1} \otimes \boldsymbol{a}'$.

The test statistic for homogeneity is

$$\frac{(\boldsymbol{R}\widehat{\boldsymbol{\gamma}})'\boldsymbol{\Sigma}^{-1}(\boldsymbol{R}\widehat{\boldsymbol{\gamma}})/\boldsymbol{a}'(\boldsymbol{X}'\boldsymbol{X})^{-1}\boldsymbol{a}}{tr\,\boldsymbol{\Sigma}^{-1}\boldsymbol{S}},$$

where $\widehat{\boldsymbol{\gamma}}$ is the LS estimator of $\boldsymbol{\gamma}$, $\boldsymbol{\Sigma}$ is the error covariance matrix, and $\boldsymbol{S}$ is the LS residual moment matrix (Theil 1971). When $\boldsymbol{\Sigma}$ is known, under the null, this test statistic is F-distributed with $(n-1)$ and $(n-1)(T-n-2)$ degrees of freedom. Usually, the error covariance matrix $\boldsymbol{\Sigma}$ is unknown and replaced by its estimator $\boldsymbol{S}$. The test statistic then becomes

$$\Psi_H = \frac{(\boldsymbol{R}\widehat{\boldsymbol{\gamma}})'\mathbf{S}^{-1}(\boldsymbol{R}\widehat{\boldsymbol{\gamma}})}{\boldsymbol{a}'(\boldsymbol{X}'\boldsymbol{X})^{-1}\boldsymbol{a}}.$$

This has an asymptotic χ^2 distribution with $(n-1)$ degrees of freedom. As Ψ_H involves $\boldsymbol{S}^{-1}$, $\boldsymbol{S}$ must be non-singular; the necessary condition for this is $T-2n \geq 1$ (Laitinen 1978). Laitinen (1978) derived the exact finite-sample distribution of Ψ_H as Hotelling's T^2, which itself is distributed as a constant multiple $\frac{(n-1)(T-n-2)}{(T-2n)}$ of $F(n-1, T-2n)$. This exact test should be used in applications where the sample size is relatively small.

Imposing homogeneity on system (7.1), we get

$$\overline{w}_{it}Dq_{it} = \theta_i DQ_t + \sum_{j=1}^{n-1}\pi_{ij}\left(Dp_{jt} - Dp_{nt}\right) + \varepsilon_{it}, \qquad i=1,\ldots,n. \tag{7.2}$$

Let $y_{it} = \overline{w}_{it}Dq_{it}$, $\gamma_i^H = [\theta_i\ \pi_{i1}\ldots\pi_{in-1}]'$ and $\boldsymbol{x}_i^H = [DQ_t\ (Dp_{1t}-Dp_{nt})\ldots(Dp_{n-1,t}-Dp_{nt})]'$. Then, the above equation can be written for $t = 1, \cdots, T$ as

$$\boldsymbol{y}_i = \boldsymbol{X}^{\boldsymbol{H}}\boldsymbol{\gamma}_i^H + \boldsymbol{\varepsilon}_i, \qquad i = 1, \cdots, n,$$

where $\boldsymbol{X}^{\boldsymbol{H}}$ is a $T \times n$ matrix whose t^{th} row is $\boldsymbol{x}_i^{H\prime}$; and $\boldsymbol{y}_i$ and $\boldsymbol{\varepsilon}_i$ are as before. As for the unconstrained case, the BLUE of the $\boldsymbol{\gamma}_i^H$'s are the single-eq. LS estimators. As before, delete the nth equation and write the above system compactly as

$$\boldsymbol{y} = (\boldsymbol{I}_{n-1} \otimes \boldsymbol{X}^{\boldsymbol{H}})\boldsymbol{\gamma}^{\boldsymbol{H}} + \varepsilon,$$

where $\boldsymbol{\gamma}^{\boldsymbol{H}} = \left[\boldsymbol{\gamma}_i^H\right]$ is a vector consisting of $(n-1)$ sub-vectors; and $\boldsymbol{y}, \boldsymbol{\varepsilon}, \boldsymbol{I}_{n-1}$ and $\otimes$ are as before.

Slutsky symmetry is

$$\pi_{ij} = \pi_{ji}, \qquad i, j = 1, \cdots, n$$

For $i, j = 1, \ldots, n - 1$, this is $\boldsymbol{R\gamma}^{\boldsymbol{H}} = \mathbf{0}$, where $\boldsymbol{R}$ is a $q \times n(n - 1)$ matrix with $q = \frac{1}{2}(n-1)(n-2)$ and each row of $\boldsymbol{R}$ consists of zeros except for a 1 and a −1 corresponding to π_{ij} and π_{ji} for some $i \neq j$. The test statistic is

$$\frac{\left(\boldsymbol{R}\hat{\gamma}^{\boldsymbol{H}}\right)'\left\{\boldsymbol{R}\left[\Sigma \otimes \left(\boldsymbol{X}^{\boldsymbol{H}\prime}\boldsymbol{X}^{\boldsymbol{H}}\right)^{-1}\right]\boldsymbol{R}'\right\}^{-1}\left(\boldsymbol{R}\hat{\gamma}^{\boldsymbol{H}}\right)}{[q/(n-1)]\boldsymbol{tr}\,\Sigma^{-1}\boldsymbol{S}},$$

where $\boldsymbol{\Sigma}$ is the error covariance matrix of model (7.2). This test statistic is F-distributed with q and $(n - 1)(T - n)$ degrees of freedom (Theil 1971).

As before, we replace $\boldsymbol{\Sigma}$ by its estimator $\boldsymbol{S}$ (when $\boldsymbol{S}$ is non-singular) and the test statistic becomes

$$\Psi_S = \left(\boldsymbol{R}\hat{\gamma}^{\boldsymbol{H}}\right)'\left\{\boldsymbol{R}\left[\Sigma \otimes \left(\boldsymbol{X}^{\boldsymbol{H}\prime}\boldsymbol{X}^{\boldsymbol{H}}\right)^{-1}\right]\boldsymbol{R}'\right\}^{-1}\left(\boldsymbol{R}\hat{\gamma}^{\boldsymbol{H}}\right),$$

which has an asymptotic χ^2 distribution with q degrees of freedom. Using simulation experiments, Meisner (1979) showed that the asymptotic test is biased against symmetry, particularly in large demand systems. Since symmetry involves cross-equation restrictions, the exact distribution of Ψ_S is complicated and has not yet been derived.

7.4 Testing Preference Independence

As discussed in Chap. 3, under preference independence the consumer's tastes can be described by means of a utility function which is the sum of n sub-utility functions, one for each good. One implication is that own-price elasticities (η_{ii}) are approximately proportional to income elasticities (η_i), with the income flexibility ϕ as the proportionality constant:

$$\eta_{ii} = \phi\, \eta_i, \qquad i = 1, \cdots, n.$$

While Deaton (1974) failed to find empirical support for proportionality of the elasticities, others have reached the opposite conclusion. These studies include Clements et al. (1984), Selvanathan (1993), Selvanathan and Selvanathan (2003), and Selvanathan et al. (2023). Testing for proportionality is an indirect test of preference independence hypothesis.

Selvanathan (1987, 1993) proposed a direct test of preference independence based on Barnard's (1963) Monte Carlo simulation procedure. The basic idea is to simulate a large number of values of the test statistic under the null to construct its distribution. The observed value of the test statistic is then compared to this distribution, rather than its asymptotic counterpart. Details of this approach are as follows.

Using the standard notation, consider the system of equations $\boldsymbol{y} = \boldsymbol{X\beta} + \boldsymbol{\varepsilon}$. Suppose we are interested in testing the null hypothesis $\boldsymbol{R\beta} = \boldsymbol{b}$ using a test statistic, τ which is a function of the estimate of the parameter vector $\boldsymbol{\beta}$. In general, the Monte Carlo procedure is:

1. Estimate the unrestricted model and obtain the data-based value τ_1 of τ.
2. Estimate the model under the null hypothesis $\boldsymbol{R\beta} = \boldsymbol{b}$ and obtain the estimate $\boldsymbol{S}$ of the covariance matrix $\boldsymbol{\Sigma}$ of the disturbances.
3. Generate quasi-normal error terms with zero means and covariance matrix $\boldsymbol{S}$. Use these errors together with the observed value of $\boldsymbol{X}$ and the restricted estimates to generate a new data set for $\boldsymbol{y}$ under the null. Use the generated data to estimate the unrestricted model.
4. Repeat Step 3 a certain number of times, N say, and in each case calculate the simulated value of the test statistic τ.
5. Let $\tau_2, \tau_3 \ldots \tau_M$ be the values of the test statistic τ obtained from the simulated data, where $M = N + 1$. For a one-tailed test, we reject the null at the α-per cent significance level if τ_1 is among the M' largest values of the τ_i's such that $\left(\frac{M'}{M}\right) \times 100 = \alpha$. If we use the $\alpha = 5$ per cent significance level and $N = 999$ simulations, for a one-tailed test, we reject the null hypothesis if the rank of τ_1 is 951, …, 999 or 1000.

Applying the Monte Carlo procedure for demand systems for a number of countries involving broad aggregates, Selvanathan (1993) is unable to reject the preference independence hypothesis in most cases.

7.5 Aggregation

Consider the situation where a consumer derives utility from the purchase of n commodities. The utility maximisation problem results in n demand equations, one for each commodity. However, as the number of commodities n could be very large, it may not be possible to analyse the demand for each good due to data limitations, difficulties in estimating a large demand system, etc. To overcome this, it is essential to aggregate the n commodities into a smaller number of broadly defined commodity groups, such as food, clothing, housing, etc. This is termed "aggregation over commodities". In order to aggregate over commodities, the structure of tastes must be block independent, meaning that the aggregate demand equation for a group must reflect the basic properties of the individual demand equations. This matter is covered in Chaps. 8 and 9.

Aggregation over commodities is one meaning of the term "aggregation". A second refers to aggregation over consumers. It has been long argued that this form of aggregation is problematic as the theoretical properties of the individual demands (such as homogeneity and Slutsky symmetry) do not carry over to the macro level. Sonnenschein (1973) concluded that with respect to market demand functions, there is little left of demand theory beyond homogeneity. In a similar vein, Shafer and Sonnenschein (1982) concluded that the conditions under which a market demand function has the same characteristics as a demand function for an individual consumer are hard to satisfy.

Responses to these criticisms will be illustrated with the popular almost ideal demand system (AIDS) and Rotterdam model, introduced in Chap. 6. The AIDS demand equation for good i and household h is

$$w_{ih} = \alpha_i + \beta_i \log\left(\frac{M_h}{k_h P}\right) + \sum_{j=1}^{n} \gamma_{ij} \log p_j. \tag{7.3}$$

The parameters k_h can be interpreted as a sophisticated measure of household size which takes account of age, household characteristics, and the economies of household size. This deflates the budget M_h/P to a "needs corrected" per capita level, allowing a limited amount of taste variation across households (Deaton and Muellbauer 1980). Multiplying both sides of (7.3) by M_h, summing over h and then dividing by $\sum_h M_h$ we get

$$\overline{w}_i = \alpha_i + \beta_i \log\left(\frac{\overline{M}}{\overline{k} P}\right) + \sum_{j=1}^{n} \gamma_{ij} \log p_j, \tag{7.4}$$

where $\log \overline{M} = \sum_h \mu_h \log M_h$, $\log \overline{k} = \sum_h \mu_h \log k_h$, and $\mu_h = \frac{M_h}{\sum_h M_h}$. The variable on the left, $\overline{w}_i = \sum_h \mu_h w_{ih}$, is the share of aggregate expenditure on good i in the aggregate budget of all households. Equation (7.4) is the macro form of the micro Eq. (7.3). If each household has the same tastes ($k_h = 1$, all h), $\overline{k} = 1$. As Eqs. (7.4) and (7.3) have exactly the same structure, AIDS aggregates "perfectly". But this conclusion applies only under the above nature of the taste parameter k_h.

Aggregation over consumers of the Rotterdam model has been severely criticised by McFadden (1964). The first response was offered by Barnett (1979a, b, 1981), followed by Mountain (1988) and Selvanathan (1991). These authors use a completely different framework known as the convergence approach that employs statistical tools. This yields more encouraging results about the properties of aggregated demand functions and details are provided in the next section.

7.6 The Convergence Approach

Recall from Chap. 6 that the Rotterdam model is a finite-change version of a system of differential demand equations. Discussion of aggregation of the Rotterdam takes place within the broader context of differential demands. Initially, Theil (1971) aggregated differential demand equations in relative prices under fairly strong assumptions about the macro parameters and variables. Barnett (1979a, b) then relaxed those assumptions but worked with absolute rather than relative prices. Selvanathan (1991) extended Theil's work under the weaker assumptions of Barnett and derived macro demand equations in relative prices. The results show that the properties of the macro coefficients are analogous to those of the micro coefficients. Below we present the findings of Barnet (1979a, b) and Selvanathan (1991) which are based on Theil's (1971, 1975/76) convergence approach to linear aggregation.

The micro demand equations of consumer c ($c = 1, \ldots, N$) in terms of his/her income M_c and the common price vector $\boldsymbol{p}$ are

$$q_{ic} = q_{ic}(M_c, \boldsymbol{p}), \qquad i = 1, \ldots, n; \qquad c = 1, \ldots, N.$$

Define the macro variables as averages of the micro counterparts:

$$\overline{q}_i = \frac{1}{N}\sum_{c=1}^{N} q_{ic}, \qquad i = 1, \ldots, n, \qquad \overline{M} = \frac{1}{N}\sum_{c=1}^{N} M_c = \frac{1}{N}\sum_{c=1}^{N}\sum_{i=1}^{n} p_i q_{ic} = \sum_{i=1}^{n} p_i \overline{q}_i.$$

If we sum the micro equation over $c = 1, \ldots, N$ and divide both sides by N, we obtain

$$\overline{q}_i = \frac{1}{N}\sum_{c=1}^{N} q_{ic}(M_c, \boldsymbol{p}) = g_i(\overline{M}, \boldsymbol{p}), \qquad i = 1, \ldots, n.$$

These equations are the per capita (or macro) analogues of the micro counterparts. While the functions g_i do not exist generally, applying the convergence approach yields such functions when the number of consumers becomes "large".

For simplicity, consider linear micro demands without prices:

$$q_{ic} = \alpha_{ic} + \beta_{ic} M_c, \qquad i = 1, \ldots, n; c = 1, \ldots, N, \tag{7.5}$$

where α_{ic} is the constant term and β_{ic} the income parameter. If we sum both sides of (7.5) over $c = 1, \ldots, N$ and divide by N, we obtain the macro relationships:

$$\overline{q}_i = \overline{\alpha}_i + \frac{1}{N}\sum_{c=1}^{N}\beta_{ic}M_c, \qquad i = 1, \ldots, n,$$

or equivalently,

$$\overline{q}_i = \overline{\alpha}_i + \frac{\sum_{c=1}^{N}\beta_{ic}M_c}{\sum_{c=1}^{N}M_c}\overline{M}, \qquad i = 1, \ldots, n, \tag{7.6}$$

where $\overline{q}_i = \frac{1}{N}\sum_{c=1}^{N} q_{ic}$ and $\overline{\alpha}_i = \frac{1}{N}\sum_{c=1}^{N}\alpha_{ic}$.

Consumer c's share in aggregate income is $\frac{M_c}{\sum_{c=1}^{N}M_c}$. Using these shares as weights, let $\overline{\beta}_i = \frac{\sum_{c=1}^{N}\beta_{ic}M_c}{\sum_{c=1}^{N}M_c}$ be a weighted average of the micro coefficients $\beta_{ic}'s$. Using Chebyshev's inequality, we can conclude that

$$\frac{\sum_{c=1}^{N}\beta_{ic}M_c}{\sum_{c=1}^{N}M_c} \text{ converges in probability to } \overline{\beta}_i.$$

Therefore, for sufficiently large N, we can write (7.6) as

$$\overline{q}_i \approx \overline{\alpha}_i + \overline{\beta}_i\overline{M}, \qquad i = 1, \ldots, n,$$

which is a linear macro version of the micro system (7.5) in the per capita variables $\overline{q}_i$ and $\overline{M}$ with constant coefficients $\overline{\alpha}_i$ and $\overline{\beta}_i$. Once again, aggregation is perfect, at least asymptotically.

7.7 Aggregating Differential Demands

The differential demand system in absolute prices for consumer c is

$$w_{ic}d(\log q_{ic}) = \theta_{ic}d(\log Q_c) + \sum_{j=1}^{n}\pi_{ijc}d(\log p_j), \qquad i = 1, \ldots, n; c = 1, \ldots, N, \tag{7.7}$$

where all consumers pay the same set of prices. The micro coefficients θ_{ic} and π_{ijc} of the micro demand equations are functions of income and prices which satisfy

$$\sum_{i=1}^{n}\theta_{ic} = 1 \quad \text{and} \quad \sum_{j=1}^{n}\pi_{ijc} = 0,$$

with $[\pi_{ijc}]$ an $n \times n$ symmetric negative semidefinite matrix of order $n - 1$.

Barnett (1979a) applies the convergence approach to yield macro demand equations in terms of macro variables and macro coefficients which are analogous to the micro demand system (7.7). He proceeds as follows:

1. Multiplying both sides of (7.7) by $\left(\frac{M_c}{N\overline{M}}\right)$ and summing over $c = 1, \ldots, N$, the ith micro demand equation becomes

$$\sum_{c=1}^{N} \frac{M_c}{N\overline{M}} w_{ic} d(\log q_{ic}) = \sum_{c=1}^{N} \frac{M_c}{N\overline{M}} \theta_{ic} d(\log Q_c) + \sum_{c=1}^{N} \sum_{j=1}^{n} \frac{M_c}{N\overline{M}} \pi_{ijc} d(\log p_j).$$

By defining

$$\overline{w}_i = \frac{p_i \overline{q}_i}{\overline{M}}, \qquad i = 1, \ldots, n,$$

the left-hand side (LHS) of the above equation becomes

$$\sum_{c=1}^{N} \frac{M_c}{N\overline{M}} w_{ic} d(\log q_{ic}) = \sum_{c=1}^{N} \frac{M_c}{N\overline{M}} \frac{p_i q_{ic}}{M_c} \frac{dq_{ic}}{q_{ic}} = \frac{p_i}{N\overline{M}} \sum_{c=1}^{N} dq_{ic} = \frac{p_i d\overline{q}_i}{\overline{M}} = \overline{w}_i d(\log \overline{q}_i),$$

which is the macro analogue of the LHS variable of the micro Eq. (7.7).

2. Using the convergence approach and applying Khinchine's theorem, the two right-hand side (RHS) variables can be simplified to (Selvanathan 1991)

$$\sum_{c=1}^{N} \frac{M_c}{N\overline{M}} \theta_{ic} d(\log Q_c) = \left[\frac{\sum_{c=1}^{N} M_c \theta_{ic}}{\sum_{c=1}^{N} M_c}\right] \left[\frac{1}{N} \sum_{c=1}^{N} d(\log Q_c)\right] = \overline{\theta}_i d(\log \overline{Q}) + O_p(1)$$

and

$$\sum_{c=1}^{N} \sum_{j=1}^{n} \frac{M_c}{N\overline{M}} \pi_{ijc} d(\log p_j) = \sum_{j=1}^{n} \left[\frac{\sum_{c=1}^{N} M_c \pi_{ijc}}{\sum_{c=1}^{N} M_c}\right] d(\log p_j) = \sum_{j=1}^{n} \overline{\pi}_{ij} d(\log p_j)$$
$$+ O_p(1),$$

where $O_p(1)$ denotes a random variable that converges in probability to 0 as $N \rightarrow \infty$,

$$d(\log \overline{Q}) = \frac{1}{N} \sum_{c=1}^{N} d(\log Q_c),$$

and the macro coefficients are defined as

$$\overline{\theta}_i = \frac{E[M_c\theta_{ic}]}{E[M_c]}, i = 1, \ldots, n; \quad \text{and} \quad \overline{\pi}_{ij} = \frac{E[M_c\pi_{ijc}]}{E[M_c]}, \qquad i,j = 1, \ldots, n.$$

3. Therefore, for sufficiently large N, the final form of the macro demand system is

$$\overline{w}_i d(\log \overline{q}_i) = \overline{\theta}_i d(\log \overline{Q}) + \sum_{j=1}^{n} \overline{\pi}_{ij} d(\log \overline{p}_j), \qquad i = 1, \ldots, n,$$

which are the macro versions of the micro Eq. (7.7).

In terms of relative prices, the differential demand for commodity i of consumer c is

$$w_{ic} d(\log q_{ic}) = \theta_{ic} d(\log Q_c) + \sum_{j=1}^{n} \nu_{ijc} \left[d(\log p_j) - \sum_{k=1}^{n} \theta_{kc} d(\log p_k) \right]. \tag{7.8}$$

The micro coefficients θ_{ic}'s satisfy $\sum_{i=1}^{n} \theta_{ic} = 1$ and the price coefficients satisfy $\sum_{j=1}^{n} \nu_{ijc} = \phi_c \theta_{ic}$, where ϕ_c is the income flexibility, and the matrix $[\nu_{ijc}]$ is symmetric negative definite for each c. Selvanathan (1991) derives the corresponding macro demand equation using the following steps:

1. Multiplying both sides of (7.8) by $\frac{M_c}{N\overline{M}}$ and summing over $c = 1, \cdots, N$ gives

$$\sum_{c=1}^{N} \frac{M_c}{N\overline{M}} w_{ic} d(\log q_{ic}) = \sum_{c=1}^{N} \frac{M_c}{N\overline{M}} \theta_{ic} d(\log Q_c) + \sum_{c=1}^{N} \sum_{j=1}^{n} \frac{M_c}{N\overline{M}} \nu_{ijc} \left[d(\log p_j) - \sum_{k=1}^{n} \theta_{kc} d(\log p_k) \right]. \tag{7.9}$$

2. We have already derived the following expressions for the LHS variable and the first term on the RHS:

$$\sum_{c=1}^{N} \frac{M_c}{N\overline{M}} w_{ic} d(\log q_{ic}) = \overline{w}_i d(\log \overline{q}_i),$$

$$\sum_{c=1}^{N} \frac{M_c}{N\overline{M}} \theta_{ic} d(\log Q_c) = \overline{\theta}_i d(\log \overline{Q}) + O_p(1).$$

3. By defining the macro coefficients as

$$\bar{\theta}_i = \frac{E[M_c\theta_{ic}]}{E[M_c]}, i = 1, \ldots, n; \quad \text{and} \quad \bar{\nu}_{ij} = \frac{E[M_c\nu_{ijc}]}{E[M_c]}, \qquad i,j = 1, \ldots, n,$$

Selvanathan (1991) showed that, under certain conditions,

$$\sum_{c=1}^{N}\sum_{j=1}^{n}\frac{M_c}{N\bar{M}}\nu_{ijc}\left[d(\log p_j) - \sum_{k=1}^{n}\theta_{kc}d(\log p_k)\right]$$
$$= \sum_{j=1}^{n}\bar{\nu}_{ij}\left[d(\log p_j) - \sum_{k=1}^{n}\bar{\theta}_k d(\log p_k)\right].$$

4. Therefore, for large N, Eq. (7.9) can be simplified as

$$\overline{w}_i d(\log \overline{q}_i) = \overline{\theta}_i d(\log \overline{Q}) + \sum_{j=1}^{n}\bar{\nu}_{ij}\left[d(\log p_j) - \sum_{k=1}^{n}\overline{\theta}_k d(\log p_k)\right],$$

which is the macro version of the micro Eq. (7.8).

Thus, under the conditions specified, the Rotterdam's aggregation is perfect, in both its absolute- and relative-price forms. Other influential work dealing with the aggregation of demand equations includes Blundell et al. (1993), Buse (1992), Chavas (1993), Heineke (1993), Lewbel (1996), Malinvaud (1993), Selvanathan (1995), and Slesnik (1998).

7.8 Tastes, Always Unchanged?

Stigler and Becker (1977) hypothesise that tastes neither change capriciously nor differ importantly between people. In an international context, this amounts to stating consumers in different countries are similar irrespective of differences in language, culture, and geography. In an innovative paper, Pollak and Wales (1987) used the quadratic expenditure system (discussed in the previous chapter) with panel data and found no support for the hypothesis of identical tastes. A number of other empirical studies such as Selvanathan and Selvanathan (1993) and Carruth et al. (1999), have also rejected the hypothesis.

Rejecting the identical/similarity hypothesis is not surprising, as proposing that similar preferences exist in a set of countries, or even within regions of the same country, is strong. Consequently, Levitt (1983) suggested a less stringent approach by asking: As globalisation might be expected to homogenise preference structures, are tastes converging or diverging? A number of studies have examined convergence with respect to specific categories of goods such as wine and beer (Aizenman and Brooks 2008; Fedoseeva 2017), food (Elsner and Hartmann 1998; Gracia and Albisu 2001; Waheeduzzaman 2011), electricity (Meng et al. 2013; Mohammadi and Ram 2012), the automobile market (Goldberg and Verboven 2005), and forestry products (Buongiorno 2009).

Some studies use a convergence approach based on budget shares to establish the long-run similarity of consumption patterns, known as preference homogeneity (for example, Kónya and Ohashi 2007; Michail 2018). The approach is based on a test of the null hypothesis of a random walk of the shares. Michail (2018) uses the following pooled regression similar to the one commonly used for the Dicky-Fuller test:

$$\Delta w_{i,c,t} = \lambda w_{i,c,t-1} + \gamma \Delta w_{i,c,t-1} + \varepsilon_{i,c,t},$$

where $w_{i,\,c,\,t}$ is the log deviation of budget share of product i ($i = 1, \ldots, n$) in country c ($c = 1, \ldots, K$) deviated from the cross-country sample average ($\overline{w}_{i,t}$) in year t. The symbol Δ signifies the first-difference operator, that is, $\Delta w_{i,\,c,\,t} = w_{i,\,c,\,t} - w_{i,\,c,\,t-1}$. Thus, consumption patterns are said to converge internationally when changes in the budget shares are stationary, that is, when $\lambda < 0$ (Busetti et al. 2006). The rate of convergence is measured by the λ coefficient with half-life $\log \frac{1}{2} / \log |\lambda|$. To apply this approach, Michail (2018) added several control variables to the RHS of the above equation, including the price of the product, income, and product and country fixed effects.

7.9 Decomposing Budget Shares

Clements et al. (2024) extended the budget-share-based-convergence approach by splitting the shares into price and quantity components, thereby identifying the source of the convergence. They show that key parameters governing budget-share convergence can be written as a linear combination of components due to prices, quantities, and price-quantity interactions. As the quantity component is under the direct control of the consumer, that is the fundamental measure of the similarity (or dissimilarity) of tastes.

This approach to taste convergence considers the budget shares of n commodities in K countries. Each share is first averaged over the K countries to measure consumption patterns in the group of countries. Then the deviation of the shares from their group counterparts is then tested for stationarity in order to ascertain if consumption is converging to a common pattern. To be more precise, denote by $p_{ict}q_{ict}$ expenditure on good i ($i = 1, \cdots, n$) in country c ($c = 1, \cdots, K$) for year t and $w_{ict} = \frac{p_{ict}q_{ict}}{M_{ct}}$ the corresponding budget share, where $M_{ct} = \sum_{i=1}^{n} p_{ict}q_{ict}$ is total consumption expenditure. Let $w'_{it} = \frac{1}{K}\sum_{c=1}^{K} w_{ict}$ be the corresponding arithmetic mean over the K countries, so that $\log\left(\frac{w_{ict}}{w'_{it}}\right)$ is the logarithmic deviation of the ith share from the mean. Then, stationarity is tested with the panel regression:

$$\Delta \log\left(\frac{w_{ict}}{w'_{it}}\right) = \lambda \log\left(\frac{w_{ic,t-1}}{w'_{i,t-1}}\right) + \gamma\Delta \log\left(\frac{w_{ic,t-1}}{w'_{i,t-1}}\right) + \varepsilon_{ict}. \tag{7.10}$$

Here, $\Delta \log\left(\frac{w_{ict}}{w'_{it}}\right) = \log\left(\frac{w_{ict}}{w'_{it}}\right) - \log\left(\frac{w_{ic,t-1}}{w'_{i,t-1}}\right)$; λ and γ are coefficients; and ε_{ict} is an error term.

Budget-share convergence involves testing the hypothesis:

$H_0 : \lambda = 0$ (there is a unit root or the budget share series is non-stationary) against
$H_A : \lambda < 0$ (there is no unit root or the budget share series is stationary).

When $\lambda < 0$, deviations from the average are eliminated over time, meaning the shares become more alike and tastes are similar internationally. This is very similar to the approach outlined in the previous section.

Equation (7.10) is formulated in terms of budget shares $w_{ict} = \frac{p_{ict}q_{ict}}{M_{ct}}$. An important question to consider is: Could both prices and quantities be non-stationary, but co-integrated, resulting in the shares being stationary? The point is, as only quantities are controllable by the consumer, how can convergence of the shares, which contain the uncontrollable price components, be solely ascribed to convergence of tastes? To investigate this, Eq. (7.10) can be reformulated so that the split between prices and quantities can be identified. Replace the cross-country arithmetic means (indicated by the primes above) with their geometric counterparts (no primes), the logarithms of which are

$$\log p_{it} = \frac{1}{K}\sum_{c=1}^{K} \log p_{ict}; \quad \log q_{it} = \frac{1}{K}\sum_{c=1}^{K} \log q_{ict};$$
$$\log M_t = \frac{1}{K}\sum_{c=1}^{K} \log M_{ct}; \quad \log w_{it} = \frac{1}{K}\sum_{c=1}^{K} \log w_{ict}.$$

As $w_{ict} = \frac{p_{ict}q_{ict}}{M_{ct}}$,

$$\log w_{ict} = \log p_{ict} + \log q_{ict} - \log M_{ct}. \tag{7.11}$$

Averaging over countries, this becomes

$$\log w_{it} = \log p_{it} + \log q_{it} - \log M_t. \tag{7.12}$$

Subtracting both sides of Eq. (7.12) from Eq. (7.11) yields

$$\log\left(\frac{w_{ict}}{w_{it}}\right) = \log\left(\frac{p_{ict}}{p_{it}}\right) + \log\left(\frac{q_{ict}}{q_{it}}\right) - \log\left(\frac{M_{ct}}{M_t}\right). \tag{7.13}$$

Next, average Eq. (7.11) over commodities:

$$\log W_{ct} = \log P_{ct} + \log Q_{ct} - \log M_{ct}, \tag{7.14}$$

where $\log W_{ct} = \frac{1}{n}\sum_{i=1}^{n} \log w_{ict}$, $\log P_{ct} = \frac{1}{n}\sum_{i=1}^{n} \log p_{ict}$, $\log Q_{ct} = \frac{1}{n}\sum_{i=1}^{n} \log q_{ict}$, and average Eq. (7.14) over countries:

$$\log W_t = \log P_t + \log Q_t - \log M_t, \tag{7.15}$$

where $\log W_t = \frac{1}{K}\sum_{c=1}^{K} \log W_{ct}$, $\log P_t = \frac{1}{K}\sum_{c=1}^{K} \log P_{ct}$and $\log Q_t = \frac{1}{K}\sum_{c=1}^{K} \log Q_{ct}$.

Subtract Eq. (7.15) from Eq. (7.14):

$$\log\left(\frac{W_{ct}}{W_t}\right) = \log\left(\frac{P_{ct}}{P_t}\right) + \log\left(\frac{Q_{ct}}{Q_t}\right) - \log\left(\frac{M_{ct}}{M_t}\right). \tag{7.16}$$

And, finally, subtract Eq. (7.16) from Eq. (7.13):

$$\log\left(\frac{w_{ict}/W_{ct}}{w_{it}/W_t}\right) = \log\left(\frac{p_{ict}/P_{ct}}{p_{it}/P_t}\right) + \log\left(\frac{q_{ict}/Q_{ct}}{q_{it}/Q_t}\right). \tag{7.17}$$

The term on the LHS of Eq. (7.17) is the logarithmic deviation of w_{ict}/W_{ct} from the average for all countries, w_{it}/W_t. Each of the two terms on the RHS has the same double-deflated form. This formulation permits the clean split into a relative price term and a relative quantity term. The two terms are both pure numbers, directly comparable across countries without reference to differing price levels or currencies. This property is not shared by the terms on the RHS variables of Eq. (7.11).

For any variable x, define $\tilde{x}_{ict} = \log\left(\frac{x_{ict}/X_{ct}}{x_{it}/X_t}\right)$. Equation (7.17) and its first difference can be written as

$$\tilde{w}_{ict} = \tilde{p}_{ict} + \tilde{q}_{ict} \tag{7.18}$$

and

$$\Delta\tilde{w}_{ict} = \Delta\tilde{p}_{ict} + \Delta\tilde{q}_{ict}. \tag{7.19}$$

The transformation $\tilde{x}_{ict}$ is also a pure number with zero means over commodities and countries, directly comparable across commodities and countries. Countries (or their consumers) are declared to be similar if $\log\left(\frac{q_{ict}}{Q_{ct}}\right)$ converges to $\log\left(\frac{q_{it}}{Q_t}\right)$, that is, if $\tilde{q}_{ict}$ is stationary.

The reformulated version of model (7.10) comprises four equations:

Budget shares

$$\Delta\tilde{w}_{ict} = \lambda^w \tilde{w}_{ict-1} + \gamma^w \Delta\tilde{w}_{ict-1} + \varepsilon^w_{ict}. \tag{7.20}$$

Prices

$$\Delta\tilde{p}_{ict} = \lambda^p \tilde{p}_{ict-1} + \gamma^p \Delta\tilde{p}_{ict-1} + \varepsilon^p_{ict}; \tag{7.21}$$

Quantities

$$\Delta\tilde{q}_{ict} = \lambda^q \tilde{q}_{ict-1} + \gamma^q \Delta\tilde{q}_{ict-1} + \varepsilon^q_{ict}; \tag{7.22}$$

Price-quantity interaction

$$\Delta\tilde{p}_{ict} = \lambda^{pq} \tilde{q}_{ict-1} + \gamma^{pq} \Delta\tilde{q}_{ict-1} + \varepsilon^{pq}_{ict}; \tag{7.23}$$

Quantity-price interaction

$$\Delta\tilde{q}_{ict} = \lambda^{qp} \tilde{p}_{ict-1} + \gamma^{qp} \Delta\tilde{p}_{ict-1} + \varepsilon^{qp}_{ict}. \tag{7.24}$$

The coefficient λ^w in Eq. (7.20) is key to the convergence of the budget shares: When $\lambda^w = 0$, there is a unit root and the shares are non-stationary. Splitting budget shares into price and quantity components means that it is possible to decompose λ^w into more basic parts due to the behaviour of prices and quantities given by Eqs. (7.21)–(7.24).

To understand further the links between the convergence of the components, write Eqs. (7.20)–(7.24) in an obvious vector form as

$$\begin{cases} \boldsymbol{y}_w = \boldsymbol{X}_w \boldsymbol{\beta}_{ww} + \boldsymbol{\varepsilon}_{ww}, \quad \boldsymbol{y}_p = \boldsymbol{X}_p \boldsymbol{\beta}_{pp} + \boldsymbol{\varepsilon}_{pp}, \quad \boldsymbol{y}_q = \boldsymbol{X}_q \boldsymbol{\beta}_{qq} + \boldsymbol{\varepsilon}_{qq} \\ \boldsymbol{y}_p = \boldsymbol{X}_q \boldsymbol{\beta}_{pq} + \boldsymbol{\varepsilon}_{pq}, \quad \boldsymbol{y}_q = \boldsymbol{X}_p \boldsymbol{\beta}_{qp} + \boldsymbol{\varepsilon}_{qp}. \end{cases} \tag{7.25}$$

Here, $\boldsymbol{\beta}_{ww} = [\lambda^w \ \gamma^w]'$, $\boldsymbol{\beta}_{pp} = [\lambda^p \ \gamma^p]'$, $\boldsymbol{\beta}_{qq} = [\lambda^q \ \gamma^q]'$, $\boldsymbol{\beta}_{pq} = [\lambda^{pq} \ \gamma^{pq}]'$, and $\boldsymbol{\beta}_{qp} = [\lambda^{qp} \ \gamma^{qp}]'$. The LS estimators of model (7.25) are

$$\begin{cases} \hat{\boldsymbol{\beta}}_{ww} = \left(\boldsymbol{X}_w'\boldsymbol{X}_w\right)^{-1}\boldsymbol{X}_w'\boldsymbol{y}_w, \quad \hat{\boldsymbol{\beta}}_{pp} = \left(\boldsymbol{X}_p'\boldsymbol{X}_p\right)^{-1}\boldsymbol{X}_p'\boldsymbol{y}_p, \quad \hat{\boldsymbol{\beta}}_{qq} = \left(\boldsymbol{X}_q'\boldsymbol{X}_q\right)^{-1}\boldsymbol{X}_q'\boldsymbol{y}_q, \\ \hat{\boldsymbol{\beta}}_{pq} = \left(\boldsymbol{X}_q'\boldsymbol{X}_q\right)^{-1}\boldsymbol{X}_q'\boldsymbol{y}_p, \quad \hat{\boldsymbol{\beta}}_{qp} = \left(\boldsymbol{X}_p'\boldsymbol{X}_p\right)^{-1}\boldsymbol{X}_p'\boldsymbol{y}_q. \end{cases} \tag{7.26}$$

Identities (7.18) and (7.19) imply

$$\boldsymbol{y}_w = \boldsymbol{y}_p + \boldsymbol{y}_q, \qquad \boldsymbol{X}_w = \boldsymbol{X}_p + \boldsymbol{X}_q. \tag{7.27}$$

Using (7.27) in (7.26), we get

$$\widehat{\boldsymbol{\beta}}_{ww} = \boldsymbol{M}_{ww}^{-1}\left(\boldsymbol{M}_{pp}\widehat{\boldsymbol{\beta}}_{pp} + \boldsymbol{M}_{pp}\widehat{\boldsymbol{\beta}}_{qp} + \boldsymbol{M}_{qq}\widehat{\boldsymbol{\beta}}_{pq} + \boldsymbol{M}_{qq}\widehat{\boldsymbol{\beta}}_{qq}\right)$$

$$= \boldsymbol{\theta}_{pp}\hat{\boldsymbol{\beta}}_{pp} + (\boldsymbol{\theta}_{pp}\hat{\boldsymbol{\beta}}_{qp} + \boldsymbol{\theta}_{qq}\hat{\boldsymbol{\beta}}_{pq}) + \boldsymbol{\theta}_{qq}\hat{\boldsymbol{\beta}}_{qq}, \quad (7.28)$$

where $\boldsymbol{M}_{ww} = \boldsymbol{X}'_w\boldsymbol{X}_w, \boldsymbol{M}_{pp} = \boldsymbol{X}'_p\boldsymbol{X}_p$ and $\boldsymbol{M}_{qq} = \boldsymbol{X}'_q\boldsymbol{X}_q$, $\boldsymbol{\theta}_{pp} = \boldsymbol{M}_{ww}^{-1}\boldsymbol{M}_{pp}$ and $\boldsymbol{\theta}_{qq} = \boldsymbol{M}_{ww}^{-1}\boldsymbol{M}_{qq}$. Equation (7.28) shows that the budget-share coefficients can be decomposed into three components represented by prices, quantities, and their interaction. The interaction term is proportional to a weighted average of the two cross-slopes: $\boldsymbol{\theta}_{pp}\hat{\boldsymbol{\beta}}_{qp} + \boldsymbol{\theta}_{qq}\hat{\boldsymbol{\beta}}_{pq} = \boldsymbol{\Theta}\bar{\boldsymbol{\beta}}$, where $\overline{\boldsymbol{\beta}} = \boldsymbol{\delta}\,\hat{\boldsymbol{\beta}}_{qp} + (\boldsymbol{I} - \boldsymbol{\delta})\hat{\boldsymbol{\beta}}_{pq}$ is the weighted average with $\boldsymbol{\delta} = (\boldsymbol{M}_{pp} + \boldsymbol{M}_{qq})^{-1}\boldsymbol{M}_{pp}$ and $\boldsymbol{\theta} = (\boldsymbol{\theta}_{pp} + \boldsymbol{\theta}_{qq})$.

7.10 The Income Flexibility

Recall from Chap. 6 the combination of Working's model and the preference-independent version of the Rotterdam model gives a system of the form

$$\overline{w}_{it}(Dq_{it} - DQ_t) = \beta_i DQ_t + \phi(\beta_i + \overline{w}_{it})\left(Dp_{it} - DP'_t\right), \qquad i = 1, \cdots, n; \quad t = 1, \ldots, T$$

Here, ϕ is the income flexibility (the inverse of the income elasticity of the marginal utility of income). The income flexibility can be obtained by estimating this system. There are some other ways of obtaining a value for this important parameter, proposed by Selvanathan (1995). A brief review of these follows.

Under the assumption of unitary income elasticities (that is, $\eta_i = 1$ or $\beta_i = 0$), the above system becomes

$$Dq_{it} - DQ_t = \phi(Dp_{it} - DP_t), \qquad i = 1, \ldots, n; \quad t = 1, \ldots, T$$

where $DP'_t = \sum_{j=1}^{n}\left(\beta_j + \overline{w}_{jt}\right)Dp_{jt} = \sum_{j=1}^{n}\overline{w}_{jt}Dp_{jt} = DP_t$ is the Divisia price index. Thus, if we regress the growth in consumption of i relative to the overall growth in consumption, $Dq_{it} - DQ_t$, against the growth in the relative prices of i, $(Dp_{it} - DP_t)$, for $t = 1, \ldots, T$, the slope coefficient can be interpreted as ϕ. This yields n such estimates, one for each commodity. These can then be combined as a weighted average to give a single estimate of ϕ for all commodities for the whole period.

Another method of estimating ϕ, based on the Divisia moments introduced in Chap. 6, is as follows. Multiply both sides of the above equation by $\overline{w}_{it}(Dp_{it} - DP_t)$ and then take the sum over $i = 1, \ldots, n$ to give

$$\sum_{i=1}^{n}\overline{w}_{it}(Dp_{it} - DP_t)(Dq_{it} - DQ_t) = \phi\sum_{i=1}^{n}\overline{w}_{it}(Dp_{it} - DP_t)^2.$$

The LHS is the Divisia price-quantity covariance, Γ_t, while the RHS is a multiple ϕ of the Divisia price variance, Π_t. Thus,

$$\Gamma_t = \phi\, \Pi_t, \qquad t = 1, \ldots, T.$$

Therefore,

$$\phi = \frac{\Gamma_t}{\Pi_t}, \qquad t = 1, \ldots, T.$$

Using the sampling distribution of ϕ, we can obtain an unbiased estimate for ϕ and its standard error.

From Chap. 6, the linear expenditure system (LES) for good i is

$$p_i q_i = p_i \gamma_i + \beta_i \left(M - \sum_{j=1}^{n} p_j \gamma_j \right).$$

Here, $p_i \gamma_i$ is "subsistence expenditure" on the commodity, $\sum_{j=1}^{n} p_j \gamma_j$ the total cost of subsistence and $M - \sum_{j=1}^{n} p_j \gamma_j$ is "supernumerary income". LES can be derived from the Stone-Geary direct utility function:

$$u(q_1, \ldots, q_n) = \sum_{i=1}^{n} \beta_i \log(q_i - \gamma_i), \tag{7.29}$$

where $\sum_{i=1}^{n} \beta_i = 1$, $0 < \beta_i < 1$, and $q_i > \gamma_i > 0$, $i = 1, \cdots, n$. The ith demand function in LES is $q_i = \gamma_i + \frac{\beta_i}{p_i} \left(M - \sum_{j=1}^{n} p_j \gamma_j \right)$, which when substituted into (7.29) gives the indirect utility function:

$$u_I(M, \boldsymbol{p}) = \sum_{i=1}^{n} \beta_i \log \left\{ \frac{\beta_i}{p_i} \left(M - \sum_{j=1}^{n} p_j \gamma_j \right) \right\}.$$

The marginal utility of income is $\frac{\partial \{u_I(M, \boldsymbol{p})\}}{\partial M} = \frac{1}{M - \sum_{j=1}^{n} p_j \gamma_j}$, to be denoted by λ. Since $\frac{\partial \lambda}{\partial M} = -\lambda^2$, the income elasticity of the marginal utility of income is

$$\frac{\partial \lambda}{\partial M} \frac{M}{\lambda} = -\frac{M}{M - \sum_{j=1}^{n} p_j \gamma_j},$$

and the income flexibility is the reciprocal:

$$\phi = -\frac{M - \sum_{j=1}^{n} p_j \gamma_j}{M} = -\left(1 - \sum_{j=1}^{n} s_j \right).$$

where $s_j = \frac{p_j \gamma_j}{M}$ is the fraction of income devoted to subsistence of j. In words, the income flexibility associated with LES is the supernumerary ratio with the sign changed.

References

Aizenman J, Brooks E (2008) Globalization and taste convergence: the cases of wine and beer. Rev Int Econ 16:217–233

Barnard GA (1963) In discussion. J R Stat Soc Ser B 25:294

Barnett WA (1979a) Theoretical foundations for the Rotterdam model. Rev Econ Stud 46:109–130

Barnett WA (1979b) The joint allocation of leisure and goods expenditure. Econometrica 47:539–563

Barnett WA (1981) Consumer demand and labour supply. North-Holland Publishing Company, Amsterdam

Barten AP (1969) Maximum likelihood estimation of a complete system of demand equations. Eur Econ Rev 1:7–73

Blundell R, Pashardes P, Weber G (1993) What do we learn about consumer demand pattern from micro data. Am Econ Rev 83:570–597

Buongiorno J (2009) International trends in forest products consumption: is there convergence? Int For Rev 11:490–500

Buse A (1992) Aggregation, distribution and dynamics in the linear and quadratic expenditure systems. Rev Econ Stat 74:45–53

Busetti F, Fabiani S, Harvey A (2006) Convergence of prices and rates of inflation. Oxf Bull Econ Stat 68:863–877

Carruth A, Gibson H, Tsakalotos E (1999) Are aggregate consumption relationships similar across the European Union? Reg Stud 33:17–26

Chavas JP (1993) On aggregation and its implication for aggregate behaviour. Ric Econ 47:201–214

Clements KW, Kappelle S, Roberts EJ (1984) Are luxuries more price elastic than necessities? McKethan-Matherly discussion paper MM6, Graduate School of Business, University of Florida, Gainesville

Clements KW, Selvanathan EA, Selvanathan S (2024) Why do consumption patterns converge? Prices quantities or their covariation?." Unpublished manuscript. The University of Western Australia, Perth

Deaton AS (1974) The analysis of consumer demand in the United Kingdom, 1900-1970. Econometrica 42:341–367

Deaton AS, Muellbauer J (1980) An almost ideal demand system. Am Econ Rev 70:312–326

Elsner K, Hartmann M (1998) Convergence of food consumption patterns between eastern and Western Europe. (No. 13) Discussion Paper, Institute of Agricultural Development in Central and Eastern Europe, Germany

Fedoseeva S (2017) In vino veritas? An alternative story of European convergence. Beverages 3:58

Goldberg PK, Verboven F (2005) Market integration and convergence to the law of one Price: evidence from the European car market. J Int Econ 65:49–73

Gracia A, Albisu LM (2001) Food consumption in the European Union: Main determinants and country differences. Agribusiness 17:469–488

Heineke JM (1993) Exact aggregation of consumer demand systems. Ric Econ 47:215–232

Kónya I, Ohashi H (2007) International consumption patterns among high-income countries: evidence from the OECD data. Rev Int Econ 15:744–757

Laitinen K (1978) Why is demand homogeneity so often rejected? Econ Lett 1:187–191

Levitt T (1983) The globalization of markets. Harv Bus Rev 61:69–81

Lewbel A (1996) Aggregation without separability: a generalised composite commodity theorem. Am Econ Rev 86:524–543

Malinvaud E (1993) A framework of aggregation theories. Ric Econ 47:107–135

McFadden D (1964) Existence conditions for Theil-type preferences. Unpublished paper, Department of Economics, University of California, Berkeley

Meisner JF (1979) Divisia moments of U.S. industry, 1947-1978. Econ Lett 4:239–242

Meng M, Payne JE, Lee J (2013) Convergence in per capita energy use among OECD countries. Energy Econ 36:536–545

Michail NA (2018) Convergence of consumption patterns in the European Union. Empir Econ 58: 979–994

Mohammadi H, Ram R (2012) Cross-country convergence in energy and electricity consumption, 1971–2007. Energy Econ 34:1882–1887

Mountain DC (1988) The Rotterdam model: an approximation in variable space. Econometrica 56: 477–484

Pollak RA, Wales TJ (1987) Specification and estimation of non separable two-stage technologies: the Leontief CES and the cobb-Douglas CES. J Polit Econ 95:311–333

Selvanathan EA (1991) Further results on aggregation of differential demand system. Rev Econ Stud 58:799–805

Selvanathan EA (1995) Data analytic techniques for consumer economics." Chapter 3. In: Selvanathan EA, Clements KW (eds) Recent developments in applied demand analysis. Springer, Berlin

Selvanathan EA, Selvanathan S (1993) A cross-country analysis of consumption patterns. Appl Econ 25:1245–1259

Selvanathan EA, Selvanathan S (2003) International consumption comparisons: OECD versus LDC. World Scientific, New York

Selvanathan S (1987) A Monte Carlo test of preference independence. Econ Lett 25:259–261

Selvanathan S (1993) A system-wide analysis of international consumption patterns. Kluwer Academic Publishers, Boston, MA

Selvanathan S, Jayasinghe M, Selvanathan EA, Rathnayaka SD (2023) Dynamic modelling of consumption patterns using LA-AIDS: a comparative study of developed versus developing countries. Empir Econ 66:75–135

Shafer W, Sonnenschein H (1982) Market demand and excess C demand functions. In: Arrow KJ, Intriligator MD (eds) Handbook of mathematical economics, vol II. North-Holland Publishing Company, Amsterdam

Slesnick DT (1998) Empirical approaches to the measurement of welfare. J Econ Lit 36:2108–2165

Sonnenschein H (1973) The utility hypothesis and market demand theory. Western Econ J 11:404–410

Stigler GJ, Becker GS (1977) De Gustibus Non Est Disputandum. Am Econ Rev 67:76–90

Theil H (1971) Principles of econometrics. Wiley, New York

Theil H (1975/76) Theory and measurement of consumer demand. North-Holland, Amsterdam

Waheeduzzaman ANM (2011) Are emerging markets catching up with the developed markets in terms of consumption? J Glob Mark 24:136–151

Chapter 8
Group Demand I: Main Results

This chapter sets out the theory of multi-stage budgeting by the consumer, group demand, conditional demand within the group and unconditional demand, and application of the theory to alcoholic beverages. The subsequent chapter gives detailed derivations, references, and sources of material covered in this chapter.

8.1 Why a Group?

A typical consumer often spends money on many goods (and services). Given the difficulty considering all these decisions simultaneously, consumers often adopt a multiple-stage budgeting approach. For simplicity, we use two steps as an example, where the consumer first allocates total expenditure into broad groups of items and then further separates group expenditure to the individual items within those groups. This two-stage budgeting system is easily generalised to higher-order structures.

This chapter first deals with the nature of preferences when goods are grouped together. Thereafter comes a fairly detailed discussion of conditional demand for goods within a group and the demand for the group as a whole. To provide a concrete example, the theory is applied to the demand for alcoholic beverages. Some of this material was previously touched on in Chap. 3 in the context of Pigou's (1910) law, whereby the more luxurious a good is, the higher its price elasticity.

8.2 Utility and Groups of Goods

Chapter 3 sets out the theory of utility maximisation under preference independence. This section extends that material to utility maximisation with two-stage budgeting.

Let q_i be the quantity demanded of good i for $i = 1, \cdots, n$ and $\boldsymbol{q}$ be the corresponding vector. Write the consumer's utility function as

K. W. Clements et al., *Short-cut Demand Elasticities and Other Convenient Approaches to Consumer Demand*, https://doi.org/10.1007/978-981-96-3588-7_8

$$u(q_1, \cdots, q_n) = u(\boldsymbol{q}).$$

Suppose the n goods are partitioned into $G \leq n$ groups such that each good belongs to one group only. Denote these groups by $\boldsymbol{S}_1, \cdots, \boldsymbol{S}_G$. Two-stage budgeting requires the preference ordering of goods within one group to be independent of consumption of goods in other groups. There then exists a sub-utility function for $\boldsymbol{S}_g$, written as $u_g(\boldsymbol{q}_g)$, where $\boldsymbol{q}_g$ refers to the members of group g. The simplest form of independence between groups is when the utility function is additive in $u_g(\cdot)$:

$$u(\boldsymbol{q}) = u_1(\boldsymbol{q}_1) + u_2(\boldsymbol{q}_2) + \cdots + u_G(\boldsymbol{q}_G). \quad (8.1)$$

According to (8.1), $\frac{\partial^2 u}{\partial q_i \partial q_j} = 0$, for $i \in \boldsymbol{S}_g, j \in \boldsymbol{S}_h$, $g \neq h$, so that the marginal utility of one good is independent of consumption of another good in a different group. When goods are ordered appropriately, this can be written in terms of a block-diagonal Hessian matrix of the utility function $\boldsymbol{U} = \frac{\partial^2 u}{\partial \boldsymbol{q} \partial \boldsymbol{q}'}$, and (8.1) is known as block independence or strong separability.

If each group contains one good, the utility function in (8.1) becomes $u(\boldsymbol{q}) = u_1(q_1) + u_2(q_2) + \cdots + u_n(q_n)$, where $u_i(q_i)$ is the sub-utility function for good i and depends only on q_i. This is the case of preference independence or additive preferences, as discussed in Chap. 3. A weaker version, weak separability, takes the form:

$$u(\boldsymbol{q}) = f(u_1(\boldsymbol{q}_1), \cdots, u_G(\boldsymbol{q}_G)),$$

where the $f(\cdot)$ is some increasing function that allows for interactions between sub-utility functions.

8.3 Conditional and Group Demands

Write the budget constraint as $\boldsymbol{p}'\boldsymbol{q} = M$, where $\boldsymbol{p} = [p_1, \cdots, p_n]'$ is the price vector and M is the total expenditure ("income" for short). Maximising utility function $u(\boldsymbol{q})$ subject to this budget constraint yields the unconditional demand equations:

$$q_i = q_i(M, \boldsymbol{P}), \text{ for } i = 1, \cdots, n.$$

These demand equations satisfy demand homogeneity and symmetry.

Under (8.1), maximising $u(\boldsymbol{q})$ subject to $\boldsymbol{p}'\boldsymbol{q} = M$ is equivalent to maximising each of the G sub-utility functions $u_g(\boldsymbol{q}_g)$ subject to the sub-budget constraint $\boldsymbol{p}_g'\boldsymbol{q}_g = M_g$, where $\boldsymbol{p}_g$ is the price vector of goods within $\boldsymbol{S}_g$ and M_g is group expenditure. This yields the demand equation for $i \in \boldsymbol{S}_g$ of the form

$$q_i = \tilde{q}_i(M_g, \boldsymbol{p}_g). \tag{8.2}$$

This shows that the demand for good $i \in \boldsymbol{S}_g$ depends on group expenditure M_g and prices of goods confined to the group $\boldsymbol{S}_g$. As the prices of goods outside the group play no role, demand equations of the form (8.2) are convenient as they are confined to variables pertaining only to the group to which the good belongs. Equation (8.2) is described as a conditional demand equation as it refers to the allocation of group expenditure to the goods within the group.

Next, the group demand equation deals with the allocation of income to groups. However, maximising the utility in (8.1) subject to budget constraint $\boldsymbol{p}'\boldsymbol{q} = M$ cannot give these group demand equations immediately as the price vector $\boldsymbol{p}$ contains prices of all n goods individually; instead, it gives unconditional demand equations of the form in $q_i = q_i(M, \boldsymbol{p})$. To obtain the group demand with a single price index for each of the groups, Gorman (1959) proposed two alternative conditions under which the group price indexes exist. The first is that the sub-utility function $u_g(\boldsymbol{q}_g)$ is homogeneous of degree one in $\boldsymbol{q}_g$; that is, the income elasticities for goods in $\boldsymbol{S}_g$ are the same, which amounts to homotheticity. The second condition is that each sub-utility function is additively separable, as given by the block independence specification in Eq. (8.1). It is to be noted that either one of these two conditions is necessary and sufficient for the existence of the price indexes of the groups.

Under either of Gorman's two conditions, there exists the price index $P_g = P(\boldsymbol{p}_g)$ and quantity index $Q_g = Q_g(\boldsymbol{q}_g)$ for group g. The group budget constraint for g is then written as $P_g Q_g = M_g$ and the total budget constraint becomes $\sum_{g=1}^{G} P_g Q_g = M$. Maximising total utility as defined by Eq. (8.1) subject to this total budget constraint yields the group demand equations

$$Q_g = Q_g(M, P_1, \cdots, P_G), \quad g = 1, \cdots, G, \tag{8.3}$$

in which the quantity demanded of the group depends on income and the price indexes of the G groups.

For the two-stage approach to be consistent, when the group and conditional demand equations are combined we should retrieve the original unconditional demand equations. To set this out formally, we multiply both sides of Eq. (8.3) by P_g to give $M_g = P_g \cdot Q_g(M, P_1, \cdots, P_G)$, and then substitute this into (8.2) to yield

$$q_i = \tilde{q}_i\left(P_g \cdot Q_g(M, P_1, \cdots, P_G), \boldsymbol{p}_g\right) = \overline{\overline{q}}_i\left(M, P_1, \cdots, P_G, \mathbf{p}_g\right).$$

If $\overline{\overline{q}}_i(\cdot) = q_i(\cdot)$, the original unconditional demand equation $q_i = q_i(M, \boldsymbol{p})$, then the two-stage budgeting approach can be described as being internally consistent.

It is to be noted that Gorman proceeds under the requirement of a single price index for each of the groups. The differential approach, to be described below, does not involve the restrictive conditions of homotheticity nor additivity of the sub-utility functions.

8.4 Differential Demands

As before, let p_i and q_i be the price and quantity demanded of good i, so that p_iq_i is expenditure on the good and if there are n goods, $M = \Sigma_{i=1}^{n} p_iq_i$ is income. Furthermore, let $w_i = \frac{p_iq_i}{M}$ be share of good i in total expenditure, which is known as the "budget share" of this good. These w_i are pure numbers, non-negative and have a unit sum. As the budget share represents spending on the good relative to all spending, it measures its economic importance as revealed by observed behaviour of the consumer. The change in the budget share can be decomposed into quantity, price and income components: $dw_i = w_i d(\log q_i) + w_i d(\log p_i) - w_i d(\log M)$.

The differential of the budget constraint, $M = \Sigma_{i=1}^{n} p_iq_i$, is $dM = \Sigma_{i=1}^{n}(p_i dq_i + q_i dp_i)$, or if we use the identity $d(\log x) = \frac{dx}{x}, x > 0$, $d(\log M) = d(\log Q) + d(\log P)$, where

$$d(\log Q) = \sum_{i=1}^{n} w_i d(\log q_i), \quad d(\log P) = \sum_{i=1}^{n} w_i d(\log p_i)$$

are Divisia indexes of quantities and prices. Thus, the change in income can be decomposed into a quantity index, $d(\log Q)$, and a price index, $d(\log P)$. The quantity index is a budget-share weighted mean of the growth in the n goods, and similarly for the price index. The weighting by the budget shares means that these indexes are representative of the relative economic importance of the individual goods. It follows that the change in money income deflated by the price index equals the quantity index, $d(\log M) - d(\log P) = d(\log Q)$. Accordingly, the quantity index defined by $d(\log Q)$ measures the change in the consumer's real income.

The consumer is taken to choose the basket $q_1, \cdots, q_n$ to maximise utility subject to the budget constraint. This leads to a demand equation for good i of the form $q_i = q_i(M, p_1, \cdots, p_n)$, which can be expressed in differential form as

$$dq_i = \frac{\partial q_i}{\partial M} dM + \sum_{j=1}^{n} \frac{\partial q_i}{\partial p_j} dp_j.$$

As shown in the next chapter, this can be expressed as

$$w_i d(\log q_i) = \theta_i d(\log Q) + \sum_{j=1}^{n} \pi_{ij} d(\log p_j). \tag{8.4}$$

Here, $\theta_i = \frac{\partial(p_iq_i)}{\partial M}$ is the ith marginal share; $d(\log Q) = \sum_{i=1}^{n} w_i d(\log q_i)$ is change in real income, as measured by the volume index; and $\pi_{ij} = \frac{p_ip_j}{M}\frac{\partial q_i^*}{\partial p_j}$ is the $(i,j)^{th}$ Slutsky coefficient, where $\frac{\partial q_i^*}{\partial p_j} = \frac{\partial q_i}{\partial p_j} + q_j \frac{\partial q_i}{\partial M}$ is the corresponding substitution effect.

The substitution term of Eq. (8.4) is expressed in absolute price changes $d(\log p_j)$. Alternatively, it can be written in relative prices by defining the Frisch (1932) price index that uses marginal shares as weights, $d(\log P') = \sum_{i=1}^{n} \theta_i d(\log p_i)$, and then using this as the deflator of the nominal price changes: $d\left(\log \frac{p_j}{P'}\right) = d\left(\log p_j\right) - d(\log P')$. The demand equation for good i then becomes

$$w_i d(\log q_i) = \theta_i d(\log Q) + \sum_{j=1}^{n} \nu_{ij} d\left(\log \frac{p_j}{P'}\right). \tag{8.5}$$

In the price term, the coefficient of the jth relative price is defined as $\nu_{ij} = \frac{\lambda u^{ij} p_i p_j}{M}$, where λ is the marginal utility of income and u^{ij} is the $(i,j)^{th}$ element of the inverse of the Hessian matrix of the utility function, $\boldsymbol{U}^{-1} = \left[\frac{\partial^2 u}{\partial q_i \partial q_j}\right]^{-1} = [u^{ij}]$. The new price coefficients ν_{ij} carry information about utility interactions of goods via u^{ij} and satisfy the constraint $\sum_{j=1}^{n} \nu_{ij} = \phi \theta_i$, where $\phi = \left(\frac{\partial \log \lambda}{\partial \log M}\right)^{-1}$ is the income flexibility, the reciprocal of the income elasticity of the marginal utility of income.

8.5 Aggregating to Group Demand

This and next section derive the demand for groups and for goods within the group. As before, let the n goods be separated into $G < n$ groups denoted by $\boldsymbol{S}_1, \cdots, \boldsymbol{S}_G$. When the G groups are block independent in the utility function, as in Eq. (8.1), the Hessian $\boldsymbol{U}$ and its inverse are both block-diagonal. Thus, the price coefficients in (8.5) for goods in different groups vanish, $\nu_{ij} = 0$ for $i \in \boldsymbol{S}_g$, $j \in \boldsymbol{S}_h$, $g \neq h$. The demand Eq. (8.5) for good $i \in \boldsymbol{S}_g$ then becomes

$$w_i d(\log q_i) = \theta_i d(\log Q) + \sum_{j \in \boldsymbol{S}_g} \nu_{ij} d\left(\log \frac{p_j}{P'}\right), \tag{8.6}$$

so only the relative prices of goods within the same group as good i play a role in the substitution term. The constraint $\sum_{j=1}^{n} \nu_{ij} = \phi \theta_i$ now takes the form $\sum_{j \in \boldsymbol{S}_g} \nu_{ij} = \phi \theta_i, i \in \boldsymbol{S}_g, g = 1, \cdots, G$.

Define the group budget and marginal shares:

$$W_g = \sum_{i \in \boldsymbol{S}_g} w_i, \quad \Theta_g = \sum_{i \in \boldsymbol{S}_g} \theta_i,$$

and the conditional shares for $i \in \boldsymbol{S}_g$ (that is, the within-group):

$$w_i^g = \frac{w_i}{W_g}, \quad \theta_i^g = \frac{\theta_i}{\Theta_g}.$$

The group budget share is the proportion of total expenditure absorbed by the group, $W_g = \sum_{i \in \boldsymbol{S}_g} p_i q_i / M$, and the conditional budget share is the proportion of group expenditure devoted to the ith member of the group, $w_i^g = p_i q_i / \sum_{i \in S_g} p_i q_i$. Similarly, the group marginal share is $\Theta_g = \partial(\sum_{i \in S_g} p_i q_i)/\partial M$ and the conditional marginal share is $\theta_i^g = \partial(p_i q_i)/\partial\left(\sum_{i \in S_g} p_i q_i\right), i \in S_g$. This θ_i^g answers the question when income increases by one-dollar resulting in a certain additional amount (Θ_g) of spending on group g as a whole, what fraction of this additional spending is devoted to good $\in S_g$? The Divisia volume index and the Frisch price index for the group are

$$d(\log Q_g) = \sum_{i \in S_g} w_i^g d(\log q_i), \quad d(\log P'_g) = \sum_{i \in S_g} \theta_i^g d(\log p_i).$$

As set out in the next chapter, the demand equation for S_g as a group is

$$W_g d(\log Q_g) = \Theta_g d(\log Q) + \phi \Theta_g d\left(\log \frac{P'_g}{P'}\right). \tag{8.7}$$

The demand for S_g accordingly depends on real income and the relative price of the group $d\left(\log P'_g/P'\right)$. The relative prices of other groups play no role under block independence.

8.6 Within-Group Demands

If the set of goods S_g is block independent in the utility function, the conditional demand for good $i \in S_g$ is a function of the volume of S_g as a whole and the prices of goods that are members of this group. That is, the conditional demand equation contains only variables pertaining to the group to which the good belongs. This section derives the conditional demand equation.

Combine Eqs. (8.6) and (8.7) to eliminate the Divisia volume index $d(\log Q)$, and then divide both sides by W_g to give:

$$w_i^g d(\log q_i) = \theta_i^g d\left(\log Q_g\right) + \sum_{j \in S_g} \nu_{ij}^g d\left(\log \frac{p_j}{P'_g}\right), \tag{8.8}$$

where $\nu_{ij}^g = \nu_{ij}/W_g$ is a new price coefficient. From the constraint $\sum_{j \in S_g} \nu_{ij} = \phi\theta_i, i \in S_g$, the ν_{ij}^g's satisfy

$$\sum_{j\in S_g}\nu_{ij}^g=\phi\eta_g\theta_i^g,\quad i\in S_g, \tag{8.9}$$

where $\eta_g = \Theta_g/W_g$ is the income elasticity of group g. Eq. (8.8) is the relative price version of the conditional demand for $i \in S_g$. The variables on the right are $d(\log Q_g)$ and $d(\log \frac{p_j}{P'_g}), j\in S_g$, which are now confined exclusively to the group to which good i belongs.

Using $d\left(\log P'_g\right)=\sum_{i\in S_g}\theta_i^g d(\log p_i)$ and (8.9), Eq. (8.8) can be expressed in absolute prices as

$$w_i^g d(\log q_i)=\theta_i^g d\left(\log Q_g\right)+\sum_{j\in S_g}\pi_{ij}^g d\left(\log p_j\right), \tag{8.10}$$

where $\pi_{ij}^g=\nu_{ij}^g-\phi\eta_g\theta_i^g\theta_j^g$ is the $(i,j)^{th}$ conditional Slutsky coefficient. It can be easily shown from Eq. (8.9) and definition $\nu_{ij}^g=\nu_{ij}/W_g$ that these π_{ij}^g's satisfy homogeneity and symmetry:

$$\sum_{j\in S_g}\pi_{ij}^g=0,\quad i\in S_g;\quad \pi_{ij}^g=\pi_{ji}^g,\quad i,j\in S_g.$$

Therefore, Eq. (8.10) is the absolute price version of the conditional demand for $i \in S_g$.

8.7 Alcohol Demand

To illustrate the econometric application of group demand and conditional demand, this section and the next examines alcoholic beverages—beer, wine, and spirits. There are at least three reasons to study the economics of alcohol consumption: (1) The magnitude of spending on alcohol by consumers; (2) the scientific challenge to determine whether conventional microeconomic theory is applicable to the case of alcohol demand; and (3) for the purpose of informing public policy in the setting of alcohol tax rates.

Alcohol is consumed worldwide, with Islamic countries being the only major exception where alcohol is prohibited/avoided for religious reasons. In many countries drinking alcohol absorbs a non-trivial part of the consumer's budget—drinking accounts for more than 10 per cent of spending on food in the United States, for example. This is not an isolated case, as will be revealed in the next chapter. The intriguing characteristic of worldwide drinking patterns is the substantial diversity across countries. To what extent can this type of diversity be explained by cross-country differences in incomes and prices? This is one challenge faced by the

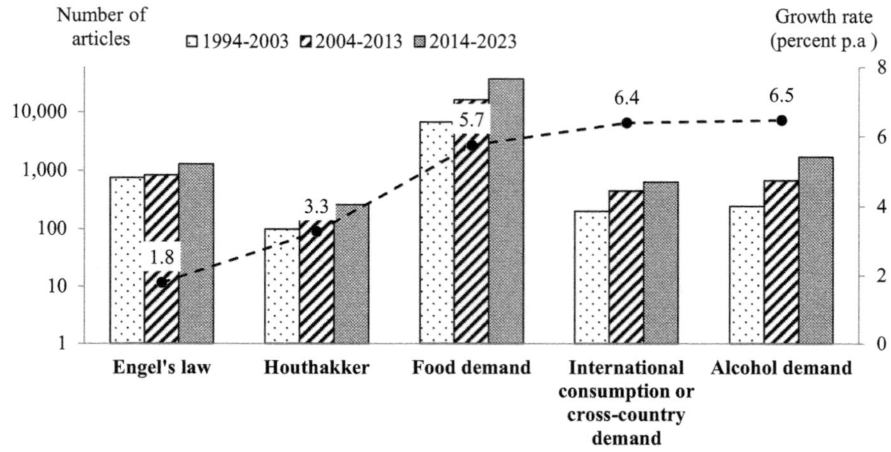

Fig. 8.1 What has been written. *Note*: This figure gives the number of items resulting from keyword searches conducted in June 2024 using Google Scholar. Houthakker refers to the article by H. S. Houthakker, "An International Comparison of Household Expenditure Patterns, Commemorating the Centenary of Engel's Law." *Econometrica*, 1957, 25: 532–51. The right-hand axis gives the annual growth rate in the number of articles, calculated as 100 times the logarithm of the ratio of the number of articles published in the period 2014–2023 to that in 1984–1993 (not included in the figure), divided by 30. *Source*: Clements et al. (2020)

economic approach to alcohol consumption patterns. Intoxication is another related issue—when consumed above a certain amount, alcohol affects cognitive abilities.

Governments of all persuasions like to tax alcohol consumption for two reasons. The first is because of the social problems associated with excessive drinking and the resources devoted to policies to solve these problems. Second, alcohol can provide a "cheap" source of revenue to the government as consumption is easy to monitor and can be taxed at source such as a brewery. Here, the term "cheap" refers to low compliance costs of the tax. Another form of economic cost of a tax is its distortionary impact. This is likely to be low for alcohol taxes as consumption is usually thought to be price inelastic. Thus, a tax-induced higher price causes consumption to fall, but the fall is not too rapid, and as the tax base does not disappear too quickly, revenue for government increases.

There is a large literature dealing with the demand for alcoholic beverages. Figure 8.1 shows the number of articles published on five food-related concepts including alcohol demand. The number of articles on Engel's law and the famous article by Houthakker (1957) over the last three decades are presented in the first two terms of the horizontal axis. These numbers experienced modest growth rates of 1.8 and 3.3 per cent per annum, respectively. In the most recent decade, the number on "food demand" was about 10,000 with a growth rate of 5.7 per cent. Although the absolute number on "international consumption patterns" or "cross-country demand" is smaller than "food demand", it grew faster at 6.4 per cent. The last term refers to "alcohol demand", which is growing at 6.5 per cent per year. Research interest in this area is growing quite rapidly due to the association of alcohol with health issues and the heavy taxes usually imposed, as discussed above. Meta-studies of alcohol demand were discussed earlier in Chap. 2.

Assuming the alcoholic beverages group is separable in the consumer's utility function, there is a two-stage budgeting hierarchy that can be represented as follows. At stage 1, consumers allocate income into alcohol and non-alcohol, where the non-alcohol items are grouped together for simplicity. Alcohol expenditure is then divided into beer, wine, and spirits at stage 2.

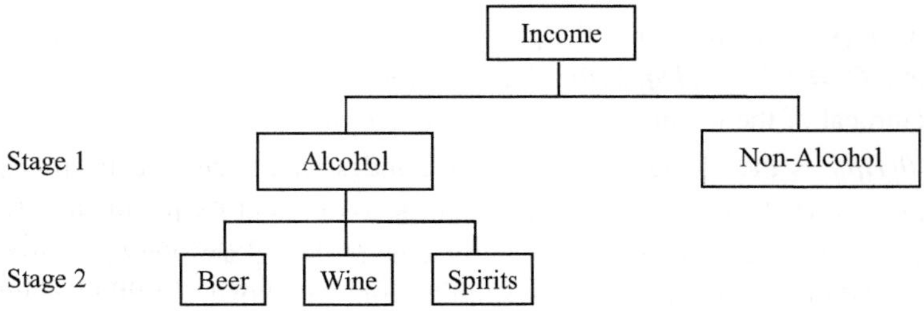

8.8 Beer, Wine, and Spirits in Australia

Clements and Johnson (1983) estimate the conditional and group demand for the three alcoholic beverages in Australia. They use conditional equations that are a slightly different version of those presented above. Recall the conditional demand for $i \in S_g$ is Eq. (8.10), $w_i^g d(\log q_i) = \theta_i^g d(\log Q_g) + \sum_{j \in S_g} \pi_{ij}^g d(\log p_j)$. Multiply by the group budget share W_g to give

$$w_i d(\log q_i) = \theta_i^g \left[W_g d(\log Q_g)\right] + \sum_{j \in S_g} \pi_{ij}^{g\prime} d(\log p_j).$$

Here, $w_i = W_g w_i^g$ is the "unconditional" budget share, θ_i^g is the conditional marginal share and $\pi_{ij}^{g\prime} = W_g \pi_{ij}^g$ is a modified conditional Slutsky coefficient. The properties of the modified system are the same as before.

To apply the above equation to finite-change data from year $t - 1$ to t, it is necessary to make some adjustments. First, w_i is replaced with $\overline{w}_{it} = (1/2) \times (w_{it} + w_{it-1})$. Second, infinitesimal changes are replaced with finite changes, that is, $d(\log x)$ with $Dx_t = \log x_t - \log x_{t-1}$. Third, to account for all other factors, a zero-mean disturbance, ε_{it}, is added to the equation. Finally, the coefficients θ_i^g and $\pi_{ij}^{g\prime}$ are taken to be constants. With S_g denoting the set of the three beverages, the estimating equation for $i \in S_g$ is

$$\overline{w}_{it}Dq_{it} = \theta_i^g\left[\overline{W}_{gt}DQ_{gt}\right] + \sum_{j\in S_g}\pi_{ij}^{g\prime}Dp_{jt} + \varepsilon_{it}.$$

The group demand equation is (8.7), $W_g d(\log Q_g) = \Theta_g d(\log Q) + \phi\Theta_g d(\log \frac{P_g'}{P'})$. With similar adjustments to those above, the estimating equation is

$$\bar{W}_{gt}DQ_{gt} = \Theta_g DQ_t + \phi\Theta_g(DP'_{gt} - DP'_t) + E_{gt}.$$

Here, $\overline{W}_{gt}DQ_{gt}$ is as defined in the previous paragraph; Θ_g is the marginal share of group g; $DQ_t = \sum_{i=1}^{n}\overline{w}_{it}Dq_{it}$ is the change in real income; ϕ is the income flexibility (the reciprocal of the income elasticity of the marginal utility of income); $DP'_{gt} = \sum_{i\in S_g}\theta_i^g Dp_{it}$ is the change in Frisch price index of g; $DP'_t = \sum_{i=1}^{n}\theta_i Dp_{it}$ with $\theta_i = \partial(p_i q_i)/\partial M$, the unconditional marginal share of i; and E_{gt} is a disturbance term with an expected value of zero. The coefficients Θ_g and ϕ are treated as constants.

The coefficient estimates and elasticities for the above modified conditional demands are presented in panel A of Table 8.1. The income elasticity of beer is 0.8, making it a conditional necessity. The value of the wine elasticity is similar, while that for spirits is substantially higher at 2.0, making it a conditional luxury. Spirits are relatively expensive in Australia, which probably accounts for their perceived luxuriousness. The own-price elasticities on the diagonal are −0.09, −0.39, and −0.41, meaning each beverage is price inelastic within the group. As the cross-price elasticities are relatively low, there is only a modest degree of substitutability between the beverages. Panel B of the table shows the estimates of group demand. The income elasticity of the group is close to unity and the price elasticity is −0.58, making alcohol price inelastic.

The unconditional demands in panel C of Table 8.1, $\overline{w}_{it}Dq_{it} = \theta_i DQ_t + \sum_{j\in S_g}\pi_{ij}Dp_{jt} + \pi_{io}Dp_{ot} + \mu_{it}$, are derived from their conditional and group counterparts. Here, π_{ij} and π_{io} are unconditional Slutsky coefficients; Dp_{ot} is the change in the price of all other goods; and μ_{it} is a disturbance term. The income elasticities are similar to conditional ones due to the group income elasticity being close to unity. The own-price elasticity for beverage i measures the response of consumption to its price change. In this context, the unconditional price change has two effects:

1. When the price increases, the direct effect via the conditional equation (which holds constant total alcohol) lowers consumption.
2. The indirect effect is to lower total alcohol consumption, which, in turn, further decreases the consumption of beverage i. Thus, the indirect effect makes the unconditional own-price elasticity more negative than the conditional one.

Specifically, the own-price elasticities for the three beverages decline from −0.09, −0.39, and −0.41 on account of conditional demand to −0.36, −0.43, −0.74, when total alcohol consumption is allowed to vary according to unconditional demand.

Table 8.1 Alcohol demand, Australia

Coefficient estimates | Elasticities

A. Conditional Demand

$$\overline{w}_{it}Dq_{it} = \theta_i^g\left[\overline{W}_{gt}DQ_{gt}\right] + \sum_{j\in S_g}\pi_{ij}^{g\prime}Dp_{jt} + \varepsilon_{it}$$

Beverage	Budget share w_i	Marginal share θ_i^g	Slutsky coefficients × 100			Income elasticity $\theta_i^g W_g/w_i$	Price elasticities		
			$\pi_{i1}^{g\prime}$	$\pi_{i2}^{g\prime}$	$\pi_{i3}^{g\prime}$		$\frac{\pi_{i1}^{g\prime}}{w_i}$	$\frac{\pi_{i2}^{g\prime}}{w_i}$	$\frac{\pi_{i3}^{g\prime}}{w_i}$
Beer	0.0424	0.590	−0.390	0.150	0.240	0.83	−0.09	0.04	0.06
Wine	0.0076	0.099		−0.293	0.144	0.78	0.20	−0.39	0.19
Spirits	0.0094	0.311			−0.384	1.97	0.26	0.15	−0.41

B. Group Demand

$$\overline{W}_{gt}DQ_{gt} = \Theta_g DQ_t + \phi\Theta_g\left(DP'_{gt} - DP'_t\right) + E_{gt}$$

Group	Budget share W_g	Marginal share Θ_g	Income flexibility ϕ	Income elasticity Θ_g/W_g	Own-price elasticity $\phi\Theta_g/W_g$
Alcohol	0.0594	0.0576	−0.595	0.97	−0.58

C. Unconditional Demand

$$\overline{w}_{it}Dq_{it} = \theta_i DQ_t + \sum_{j\in S_g}\pi_{ij}Dp_{jt} + \pi_{io}Dp_{ot} + \mu_{it}$$

Beverage	Budget share w_i	Marginal share θ_i	Slutsky coefficients × 100				Income elasticity θ_i/w_i	Price elasticities			
			π_{i1}	π_{i2}	π_{i3}	π_{io}		$\frac{\pi_{i1}}{w_i}$	$\frac{\pi_{i2}}{w_i}$	$\frac{\pi_{i3}}{w_i}$	$\frac{\pi_{io}}{w_i}$
Beer	0.0424	0.0340	−1.514	−0.039	−0.353	1.906	0.80	−0.36	−0.01	−0.08	0.45
Wine	0.0076	0.0057		−0.325	0.044	0.319	0.75	−0.05	−0.43	0.06	0.42
Spirits	0.0094	0.0179			−0.697	1.006	1.91	−0.38	0.05	−0.74	1.07

Notes

1. *Panel A*: The left side of the panel contains estimates using annual Australian data, 1955–1977, of the conditional demand equation for beverage $i \in S_g$ at time t, $\overline{w}_{it}Dq_{it} = \theta_i^g\left[\overline{W}_{gt}DQ_{gt}\right] + \sum_{j\in S_g}\pi_{ij}^{g\prime}Dp_{jt} + \varepsilon_{it}$. The variable on the left is $\overline{w}_{it}Dq_{it}$. Here, $\overline{w}_{it} = (1/2)(w_{it} + w_{it-1})$ is the arithmetic average of the budget share of alcoholic beverage i in years t and t-1. The term $Dq_{it} = \log q_{it} - \log q_{it-1}$ is the log-change in the quantity demanded. There are three terms on the right

(continued)

of the equation. The first is $\theta_i^g\left[\overline{W}_{gt}DQ_{gt}\right]$, with θ_i^g the conditional marginal share of $i \in \boldsymbol{S}_g$ and $\overline{W}_{gt}DQ_{gt} = \sum_{i\in \boldsymbol{S}_g}\overline{w}_{it}Dq_{it}$. The second term is $\sum_{j\in \boldsymbol{S}_g}\pi_{ij}^{g\prime}Dp_{jt}$, where $\pi_{ij}^{g\prime}$ is a modified conditional Slutsky coefficient and $Dp_{jt} = \log p_{jt} - \log p_{jt-1}$ is the log-change in the price of j. Finally, ε_{it} is a disturbance term with zero mean. The right side of the panel contains the corresponding elasticities (evaluated at sample means of the budget shares).

2. *Panel B*: The left side of the panel contains estimates of the group demand equation for alcohol as a whole at time t, $\overline{W}_{gt}DQ_{gt} = \Theta_g DQ_t + \phi\Theta_g\left(DP'_{gt} - DP'_t\right) + E_{gt}$. The term on the left of this equation is defined above. The first term on the right is $\Theta_g DQ_t$, where Θ_g is the marginal share of the group and $DQ_t = \sum_{i=1}^n \overline{w}_{it}Dq_{it}$ is the change in real income. The second term is $\phi\Theta_g\left(DP'_{gt} - DP'_t\right)$, where ϕ is the income flexibility (the reciprocal of the income elasticity of the marginal utility of income) and $DP'_{gt} - DP'_t$ is the change in the Frisch relative price of g, with $DP'_{gt} = \sum_{i\in \boldsymbol{S}_g}\theta_i^g Dp_{it}$, $DP'_t = \sum_{i=1}^n \theta_i Dp_{it}$ and $\theta_i = \partial(p_i q_i)/\partial M$ the unconditional marginal share of i. The third term is the disturbance E_{gt}. Elasticities are given on the right side of the panel.

3. *Panel C*: The left side of this panel contains the corresponding estimates of the unconditional demand equation for beverage i, $\overline{w}_{it}Dq_{it} = \theta_i DQ_t + \sum_{j\in \boldsymbol{S}_g}\pi_{ij}Dp_{jt} + \pi_{io}Dp_{ot} + \mu_{it}$. Here, π_{ij} and π_{io} are unconditional Slutsky coefficients, defined as $\pi_{ij} = \nu_{ij} - \phi\theta_i\theta_j = W_g\pi_{ij}^g + \phi\Theta_g(1-\Theta_g)\theta_i^g\theta_j^g, i, j \in \boldsymbol{S}_g$; and $\pi_{io} = -\phi\theta_i\theta_0$, $i \in \boldsymbol{S}_g$, where the subscript o refers to all other goods. The variable Dp_{ot} is the log-change in the price of all other goods, while μ_{it} is a disturbance term. The coefficients here are obtained by substituting the right-hand side of the group equation for $\overline{W}_{gt}DQ_{gt}$ on the right of the conditional equations. Elasticities are given on the right side of the panel.

4. Intercepts (which represent trend-like changes in consumption) are included, but not presented.

Source: Clements and Johnson (1983).

References

Clements KW, Johnson LW (1983) The demand for beer, wine, and spirits: a systemwide analysis. J Bus 56:273–304
Clements KW, Lan Y, Liu H (2020) Understanding alcohol consumption across countries. Appl Econ 52:4421–4439
Frisch R (1932) New methods of measuring marginal utility. J. C. B. Mohr, Tubingen
Gorman WM (1959) Separability utility and aggregation. Econometrica 27:469–481
Houthakker HS (1957) An international comparison of household expenditure patterns, commemorating the centenary of Engel's law. Econometrica 25:532–551
Pigou AC (1910) A method of determining the numerical value of demand elasticities. Econ J 20: 636–640

Chapter 9
Group Demand II: Further Results and Details

9.1 More on Multi-Stage Budgeting

Some further details on Gorman's (1959) results are as follows. Suppose the price index for group g is $P_g(\boldsymbol{p}_g)$, where $\boldsymbol{p}_g$ is the price vector of goods within group g, $g = 1, \ldots, G$, and M_g is group expenditure/income. Gorman shows that the indirect sub-utility function for group g takes the form

$$v_g(M_g, \boldsymbol{p}_g) = G_g\left(\frac{M_g}{P_g(\boldsymbol{p}_g)}\right) + Q_g(\boldsymbol{p}_g), \tag{9.1}$$

where $Q_g(\boldsymbol{p}_g)$ is homogeneous of degree zero in $\boldsymbol{p}_g$. Equation (9.1) is known as the "generalised polar form".

As indicated in the previous chapter, Gorman proposed two alternative conditions for the existence of the index $P_g(\boldsymbol{p}_g)$. For convenience, we reverse the order of the two conditions and first discuss the second condition relating to separability. That is, if the G indirect sub-utility functions take the full generalised form (9.1), the functions are required to be additively separable in the overall indirect utility function. The alternative existence condition relates to homogeneity. This requires that indirect sub-utility functions, Eq. (9.1) for $g = 1, \cdots, G$, do not contain the term $Q_g(\boldsymbol{p}_g)$ and so take the simpler form $v_g(M_g, \boldsymbol{p}_g) = G_g\left(\frac{M_g}{P_g(\boldsymbol{p}_g)}\right)$. This simpler form implies homothetic preferences. Taken together, the two conditions state that groups are either additively separable in the (indirect) utility function or homothetic. It is also worth noting that the two conditions can be applied to the G groups in a simultaneous manner; that is, some groups can be separable and others homothetic.

Many studies use Gorman's approach. Prominent applications to food demand include Edgerton (1997) and Edgerton et al. (1996), who follow the homothetic condition. Carpentier and Guyomard (2001) relax the homothetic condition with an approximation approach.

K. W. Clements et al., *Short-cut Demand Elasticities and Other Convenient Approaches to Consumer Demand*, https://doi.org/10.1007/978-981-96-3588-7_9

9.2 Differential Demands

As discussed in earlier chapters, the consumer is taken to choose the basket $q_1, \cdots, q_n$ to maximise utility subject to the budget constraint. This leads to a demand equation for good i of the form $q_i = q_i(M, p_1, \cdots, p_n)$, which can be expressed in differential form as

$$dq_i = \frac{\partial q_i}{\partial M} dM + \sum_{j=1}^{n} \frac{\partial q_i}{\partial p_j} dp_j.$$

The Slutsky equation is $\frac{\partial q_i}{\partial p_j} = \frac{\partial q_i^*}{\partial p_j} - q_j \frac{\partial q_i}{\partial M}$ with $\frac{\partial q_i^*}{\partial p_j}$ the substitution effect. This can be used to write the above as

$$dq_i = \frac{\partial q_i}{\partial M}\left(dM - \sum_{j=1}^{n} q_j dp_j\right) + \sum_{j=1}^{n} \frac{\partial q_i^*}{\partial p_j} dp_j.$$

Multiplying both sides of the above equation by $\frac{1}{q_i}$ and using $d(\log x) = \frac{dx}{x}$, we obtain

$$d(\log q_i) = \frac{M}{q_i}\frac{\partial q_i}{\partial M}\left[d(\log M) - \sum_{j=1}^{n} \frac{p_j q_j}{M} d(\log p_j)\right] + \sum_{j=1}^{n} \frac{p_j}{q_i}\frac{\partial q_i^*}{\partial p_j} d(\log p_j).$$

The term in the square brackets on the right-hand side is the change in money income relative to a weighted sum of the n price changes. As the weights are the budget shares, this weighted sum is the Divisia price index $d(\log P)$. It then follows from the differential version of the budget constraint, $d(\log M) = d(\log Q) + d(\log P)$, that the term in square brackets is the change in real income $d(\log Q)$. Thus, we write the equation as

$$d(\log q_i) = \eta_i d(\log Q) + \sum_{j=1}^{n} \eta_{ij} d(\log p_j), \tag{9.2}$$

where $\eta_i = \frac{\left(\frac{\partial q_i}{q_i}\right)}{\left(\frac{\partial M}{M}\right)} = \frac{\partial(\log q_i)}{\partial(\log M)}$ is the income elasticity of good i and $\eta_{ij} = \left(\frac{p_j}{q_i}\right)\frac{\partial q_i^*}{\partial p_j} = \frac{\partial(\log q_i^*)}{\partial(\log p_j)}$ is the $(i,j)^{th}$ price elasticity (income compensated). Multiplying both sides of Eq. (9.2) by the budget share $w_i = \frac{p_i q_i}{M}$ gives the differential demand equation for good i:

$$w_i d(\log q_i) = \theta_i d(\log Q) + \sum_{j=1}^{n} \pi_{ij} d(\log p_j).$$

9.3 Group Demand

The demand equation for good $i \in \boldsymbol{S}_g$ is (8.6), which we reproduce:

$$w_i d(\log q_i) = \theta_i d(\log Q) + \sum_{j \in \boldsymbol{S}_g} \nu_{ij} d\left(\log \frac{p_j}{P'}\right). \tag{9.3}$$

Sum both sides of Eq. (9.3) over $i \in \boldsymbol{S}_g$:

$$\sum_{i \in \boldsymbol{S}_g} w_i d(\log q_i) = \sum_{i \in \boldsymbol{S}_g} \theta_i d(\log Q) + \sum_{i \in \boldsymbol{S}_g} \sum_{j \in \boldsymbol{S}_g} \nu_{ij} d\left(\log \frac{p_j}{P'}\right).$$

Using $w_i = W_g w_i^g$, $W_g = \sum_{i \in \boldsymbol{S}_g} w_i$ and $d\left(\log Q_g\right) = \sum_{i \in \boldsymbol{S}_g} \frac{w_i}{W_g} d(\log q_i)$, the left-hand side becomes $W_g d(\log Q_g)$. On the right, the income term becomes $\Theta_g d(\log Q)$, with $\Theta_g = \sum_{i \in \boldsymbol{S}_g} \theta_i$, while the substitution term is

$$\sum_{i \in \boldsymbol{S}_g} \sum_{j \in \boldsymbol{S}_g} \nu_{ij} d\left(\log \frac{p_j}{P'}\right) = \sum_{i \in \boldsymbol{S}_g} \sum_{j \in \boldsymbol{S}_g} \nu_{ij} d(\log p_j) - \sum_{i \in \boldsymbol{S}_g} \sum_{j \in \boldsymbol{S}_g} \nu_{ij} d(\log P'). \tag{9.4}$$

The first term on the right of the above can be expressed as

$$\sum_{i \in \boldsymbol{S}_g} \sum_{j \in \boldsymbol{S}_g} \nu_{ij} d(\log p_j) = \sum_{j \in \boldsymbol{S}_g} \sum_{i \in \boldsymbol{S}_g} \nu_{ji} d(\log p_j) = \sum_{j \in \boldsymbol{S}_g} \phi \theta_j d(\log p_j) = \phi \Theta_g d\left(\log P'_g\right).$$

The first equals sign of the above is based on the symmetry of the ν_{ij}'s, the second follows from constraint $\sum_{j \in \boldsymbol{S}_g} \nu_{ij} = \phi \theta_i, i \in \boldsymbol{S}_g$, and the third uses $\theta_j = \theta_j^g \Theta_g$ and $d\left(\log P'_g\right) = \sum_{i \in \boldsymbol{S}_g} \theta_i^g d(\log p_i)$. In view of $\sum_{j \in \boldsymbol{S}_g} \nu_{ij} = \phi \theta_i, i \in \boldsymbol{S}_g$, $\sum_{i \in \boldsymbol{S}_g} \sum_{j \in \boldsymbol{S}_g} \nu_{ij} = \phi \sum_{i \in \boldsymbol{S}_g} \theta_i = \phi \Theta_g$. Thus, the last term on the right of Eq. (9.4) is

$$\sum_{i \in \boldsymbol{S}_g} \sum_{j \in \boldsymbol{S}_g} \nu_{ij} d(\log P') = \phi \Theta_g d(\log P').$$

Accordingly, the whole substitution term (9.4) simplifies to

$$\sum_{i \in \boldsymbol{S}_g} \sum_{j \in \boldsymbol{S}_g} \nu_{ij} d\left(\log \frac{p_j}{P'}\right) = \phi \Theta_g d\left(\log P'_g\right) - \phi \Theta_g d(\log P') = \phi \Theta_g d\left(\log \frac{P'_g}{P'}\right).$$

Retracing our steps, the demand equation for $\boldsymbol{S}_g$ as a group is

$$W_g d(\log Q_g) = \Theta_g d(\log Q) + \phi\Theta_g d\left(\log \frac{P'_g}{P'}\right).$$

9.4 Back to Ordinary Demands

Recall the conditional system for $\boldsymbol{S}_g$ in absolute-price form, that is, Eq. (8.10) for $i \in \boldsymbol{S}_g$, $w_i^g d(\log q_i) = \theta_i^g d(\log Q_g) + \sum_{j \in \boldsymbol{S}_g} \pi_{ij}^g d(\log p_j)$. Multiply both sides by W_g and use $W_g w_i^g = w_i$ to give

$$w_i d(\log q_i) = \theta_i^g W_g d(\log Q_g) + \sum_{j \in \boldsymbol{S}_g} W_g \pi_{ij}^g d(\log p_j).$$

For the term $W_g d(\log Q_g)$ on the right, substitute the right-hand side of the group demand given by (8.7), $W_g d(\log Q_g) = \Theta_g d(\log Q) + \phi\Theta_g d\left(\log \frac{P'_g}{P'}\right)$, which was also derived in the previous section. This yields

$$w_i d(\log q_i) = \theta_i^g \left[\Theta_g d(\log Q) + \phi\Theta_g d\left(\log \frac{P'_g}{P'}\right)\right] + \sum_{j \in \boldsymbol{S}_g} W_g \pi_{ij}^g d(\log p_j). \quad (9.5)$$

To simplify the relative price term, write the Frisch price index as $d(\log P') = \sum_{g=1}^{G} \Theta_g d(\log P'_g)$, where $d\left(\log P'_g\right) = \sum_{j \in \boldsymbol{S}_g} \theta_j^g d(\log p_j)$, as before. Thus,

$$d(\log P') = \sum_{g=1}^{G} \Theta_g d(\log P'_g) = \Theta_g \sum_{j \in \boldsymbol{S}_g} \theta_j^g d(\log p_j) + \sum_{j \notin \boldsymbol{S}_g} \theta_j d(\log p_j).$$

The term $\phi\Theta_g \theta_i^g d(\log \frac{P'_g}{P'})$ in Eq. (9.5) then becomes

$$\phi\Theta_g \theta_i^g d\left(\log \frac{P'_g}{P'}\right) = \phi\Theta_g \theta_i^g \left[(1 - \Theta_g) \sum_{j \in \boldsymbol{S}_g} \theta_j^g d(\log p_j) - \sum_{j \notin \boldsymbol{S}_g} \theta_j d(\log p_j)\right].$$

Substituting this into Eq. (9.5) and collecting terms gives

$$w_i d(\log q_i) = \theta_i d(\log Q) + \sum_{j \in S_g} [\phi \theta_i^g \theta_j^g \Theta_g (1 - \Theta_g) + W_g \pi_{ij}^g] d(\log p_j)$$
$$+ \sum_{j \notin S_g} - \phi \theta_i \theta_j d(\log p_j) = \theta_i d(\log Q) + \sum_j \pi_{ij} d(\log p_j).$$

The Slutsky coefficients here are defined as

$$\pi_{ij} = W_g \pi_{ij}^g + \phi \Theta_g (1 - \Theta_g) \theta_i^g \theta_j^g, \quad i, j \in S_g; \quad \pi_{ij} = -\phi \theta_i \theta_j, \quad i \in S_g, j \notin S_g.$$

It can be easily shown that these coefficients satisfy homogeneity and symmetry. In Table 8.1 the coefficient $\pi_{ij} = -\phi \theta_i \theta_j$, $i \in S_g$, $j \notin S_g$ was denoted by π_{io}.

The above three sections presented three types of demand equations—unconditional, group and conditional. These are summarised in Table 9.1.

9.5 Geometry of Drinking

The drinking pattern of alcohol can be illustrated with a simple geometric device. According to the Passport GMID Database (2005), in the USA the within-alcohol budget shares for beer, wine, and spirits are 51, 28, and 21 per cent, respectively. Thus, American drinkers allocate more than half of their alcohol spending to beer, while the remaining half is roughly equally divided between wine and spirits. As the three shares are non-negative with a unit sum, we can plot them in a tetrahedron, as in panel A of Fig. 9.1. As the USA spends more than 50 per cent on beer, it can be classified as a beer-drinking country. This is indicated in the figure by the point for the USA being located in the bottom left sub-triangle; all points in this sub-triangle correspond to a beer share of more than 50 per cent. The sub-triangles for wine and spirits correspond to the dominance of those beverages. In addition to these three sub-triangles, there is a fourth sub-triangle, the centre region where consumption is not dominated by any single beverage.

If a country falls in one of the three sub-triangles nearest to a vertex, its alcohol consumption is "intensive" in the relevant beverage. If a country is located in the centre sub-triangle, it is diversified as no beverage absorbs more than 50 per cent of the total. To emphasise the four different regions, panel B of Fig. 9.1 splits the overall triangle into the four sub-triangles. The budget share vector for each of 110 countries is located in one of the four regions, so countries are accordingly classified. Also displayed in this panel is the fraction of the 110 countries in each region. Thus, 41 per cent of countries are beer intensive, 12 per cent wine intensive, 11 per cent spirits intensive, and the remaining 36 per cent are diversified. Thus, beer can be dubbed the "global beverage". The interesting conclusion from this figure is the extent of "specialisation" in consumption, as only slightly more than one-third of countries diversify the composition of their drinking.

Table 9.1 Four types of demands

Concept	Expression	Interpretation
A. ***Unconditional demand***		
$w_i d(\log q_i) = \theta_i d(\log Q) + \sum_{j=1}^{n} \nu_{ij} d(\log p_j/P') = \theta_i d(\log Q) + \sum_{j=1}^{n} \pi_{ij} d(\log p_j)$		
What is allocated?	$M = \sum_{i=1}^{n} p_i q_i$	Total consumption expenditure
Number of goods	n	
Budget share of good i	$w_i = (p_i q_i)/M, \sum_{i=1}^{n} w_i = 1$	Share of total expenditure
Change in quantity of i	$d(\log q_i)$	
Change in total consumption	$d(\log Q) = \sum_{i=1}^{n} w_i d(\log q_i)$	Growth in volume index
Change in price of j	$d(\log p_j)$	
Marginal share of i	$\theta_i = \partial(p_i q_i)/\partial M, \sum_{i=1}^{n} \theta_i = 1$	
Price coefficient	$\nu_{ij} = \lambda u^{ij} p_i p_j / M, [u^{ij}] = [\partial^2 u/\partial q_i \partial q_j]^{-1}, \sum_{j=1}^{n} \nu_{ij} = \phi\theta_i$	
Marginal utility of income	$\lambda = \partial u/\partial M$, $u =$ utility	Shadow price of additional income
Income flexibility	$\phi = (\partial \log \lambda / \partial \log M)^{-1}$	Reciprocal of income elasticity of λ
Change in relative price of j	$d(\log p_j/P') = d(\log p_j) - \sum_{j=1}^{n} \theta_j d(\log p_j)$	
Slutsky coefficient	$\pi_{ij} = \nu_{ij} - \phi\theta_i\theta_j$	
Demand homogeneity	$\sum_{j=1}^{n} \pi_{ij} = 0, i = 1, \ldots, n$	
Slutsky symmetry	$\pi_{ij} = \pi_{ji}, i, j = 1, \ldots, n$	
B. ***Group demand under block independence***		
$W_g d(\log Q_g) = \Theta_g d(\log Q) + \phi\Theta_g d(\log P'_g/P')$		
What is allocated?	$M = \sum_{i=1}^{n} p_i q_i$	Total consumption expenditure
Number of groups	G	
Budget share of group g	$W_g = M_g/M, M_g = \sum_{i \in S_g} p_i q_i$, $S_g =$ goods in group g, $\sum_{g=1}^{G} W_g = 1$	Group share of total expenditure
Change in quantity of g	$d(\log Q_g) = \sum_{i \in S_g} w_i^g d(\log q_i), w_i^g = p_i q_i / M_g$	
Change in total consumption	$d(\log Q) = \sum_{g=1}^{G} W_g \, d(\log Q_g)$	Growth in volume index
Marginal share of g	$\Theta_g = \sum_{i \in S_g} \theta_i, \sum_{g=1}^{G} \Theta_g = 1$	
Price coefficient	$\phi\Theta_g, \sum_{g=1}^{G} \phi\Theta_g = \phi$	
Change in relative price of g	$d(\log P'_g/P') = \sum_{j \in S_g} \theta_j^g d(\log p_j) - \sum_{j=1}^{n} \theta_j d(\log p_j), \theta_j^g = \theta_j/\Theta_g$	

C. *Conditional demand*		
$w_i^g d(\log q_i) = \theta_i^g d(\log Q_g) + \sum_{j \in S_g} \nu_{ij}^g d\left(\log p_j / P_g'\right) = \theta_i^g d(\log Q_g) + \sum_{j \in S_g} \pi_{ij}^g d(\log p_j), i \in \boldsymbol{S}_g$		
What is allocated?	$M_g = \sum_{i \in s_g} p_i q_i$, $\boldsymbol{S}_g$= goods in group g	Group expenditure
Number of goods	n_g	
Budget share of good i	$w_i^g = p_i q_i / M_g, \sum_{i \in s_g} w_i^g = 1$	Share within group
Marginal share of i	$\theta_i^g = \partial (p_i q_i) / \partial M_g, \sum_{i \in S_g} \theta_i^g = 1$	
Price coefficient	$\nu_{ij}^g = \nu_{ij} / W_g, \sum_{j \in S_g} \nu_{ij}^g = \phi \Theta_g \theta_i^g / W_g$	
Change in relative price of j	$d\left(\log p_j / P_g'\right) = d(\log p_j) - \sum_{j \in S_g} \theta_j^g d(\log p_j)$	
Slutsky coefficient	$\pi_{ij}^g = \nu_{ij}^g - \phi \eta_g \theta_i^g \theta_j^g, \eta_g = \Theta_g / W_g$	
Demand homogeneity	$\sum_{j=1}^{n_g} \pi_{ij}^g = 0$	
Slutsky symmetry	$\pi_{ij}^g = \pi_{ji}^g, i, j = 1, \ldots, n_g$	
D. *Unconditional demand under block independence*		
$w_i d(\log q_i) = \theta_i d(\log Q) + \sum_{j \in S_g} \nu_{ij} d\left(\log p_j / P'\right) = \theta_i d(\log Q) + \sum_{j \in S_g} \pi_{ij} d(\log p_j) + \sum_{j \notin S_g} \pi_{ij} d(\log p_j)$		
Slutsky coefficient	$\pi_{ij} = \begin{cases} \nu_{ij} - \phi \theta_i \theta_j = W_g \pi_{ij}^g + \phi \Theta_g (1 - \Theta_g) \theta_i^g \theta_j^g, & i, j \in \boldsymbol{S}_g \\ - \phi \theta_i \theta_j = - \phi \Theta_g \Theta_h \theta_i^g \theta_j^h, & i \in \boldsymbol{S}_g, j \in \boldsymbol{S}_h, g \neq h \end{cases}$	
Demand homogeneity	$\sum_{j=1}^{n} \pi_{ij} = 0, i = 1, \ldots, n$	
Slutsky symmetry	$\pi_{ij} = \pi_{ji}, i, j = 1, \ldots, n$	

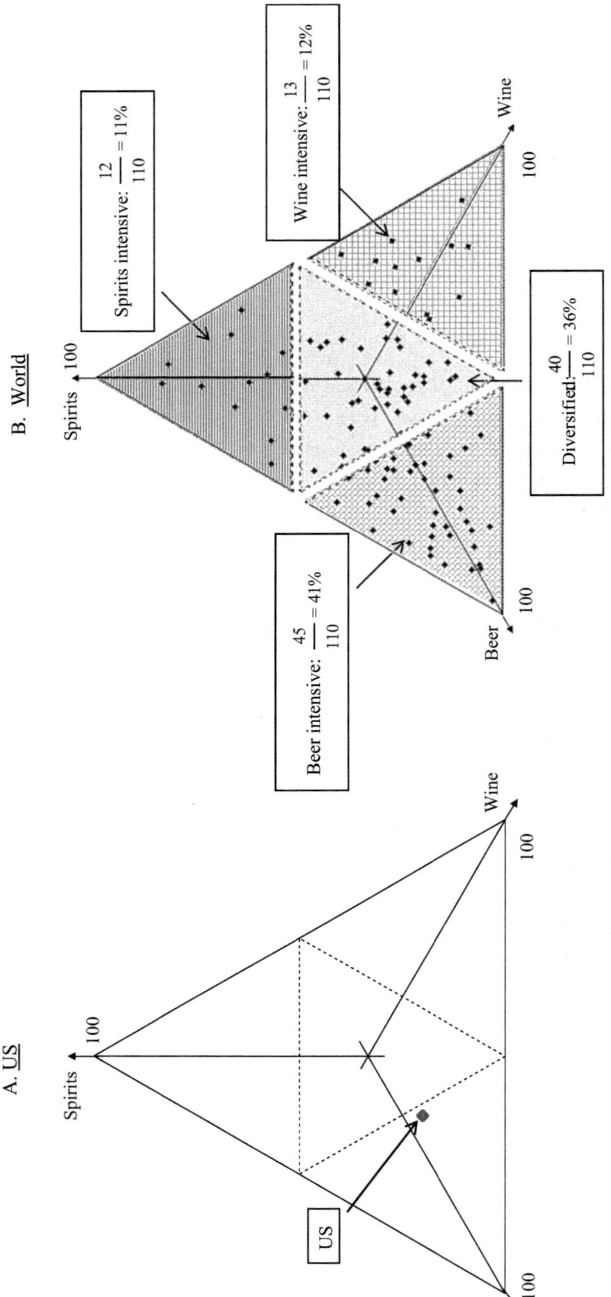

Fig. 9.1 Geometry of drinking. *Source*: Clements et al. (2020)

9.6 The Econometrics of Adding-Up

The above demand equations derived from multi-stage budgeting deal with allocation of expenditure at different stages (or levels). These equations belong to a class of models that Bewley (1986) calls "allocation models". At the start of his book, Bewley characterises these in the following terms:

> All allocation models are subject to a basic identity: The sum of the component equals the aggregate. (Page 1)

He subsequently elaborates by writing

> A system of equations purporting to explain the distribution of a predetermined aggregate among its components must satisfy the constraint that the sum of the individual components equals the aggregate. Since the data for an allocation model naturally obey this identity, the implication for model specification is that the components predicted or implied by the model sum exactly to the predetermined aggregate. This rule, which governs the specification of an allocation model, is known as the adding-up criterion. (Page 10)

Bewley (p. 3) notes the generality of allocation models in economics. These occur in a range of areas including consumer demand models that are subject to the budget constraint, asset market models (where a balance-sheet constraint applies), market-share models (the shares have a unit sum), international trade models (imports of all goods in all countries equal total exports), and regional migration models (flows of total departures from source must balance arrivals at destination). The importance of the adding-up criterion in allocation models was first emphasised by Nicholson (1949, 1957). Subsequent contributions were made by Berndt and Savin (1975), Powell (1969), and Worswick and Champernowne (1954). Although this section is part of a chapter on groups of goods, it should be clear that it is more broadly applicable to all demand systems.

To illustrate a specific example of an allocation model, consider the demand equation system:

$$w_{ic}(d(\log q_{ic}) - d(\log Q_c)) = \theta_i d(\log Q_c) + \sum\nolimits_{j=1}^{n} \pi_{ij} d(\log p_{jc})$$

for $i = 1, \cdots, n$. The variable on the left is $w_{ic}(d(\log q_{ic}) - d(\log Q_c))$. As $\sum_{i=1}^{n} w_{ic} = 1$ and $\sum_{i=1}^{n} w_{ic} \log q_{ic} = \log Q_c$, the left-hand side variable sums over commodities to zero, $\sum_{i=1}^{n} w_{ic}(d(\log q_{ic}) - d(\log Q_c)) = 0$. This reflects that total consumption $\log Q_c$ is allocated to the n elements $\log q_{1c}, \cdots, \log q_{nc}$ and $\sum_{i=1}^{n} w_{ic}(d(\log q_{ic}) - d(\log Q_c))$ is the weighted deviation of all items from the total. Another example is the division of total expenditure on a group to the components. This division is measured by the n_g within-group-g budget shares for country c, $w_{1c}^{g}, \cdots, w_{n_g c}^{g}$, which have a unit sum. This section and next two contain a unified account of the econometric issues associated with these models, as well as some new results. The approach is to start with the general case and then consider several special cases.

Starting with the generic case, consider a simple linear demand model for commodity i ($i = 1, \cdots, n$) in country c ($c = 1, \cdots, C$):

$$y_{ic} = \alpha_i + \beta_i x_c + \varepsilon_{ic}. \tag{9.6}$$

Define the following vectors

$$\boldsymbol{y}_i = \begin{bmatrix} y_{i1} \\ \vdots \\ y_{iC} \end{bmatrix}, \boldsymbol{\iota} = \begin{bmatrix} 1 \\ \vdots \\ 1 \end{bmatrix}, \boldsymbol{x} = \begin{bmatrix} x_1 \\ \vdots \\ x_C \end{bmatrix}, \boldsymbol{\gamma}_i = \begin{bmatrix} \alpha_i \\ \beta_i \end{bmatrix}, \boldsymbol{\varepsilon}_i = \begin{bmatrix} \varepsilon_{i1} \\ \vdots \\ \varepsilon_{iC} \end{bmatrix}.$$

Then, the vector form of (9.6) is

$$\boldsymbol{y}_i = \alpha_i \boldsymbol{\iota} + \beta_i \boldsymbol{x} + \boldsymbol{\varepsilon}_i = \boldsymbol{X}\boldsymbol{\gamma}_i + \boldsymbol{\varepsilon}_i.$$

Here,

$$\boldsymbol{X} = [\boldsymbol{\iota}\ \ \boldsymbol{x}] = \begin{bmatrix} 1 & x_1 \\ \vdots & \vdots \\ 1 & x_C \end{bmatrix}$$

is a $C \times 2$ matrix of the independent "variables".

Define

$$\Delta = C\sum x_c^2 - \left(\sum x_c\right)^2. \tag{9.7}$$

Then, the moment matrix of $\boldsymbol{X}$, its inverse and the vector of cross-products are

$$\boldsymbol{X}'\boldsymbol{X} = \begin{bmatrix} 1 & \cdots & 1 \\ x_1 & \cdots & x_C \end{bmatrix} \begin{bmatrix} 1 & x_1 \\ \vdots & \vdots \\ 1 & x_C \end{bmatrix} = \begin{bmatrix} C & \sum x_c \\ \sum x_c & \sum x_c^2 \end{bmatrix},$$

$$(\boldsymbol{X}'\boldsymbol{X})^{-1} = \Delta^{-1} \begin{bmatrix} \sum x_c^2 & -\sum x_c \\ -\sum x_c & C \end{bmatrix}$$

and

$$\boldsymbol{X}'\boldsymbol{y}_i = \begin{bmatrix} 1 & \cdots & 1 \\ x_1 & \cdots & x_C \end{bmatrix} \begin{bmatrix} y_{i1} \\ \vdots \\ y_{iC} \end{bmatrix} = \begin{bmatrix} \sum_c y_{ic} \\ \sum_c x_c y_{ic} \end{bmatrix}.$$

The least-squares (LS) estimator of $\boldsymbol{\gamma}_i$ is $\widehat{\boldsymbol{\gamma}}_i = (\boldsymbol{X}'\boldsymbol{X})^{-1}\boldsymbol{X}'\boldsymbol{y}_i$ and its sum over $i = 1, \cdots, n$ is

$$\begin{aligned} \sum\nolimits_i \widehat{\boldsymbol{\gamma}}_i &= \sum\nolimits_i (\boldsymbol{X}'\boldsymbol{X})^{-1}\boldsymbol{X}'\boldsymbol{y}_i = (\boldsymbol{X}'\boldsymbol{X})^{-1}\boldsymbol{X}'\sum\nolimits_i \boldsymbol{y}_i \\ &= \Delta^{-1} \begin{bmatrix} \sum x_c^2 & -\sum x_c \\ -\sum x_c & C \end{bmatrix} \begin{bmatrix} \sum_c \sum_i y_{ic} \\ \sum_c x_c \sum_i y_{ic} \end{bmatrix}. \end{aligned} \tag{9.8}$$

In what follows, we apply (9.8) to specific models to examine how the budget constraint affects the sum of $\widehat{\gamma}_i$.

If we set $y_{ic} = p_{ic}q_{ic}$, expenditure on good i in country c, and $x_c = \sum_{i=1}^{n} p_{ic}q_{ic}$, income in country c, to be denoted by M_c, Eq. (9.6) becomes:

$$p_{ic}q_{ic} = \alpha_i + \beta_i M_c + \varepsilon_{ic}. \tag{9.9}$$

Summing both sides over $i = 1, \cdots, n$ we obtain $M_c = \sum_i \alpha_i + \sum_i \beta_i M_c + \sum_i \varepsilon_{ic}$, which implies

$$\sum_i \alpha_i = 0, \quad \sum_i \beta_i = 1, \quad \sum_i \varepsilon_{ic} = 0. \tag{9.10}$$

In Eq. (9.9), the parameter $\beta_i = \partial(p_{ic}q_{ic})/\partial M_c$ is the ith marginal share, which answers how much of a one-dollar increase in income is spent on the good. As this additional income is spent in total on some or all of the n goods, the marginal shares have a unit sum, as indicated by the second member of Eq. (9.10). The marginal shares are taken to be constants in (9.9). Stone's (1954) linear expenditure system (LES) is $p_{ic}q_{ic} = \gamma_i p_{ic} + \beta_i \left(M_c - \sum_{j=1}^{n} \gamma_j p_{jc} \right) + \varepsilon_{ic}, i = 1, \cdots, n$. If prices are constant at $p_1, \cdots, p_n$, then LES takes the form of Eq. (9.9) with $\alpha_i = \sum_j (\delta_{ij} - \beta_i)\gamma_j p_j$, where δ_{ij} is the Kronecker delta ($\delta_{ij} = 1$ if $i = j$, 0 otherwise). Constant marginal shares are a characteristic of LES.

The Rotterdam model, due to Barten (1964) and Theil (1965), also possesses constant marginal shares, like Eq. (9.9). The Rotterdam model is formulated in terms of transitions over time from period $t - 1$ to t and its ith equation is

$$\overline{w}_{it} Dq_{it} = \beta_i DQ_t + \sum_{j=1}^{n} \pi_{ij} Dp_{jt} + \varepsilon_{it},$$

where $\overline{w}_{it} = (1/2)(w_{it} + w_{it-1})$, $Dq_{it} = \log(q_{it}/q_{it-1})$, $DQ_t = \sum_{i=1}^{n} \overline{w}_{it} Dq_{it}$, $Dp_{jt} = \log(p_{jt}/p_{jt-1})$, and β_i and π_{ij} are constant parameters. Here, β_i is equal to the marginal share $\partial(p_{ic}q_{ic})/\partial M_c$. To see this, divide both sides by $\overline{w}_{it}$ to give

$$Dq_{it} = (\beta_i/\overline{w}_{it}) DQ_t + \sum_{j=1}^{n} (\pi_{ij}/\overline{w}_{it}) Dp_{jt} + \varepsilon_{it}/\overline{w}_{it}.$$

This shows that $\beta_i/\overline{w}_{it}$ is the income elasticity of i and that $\beta_i = \overline{w}_{it}(\beta_i/\overline{w}_{it})$ is the elasticity weighted by the corresponding share. As this income elasticity is defined as $\eta_i = \partial(\log q_i)/\partial(\log M) = (\partial q_i/\partial M) \cdot (M/q_i)$, and as $w_i = p_i q_i/M$, the weighted elasticity is

$$w_i \eta_i = (p_i q_i/M) \cdot (\partial q_i/\partial M) \cdot (M/q_i) = \partial(p_i q_i)/\partial M,$$

which is the marginal share. If prices are constant, then $Dp_{jt} = 0, j = 1, \cdots, n$, and the Rotterdam equation becomes

$$\overline{w}_{it}Dq_{it} = \beta_i DQ_t + \varepsilon_{it}.$$

As $\sum_{i=1}^{n} \overline{w}_{it}Dq_{it} = DQ_t$, it follows that $\sum_i \beta_i = 1$ and $\sum_i \varepsilon_{it} = 0$. Thus, the above equation has the same basic property as Eq. (9.9), viz., the sum of the variable on the left-hand side equals the variable on the right.

As Eq. (9.9) relates to both LES and the Rotterdam model, following discussion that refers to (9.9) can also be taken to have implications for those two models. In (9.9), $\sum_i y_{ic} = \sum_i p_{ic} q_{ic} = M_c = x_c$. Thus, the 2×1 vector on the far right of (9.8) becomes

$$\begin{bmatrix} \sum_c \sum_i y_{ic} \\ \sum_c x_c \sum_i y_{ic} \end{bmatrix} = \begin{bmatrix} \sum_c x_c \\ \sum_c x_c^2 \end{bmatrix}.$$

We substitute this into (9.8) to obtain

$$\begin{aligned} \sum_i \widehat{\gamma}_i = \sum_i \begin{bmatrix} \widehat{\alpha}_i \\ \widehat{\beta}_i \end{bmatrix} &= \Delta^{-1} \begin{bmatrix} \sum x_c^2 & -\sum x_c \\ -\sum x_c & C \end{bmatrix} \begin{bmatrix} \sum x_c \\ \sum x_c^2 \end{bmatrix} \\ &= \Delta^{-1} \begin{bmatrix} 0 \\ C\sum x_c^2 - \left(\sum x_c\right)^2 \end{bmatrix} = \begin{bmatrix} 0 \\ 1 \end{bmatrix}, \end{aligned} \tag{9.11}$$

where the last step follows from definition (9.7). In words, Eq. (9.11) shows that the estimated intercepts $\widehat{\alpha}_i$ add over the commodities (equations) to zero, while the slope coefficients $\widehat{\beta}_i$ add to unity. Define the $C \times 1$ vector of residuals for demand equation i as $\widehat{\boldsymbol{\varepsilon}}_i = \boldsymbol{y}_i - \boldsymbol{X}\widehat{\boldsymbol{\gamma}}_i$. In view of result (9.11) and as

$$\sum_i \boldsymbol{y}_i = \begin{bmatrix} M_1 \\ \vdots \\ M_C \end{bmatrix} = \boldsymbol{M} \text{ and } \boldsymbol{X}\begin{bmatrix} 0 \\ 1 \end{bmatrix} = \begin{bmatrix} 1 & M_1 \\ \vdots & \vdots \\ 1 & M_C \end{bmatrix} \begin{bmatrix} 0 \\ 1 \end{bmatrix} = \begin{bmatrix} M_1 \\ \vdots \\ M_C \end{bmatrix} = \boldsymbol{M},$$

we have

$$\sum_i \widehat{\boldsymbol{\varepsilon}}_i = \sum_i \boldsymbol{y}_i - \boldsymbol{X}\sum_i \widehat{\boldsymbol{\gamma}}_i = \boldsymbol{M} - \boldsymbol{X}\begin{bmatrix} 0 \\ 1 \end{bmatrix} = \boldsymbol{0}.$$

That is, the residuals for each country sum over the n equations to zero. Accordingly, we have shown that as an implication of the budget constraint, the LS estimators of model (9.9) for $i = 1, \cdots, n$ satisfy (9.10).

Next, suppose the ith share is a linear function of the logarithm of income:

$$w_{ic} = \alpha_i + \beta_i \log M_c + \varepsilon_{ic}, \tag{9.12}$$

so that in terms of Eq. (9.6), now $y_{ic} = w_{ic}$, $\sum_i y_{ic} = \sum_i w_{ic} = 1$, and $x_c = \log M_c$. Eq. (9.12) is the Working (1943) - Leser (1963) Engel curve, which is the income part of the almost ideal demand model of Deaton and Muellbauer (1980a), $w_{ic} = \alpha_i + \beta_i \log(M_c/P_c) + \sum_{j=1}^{n} \gamma_{ij} \log p_{jc} + \varepsilon_{ic}$, where P_c is a price index.

Summing (9.12) over commodities gives $1 = \sum \alpha_i + \sum \beta_i \log M_c + \sum \varepsilon_{ic}$, so that adding-up requires $\sum_i \alpha_i = 1$, $\sum_i \beta_i = 0$, and $\sum_i \varepsilon_{ic} = 0$.

In the context of model (9.12),

$$\begin{bmatrix} \sum_c \sum_i y_{ic} \\ \sum_c x_c \sum_i y_{ic} \end{bmatrix} = \begin{bmatrix} \sum_c \sum_i w_{ic} \\ \sum_c x_c \sum_i w_{ic} \end{bmatrix} = \begin{bmatrix} C \\ \sum_c x_c \end{bmatrix},$$

which when substituted into (9.8) gives

$$\sum_i \widehat{\gamma}_i = \Delta^{-1} \begin{bmatrix} \sum x_c^2 & -\sum x_c \\ -\sum x_c & C \end{bmatrix} \begin{bmatrix} C \\ \sum_c x_c \end{bmatrix} = \Delta^{-1} \begin{bmatrix} C \sum x_c^2 - \left(\sum x_c\right)^2 \\ 0 \end{bmatrix} = \begin{bmatrix} 1 \\ 0 \end{bmatrix}.$$

In contrast to the expenditure system, the estimated intercepts $\widehat{\alpha}_i$ in this case add over commodities to unity, while the slope coefficients $\widehat{\beta}_i$ add to zero.

The sum of the $C \times 1$ vector of residuals for demand equation i, $\widehat{\boldsymbol{\varepsilon}}_i$, over i is:

$$\sum_i \widehat{\boldsymbol{\varepsilon}}_i = \sum_i \boldsymbol{y}_i - \boldsymbol{X} \sum_i \widehat{\boldsymbol{\gamma}}_i = \begin{bmatrix} 1 \\ \vdots \\ 1 \end{bmatrix} - \begin{bmatrix} 1 & \log M_1 \\ \vdots & \vdots \\ 1 & \log M_C \end{bmatrix} \begin{bmatrix} 1 \\ 0 \end{bmatrix} = \mathbf{0},$$

so again, the least-square estimators satisfy the budget constraint.

Suppose $y_{ic} = w_{ic}(\log q_{ic} - \log Q_c)$, relative consumption $\log q_{ic} - \log Q_c$ weighted by budget share w_{ic}, is a linear function of real income $x_c = \log Q_c$. Equation (9.6) becomes:

$$w_{ic}(\log q_{ic} - \log Q_c) = \alpha_i + \beta_i \log Q_c + \varepsilon_{ic}. \tag{9.13}$$

Summing (9.13) over commodities, we have $0 = \sum_i \alpha_i + \sum_i \beta_i \log Q_c + \sum_i \varepsilon_{ic}$, so adding-up requires $\sum_i \alpha_i = 0$, $\sum_i \beta_i = 0$, and $\sum_i \varepsilon_{ic} = 0$.

Now since $\sum_i y_{ic} = \sum_i w_{ic}(\log q_{ic} - \log Q_c) = 0$,

$$\begin{bmatrix} \sum_c \sum_i y_{ic} \\ \sum_c x_c \sum_i y_{ic} \end{bmatrix} = \begin{bmatrix} \sum_c \sum_i w_{ic}(\log q_{ic} - \log Q_c) \\ \sum_c x_c \sum_i w_{ic}(\log q_{ic} - \log Q_c) \end{bmatrix} = \begin{bmatrix} 0 \\ 0 \end{bmatrix}.$$

Substitute this into (9.8) to obtain:

$$\sum_i \widehat{\gamma}_i = \Delta^{-1} \begin{bmatrix} \sum x_c^2 & -\sum x_c \\ -\sum x_c & C \end{bmatrix} \begin{bmatrix} 0 \\ 0 \end{bmatrix} = \begin{bmatrix} 0 \\ 0 \end{bmatrix} \text{ and}$$

$$\sum_i \widehat{\boldsymbol{\varepsilon}}_i = \sum_i \boldsymbol{y}_i - \boldsymbol{X} \sum_i \widehat{\boldsymbol{\gamma}}_i = \begin{bmatrix} 0 \\ \vdots \\ 0 \end{bmatrix} - \boldsymbol{X} \begin{bmatrix} 0 \\ 0 \end{bmatrix} = \mathbf{0}.$$

In this case, the estimated intercepts, slope coefficients, and residuals all add to 0.

If prices are included in right-hand side of (9.13), do the above constraints still hold? Instead of defining $x_c = \log Q_c$ in (9.13), x_c becomes a vector of real income and prices, which leads to a change in the definition of the matrix $\boldsymbol{X}$.

However, as $\sum_i y_{ic} = \sum_i w_{ic}(\log q_{ic} - \log Q_c) = 0$ continues to hold, the sum of the LS estimator is still zero: $\sum_i \widehat{\boldsymbol{\gamma}}_i = (\boldsymbol{X}'\boldsymbol{X})^{-1}\boldsymbol{X}'\sum_i \boldsymbol{y}_i = (\boldsymbol{X}'\boldsymbol{X})^{-1}\boldsymbol{X}'\boldsymbol{0} = \boldsymbol{0}$. Thus, no matter how $\boldsymbol{X}$ is defined, in this case, the sum of the coefficients is always 0. The same applies to the residuals.

One further point should be noted regarding model (9.13). The time-series version of the model with prices is $\overline{w}_{it}(Dq_{it} - DQ_t) = \beta_i DQ_t + \sum_{j=1}^{n} \pi_{ij} Dp_{jt} + \varepsilon_{it}$, where the notation is as before. As the sum of the left-hand side variable is zero, it follows that the results of this section are clearly applicable here also.

9.7 Multiple Consuming Units

The term "consuming units" refers here to groups of consumers or countries; in what follows we consider the case of multiple groups of countries. Accounting for multiple groups involves adding multiple intercepts in each equation of the general model.

Let the $c = 1, \cdots, C$ countries are allocated into $r < C$ groups. Denote these r groups by $\boldsymbol{S}_1, \cdots, \boldsymbol{S}_r$ and let C_k be the number of countries in $\boldsymbol{S}_k$ with $\sum_{k=1}^{r} C_k = C$. Country c can be "located" by the indicator variable

$$I_k(c \in \boldsymbol{S}_k) = \begin{cases} 1 \text{ if } c \in \boldsymbol{S}_k \\ 0 \text{ otherwise} \end{cases}, \text{ for } k = 1, \cdots, r.$$

If each country is included in one of groups, then $\sum_{k=1}^{r} I_k(c \in \boldsymbol{S}_k) = 1$ for $c = 1, \cdots, C$. This situation could be described as a "complete allocation". A special case is when countries are classified according to the "intensity" of their consumption patterns, as discussed in Sect. 9.5 for the case of alcohol. Country c belongs to group k if it is intensive in the consumption of good k ($k = 1, \cdots, n$, the number of goods); if the country is not intensive in any good, that is, if its consumption is "diversified", then it belongs to group $n + 1$, so that $r = n + 1$.

The extension of the generic model (9.6) to incorporate the indicator variables is:

$$y_{ic} = \sum_{k=1}^{r} \alpha_{ik} I_k(c \in \boldsymbol{S}_k) + \beta_i x_c + \varepsilon_{ic}. \tag{9.14}$$

Define the following vectors:

$$\boldsymbol{y}_i = \begin{bmatrix} y_{i1} \\ y_{i2} \\ \vdots \\ y_{iC} \end{bmatrix}, \boldsymbol{x} = \begin{bmatrix} x_1 \\ x_2 \\ \vdots \\ x_C \end{bmatrix}, \boldsymbol{\gamma}_i = \begin{bmatrix} \alpha_{i1} \\ \alpha_{i2} \\ \vdots \\ \alpha_{ir} \\ \beta_i \end{bmatrix}, \boldsymbol{\varepsilon}_i = \begin{bmatrix} \varepsilon_{i1} \\ \varepsilon_{i2} \\ \vdots \\ \varepsilon_{iC} \end{bmatrix},$$

as well as the $C \times 1$ vector of binary values of the kth indicator function, to be written $\boldsymbol{\imath}_k$, whose c^{th} element is one if $c \in \boldsymbol{S}_k$ and is zero otherwise. The sum of all the

C elements of $\boldsymbol{\iota}_k$ is $\boldsymbol{\iota}_k'\boldsymbol{\iota}_k = C_k$, the number of countries in $\boldsymbol{S}_k$. Then, the vector form of (9.14) is

$$\boldsymbol{y}_i = \sum_{k=1}^{r} \alpha_{ik}\boldsymbol{\iota}_k + \beta_i\boldsymbol{x} + \boldsymbol{\varepsilon}_i = \boldsymbol{X}\boldsymbol{\gamma}_i + \boldsymbol{\varepsilon}_i,$$

where $\boldsymbol{X} = \begin{bmatrix} \boldsymbol{\iota}_1 & \boldsymbol{\iota}_2 & \cdots & \boldsymbol{\iota}_r & \boldsymbol{x} \end{bmatrix}$.

Defining the following:

$$\boldsymbol{A} = \begin{bmatrix} C_1 & 0 & \cdots & 0 \\ 0 & C_2 & \cdots & 0 \\ \vdots & \vdots & \cdots & \vdots \\ 0 & 0 & \cdots & C_r \end{bmatrix}, \quad \boldsymbol{b} = \begin{bmatrix} \sum_{c\in \boldsymbol{S}_1} x_c \\ \sum_{c\in \boldsymbol{S}_2} x_c \\ \vdots \\ \sum_{c\in \boldsymbol{S}_r} x_c \end{bmatrix}, \quad d = \left(\sum x_c^2 - \boldsymbol{b}'\boldsymbol{A}^{-1}\boldsymbol{b}\right)^{-1},$$

the moment matrix of $\boldsymbol{X}$, its inverse and the vector of cross-products are

$$\boldsymbol{X}'\boldsymbol{X} = \begin{bmatrix} \boldsymbol{A} & \boldsymbol{b} \\ \boldsymbol{b}' & \sum x_c^2 \end{bmatrix}, \quad (\boldsymbol{X}'\boldsymbol{X})^{-1} = d\begin{bmatrix} d^{-1}\boldsymbol{A}^{-1} + \boldsymbol{A}^{-1}\boldsymbol{b}\boldsymbol{b}'\boldsymbol{A}^{-1} & -\boldsymbol{A}^{-1}\boldsymbol{b} \\ -\boldsymbol{b}'\boldsymbol{A}^{-1} & 1 \end{bmatrix} \text{ and}$$

$$\boldsymbol{X}'\boldsymbol{y}_i = \begin{bmatrix} \boldsymbol{\iota}_1' \\ \boldsymbol{\iota}_2' \\ \vdots \\ \boldsymbol{\iota}_r' \\ \boldsymbol{x}' \end{bmatrix} \begin{bmatrix} y_{i1} \\ \vdots \\ y_{iC} \end{bmatrix} = \begin{bmatrix} \sum_{c\in \boldsymbol{S}_1} y_{ic} \\ \sum_{c\in \boldsymbol{S}_2} y_{ic} \\ \vdots \\ \sum_{c\in \boldsymbol{S}_r} y_{ic} \\ \sum_c x_c y_{ic} \end{bmatrix}.$$

The sum of the LS estimator of $\boldsymbol{\gamma}_i$ is:

$$\sum_{i=1}^{n} \widehat{\boldsymbol{\gamma}}_i = (\boldsymbol{X}'\boldsymbol{X})^{-1}\sum_{i=1}^{n} \boldsymbol{X}'\boldsymbol{y}_i = \begin{bmatrix} \boldsymbol{A}^{-1} + d\boldsymbol{A}^{-1}\boldsymbol{b}\boldsymbol{b}'\boldsymbol{A}^{-1} & -d\boldsymbol{A}^{-1}\boldsymbol{b} \\ -d\boldsymbol{b}'\boldsymbol{A}^{-1} & d \end{bmatrix} \begin{bmatrix} \sum_{c\in \boldsymbol{S}_1}\sum_i y_{ic} \\ \sum_{c\in \boldsymbol{S}_2}\sum_i y_{ic} \\ \vdots \\ \sum_{c\in \boldsymbol{S}_r}\sum_i y_{ic} \\ \sum_c x_c \sum_i y_{ic} \end{bmatrix}. \tag{9.15}$$

Next, we apply (9.15) to two of the previous demand systems to examine how the budget constraint impinges on $\sum_i \widehat{\boldsymbol{\gamma}}_i$ and the sum of the residuals. The share system Eq. (9.12) with country groups is:

$$w_{ic} = \sum_{k=1}^{r} \alpha_{ik} I_k(c \in \boldsymbol{S}_k) + \beta_i \log M_c + \varepsilon_{ic}. \tag{9.16}$$

Summing both sides over i, we have $1 = \sum_i \sum_{k=1}^{r} \alpha_{ik} I_k(c \in \boldsymbol{S}_k) + \sum_i \beta_i \log M_c + \sum_i \varepsilon_{ic}$. This implies $\sum_i \alpha_{ik} = 1$, $k = 1, \cdots, r$, $\sum_i \beta_i = 0$ and $\sum_i \varepsilon_{ic} = 0$.

In (9.16), $\sum_{i=1}^{n} y_{ic} = \sum_{i=1}^{n} w_{ic} = 1$, which is substituted into (9.15) to obtain:

$$\sum_{i=1}^{n} \widehat{\boldsymbol{\gamma}}_i = \begin{bmatrix} \boldsymbol{A}^{-1} + d\boldsymbol{A}^{-1}\boldsymbol{bb}'\boldsymbol{A}^{-1} & -d\boldsymbol{A}^{-1}\boldsymbol{b} \\ -d\boldsymbol{b}'\boldsymbol{A}^{-1} & d \end{bmatrix} \begin{bmatrix} C_1 \\ C_2 \\ \vdots \\ C_r \\ \sum_c x_c \end{bmatrix}.$$

To simplify this expression, note that

$$\boldsymbol{A\iota} = \begin{bmatrix} C_1 & 0 & \cdots & 0 \\ 0 & C_2 & \cdots & 0 \\ \vdots & \vdots & \cdots & \vdots \\ 0 & 0 & \cdots & C_r \end{bmatrix} \begin{bmatrix} 1 \\ 1 \\ \vdots \\ 1 \end{bmatrix} = \begin{bmatrix} C_1 \\ C_2 \\ \vdots \\ C_r \end{bmatrix} \text{ and } \boldsymbol{b}'\boldsymbol{\iota} = \sum_{c=1}^{C} x_c,$$

where $\boldsymbol{\iota}$ is an $r \times 1$ vector of unit elements. Thus,

$$\sum_{i=1}^{n} \widehat{\boldsymbol{\gamma}}_i = \begin{bmatrix} \boldsymbol{A}^{-1} + d\boldsymbol{A}^{-1}\boldsymbol{bb}'\boldsymbol{A}^{-1} & -d\boldsymbol{A}^{-1}\boldsymbol{b} \\ -d\boldsymbol{b}'\boldsymbol{A}^{-1} & d \end{bmatrix} \begin{bmatrix} \boldsymbol{A\iota} \\ \sum_c x_c \end{bmatrix} = \begin{bmatrix} \boldsymbol{\iota} + d\boldsymbol{A}^{-1}\boldsymbol{bb}'\boldsymbol{\iota} - d\boldsymbol{A}^{-1}\boldsymbol{b}\sum_c x_c \\ -d\boldsymbol{b}'\boldsymbol{\iota} + d\sum_c x_c \end{bmatrix} = \begin{bmatrix} \boldsymbol{\iota} \\ 0 \end{bmatrix}.$$

The sum of the residuals is:

$$\sum_i \widehat{\boldsymbol{\varepsilon}}_i = \sum_i \boldsymbol{y}_i - \boldsymbol{X}\sum_i \widehat{\boldsymbol{\gamma}}_i = \begin{bmatrix} 1 \\ \vdots \\ 1 \end{bmatrix} - \begin{bmatrix} \boldsymbol{\iota}_1 & \cdots & \boldsymbol{\iota}_r & x_c \end{bmatrix} \begin{bmatrix} \boldsymbol{\iota} \\ 0 \end{bmatrix}.$$

As complete allocation means that $\sum_{k=1}^{r} I_k(c \in \boldsymbol{S}_k) = 1$, we have $\begin{bmatrix} \boldsymbol{\iota}_1 & \cdots & \boldsymbol{\iota}_r \end{bmatrix}\boldsymbol{\iota} = \boldsymbol{\iota}_1 + \boldsymbol{\iota}_2 + \cdots \boldsymbol{\iota}_r = \boldsymbol{\iota}$, which implies

$$\sum_i \widehat{\boldsymbol{\varepsilon}}_i = \boldsymbol{\iota} - \boldsymbol{\iota} = \boldsymbol{0}.$$

Thus, under complete allocation, the LS estimator satisfies the adding-up constraint.

The relative consumption system Eq. (9.13) for groups of countries is:

$$w_{ic}(\log q_{ic} - \log Q_c) = \sum_{k=1}^{r} \alpha_{ik} I_k(c \in \boldsymbol{S}_k) + \beta_i \log Q_c + \varepsilon_{ic}. \tag{9.17}$$

Summing (9.17) both sides over i gives $0 = \sum_i \sum_{k=1}^{r} \alpha_{ik} I_k(c \in \boldsymbol{S}_k) + \sum_i \beta_i \log Q_c + \sum_i \varepsilon_{ic}$, which implies $\sum_i \alpha_{ik} = 0$, $k = 1, \ldots, r$, $\sum_i \beta_i = 0$ and $\sum_i \varepsilon_{ic} = 0$. In Eq. (9.17), $\sum_i y_{ic} = \sum_i w_{ic}(\log q_{ic} - \log Q_c) = 0$, so that:

$$\begin{bmatrix} \sum_{c\in S_1}\sum_i y_{ic} \\ \sum_{c\in S_2}\sum_i y_{ic} \\ \vdots \\ \sum_{c\in S_r}\sum_i y_{ic} \\ \sum_c x_c \sum_i y_{ic} \end{bmatrix} = \begin{bmatrix} 0 \\ 0 \\ \vdots \\ 0 \\ 0 \end{bmatrix} = \mathbf{0}.$$

Substituting this into (9.15) gives

$$\sum_{i=1}^{n} \widehat{\boldsymbol{\gamma}}_i = (\boldsymbol{X}'\boldsymbol{X})^{-1} \sum_{i=1}^{n} \boldsymbol{X}'\boldsymbol{y}_i = \begin{bmatrix} \boldsymbol{A}^{-1} + d\boldsymbol{A}^{-1}\boldsymbol{b}\boldsymbol{b}'\boldsymbol{A}^{-1} & -d\boldsymbol{A}^{-1}\boldsymbol{b} \\ -d\boldsymbol{b}'\boldsymbol{A}^{-1} & d \end{bmatrix} \mathbf{0} = \mathbf{0}.$$

The sum of the residuals is:

$$\sum_i \widehat{\boldsymbol{\varepsilon}}_i = \sum_i \boldsymbol{y}_i - \boldsymbol{X} \sum_i \widehat{\boldsymbol{\gamma}}_i = \begin{bmatrix} 0 \\ \vdots \\ 0 \end{bmatrix} - \boldsymbol{X} \begin{bmatrix} 0 \\ \vdots \\ 0 \end{bmatrix} = \mathbf{0}.$$

The estimated intercepts, slope coefficients, and residuals all sum to 0.

9.8 Implications and Summary of Adding Up

In conventional allocation models, the budget constraint implies "adding-up" constraints on the coefficients and the disturbance terms. It is well known that the LS estimator satisfies these constraints. We considered the new case in which indicator variables are included as intercept shifters. For the adding-up result to carry over to this case, we established the following:

1. In a share system, the indicator variables must have a unit sum for each observation. In a cross-country application, this means that each country has to be allocated to some group.
2. In a relative consumption system, the left-hand side variables sum to zero. There is no such restriction on the number of indicator variable in this case—the adding-up constraints are satisfied by the LS estimator no matter how the right side of the equation is specified. This interesting result seems new.

These results are summarised in Table 9.2.

9.9 Sources

Much of Chaps. 8 and 9 material is from Liu (2018).

The empirical implications of the utility function $u(\boldsymbol{q}) = f(u_1(\boldsymbol{q}_1), \cdots, u_G(\boldsymbol{q}_G))$ were studied by Strotz (1957). Block independence is a specific case of this utility function.

Table 9.2 Implications of adding up

Model	Sum of Dependent variable $\sum_{i=1}^{n} y_{ic}$	Estimated intercepts $\sum_{i=1}^{n}\widehat{\alpha}_i$, $\sum_{i=1}^{n}\widehat{\alpha}_{ik}$	Estimated slopes $\sum_{i=1}^{n}\widehat{\beta}_i$	Residuals $\sum_{i=1}^{n}\widehat{\varepsilon}_{ic}$
A. *One intercept*				
$y_{ic} = \alpha_{ic} + \beta_i x_c + \varepsilon_{ic}$				
1. Expenditure system	x_c	0	1	0
2. Share system	1	1	0	0
3. Relative consumption	0	0	0	0
B. *Multiple intercepts*				
$y_{ic} = \sum_{k=1}^{r}\alpha_{ik} I_k(c \in S_k) + \beta_i x_c + \varepsilon_{ic}$, $\sum_{k=1}^{r} I_k(c \in S_k) = 1$, $c = 1, \ldots, C$				
1. Share system	1	1	0	0
2. Relative consumption	0	0	0	0

Note: There are $i = 1, \ldots, n$ goods and $c = 1, \ldots, C$ countries. For each model, the dependent variable y_{ic} is defined as:

Model	Dependent variable
1. Expenditure system	$p_{ic}q_{ic}$, expenditure in good i in country c
2. Share system	$w_i = p_i q_i / M$, budget share of i in c
3. Relative consumption system	$w_{ic}(\log q_{ic} - \log Q_c)$, weighted deviation of $\log q_{ic}$ from the weighted average

Weak separability is also known as block-wise independence. Strotz (1957) showed that weak separability is necessary and sufficient for two-stage budgeting.

The foundations of utility theory for groups of goods in Sect. 8.2 derive from Barten and Turnovsky (1966), Gorman (1959), Leontief (1947a, b), Sono (1961), Strotz (1957), and Theil (1975/76). For related material, see Pollak (1969), and for a survey, see Deaton and Muellbauer (1980b). Further details of conditional and group demand are in Clements (1987).

Figure 8.1 is an updated version of Clements et al. (2020, Fig. 1). Figure 9.1 is also from Clements et al. (2020).

References

Barten AP (1964) Consumer demand functions under conditions of almost additive preferences. Econometrica 32:1–38

Barten AP, Turnovsky SJ (1966) Some aspects of the aggregation problem for composite demand equations. Int Econ Rev 7:231–259

Berndt ER, Savin NE (1975) Estimation and hypothesis testing in singular equation systems with autoregressive disturbances. Econometrica 43:937–956

Bewley R (1986) Allocation models: specification, estimation, and applications. Ballinger, Cambridge, MA

Carpentier A, Guyomard H (2001) Unconditional elasticities in two-level demand systems: an approximate solution. Am J Agric Econ 83:222–229

Clements KW (1987) The demand for groups of goods and conditional demand." Chapter 4. In: Theil H, Clements KW (eds) Applied demand analysis: results from system-wide approaches. Ballinger, Cambridge, MA, pp 163–184

Clements KW, Lan Y, Liu H (2020) Understanding alcohol consumption across countries. Appl Econ 52:4421–4439

Deaton AS, Muellbauer J (1980a) An almost ideal demand system. Am Econ Rev 70:312–326

Deaton AS, Muellbauer J (1980b) Economics and consumer behaviour. Cambridge University Press, Cambridge

Edgerton DL (1997) Weak separability and the estimation of elasticities in multilevel demand systems. Am J Agric Econ 79:62–79

Edgerton DL, Assarsson B, Hummelmose A, Laurila IP, Rickertsen K, Vale PH (1996) The econometrics of demand systems: with applications to food demand in the nordic countries. Springer Science and Business Media

Gorman WM (1959) Separability utility and aggregation. Econometrica 27:469–481

Leontief WW (1947a) A note on the interrelationship of subsets of independent variables of a continuous function with continuous first derivatives. Bull Am Math Soc 53:343–350

Leontief WW (1947b) Introduction to a theory of the internal structure of functional relationships. Econometrica 15:361–373

Leser CEV (1963) Forms of Engel functions. Econometrica 31:694–703

Liu H (2018) Cross-country food consumption patterns: theory and measurement. PhD thesis, The University of Western Australia

Nicholson JL (1949) Variations in working class family expenditure. J R Stat Soc Ser A 112:359–418

Nicholson JL (1957) The general form of the adding-up criterion. J R Stat Soc Ser A 120:84–85

Passport GMID Database (2005). Consumer expenditure on alcoholic beverages. http://www.portal.euromonitor.com/portal/magazine/homemain

Pollak RA (1969) Conditional demand functions and consumption theory. Q J Econ 83:60–78

Powell A (1969) Aitken estimators as a tool in allocating predetermined aggregates. J Am Stat Assoc 64:913–922

Sono M (1961) The effect of price changes on the demand and supply of separable goods. Int Econ Rev 2:239–271

Stone R (1954) Linear expenditure systems and demand analysis: an application to the pattern of British demand. Econ J 64:511–527

Strotz RH (1957) The empirical implications of a utility tree. Econometrica 27:269–280

Theil H (1965) The information approach to demand analysis. Econometrica 33:67–87

Theil H (1975/76) Theory and measurement of consumer demand. Two volumes. North-Holland Publishing Company, Amsterdam

Working H (1943) Statistical laws of family expenditure. J Am Stat Assoc 38:43–56

Worswick GDN, Champernowne DG (1954) A note on the adding-up criterion. Rev Econ Stud 22: 57–60

Chapter 10
Demand Analysis for CGE Modelling and EDM I: Main Results

10.1 Introduction

Numerical macroeconomic models like computable (or applied) general equilibrium (CGE) models and equilibrium displacement models (EDM) comprehensively represent price substitutability in many parts of the economy. The demand equations in these models use price elasticities to quantify the responsiveness of economic agents to relative price changes. For example, households (firms) maximise utility (minimise costs) by substituting more expensive goods (inputs) with cheaper ones subject to income and preferences (revenue and technology). The degree of substitutability is represented by the price elasticities of demand. This chapter provides applications of demand elasticities within a CGE framework. These applications draw heavily from the works of Clements et al. (2021, 2022) and Mariano et al. (2024). These demand elasticities are also applicable to EDM. Thus, this chapter provides an overview of EDM and how the application of these demand elasticities applies to EDM.

This chapter focuses on the main results of the econometric estimation and the model application of demand elasticities. The subsequent chapter provides a more in-depth discussion of the results.

10.2 Computable General Equilibrium Models

CGE models apply the principles of general equilibrium theory in their depiction of the whole economy. They capture all the flows in the economy by representing different agents such as households, government, foreigners, and businesses. These economic agents make decentralised decisions on their consumption or production activities but are interconnected through upstream and downstream flows of goods and services in commodity markets or the demand for and supply of primary inputs

K. W. Clements et al., *Short-cut Demand Elasticities and Other Convenient Approaches to Consumer Demand*, https://doi.org/10.1007/978-981-96-3588-7_10

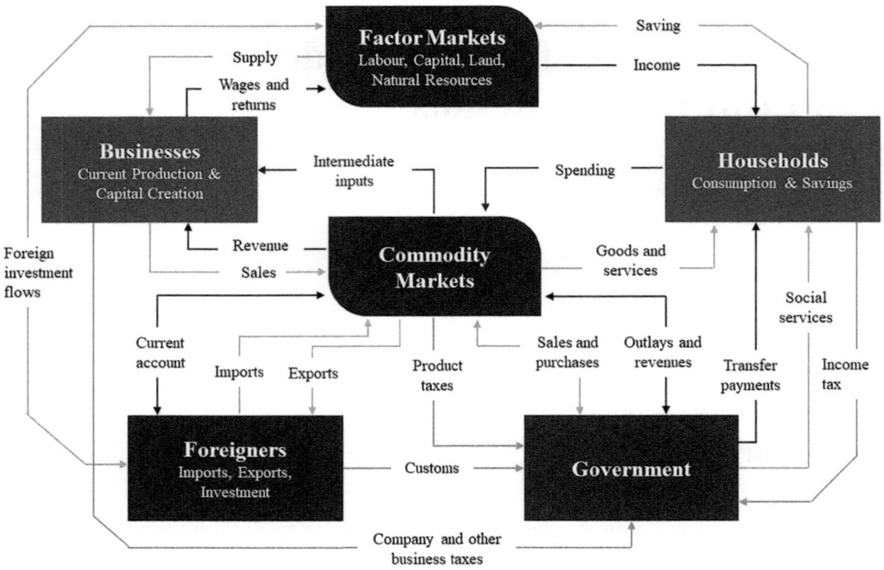

Fig. 10.1 Interrelationships of economic activities in a CGE model

in the factor market. The decisions of all economic agents sum to give the macroeconomic behaviour of an economy, such as changes in gross domestic product (GDP), government tax revenue and spending, aggregate savings and investment, and the balance of trade (Burfisher 2021). Figure 10.1 shows the interdependence of agents in the economy with fundamental links in production structure, consumption patterns, and income flows. With the economy represented as a system of interdependent components, CGE models recognise that a shock on one component will create ripple effects throughout the entire economic system. Prices, outputs, and incomes are endogenously determined by the interaction of optimising units of production and consumption.

One of the key features of CGE models is the representation of optimising behaviour by households and firms in the context of competitive markets with explicit resource and budget constraints. Households decide on the demand for commodities and the supply of endowments in order to maximise utility while firms decide on the demand for inputs and the supply of outputs in order to maximise profits. These optimising behaviours are influenced by prices, which are determined by market-clearing conditions in commodity and factor markets. For example, commodity prices are determined by a market-clearing condition where total sales equal total output for a given commodity. The level of income, preferences, and prices jointly determine aggregate demand while the cost of inputs and demand for output determines aggregate supply. Similarly, factor prices such as the wage and (capital) rental rate are also determined by a market equilibrium where demand equals supply for a given primary factor.

To produce numerical results, CGE models are calibrated with real-world data, hence the adjective "computable" in computable general equilibrium. There are two sets of data used in the calibration process. One is the data coefficients that calibrate the flows and stocks in the economy such as the purchases of final goods and services by households for consumption, demands for intermediate inputs and primary factors by firms for production, the collection of taxes and the payment of income support by the government, and procurements of foreign goods and capital investments. These economic flows are published in input-output tables, national accounts, financial data, and household surveys, among other sources. Another set of data are the elasticities that calibrate the behavioural responses of economic agents in relation to price and income changes. Many CGE models rely extensively on literature-based estimates for these parameter values. These behavioural parameters can be econometrically estimated using empirical data. Once calibrated, the initial database provides an initial solution to the model. The initial solution is used as a benchmark to which the results of a counterfactual scenario are compared. That is, the model's counterfactual solution provides a measure of how the economy would respond to a change in policy or economic events in reference to the initial solution as calibrated by the model's benchmark data and parameters.

10.3 Strengths and Weaknesses of CGE

CGE models have been widely used to address policy questions in taxation, international trade, income inequality, and the environment among others. Prior to CGE modelling, input-output (IO) analysis was a popular tool for policy analysis. The IO model was developed by Leontief (1936) who formalised the integration of Walrasian general equilibrium theory and the concept of interindustry linkages (Miller and Blair 2009). These models were used extensively in the 1950s providing static multiplier coefficients to derive estimates of the total response of the economy as a result of some specified event, policy or activity (e.g. Leontief et al. 1953). However, the use of IO multipliers for this purpose is now recognised as misleading due to their inherent simplifying assumptions. Shortcomings of IO analysis are outlined in detail by Clark (2018), Layman (2002), Gretton (2013), and ABS (2021). The obvious drawback of an IO model is that the input-output coefficients are assumed fixed. This assumption is unrealistic since technology changes over time make the ratios for intermediate inputs and production non-constant. Another unrealistic assumption is that there are no supply-side constraints (via limits on the supply of primary factors) so that industries face no limits on how much they can expand. It is assumed that extra output can be produced in one area without taking resources (capital and labour) away from other activities. These assumptions rule out changes in prices and input substitutability.

Constraints on the availability of inputs require prices to act as a rationing device as in general equilibrium theory. However, as factors of production are assumed to be in limitless supply, this rationing response is assumed not to occur in IO analysis.

With fixed prices, firms have no incentive to substitute expensive inputs with cheaper ones; hence, the notion of cost minimisation is implicitly neglected. These limitations motivated the development of computable general equilibrium models that lacked these limitations by adopting more realistic and sophisticated economic assumptions. The onset of CGE modelling in the 1970s was facilitated by the increased efficiency of computing technology and software over this period. CGE models gained increasing popularity over IO models because they incorporated more desirable theoretical features such as optimisation theory, recognition of resource and budget constraints, and the allowance for price-induced behavioural responses. These features mean that CGE models distribute shocks across price and quantity effects compared to the pure quantity effects observed in IO models. This means the impact (i.e. quantity response) of a shock is much smaller when analysed within a CGE framework compared to IO as some of the shock leads to price changes, which is ruled out by assumption in the IO framework. This feature means that the results are much less likely to be overstated particularly in the medium to long run.

10.4 Recent Advances

The advances in solution techniques to solve non-linear models led to the exponential growth of CGE applications in the 1970s and 1980s. There are two broad approaches in solving a multi-sectoral, economy-wide non-linear general equilibrium models: the levels approach and the linearised approach. In the levels approach the model equations remain in their original non-linear form and are solved simultaneously. Examples of this are the pioneering works of Scarf and his doctoral students (Scarf and Hansen 1973; Scarf and Shoven 1983). Scarf's approach applies a fixed-point algorithm where the model is solved by finding a fixed point in a mapping of prices through excess demand equations. Early applications of this approach were on tax policy analysis (Scarf and Hansen 1973; Scarf and Shoven 1983; Shoven and Whalley 1984). The levels approach is used widely in North America and Europe. It is often implemented with the GAMS (General Algebraic Modelling System) software (Bisschop and Meeraus 1982).

In the linearised approach the model equations (which are typically highly non-linear) are linearised and an approximate model solution is obtained by matrix inversion. The linear approximation technique was first applied by Johansen (1960) in his model of Norway. The linearised approach is subject to linearisation error. This limitation was overcome by Dixon and his colleagues by the application of accurate solution methods by solving the linearised equations using multi-step algorithms. The linearised approach was popularised in Australia with the development of the ORANI and MONASH models (Dixon et al. 1982, 1992) and related developments in many Asian countries. The linearised approach is typically solved using the GEMPACK (General Equilibrium Modelling Package) software (Harrison and Pearson 1996). Alternative programming techniques to solve CGE models are described in Ginsburgh and Waelbroeck (1981).

CGE modelling has evolved to become one of the most influential tools in applied economics. As an established field, its features have advanced in terms of geographical coverage, theoretical developments, database calibration and parametrisation, and cutting-edge applications. Depending on the spatial representation, a CGE model can be categorised as a national (single-country) model, a national model with multiple subnational regions or a global model with multiple national regions. Many CGE models represent individual countries to examine domestic policies. Dixon and Jorgenson (2013) provide references to single-country models. A multi-regional single-country model is one where the national economy is disaggregated to represent individual subnational regions. These models are specifically designed for implementing spatially heterogeneous shocks and analysing regional outcomes. They account for inter-regional labour migration, inter-regional ownership of capital and land, regionally specified transport margin services, and different tiers of government. Giesecke and Madden (2013) provide examples of regional CGE models. Global CGE models represent the world economy by representing the global economy with multiple regions that can represent individual countries (e.g. USA) or country groupings (e.g. Europe, Asia, America, Oceania, Africa, etc.). The popularity of global CGE models has been motivated by the significance of global policy issues such as climate change, international trade, immigration, and food security, among others. Notable examples of global CGE models are the GTAP model developed at Purdue University (Hertel 2013), the GTEM model developed at CSIRO (Cai et al. 2015), the ENVISAGE and LINKAGE models of the World Bank (van der Mensbrugghe 2011) and the G-Cubed model (McKibbin and Wilcoxen 2013). In terms of methodological advancements, two key developments in CGE modelling are integrated assessment models for climate and energy analysis, and microsimulation models for distributional analysis.

In relation to modelling consumer demands, capturing heterogeneous behaviour across households is a necessary condition for improving the richness and rigour of consumption modelling and evaluating the distributional impact of policies or economic development. Most CGE models represent households using a single representative agent. This generic household representation gives no insight into how aggregate changes in the economy affect individual households or household types. To overcome this limitation, a large literature has emerged where CGE models are linked with a microsimulation model as represented by the works of Decaluwé et al. (1999), Cogneau and Anne-Sophie (2000), Cockburn (2001), Cororaton (2003), Bussolo and Lay (2003), Jensen and Tarr (2003), Boccanfuso et al. (2008), Bouët et al. (2011), and Clements et al. (2021). These microsimulation-CGE models disaggregate private final demand and income across multiple households to capture distributional effects. For instance, for five developing countries (Brazil, Pakistan, Tanzania, Uruguay, Vietnam), the MIRAGE model of the world economy represents 40 households distinguished according to income and consumption patterns (Bouët et al. 2011). For Australia, Clements et al. (2021) replace the single representative household agent in a CGE model with 10,046 households. A common conclusion in these studies is that the disaggregated model better captures the richness of diverse household demand behaviour and income flows.

10.5 Equilibrium Displacement Models

EDMs are an elasticity form of comparative-static results derived from economic theory (Wohlgenant 2011). For example, the famous Slutsky equation separates the substitution and income effects of the consumer's total response to a relative price change. This is a comparative-static result based on the theory of optimisation by a utility-maximising consumer facing a budget constraint. A popular approach to operationalising this result to a particular market involves developing an elasticity form of the Slutsky equation by totally differentiating the first-order conditions; this approach interprets the first-order conditions as equilibrium equations. The resulting equations are linear (i.e. linearised versions of the underlying non-linear equations) and require estimates of price and income elasticities. Thus, EDMs are also known as linear elasticity models (Brester et al. 2023). The Slutsky-based model described above can be used to analyse the displacement of equilibrium (i.e. initial prices and quantities) of a change in an exogenous variable (e.g. a commodity price). This explains the derivation of the term EDM.

EDMs can be applied to a single market or multiple markets. When applied to multiple markets these can represent either vertical relationships (i.e. upstream and downstream producers in a value chain) or horizontal relationships (i.e. upstream and downstream producers, importers, and exporters). In this sense, EDMs can be thought of less comprehensive than CGE models as they cannot be used to analyse changes in whole economic systems. However, EDMs are similar to other partial equilibrium approaches in that they require less data and less computational resources (Brester et al. 2023).

Below we discuss how demand systems are incorporated into CGE models and EDMs. Both modelling strategies require elasticities to calibrate the system of equations. Thus, the discussion to follow should be interpreted as applying to both modelling strategies. Later, we also present a simplified example of an EDM.

10.6 Incorporating Demand Systems

CGE models are represented by a system of non-linear equations specifying the behaviour of different economic agents. This equation system includes the optimisation theories that directs the consumption decisions of consumers, i.e. the consumption of final goods (intermediates inputs) by households (firms). Figures 10.2 and 10.3 provide an overview of the demand structure of households and firms. The demand system is divided into a two-level (or two-stage) consumption decision problem. At the first level, households decide on the amount of commodity composites for a given budget and price. Then, on the second level, demands for each commodity is further divided into domestic and imported products. For firms, their use of intermediate commodities is complemented with primary factors input to produce an output.

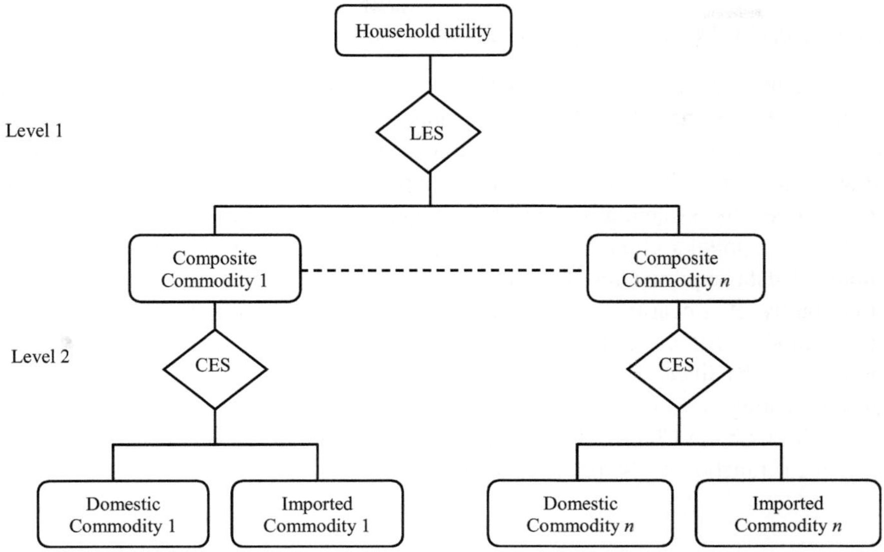

Fig. 10.2 Household demand structure

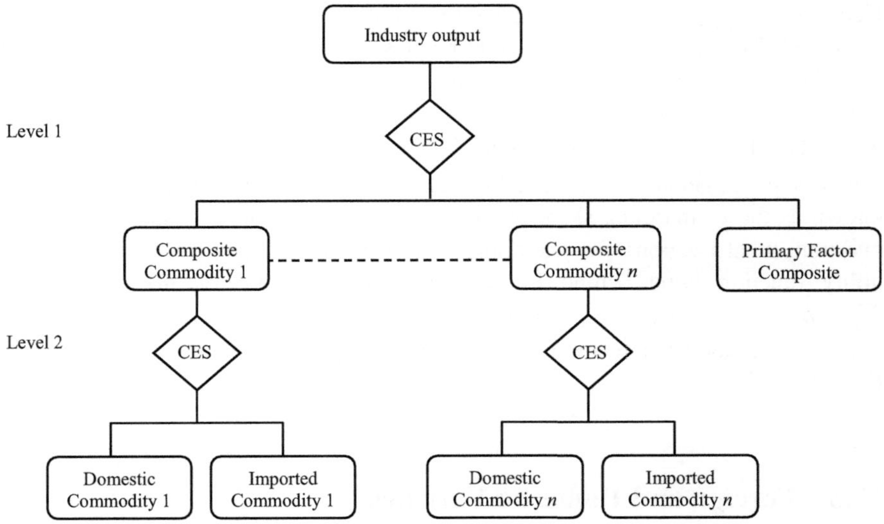

Fig. 10.3 Industry production structure

10.7 Household Demands

Let q_i the quantity demanded for commodity $i = 1, \cdots, n$ and the price denoted as p_i. Consumer theory indicates that household demand for commodity i is obtained by the maximisation of a utility function $u(\boldsymbol{q})$ where $\boldsymbol{q}$ is the quantity vector, subject to the budget constraint $M = \sum_{i=1}^{n} p_i.q_i$. Several models are currently in use to represent the household demand system in a CGE model. This includes the linear expenditure system (LES, Stone 1954), Rotterdam model (Barten 1964; Theil 1965), translog model (Christensen et al. 1975), and almost ideal model (Deaton and Muellbauer 1980). These models were described in Chap. 6. Here, we focus our discussion on the LES demand system as this has been highly influential to CGE practitioners.

LES is a popular choice among CGE modellers due to its simplicity and parsimony of data requirements. It is also reasonably straightforward to estimate and, importantly, its linearity makes it easy to interpret and incorporate in larger economic models. But the model struggles to deal adequately with heterogeneity mainly because of its linear Engel curves. In next chapter we deal with the issue by disaggregating consumers according to their income.

As discussed in Chap. 6, LES expresses expenditure on good i $(p_i q_i, i = 1, \cdots, n)$ as a linear function of the prices and income:

$$p_i q_i = p_i \gamma_i + \beta_i \left(M - \sum_{j=1}^{n} p_j \gamma_j \right), \quad i = 1, \cdots, n. \tag{10.1}$$

Here, $M = \sum_{i=1}^{n} p_i q_i$ is total expenditure, but is conventionally referred to as "income". The first term on the right-hand side of $p_i \gamma_i$ is expenditure on good i unrelated to income. This can be interpreted as the cost of "subsistence consumption" of the good. Thus, according to Eq. (10.1), the consumer first spends $\sum_{j=1}^{n} p_j \gamma_j$ to satisfy all subsistence requirements. The remaining amount, $M - \sum_{j=1}^{n} p_j \gamma_j$, is called "supernumerary income", and a fraction β_i of this is spent on good i. This β_i is known as the ith marginal share, with $\sum_{i=1}^{n} \beta_i = 1$, $0 < \beta_i < 1$, and answers the question, what fraction of a one-dollar rise in income is spent on the good? The utility function lying behind Eq. (10.1) is the Stone-Geary, $u(q_1, \cdots, q_n) = \sum_{i=1}^{n} \beta_i \log(q_i - \gamma_i), q_i > \gamma_i$. This takes the Cobb-Douglas form if $\gamma_i = 0$, $i = 1$, $\cdots$, n. Comprehensive accounts of LES are contained in Goldberger (1987) and Powell (1973).

10.8 Foreign and Domestic Varieties

Once the composite LES demand has been determined, the household chooses the cost-minimising combination of imported and domestic varieties of each commodity. The demand for domestically produced and imported goods is typically based on an Armington (1969) structure. Here, the domestic variety of a particular good is distinguished from its imported counterpart and the two are treated as imperfect substitutes within a constant-elasticity-of-substitution (CES) framework. The CES utility function is represented as:

$$u_i(\boldsymbol{q}_i) = \left(\sum_{j \in \boldsymbol{S}_i} \alpha_j q_j^{-\rho} \right)^{-\frac{1}{\rho}}, \quad \alpha_j > 0, \rho \geq -1, \rho \neq 0. \tag{10.2}$$

Here, $\boldsymbol{S}_i$ is the set of varieties of good i. The elasticity of substitution is $\sigma = \frac{1}{1+\rho} > 0$ and the corresponding conditional demands are:

$$q_j = \frac{M_i \alpha_j^{\sigma} p_j^{-\sigma}}{\sum_{k \in \boldsymbol{S}_i} \alpha_k^{\sigma} p_k^{1-\sigma}}, \quad j \in \boldsymbol{S}_i, \tag{10.3}$$

where q_j is the quantity demanded of $j \in \boldsymbol{S}_i$, $M_i = \sum_{k \in \boldsymbol{S}_i} p_k q_k$ is total expenditure on group of goods in $\boldsymbol{S}_i$ and p_k is the price of $k \in \boldsymbol{S}_i$. When prices are constant, consumption is proportional to group expenditure, which means conditional income elasticities are all unity. Eq. (10.3) can be expressed more compactly by defining the group price index as $P_i^* = \left(\sum_{k \in \boldsymbol{S}_i} \alpha_k^{\sigma} p_k^{1-\sigma} \right)^{\frac{1}{1-\sigma}}$. The denominator in Eq. (10.3), $\sum_{k \in \boldsymbol{S}_i} \alpha_k^{\sigma} p_k^{1-\sigma}$, can then be replaced with $P_i^{1-\sigma}$ to give

$$q_j = \alpha_j^{\sigma} \frac{M_i}{P_i^*} \left(\frac{p_j}{P_i^*} \right)^{-\sigma}, \quad j \in \boldsymbol{S}_i. \tag{10.4}$$

This makes clear the dependence of consumption on real expenditure on the group, $\frac{M_i}{P_i^*}$, and the own-relative price, $\frac{p_j}{P_i^*}$. The demand Eq. (10.4) applies to both households and firms. CGE applications of this Armington structure can be found in Clements et al. (2021), Dixon et al. (2016), Zhai (2008), Lloyd and Zhang (2006), Zhang and Verikios (2006), Shiells and Reinert (1993), and Bandara (1991). Chapter 3 contains a detailed discussion of the CES.

10.9 Intermediate Demands

For firms, the demand for intermediate commodities is also governed by a specified form of the production technology. Many CGE models employ the traditional assumption of Leontief technology where the demand for inputs is a fixed proportion of output. As demonstrated by Mariano et al. (2024), relying on this assumption can seriously mislead the economic implications of CGE results. A more realistic assumption is to apply a function that yields non-zero input demand elasticities such as the CES and the constant ratios of elasticity of substitution, homothetic (CRESH, Hanoch 1971). Both CES and CRESH are generalisation of the Cobb-Douglas function by allowing elasticity of substitution to differ from unity.

The CES production function is similar to Eq. (10.2) and the cost-minimising demand for input *j* is similar to Eq. (10.3). The price elasticity of demand (σ) governs the substitution between commodity inputs. Note that the CES can accommodate a wide range of behaviour, from approaching no substitution ($\sigma \to 0$, the Leontief case), to Cobb-Douglas ($\sigma \to 1$), to perfect substitution ($\sigma \to \infty$, linearity). A limitation of the CES production function is that the elasticities across all pairs of inputs are the same. The CRESH function relaxes this assumption by allowing substitutability between more than two inputs. Using a CRESH function, the optimal mix of commodity inputs is represented as

$$\sum\nolimits_i \left[\frac{q_{ij}}{q_j \alpha_{ij}}\right]^{\beta_i} \frac{\gamma_i}{\beta_i} = \eta, \quad 0 < \beta_i < 1, \gamma_i > 0, \sum\nolimits_i \gamma_i = 1, \ \eta > 0 \tag{10.5}$$

where q_{ij} is the demand for intermediate input i by industry j, q_j is demand for the intermediate input composite, α_{ij} is factor-specific unit input requirements, and γ_i, β_i and η are parameters. The elasticity of substitution across intermediate inputs is $\frac{\sigma_i \sigma_j}{\sum_k a_k \sigma_k}$ where $\sigma_i = \frac{1}{1-\beta_i}$ is the CRESH parameter associated with input i and a_k is the k- *th* input's cost share. Firms have some choice with respect to the production technology and will alter the pattern of intermediate usage in production if relative prices change. In the special case when all σ_i have the same value, the CRESH system is equivalent to CES.

10.10 A Stylised EDM

The numerical implementation of equilibrium displacement models (EDMs) can be illustrated with a stylised demand-and-supply framework.

Consider a single industry where demand for the product depends on the relative price p and real income y, while supply depends on the price and technology t. In differential form, we have

$$dq^d = -a^d dp + b^d dy, \quad a^d, b^d > 0; \quad dq^s = a^s dp + b^s dt, \quad a^s, b^s > 0.$$

The model is closed with the market-clearing condition,

$$dq^d = dq^s.$$

The endogenous variables to be determined are the changes in the equilibrium quantity dq and price dp, while the exogenous variables, taken as given, are income and technology. By substitution, the solution for the price is

$$dp = \frac{1}{a^d + a^s}\left(b^d dy - b^s dt\right). \tag{10.6}$$

Using the identity $\frac{dx}{x} = d(\log x)$, result Eq. (10.6) can be expressed in more familiar elasticity form by defining the price elasticity of demand as

$$\eta_p^d = \frac{\partial\left(\log q^d\right)}{\partial\left(\log p\right)} = \frac{\partial q^d}{\partial p}\frac{p}{q^d} = -a^d\frac{p}{q^d} < 0.$$

Similarly, the income elasticity of demand is $\eta_y^d = b^d\frac{y}{q^d} > 0$, while for supply, the price and technology elasticities are $\eta_p^s = a^s\frac{p}{q^s} > 0$ and $\eta_t^s = b^s\frac{t}{q^s} > 0$. Result (10.6) is then equivalent to

$$d(\log p) = \frac{1}{\eta_p^s - \eta_p^d}\left[\eta_y^d d(\log y) - \eta_t^s d(\log t)\right], \quad \eta_p^s - \eta_p^d > 0. \tag{10.7}$$

Suppose, for example, all elasticities are unitary so that $\eta_p^s - \eta_p^d = 1 - (-1) = 2$ and $\eta_y^d = \eta_t^s = 1$. From Eq. (10.7),

$$d(\log p) = \frac{1}{2}[d(\log y) - d(\log t)].$$

In this case, when technology is unchanging, a 10-per cent increase in income leads to the price rising by 5 per cent; larger price elasticities have the effect of damping the equilibrium price response. If income and technology both increase at the same rate, one offsets the other and the price remains unchanged.

In EDM format, the model and its solution are

$$\begin{bmatrix} 1 & 0 & a^d \\ 0 & 1 & -a^s \\ 1 & -1 & 0 \end{bmatrix}\begin{bmatrix} dq^d \\ dq^s \\ dp \end{bmatrix} = \begin{bmatrix} b^d dy \\ b^s dt \\ 0 \end{bmatrix}, \quad \begin{bmatrix} dq^d \\ dq^s \\ dp \end{bmatrix} = \begin{bmatrix} 1 & 0 & a^d \\ 0 & 1 & -a^s \\ 1 & -1 & 0 \end{bmatrix}^{-1}\begin{bmatrix} b^d dy \\ b^s dt \\ 0 \end{bmatrix}.$$

The inverse of the matrix of coefficients is

$$\begin{bmatrix} 1 & 0 & a^d \\ 0 & 1 & -a^s \\ 1 & -1 & 0 \end{bmatrix}^{-1} = \frac{1}{\phi}\begin{bmatrix} \phi - a^d & a^d & a^d \\ a^s & \phi - a^s & -a^s \\ 1 & -1 & -1 \end{bmatrix}, \quad \phi = a^d + a^s > 0.$$

Thus, the explicit solution is

$$\begin{bmatrix} dq^d \\ dq^s \\ dp \end{bmatrix} = \frac{1}{\phi}\begin{bmatrix} \phi - a^d & a^d & a^d \\ a^s & \phi - a^s & -a^s \\ 1 & -1 & -1 \end{bmatrix}\begin{bmatrix} b^d dy \\ b^s dt \\ 0 \end{bmatrix}.$$

From the last row of the above,

$$dp = \frac{1}{\phi}\left(b^d dy - b^s dt\right) = \frac{1}{a^d + a^s}\left(b^d dy - b^s dt\right),$$

$$\text{or } d(\log p) = \frac{1}{\eta_p^s - \eta_p^d}\left[\eta_y^d d(\log y) - \eta_t^s d(\log t)\right].$$

These expressions coincide with Eqs. (10.6) and (10.7), as they should.

While simple, this example shows how EDMs require numerical values of elasticities. It would be straightforward to extend the example to allow for multiple products that are substitutes or complements in consumption. Chapter 8 presented income and price elasticities of demand for alcoholic beverages, comprising beer, wine, and spirits. These elasticities could be incorporated in an EDM of the alcohol industry.

10.11 Estimating Elasticities

Elasticity parameters are exogenously specified in the CGE model to calibrate the behaviour of consumers and producers. The goal of this calibration is to link the specification of the demand functions in the model with empirical data. Two kinds of numerical values are necessary in CGE models as summarised by Devarajan and Robinson (2005). First are the share coefficients describing the structure of the economy in a particular period. These data coefficients are derived from the value of economic flows published in input-output (IO) tables or social accounting matrix (SAM). Second are the elasticity parameters describing the behaviour of economic agents in the model. Shoven and Whalley (1992) and McKitrick (1998) argue that appropriate estimates of these behavioural parameters are critical as they substantially affect the empirical validity of the model results. The paucity of data together with the theoretical and computational complications in the estimation of behavioural parameters have been cited by CGE modellers as challenging barriers to application of appropriate econometric techniques (Arndt et al. 2002).

Many CGE modellers rely on literature-based estimates or arbitrarily assign a value that could either be high or low. As noted by McKitrick (1998), this approach has been criticised by many scholars (Jorgenson 1984; Lau 1984, Jorgensen et al. 1992; Diewert and Lawrence 1994) for a number of reasons. First, elasticities borrowed from surveyed literature have inconsistent sectoral classification, are estimated for countries not represented by the model and are estimated from obsolete data. Second, functional forms used in estimating the elasticities are not coherent with the theoretical representation of the demand system in the model. These critiques, if not addressed, pose serious consequences for the validity of numerical results generated by the model. In the next several sections, we provide econometric applications of estimating the key parameters in a CGE model. The methodological approach used is sufficiently general to be applicable to other countries.

10.12 Household Elasticities

For the household demand system, we demonstrate with the estimation of LES. The LES demand system (10.1) can be rewritten more compactly as

$$p_i q_i = \alpha_i + \beta_i M, \quad i = 1, \cdots, n, \tag{10.8}$$

where

$$\alpha_i = \sum_{j=1}^{n} (\delta_{ij} - \beta_i) p_j \gamma_j, \quad i = 1, \cdots, n. \tag{10.9}$$

The coefficients of Eq. (10.8) satisfy $\sum_{i=1}^{n} \alpha_i = 0$ and $\sum_{i=1}^{n} \beta_i = 1$. The Kronecker delta δ_{ij} in Eq. (10.9) is equal to unity if $i = j$, or 0 otherwise. When households face the same prices, household survey data can be used with system (10.8) to estimate the n marginal shares, $\beta_1, \cdots, \beta_n$, as well as the n intercepts, $\alpha_1, \cdots, \alpha_n$. However, because there are only $n - 1$ independent values of the intercepts (one is constrained by $\sum_{i=1}^{n} \alpha_i = 0$), there is insufficient information to determine the n subsistence expenditures, $p_1\gamma_1, \cdots, p_n\gamma_n$ (Powell 1973; Howe 1975; Pollak and Wales 1978).

Identification obviously requires the introduction of some additional information. Clements et al. (2022) discuss different approaches of dealing with the identification issue. First, as mentioned in Chap. 6, Betancourt (1973) and Howe (1975) showed that taking savings to be another "good" in the LES and setting its $\gamma = 0$ produces the ELES (Lluch 1973). This zero restriction achieves identification. Second, Howe (1975) uses the minimum-cost diet to determine subsistence food expenditure. The third approach exploits whatever cross-sectional price variation is available. For example, Betancourt (1971) uses the variation in wages (the opportunity cost of leisure) across households; Lluch (1971) uses regional price variation; and Kravis et al. (1982, Chap. 9) employ cross-country price variation. See also Pollak and Wales (1978). Fourth, with information on the total cost of subsistence, the value of the income elasticity of the marginal utility of income (referred to as "Frisch parameter") can be determined, from which the LES parameters can be identified.

Using a cross-sectional household survey, Clements et al. (2022) used a modified version of the last approach above to derive the LES parameters. Rather than specifying the value of the cost of subsistence, $\boldsymbol{p}'\boldsymbol{\gamma} = \sum_{i=1}^{n} p_i q_i$, they specified the

Frisch parameter itself. In LES, the Frisch "parameter" is the negative inverse of the supernumerary ratio:

$$\omega = -\frac{M}{M - \boldsymbol{p}'\boldsymbol{\gamma}} < 0. \tag{10.10}$$

Clements et al. (2022) use a Frisch parameter value of $\omega = -2$. The basis for this is the accumulation of evidence mostly from estimates of the Rotterdam model. Once the value of ω is known, all the parameters of LES can be estimated from a single household expenditure survey. First, the α_i intercepts and β_i coefficients in Eq. (10.8) can be estimated using n separate least-squares regressions of $p_i q_i$ on M. Second, given ω, the total cost of subsistence is determined from Eq. (10.10) as $\boldsymbol{p}'\boldsymbol{\gamma} = \left(1 + \frac{1}{\omega}\right)M$. Third, writing Eq. (10.9) as $\alpha_i = p_i\gamma_i - \beta_i \boldsymbol{p}'\boldsymbol{\gamma} = p_i\gamma_i - \beta_i\left(1 + \frac{1}{\omega}\right)M$, the value of subsistence expenditure for each good can then be recovered from the estimates of α_i and β_i as

$$p_i\gamma_i = \alpha_i + \beta_i(1 + \frac{1}{\omega})M, \quad i = 1, \cdots, n. \tag{10.11}$$

To derive the income and price elasticities, let $w_i = \frac{p_i q_i}{M}$ be the budget share of good i, $s_i = \frac{p_i \gamma_i}{M}$ be the fraction of income devoted to the subsistence consumption of i and $r = 1 - \sum_{j=1}^{n} s_j = \frac{M - \sum_{j=1}^{n} p_j\gamma_j}{M}$ be the supernumerary ratio. The LES of Eq. (10.1) can then be expressed in share form as

$$w_i = (1 - r)\frac{p_i\gamma_i}{\boldsymbol{p}'\boldsymbol{\gamma}} + r\beta_i.$$

Applying these shares to the logarithmic differential of Eq. (10.1) gives:

$$d(\log q_i) = \frac{\beta_i}{w_i} d(\log M) + \sum_{j=1}^{n} \left[\delta_{ij}\left(\frac{s_i}{w_i} - 1\right) - \frac{\beta_i}{w_i} s_j\right] d\left(\log p_j\right),$$

where δ_{ij} is again the Kronecker delta. This shows that $\eta_i = \frac{\beta_i}{w_i}$ is the income elasticity of good i. The corresponding Marshallian (uncompensated) and Slutsky (compensated) price elasticities are:

$$\eta_{ij} = \delta_{ij}\left(\frac{s_i}{w_i} - 1\right) - \frac{\beta_i}{w_i} s_j, \quad \eta_{ij}^{*} = \delta_{ij}\left(\frac{s_i}{w_i} - 1\right) + \frac{\beta_i}{w_i}\left(w_j - s_j\right).$$

Table 10.1 summarises the LES estimates of Clements et al. (2022) for 20 goods. Columns 2 and 3 present the LES coefficients which are all significant. Column 4 provides the income elasticities. Higher income elasticities are observed for

Table 10.1 LES coefficients and derived elasticities, Australia

Commodity group (1)	Coefficients of $p_iq_i = \alpha_i + \beta_iM$ (Standard errors): Intercept α_i (2)	Slope $\beta_i \times 100$ (3)	Income elasticity (4)	Own-price elasticities: Marshallian (5)	Slutsky (6)
1. Food	1476 (29.24)	7.95 (0.13)	0.806	−0.408	−0.328
2. Beverages and tobacco	67 (23.03)	3.45 (0.10)	1.077	−0.498	−0.463
3. Clothing and footwear	−179 (19.12)	3.63 (0.09)	1.171	−0.576	−0.539
4. Light goods manufactures	−349 (30.38)	8.36 (0.13)	1.120	−0.587	−0.504
5. Heavy goods manufactures	295 (19.62)	5.48 (0.09)	0.999	−0.478	−0.423
6. Utilities	1252 (14.71)	1.51 (0.07)	0.373	−0.191	−0.176
7. Housing	−132 (67.93)	16.31 (0.29)	0.954	−0.589	−0.426
8. Hotels and restaurants	−352 (23.3)	7.47 (0.10)	1.146	−0.590	−0.515
9. Private transportation	−542 (31.14)	4.51 (0.14)	1.198	−0.690	−0.645
10. Public transportation	−152 (17.73)	2.89 (0.08)	1.122	−0.576	−0.548
11. Communications	531 (13.14)	3.05 (0.06)	0.795	−0.383	−0.352
12. Finance	−795 (33.31)	7.85 (0.15)	1.266	−0.668	−0.590
13. Insurance	−39 (38.83)	9.62 (0.17)	0.908	−0.552	−0.456
14. Professional services	−43 (15.6)	1.26 (0.07)	1.032	−0.545	−0.533
15. Admin and support services	−166 (22.64)	2.48 (0.10)	1.124	−0.595	−0.570
16. Public a dministration	90 (8.9)	0.93 (0.04)	0.871	−0.419	−0.410
17. Education	−275 (21.23)	2.72 (0.10)	1.133	−0.650	−0.623
18. Health	−154 (19.9)	2.77 (0.09)	1.114	−0.580	−0.553
19. Recreation	−79 (12.91)	1.81 (0.06)	1.154	−0.560	−0.542
20. Other services	−457 (31.99)	6.06 (0.14)	1.122	−0.622	−0.561
Sum	0	100			

Note: Standard errors in parentheses

finance, private vehicles, apparel, recreation, and hotel and restaurants. Columns 5 and 6 give the own-price elasticities. These are all less than one in absolute value, as is to be expected for these fairly broad categories. The Marshallian elasticities are all larger than the Slutsky versions, but the differences are not substantial. As the difference between the two is $\eta_{ii} - \eta^{*}_{ii} = \beta_i$, the reason for the similarity is that many of the marginal shares necessarily tend to be modest when there are 20 goods. These results are further discussed in Chap. 11 with additional estimates of LES across income quintiles.

10.13 Intermediate Input Substitution

Next, we describe the estimation of the substitution elasticities in the input demand system of industries. Two estimation procedures are described here—one is the index-number approach of Selvanathan et al. (2024) and the other an econometric method.

If there are n intermediates, $C_j = \sum_{i=1}^{n} p_{ij} q_{ij}$ is the total cost of intermediate inputs used by industry j. The differential of total cost is $dC_j = \sum_{i=1}^{n} q_{ij} dp_{ij} + \sum_{i=1}^{n} p_{ij} dq_{ij}$. Dividing by C_j and using $\frac{dx}{x} = d\log x$, this becomes

$$d\left(\log C_j\right) = \sum_{i=1}^{n} a_{ij} d\left(\log p_{ij}\right) + \sum_{i=1}^{n} a_{ij} d\left(\log q_{ij}\right). \tag{10.12}$$

where $a_{ij} = \frac{p_{ij} q_{ij}}{C_j}$ is the share of intermediate input i in the total cost of intermediates with $0 < a_{ij} < 1$ and $\sum_{i=1}^{n} a_{ij} = 1$. The Divisia price and volume indexes are

$$d\left(\log P_j\right) = \sum_{i=1}^{n} a_{ij} d\left(\log p_{ij}\right), \quad d\left(\log Q_j\right) = \sum_{i=1}^{n} a_{ij} d\left(\log q_{ij}\right). \tag{10.13}$$

Equation (10.12) can thus be written as $d(\log C_j) = d(\log P_j) + d(\log Q_j)$, which shows that the change in total cost can be cleanly split into price and volume components.

We shall repeat some material from Chap. 6 after making obvious notational changes. The companion measures of dispersion are the Divisia second-order moments, the variances of prices (Π_j) and quantities (K_j), and the corresponding covariance (Γ_j):

$$\begin{cases} \Pi_j = \sum_{i=1}^{n} a_{ij}\{d(\log p_{ij}) - d(\log P_j)\}^2, \\ K_j = \sum_{i=1}^{n} a_{ij}\{d(\log q_{ji}) - d(\log Q_j)\}^2, \\ \Gamma_j = \sum_{i=1}^{n} a_{ij}\{d(\log p_{ij}) - d(\log P_j)\}\{d(\log q_{ij}) - d(\log Q_j)\}. \end{cases} \tag{10.14}$$

If there is substitutability between inputs, more expensive inputs can be economised on with cheaper ones, and the price-quantity covariance Γ_j would tend to be negative.

For a particular industry, the CES production function is represented by Eq. (10.2). The industry chooses the input mix to minimise total cost, $C = \sum_{i=1}^{n} p_i q_i$. The cost-minimising demand for input i is

$$q_i = \alpha_i^{\sigma} \frac{C}{P^*}\left(\frac{p_i}{P^*}\right)^{-\sigma}, \tag{10.15}$$

while the cost-minimising share for input i is $a_i = \frac{\alpha_i^{\sigma} p_i^{1-\sigma}}{\sum_{k=1}^{n} \alpha_k^{\sigma} p_k^{1-\sigma}}$, which we write as

$$a_i = \alpha_i^{\sigma}\left(\frac{p_i}{P^*}\right)^{1-\sigma}, \tag{10.16}$$

where P^* is the CES price index

$$P^* = \left(\sum_{j=1}^{n} \alpha_j^{\sigma} p_j^{1-\sigma}\right)^{\frac{1}{1-\sigma}}. \tag{10.17}$$

From Eq. (10.15), the price elasticity of demand is $-\sigma$. Eq. (10.16) shows that the share a_i is constant when $\sigma = 1$, as it is under Cobb-Douglas technology, while when there is no substitution, $\sigma = 0$ (the Leontief assumption) and the share is unit elastic. Eq. (10.15) is the same as Eq. (10.4) with appropriate reinterpretation.

The logarithmic differential of the CES price index (10.17) is

$$d\log P^* = d\log\left(\sum_{j=1}^{n} \alpha_j^{\sigma} p_j^{1-\sigma}\right)^{\frac{1}{1-\sigma}} = \sum_{j=1}^{n} \frac{\alpha_j^{\sigma} p_j^{1-\sigma}}{(P^*)^{1-\sigma}} d\log p_j.$$

Using Eq. (10.16), the price index simplifies to

$$d\log P^* = \sum_{j=1}^{n} a_j d\log p_j,$$

so that this CES price index coincides with the Divisia price index $d\log P$ in Eq. (10.13).

The differential of Eq. (10.15) gives the linearised demand equation

$$d\log q_i - d\log Q = -\sigma(d\log p_i - d\log P), \tag{10.18}$$

where $d\log Q = d\log C - d\log P$ and σ is the elasticity of input substitution. Multiplying both sides of Eq. (10.18) by $d\log p_i - d\log P$, weighting by a_i and then summing over $i = 1, \cdots, n$, gives

$$\sum_{i=1}^{n} a_i\{d(\log p_i) - d(\log P)\}\{d(\log q_i) - d(\log Q)\}$$

$$= -\sigma \sum_{i=1}^{n} a_i\{d(\log p_i) - d(\log P)\}^2.$$

In view of the Divisia second-order moments in Eq. (10.14), the above equation can be simplified into $\Gamma = -\sigma\Pi$, or

$$\sigma = -\frac{\Gamma}{\Pi}. \tag{10.19}$$

Equation (10.19) implies that when CES and Divisia are combined, the elasticity of substitution emerges as the ratio of the weighted covariance to variance with the sign changed, an attractively simple result. Using the means of the Divisia moments, Eq. (10.19) can be used to provide convenient preliminary estimates of the elasticity of input substitution. However, a limitation of this is it does not provide an indication the statistical accuracy of the calculated σ' s.

A more rigorous approach is to use an econometric method that allows testing statistical significance. To econometrically estimate the CES demand system in Eq. (10.18), we replace infinitesimal logarithmic changes with discrete changes and weight observations by multiplying both sides by the cost share of *i*. This yields the system of *n* equations:

$$\bar{a}_{it}(Dq_{it} - DQ_t) = \gamma\{\bar{a}_{it}(Dp_{it} - DP_t)\} + \varepsilon_{it}, \quad i = 1, \cdots, n; t = 2, \cdots, T, \tag{10.20}$$

where $\bar{a}_{it} = \frac{1}{2}(a_{it} + a_{i,t-1})$ is the average of the shares in two consecutive years; $Dq_{it} = \log q_{it} - \log q_{i,t-1}$ is the log-change in the quantity; $Dp_{it} = \log p_{it} - \log p_{i,t-1}$ is the log-change in the price; $DP_t = \sum_{i=1}^{n} \bar{a}_{it} Dp_{it}$ is the discrete Divisia price index of inputs; $DQ_t = \sum_{i=1}^{n} \bar{a}_{it} Dq_{it}$ is the discrete Divisia quantity index; $\gamma = -\sigma$ is the elasticity of substitution with the sign changed; and ε_{it} is a disturbance term.

A noteworthy feature of system (10.20) is the price term in each equation contains only the own-relative price, with cross-price effects absorbed into the price index. A related property is that the price coefficient γ takes the same value in each equation. Equation (10.20) can be estimated as a system of seemingly unrelated regression equations for each using industry. To take account of any residual trend-like changes in the input mix, an intercept θ_i is added to each equation with $\sum_{i=1}^{n}\theta_i = 0$. Equation (10.20) is consistent with the CES framework as demonstrated by Selvanathan (1985).

Mariano et al. (2024) employed both the index-number and econometric approaches to estimate the substitution elasticities for 30 industries. The results are in Table 10.2. Column 2 gives the first set of elasticity estimates derived from the index-number approach. All the elasticities deviate from zero and are less than unity. These non-zero values of sigma reflect that input shares respond to relative changes in prices. Column 3 provides the second set derived from econometrically estimating the parameters of the CES input demand system. Twenty-four of the 31 coefficients are significantly positive. There are two insignificant negative estimates. Comparing the two sets of elasticities, the weighted means are quite close: 0.476 for the elasticities from the index-number approach, and 0.402 for the econometric estimates. Nonetheless, the econometric estimates might be judged to be more precise as indicated by a lower root-mean-square error (RMSE) of 0.024 as compared to 0.075 for the index-number approach. The subsequent chapter provides more detailed discussion of the data and estimation results.

10.14 Import-Domestic Substitution

Goods demanded by households and firms are differentiated as domestically produced or imported from other countries. Using the Armington framework, this product differentiation is usually represented in CGE models as a CES aggregate of the domestic and foreign varieties. As previously described, the CES utility function for good i is represented by Eq. (10.2) and the corresponding demand equation is given by Eq. (10.4). With two varieties of good i (i.e. domestic = 1 and imported = 2), the CES demand equations can be written as

$$q_i^1 = \left(\alpha_i^1\right)^{\sigma_i} \frac{M_i}{P_i^*}\left(\frac{p_i^1}{P_i^*}\right)^{-\sigma_i}, q_i^2 = \left(\alpha_i^2\right)^{\sigma_i} \frac{M_i}{P_i^*}\left(\frac{p_i^2}{P_i^*}\right)^{-\sigma_i},$$

where superscripts represent the corresponding prices of the domestic and imported varieties of the good. Taking logs then gives the relative demand for the goods:

$$\log\left(\frac{q_i^1}{q_i^2}\right) = \beta_i - \sigma_i \log\left(\frac{p_i^1}{p_i^2}\right), \tag{10.21}$$

Table 10.2 Elasticity of input substitution, Australia

	Using industry (1)	Index-number estimates (2)	Econometric estimates (3)
1	Sheep, grains, cattle, poultry, and other livestock	0.522	0.515 (0.052)
2	Forestry, fishery, and agriculture services	0.542	0.579 (0.074)
3	Energy and mineral mining	0.435	0.391 (0.051)
4	Food, beverage, and tobacco	0.297	0.300 (0.080)
5	Textile, cloth, and footwear	0.597	0.556 (0.111)
6	Wood and paper	0.360	0.357 (0.066)
7	Chemical and non-metal manufacturing	0.563	0.587 (0.079)
8	Metal products manufacturing	0.583	1.005 (0.081)
9	Transport equipment	0.072	−0.230 (0.146)
10	Machinery and other equipment	0.104	0.121 (0.106)
11	Furniture and other manufacturing	0.267	0.377 (0.105)
12	Construction services	0.332	0.324 (0.061)
13	Wholesale and retail trade	0.687	0.724 (0.040)
14	Accommodation and food services	0.545	0.431 (0.056)
15	Transport services	0.289	0.283 (0.050)
16	Information media and telecommunication	0.463	0.463 (0.068)
17	Finance and insurance services	0.203	0.753 (0.100)
18	Rental and hire services	0.174	0.176 (0.063)
19	Dwelling and real estate	0.507	0.893 (0.127)
20	Professional, scientific, and technical services	0.206	0.383 (0.056)
21	Administrative and support services	0.348	0.350 (0.057)
22	Public administration, defence, and security	0.419	0.396 (0.046)
23	Primary and secondary education	0.219	0.018 (0.092)
24	Tertiary and vocational education	0.470	−0.111 (0.131)
25	Other education and training services	0.359	0.565 (0.111)
26	Health care services	0.317	0.040 (0.067)
27	Heritage, creative, and performing arts	0.449	0.166 (0.109)
28	Sports and recreation	0.700	0.799 (0.071)
29	Repair and maintenance	0.595	0.674 (0.062)
30	Other services	0.580	0.553 (0.056)
31	Weighted mean	0.476	0.402 (0.035)
	RMSE	0.075	0.024

Note: Standard errors in parentheses

where $\beta_i = \sigma_i \log\left(\frac{\alpha_i^1}{\alpha_i^2}\right)$ is an intercept. This equation implies that for good *i*, a 1-per cent increase in the price of the domestic variety (p_i^1), relative to the foreign one (p_i^2), leads to a fall in the volume of domestic sales (q_i^1) relative to foreign sales (q_i^2) of σ_i per cent. Equation (10.21) is the most common form used to estimate the elasticity of

Table 10.3 Single-equation OLS and panel estimates of Armington elasticities

	Commodity (1)	OLS estimates (2)	Panel estimates (3)
1	Meat products	1.000 (0.160)	1.133 (0.185)
2	Dairy products and egg	0.906 (0.189)	1.051 (0.203)
3	Fish products	0.608 (0.239)	0.839 (0.230)
4	Other food products	0.710 (0.129)	1.013 (0.331)
5	Beverage and tobacco	1.009 (0.292)	1.268 (0.462)
6	Coal, petroleum, and gas	0.642 (0.098)	0.747 (0.093)
7	Basic chemicals	0.637 (0.137)	0.849 (0.251)
8	Pharmaceutical products	0.523 (0.471)	0.730 (0.603)
9	Textile and leather	0.682 (0.213)	1.004 (0.282)
10	Clothing and footwear	0.775 (0.165)	1.033 (0.295)
11	Wood and products	0.823 (0.333)	1.210 (0.413)
12	Paper products	0.858 (0.157)	1.009 (0.303)
13	Furniture	0.826 (0.170)	0.991 (0.279)
14	Non-metals	0.552 (0.107)	0.777 (0.273)
15	Iron steel	0.301 (0.202)	0.494 (0.235)
16	Non-ferrous metals	1.002 (0.434)	1.048 (0.174)
17	Machinery equipment	0.742 (0.162)	0.978 (0.33)
18	Motor vehicles and parts	0.143 (0.525)	0.355 (0.728)
19	Transport equipment	2.056 (0.660)	2.246 (0.306)
20	Other manufactures	0.742 (0.180)	0.905 (0.264)

Note: Standard errors in parentheses

substitution between domestic and imported goods. This can be estimated with time-series data by a single-equation least-squares regression or a panel approach.

Clements et al. (2021) econometrically estimated the Armington elasticities for 20 commodity groups and Table 10.3 summarises the results. Column 2 gives the least single-equation estimates. All of the substitution elasticities are positive and mostly significant, where they range from 0.14 for Motor Vehicles to 2.06 for Transport Equipment, and the majority of the significant estimates are either less than unity or very close to it. Column 3 gives the results for the panel approach, which has two advantages over the single-equation estimates. First, it allows for the easy incorporation of a time effect for each year that affects all goods simultaneously such as a transport disruption that delays the delivery of all imported goods. A second advantage is that the panel approach facilitates the testing of hypotheses covering multiple sectors, as demonstrated in Chap. 11. Relative to the single-equation estimates, the elasticities from the panel approach tend to be more significant and larger, ranging from 0.36 to 2.25.

10.15 Elasticities Matter I: Households

The remaining sections of the chapter demonstrate how elasticity values influence the outcomes of policy simulations in a CGE model. Further details of the results to be discussed are contained in the next chapter. One of the significant advances in the CGE field is the incorporation of a microsimulation capability through an explicit representation of household heterogeneity. Modelling heterogeneous behaviour across households is necessary in evaluating the distributional impact of policies or economic development. Using a multi-household CGE model, Clements et al. (2022) tested the sensitivity of modelling results to two sets of LES estimates. The first simulation applies a single LES model such that all households have uniform elasticities for each good. The second simulation splits households into quintile groups and assigns the quintile LES estimates, thereby allowing elasticities to vary across household groups. Each simulation moves the Australian economy along a cyclically balanced 30-year growth path beginning in 2020.

Modelling results show a rise in GDP of 2.2 per cent per annum over the 30-year period. This GDP growth reflects higher incomes for households receiving income from primary factors inputs. Higher disposable incomes indicate higher purchasing power and thus an increase in consumption for a constant saving rate. This increase in household income drives a substantial change in the structure of the economy over 30 years as revealed by the changes in household budget shares, as shown in Fig. 10.4. With the increasing incomes, the shares of luxuries and necessities increase and decrease, respectively. However, household disaggregation results in a systematic difference: when the demand responses are allowed to vary over the

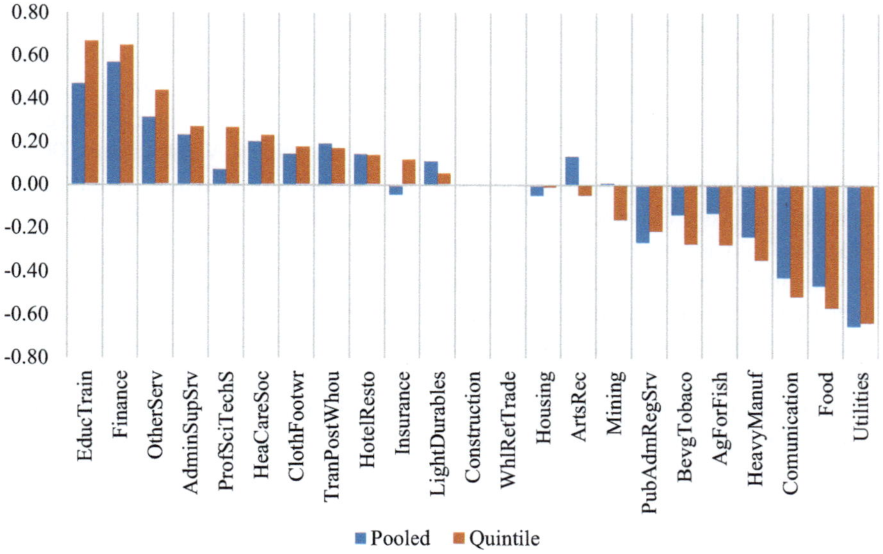

Fig. 10.4 Average annual change in budget shares (%)

income distribution, the greater dispersion of income elasticities means the rise (fall) in the shares of luxuries (necessities) tends to be larger. In other words, the differences in budget-share changes are positively correlated with income elasticities. This finding indicates disaggregation amplifies structural change.

10.16 Elasticities Matter II: Producers

The input demand elasticities in a CGE model influence the magnitude of demand responses of producers to changes in input prices. A high (low) input elasticity value means that sectors are more (less) sensitive to changes in input prices. Mariano et al. (2024) demonstrated the implications of input demand elasticities on modelling results. Their CGE simulation mimics a carbon price policy by applying a 100-per cent ad valorem sales tax on the use of fossil-based fuel products as a production input. This simulation was undertaken four times using four sets of input substitution elasticities. First is where $\sigma_j = 0$ based on Leontief production technology. Second is where $\sigma_j = 0.25$ based on elasticities applied in Verikios et al. (2021) and supported by the work of Bruno (1984) and Atalay (2017). The third is a wider range of CES elasticities $0.07 < \sigma_j < 1$, based on the econometric estimates of Mariano et al. (2024). Fourth is setting $\sigma_j = 1$ based on Cobb-Douglas production technology. All other parameters in the CGE model are held constant in each of the four simulations; thus, the differences in results across simulations are purely due to the differences in the values of the elasticity input substitution.

In general, the first-round effect of the sales tax is to raise the relative price of fuel products. Starting with the Leontief assumption where sigma is zero, the modelling results show a 2.33-per cent increase in output price of fuel products. Such a price increase should provide an incentive for producers to switch to another energy source such as electricity. However, Leontief technology assumes zero substitutability for intermediate inputs (i.e. $\sigma = 0$). So the first-round effect on higher fuel prices will just flow through to higher output prices. The largest changes in output price are observed for industries that are the most intensive users of fossil fuels such as manufacturing and transport services. These industries generally experience the largest contraction in economic activity due to a large price-induced fall in demand.

As substitution possibilities increase (i.e. σ increases), all industries are able to substitute electricity for other fuels to a greater extent. Modelling results indicate an increase in the demand for electricity; i.e. this sector expands by 10.5 per cent with Cobb-Douglas technology compared to a contraction of 7.1 per cent with Leontief technology. It is clear in Fig. 10.5 that there is a reversal of output effects for alternative fuels (i.e. electricity), from a contraction to a significant expansion. Figure 10.6 shows the effects on economy-wide price and output changes as sigma increases. On average, the price and volume decreases are smaller as σ rises: For $\sigma = 1$ the mean reduction in price is -3.2 per cent while for volumes the reduction is 2.2 per cent. This demonstrates that taking the traditional Leontief

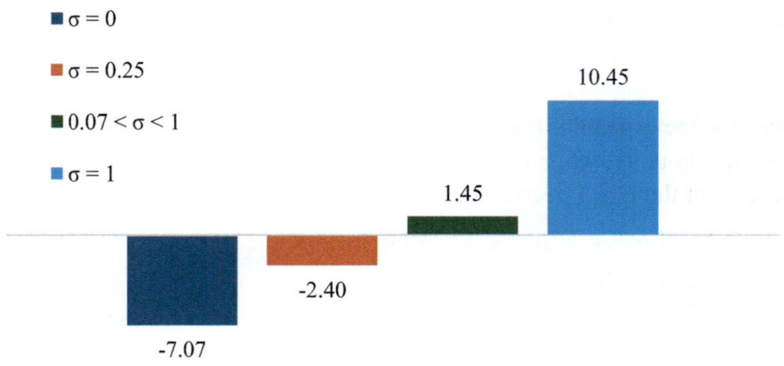

Fig. 10.5 Percentage change in electricity output

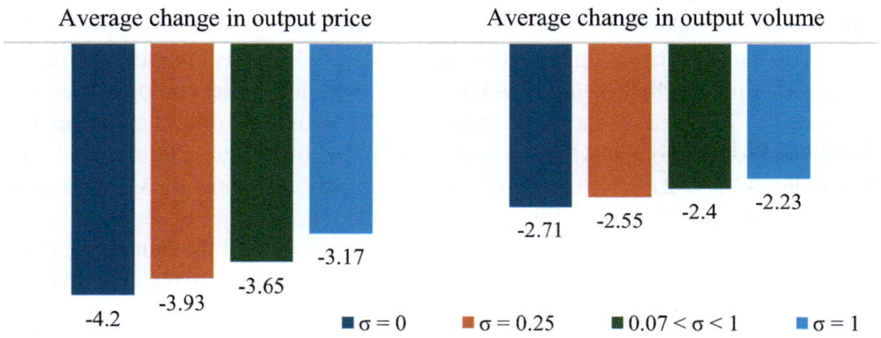

Fig. 10.6 Percentage change in economy-wide price and quantity

assumption where the IO coefficients are fixed can have misleading economic implications.

10.17 Elasticities Matter III: Armington Elasticities

The Armington elasticities play a critical role in determining results in a CGE model, particularly in assessing the economic impacts of international policies. The Armington approach of product differentiation captures the frequently observed phenomenon of "cross-hauling" where a country simultaneously imports and exports the same commodities. A common explanation for this is product differentiation, where the domestic variety of a particular good and its imported counterpart are imperfectly substitutable due to their heterogeneous nature. The degree of heterogeneity is reflected by the elasticity of substitution: Higher elasticity values imply less heterogeneity, and more heterogeneity for lower values. For consumers,

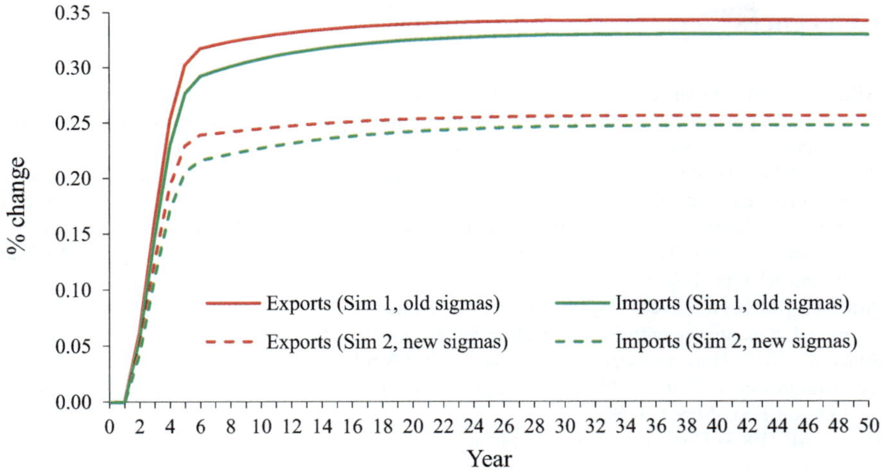

Fig. 10.7 Imports and exports, percentage deviation from baseline

the Armington elasticities determine how a given income is allocated between domestic and imported products.

Clements et al. (2021) demonstrated the sensitivity of modelling results to different values of Armington elasticities. Using a CGE model, they simulated a trade liberalisation policy where all tariffs levied on imported products are completely removed. This trade liberalisation experiment is applied twice: Simulation 1 uses old Armington elasticities from Alaouze et al. (1977) and Simulation 2 uses new elasticities from Clements et al. (2021). There has been remarkable growth in the market shares of goods imported into Australia over the past decades. This change in market structure alters the way consumers respond to the relative price of domestic and imported products. The new estimates of Armington elasticities (Simulation 2) reveal that consumers are less responsive to recent changes in the relative price of domestic and imported goods as indicated by a lower average of the new elasticities (1.16) relative to the old ones (1.54). In terms of the modelling results, as shown in Fig. 10.7, this finding generates smaller price-induced responses in quantity variables relative to the old estimates of elasticities (Simulation 1).

A similar trade liberalisation experiment is also conducted by Zhang and Verikios (2006) using a global CGE model—GTAP. They tested the effect of two sets of new elasticities (one is CES and the other is CRESH) relative to the original GTAP elasticities. The new elasticities are region-specific while the original elasticities are region-generic. Their modelling results show that, compared with the standard GTAP elasticities, the new elasticities generate more diversified changes in imports across regions. In particular, there is more (less) substitutability between domestic and imported goods in developed (developing) countries in response to changes in their relative price.

References

ABS (2021) Australian Bureau of statistics, National Accounts data. Available online at https://www.abs.gov.au/statistics/economy/national-accounts/australian-national-accounts-input-output-tables/2018-19#input-output-multipliers

Alaouze CM, Marsden JS, Zeitsch J (1977) Estimates of the elasticity of substitution between imported and domestically produced commodities at the four digit ASIC level. IMPACT project, Industries Assistance Commission, Working paper no. 0–11, Melbourne, January

Armington PS (1969) The geographic pattern of trade and the effects of price changes. IMF Staff Papers XVI, pp 176–99

Arndt C, Robinson S, Tarp F (2002) Parameter estimation for a computable general equilibrium model: a maximum entropy approach. Econ Model 19:375–398

Atalay E (2017) How important are sectoral shocks? Am Econ J Macroecon 9:254–280

Bandara JS (1991) Computable general equilibrium models for development policy analysis in LDCs. J Econ Surv 5:3–69

Barten AP (1964) Consumer demand functions under conditions of almost additive preferences. Econometrica 32:1–38

Betancourt RR (1971) The estimation of price elasticities from cross-section data under additive preferences. Int Econ Rev 12:283–292

Betancourt RR (1973) The analysis of patterns of consumption in underdeveloped countries. Paper presented to the ECIEL conference on consumption, prices, and economic development, Hamburg, Germany

Bisschop J, Meeraus A (1982) On the development of a general algebraic modelling system in a strategic planning environment. Math Program Stud 20:1–29

Boccanfuso D, Decaluwé B, Savard L (2008) Poverty, income distribution and CGE micro-simulation modeling: does the functional form of distribution matter? J Econ Inequal 6:149–184

Bouët A, Estrades C, Laborde D (2011) Households heterogeneity in a global CGE model: an illustration with the MIRAGE poverty module. Paper presented at the 14th annual conference on global economic analysis, Venice, Italy

Brester GW, Atwood JA, Boland MA (2023) Equilibrium displacement models: theory, applications and policy analysis. University of Minnesota Libraries Publishing

Bruno M (1984) Raw materials, profits, and the productivity slowdown. Q J Econ 99:1–30

Burfisher ME (2021) Introduction to computable general equilibrium models. Cambridge University Press, Cambridge

Bussolo M, Lay J (2003) Globalisation and poverty changes in Colombia. Working paper 28734. World Bank Group, Washington, DC

Cai Y, Newth D, Finnigan D, Gunasekera D (2015) A hybrid energy-economy model for global integrated assessment of climate change, carbon mitigation and energy transformation. Appl Energy 148:381–395

Christensen L, Jorgenson D, Lau L (1975) Transcendental logarithmic utility functions. Am Econ Rev 65:367–383

Clark M (2018) Whole-of-economy modelling: beyond the black box. Staff Research Paper, Queensland Productivity Commission, Queensland

Clements KW, Mariano MJM, Verikios G (2021) Foreign-domestic substitution, import penetration, and CGE modelling. Appl Econ 53:209–231

Clements KW, Mariano MJM, Verikios G (2022) Expenditure patterns, heterogeneity and long-term structural change. Econ Model 113

Cockburn J (2001) Trade liberalization and poverty in Nepal: a computable general equilibrium micro simulation analysis. Centre for the Study of African Economies and Nuffield College

Cogneau D, Anne-Sophie R (2000) Income distribution, poverty and growth in madagascar: learning from a microsimulation model in a general equilibrium framework. Trade and Macroeconomic Division (TMD) Discussion Paper No. 61. IFPRI, Washington, DC

Cororaton C (2003) Analysis of trade reforms, income inequality and poverty using microsimulation approach: the case of The Philippines. Philippines Institute of Development Studies, paper no. 2003–09

Deaton AS, Muellbauer J (1980) Economics and consumer behaviour. Cambridge University Press, Cambridge

Decaluwé B, Dumont JC, Savard L (1999) How to measure poverty and inequality in general equilibrium framework. Laval University, CREFA Working Paper 9920

Devarajan S, Robinson S (2005) The influence of computable general equilibrium models on policy. In: Kehoe TJ, Srinivasan TN, Whalley J (eds) Frontiers in applied general equilibrium modeling: in honor of Herbert Scarf. Cambridge University Press, Cambridge, pp 402–428

Diewert WE, Lawrence D (1994) The marginal costs of taxation in New Zealand. Report prepared for the New Zealand Business Round Table by Swan Consultants Pty Ltd., Canberra

Dixon PB, Jorgenson D (2013) Handbook of CGE modeling, vol 1, Amsterdam, pp 995–1068

Dixon PB, Parmenter BR, Powell AA, Wilcoxen PJ (1992) Notes and problems in applied general equilibrium economics, Amsterdam

Dixon PB, Parmenter BR, Sutton J, Vincent DP (1982) ORANI: a Multisectoral model of the Australian economy, Amsterdam

Dixon PB, Jerie M, Rimmer MT (2016) Modern trade theory for CGE modelling: the Armington, Krugman and Melitz models. J Glob Econ Anal 1:1–110

Giesecke JA, Madden JR (2013) Regional computable general equilibrium modeling. In: Dixon PB, Jorgenson D (eds) Handbook of CGE modeling, vol 1, Amsterdam, pp 379–475

Ginsburgh V, Waelbroeck J (1981) Activity analysis and general equilibrium modelling. Amsterdam

Goldberger AS (1987) Functional form and utility: a review of consumer demand theory. Westview Press, Boulder and London

Gretton P (2013). On input-output tables: uses and abuses. Staff Research Note, Productivity Commission, Canberra

Hanoch G (1971) CRESH production functions. Econometrica 39:695–712

Harrison WJ, Pearson RK (1996) Computing solutions for large general equilibrium models using GEMPACK. Comput Econ 9:83–127

Hertel TW (2013) Global applied general equilibrium analysis using the global trade analysis project framework. In: Dixon PB, Jorgenson D (eds) Handbook of CGE modeling, vol 1, Amsterdam, pp 815–876

Howe H (1975) Development of the extended linear expenditure system from simple saving assumptions. Eur Econ Rev 6:305–310

Jensen J, Tarr D (2003) Trade, exchange rate, and energy pricing reform in Iran: potentially large efficiency effects and gains to the poor. Rev Dev Econ 7:543–562

Johansen L (1960) A multisectoral study of economic growth, Amsterdam

Jorgensen DW (1984) Econometric methods for applied general equilibrium analysis. In: Scarf H, Shoven JB (eds) Applied general equilibrium analysis. Cambridge University Press, New York, pp 139–203

Jorgensen DW, Slesnick DT, Wilcoxen PJ (1992) Carbon taxes and economic welfare. Harvard Institute of Economic Research Discussion Paper 1589

Kravis IB, Heston A, Summers R (1982) World product and income: international comparisons of real gross product. Johns Hopkins University Press, Baltimore, MD

Layman B (2002) The use and abuse of input-output multipliers. Economic Research Articles, Department of Treasury and Finance, Western Australia

Lau L (1984) Comments on Mansur and Whalley (1984). In: Scarf H, Shoven JB (eds) Applied general equilibrium analysis. Cambridge University Press, New York, pp 127–137

Leontief WW (1936) Quantitative input-output relations in the economic system of the United States. Rev Econ Stat 18:105–125

Leontief W, Chenery HB, Clark PG, Duesenberry JS, Ferguson AR, Grosse AP, Grosse RN, Holzman M, Isard W, Kisten H (1953) Studies in the structure of the American economy. Oxford University Press, New York

Lloyd PJ, Zhang XG (2006) The Armington model. Productivity Commission. Staff Working Paper, Melbourne, January

Lluch C (1971) Consumer demand functions, Spain, 1958-1964. Eur Econ Rev 2:277–302

Lluch C (1973) The extended linear expenditure system. Eur Econ Rev 4:21–32

Mariano MJM, Verikios G, Clements KW (2024) Are input-output coefficients really fixed? Appl Econ:1–24

McKibbin WJ, Wilcoxen PJ (2013) A global approach to energy and the environment: the G-cubed model. In: Dixon PB, Jorgenson D (eds) Handbook of CGE modeling, vol 1, Amsterdam, pp 995–1068

McKitrick RR (1998) The econometric critique of computable general equilibrium modeling: the role of functional forms. Econ Model 15:543–573

Miller RE, Blair PD (2009) Input-output analysis: foundations and extensions, 2nd edn. Cambridge University Press, Cambridge

Pollak RA, Wales TJ (1978) Estimation of complete demand systems from household budget data: the linear and quadratic expenditure systems. Am Econ Rev 68:348–359

Powell AA (1973) Estimation of Lluch's extended linear expenditure system from cross-sectional data. Aust J Stat 15:111–117

Scarf HE, Shoven JB (1983) Applied general equilibrium analysis. Cambridge University Press, New York

Scarf HE, Hansen T (1973) The computation of economic equilibria. Yale University Press, New Haven, CT

Selvanathan EA (1985) An even simpler differential demand system. Econ Lett 19:343–347

Selvanathan EA, Selvanathan S, Clements KW (2024) Estimating the elasticity of substitution: an index number approach. J Int Trade Econ Dev. forthcoming

Shiells CR, Reinert KA (1993) Armington models and terms-of-trade effects: some econometric evidence for North America. Can J Econ 26:299–316

Shoven JB, Whalley J (1984) Applied general-equilibrium models of taxation and international trade: an introduction and survey. J Econ Lit 22:1007–1051

Shoven JB, Whalley J (1992) Applying general equilibrium. Cambridge University Press, Cambridge

Stone R (1954) Linear expenditure systems and demand analysis: an application to the pattern of British demand. Econ J 64:511–527

Theil H (1965) The information approach to demand analysis. Econometrica 33:67–87

van der Mensbrugghe D (2011) LINKAGE technical reference document: version 7.1. The World Bank, Washington, DC

Verikios G, Hanslow K, Mariano MJM, Clements KW (2021) Understanding the Australian economy: a computable general equilibrium model with updated data and parameters. Department of Accounting, finance and economics, discussion paper series 2021–06, Griffith University

Wohlgenant MK (2011) Consumer demand and welfare in equilibrium displacement models. Chapter 11. In: Lusk JL, Roosen J, Shogren JF (eds) The Oxford handbook of the economics of food consumption and policy. Oxford University Press, Oxford

Zhai F (2008) Armington meets Melitz: introducing firm heterogeneity in a global CGE model of trade. J Econ Integr 23:575–604

Zhang X, Verikios G (2006) Armington parameter estimation for a computable general equilibrium model: a database consistent approach. Economics Discussion Paper 06-10, The University of Western Australia

Chapter 11
Demand Analysis for CGE Modelling and EDM II: Further Results and Details

This chapter provides more details and elaboration of the ideas and results of the previous chapter. While the focus is on the estimation of demand systems and their use in CGE, much of the material on demand modelling is sufficiently general to be useful for EDMs also.

11.1 Household Demands: The Linear Expenditure System

As discussed in the previous chapter, the linear expenditure system (LES) is a popular model for analysing consumer behaviour. The model takes the form

$$p_i q_i = p_i \gamma_i + \beta_i \left(M - \sum_{j=1}^{n} p_j \gamma_j \right), \quad i = 1, \cdots, n, \tag{11.1}$$

where $p_i q_i$ is expenditure on good i, p_i is the price of the good, M is income, $p_i \gamma_i$ is the cost of subsistence, and n is the number of goods. If citations are a measure of success, then according to Google Scholar (July 2024), the original Stone (1954) article alone has more than 2300 citations. This popularity of LES is partly due to its status in history: It was the first demand system satisfying the "triad" requirements of microeconomics of the budget constraint, homogeneity of degree zero, and symmetry of the substitution effects, as well being consistent with Engel's law (the income elasticity of food demand less than unity). The Cobb-Douglas and CES models also satisfy the triad, but as all income elasticities are unity, they violate the Engel's law.

There are several other reasons accounting for the prominence of LES:

- *Linearity in variables*: As its name indicates, LES expresses expenditures as a linear function of income and the prices. This leads to straightforward algebraic

K. W. Clements et al., *Short-cut Demand Elasticities and Other Convenient Approaches to Consumer Demand*, https://doi.org/10.1007/978-981-96-3588-7_11

manipulation, as well as ease of use when the system is embedded as part of a larger model.

- *Clear interpretation*: As mentioned above, the γ_i's can be interpreted as subsistence quantities (when $\gamma_i > 0$), the minima needed to generate utility. According to LES, total expenditure is first allocated to subsistence and then to supernumerary requirements. The coefficients attached to supernumerary income, the β_i's, are marginal shares, and the ratio of these to the corresponding budget shares are the income elasticities. The utility function underlying the LES is Stone-Geary, $u(q_1, \cdots, q_n) = \sum_{i=1}^{n} \beta_i \log(q_i - \gamma_i)$, with $\sum_{i=1}^{n} \beta_i = 1$. Clearly, this requires $q_i > \gamma_i$, $i = 1, \ldots, n$. There is no problem when $\gamma_i < 0$, but the subsistence interpretation is not applicable.
- *Parsimony of parameters*: In general, the $n \times n$ matrix of compensated price slopes of n demand functions is symmetric, negative semi-definite with $\frac{1}{2}n(n-1)$ free elements. Adding the n income responses gives a total of $\frac{1}{2}n(n+1)$ free parameters, which for $n = 10$ is 55. By contrast, LES contains n γ_i's and $(n - 1)$ β_i's (one is constrained by $\sum_{i=1}^{n} \beta_i = 1$), or $2n - 1 = 19$ for $n = 10$. There is thus a substantial economy of parameterisation in LES, which is attractive for econometric estimation, especially for medium- to large-size systems and/or when the model is applied to data with modest variability.
- *Mildly non-linear in the parameters*: As the marginal shares and γ_i's appear as a product in LES, non-linear optimisation approaches are needed for estimation. But modern software can handle this challenge fairly easily.

The above attractive features come at some cost, however—there are no free lunches. The main limitations of LES are:

- *Additive utility*: The Stone-Geary utility function is additive in the n goods, meaning that each marginal utility depends only on consumption of the good in question, not the others (i.e. preference independence). This is usually taken to imply that LES can be applied to the consumption of broadly defined commodities only, not more narrow ones that would be more likely to have utility interactions with others. Additive utility leads to the following two restrictions on demand.
- *Income effects*: All goods are normal, as from the Stone-Geary each $\beta_i > 0$. This restriction is possibly a mild one for all but a few minor goods.
- *Price substitution*:

  (i) *Goods are substitutes*: On the basis of the income-compensated substitution effect, all pairs of goods are substitutes, there can be no complementarity. This means the Slutsky cross-price elasticities are all positive.

  (ii) *Price inelasticity*: Each Marshallian own-price elasticity (which combines the income and substitution effects) is less than unity in absolute value when the associated $\gamma_i > 0$, as is usually the case.

- *Functional form*: Linearity is one of the above advantages of LES, but linear Engel curves is a restrictive property when the range of income is substantial.

All models have their strengths and weaknesses as they are only imperfect approximations to actual behaviour. The LES is not perfect, but when applied with care, the model can shed considerable light on the determinants of consumption patterns.

11.2 An Identification Problem

Consider a household survey in which all households face the same prices. LES (11.1) simplifies to

$$p_i q_i = \alpha_i + \beta_i M, \quad i = 1, \cdots, n \tag{11.2}$$

where

$$\alpha_i = \sum_{j=1}^{n} (\delta_{ij} - \beta_i) p_j \gamma_j, \quad i = 1, \cdots, n. \tag{11.3}$$

Here, δ_{ij} is the Kronecker delta ($\delta_{ij} = 1$ if $i = j, 0$ otherwise).

From the budget constraint $\sum_{i=1}^{n} p_i q_i = M$, there are adding-up constraints on the coefficients, viz., $\sum_{i=1}^{n} \alpha_i = 0$ and, as before, $\sum_{i=1}^{n} \beta_i = 1$. Cross-sectional data can be used to estimate system (11.2) to give the n marginal shares, $\beta_1, \cdots, \beta_n$, as well as the n intercepts, $\alpha_1, \cdots, \alpha_n$. The question is, can we then recover from these estimates the n subsistence parameters, $\gamma_1, \cdots, \gamma_n$, by using relationship (11.3)? The answer is no. To establish this negative result, define the $n \times 1$ vectors $\boldsymbol{\alpha} = [\alpha_1, \cdots, \alpha_n]'$, $\tilde{\boldsymbol{\gamma}} = [p_1 \gamma_1, \cdots, p_n \gamma_n]'$, and $\boldsymbol{\beta} = [\beta_1, \cdots, \beta_n]'$. We can then write Eq. (11.3) in vector form as $\boldsymbol{\alpha} = (\boldsymbol{I} - \boldsymbol{\beta}\boldsymbol{\iota}')\tilde{\boldsymbol{\gamma}}$, where $\boldsymbol{I}$ is the $n \times n$ identity matrix and $\boldsymbol{\iota}' = [1, \cdots, 1]$, or

$$\boldsymbol{\alpha} = \boldsymbol{A}\tilde{\boldsymbol{\gamma}}, \quad \boldsymbol{A} = \boldsymbol{I} - \boldsymbol{\beta}\boldsymbol{\iota}'.$$

The $\boldsymbol{A}$ matrix has zero column sums, that is,

$$\boldsymbol{\iota}'\boldsymbol{A} = \boldsymbol{\iota}'\boldsymbol{I} - \boldsymbol{\iota}'\boldsymbol{\beta}\boldsymbol{\iota}' = \boldsymbol{\iota}' - \boldsymbol{\iota}' = \boldsymbol{0}',$$

where the second step follows from $\sum_{i=1}^{n} \beta_i = 1$, or $\boldsymbol{\iota}'\boldsymbol{\beta} = 1$. This means $\boldsymbol{A}$ is singular and $\tilde{\boldsymbol{\gamma}}$ cannot be recovered as $\boldsymbol{A}^{-1}\boldsymbol{\alpha}$. The basic problem is that there are only $n - 1$ independent values of the intercepts, as one is constrained by $\sum_{i=1}^{n} \alpha_i = 0$, which provide insufficient information to determine the n subsistence expenditures.

These matters have been discussed by Howe (1975), Pollak and Wales (1978), and Powell (1973).

As briefly discussed in the previous chapter, the parameters of LES can be identified once the cost of subsistence is known. Within the LES framework, the total cost of subsistence is implied by a measure of the income curvature of the utility function that is related to the overall degree of substitutability among goods. The utility function corresponding to LES is $u(q_1, \cdots, q_n) = \sum_{i=1}^{n} \beta_i \log(q_i - \gamma_i)$. The marginal utility of good i is $\frac{\partial u}{\partial q_i} = \frac{\beta_i}{q_i - \gamma_i}$. For this to be positive, $q_i > \gamma_i$, or $p_i q_i > p_i \gamma_i$ (assuming $\beta_i > 0$). Summing over $i = 1, \cdots, n$, this implies

$$M > \boldsymbol{p}'\boldsymbol{\gamma}, \tag{11.4}$$

where $\boldsymbol{p}'\boldsymbol{\gamma} = \sum_{i=1}^{n} p_i \gamma_i$ is the cost of subsistence. Income exceeding subsistence means supernumerary income, $M - \boldsymbol{p}'\boldsymbol{\gamma}$, is positive.

For a budget-constrained maximum, each marginal utility is proportional to the corresponding price, that is, $\frac{\beta_i}{q_i - \gamma_i} = \lambda p_i, i = 1, \cdots, n$, where λ is the marginal utility of income $\frac{\partial u}{\partial M}$. Multiplying through by $q_i - \gamma_i$ and then summing over $i = 1, \cdots, n$ gives $\sum_{i=1}^{n} \beta_i = \lambda(M - \boldsymbol{p}'\boldsymbol{\gamma})$. As $\sum_{i=1}^{n} \beta_i = 1$, the reciprocal of supernumerary income is $\lambda = \frac{1}{M - \boldsymbol{p}'\boldsymbol{\gamma}}$, which itself is positive under condition Eq. (11.4). Since $\frac{\partial \lambda}{\partial M} = -\lambda^2 < 0$, the income elasticity of the marginal utility of income is $\frac{\partial \lambda}{\partial M} \frac{M}{\lambda} = -\frac{M}{M - \boldsymbol{p}'\boldsymbol{\gamma}}$, the negative inverse of the supernumerary ratio. This elasticity is referred to as the "Frisch parameter" (ω):

$$\omega = -\frac{M}{M - \boldsymbol{p}'\boldsymbol{\gamma}}. \tag{11.5}$$

A rise in income leads to a decrease in $|\omega|$. Chapter 7 also derived expression (11.5) from the indirect utility function.

LES implies that ω is not constant, but dependent upon income and prices. From Eq. (11.5), the income elasticity of ω is

$$\frac{\partial \log|\omega|}{\partial \log M} = 1 + \omega < 0.$$

The negative value of this elasticity follows from condition (11.4) which implies $\omega < -1$. As stated above, the marginal utility of income is always positive and always declines with additional income (that is, $\omega < 0$). But according to the above equation, the decline in $|\omega|$ is damped as the consumer becomes richer. Again from Eq. (11.5), the price elasticity of ω is

$$\frac{\partial \log|\omega|}{\partial \log p_i} = -\omega \frac{p_i \gamma_i}{M} > 0, \quad i = 1, \cdots, n.$$

Thus, the effect on $|\omega|$ of a price increase has the opposite sign to an income increase. As $\sum_{i=1}^{n} \frac{\partial \log|\omega|}{\partial \log p_i} = -\omega \frac{p'\gamma}{M} = -(1+\omega)$, an equiproportional rise in income and all prices leaves the Frisch parameter unchanged. This, of course, simply reflects the homogeneity of expression (11.5).

Rearrangement of Eq. (11.5) yields a simple expression for the cost of subsistence as a proportion of income

$$\frac{p'\gamma}{M} = 1 + \frac{1}{\omega}. \tag{11.6}$$

This reveals that once the value of ω is known, the subsistence share of income can be determined; and given income, we can infer $\boldsymbol{p}'\boldsymbol{\gamma}$. Writing Eq. (11.3) as $\alpha_i = p_i \gamma_i - \beta_i \boldsymbol{p}'\boldsymbol{\gamma}$, the value of subsistence expenditure for each good can then be recovered from the estimated intercept and marginal share as

$$p_i \gamma_i = \alpha_i + \beta_i \boldsymbol{p}'\boldsymbol{\gamma}, \quad i = 1, \cdots, n. \tag{11.7}$$

To use Eqs. (11.6) and (11.7) for identification, the value of the Frisch parameter ω is needed. The next several sections present different sources of this parameter value.

11.3 The Frisch Conjecture

Chapter 3 briefly discussed Frisch's famous speculation regarding how the income elasticity of the marginal utility of income might vary with the affluence of consumers. This and related matters shall now be considered.

In what has become known as the "Frisch conjecture", Frisch (1959, p. 189) viewed the marginal utility of income for the poor as highly sensitive to income, while that for the rich is relatively insensitive. That is, the elasticity of the marginal utility, ω, takes a large negative value for the poor and then moves in the direction of zero as consumers become more affluent. In his words:

> We may, perhaps, assume that in most cases the [Frisch parameter] has values of the order of magnitude given below.

$\omega = -10$	for the extremely poor and apathetic part of the population
$\omega = -4$	for the slightly better-off but still poor part of the population with a fairly pronounced desire to become better off
$\omega = -2$	for the middle-income bracket, "the median part" of the population
$\omega = -0.7$	for the better-off part of the population
$\omega = -0.1$	for the rich part of the population with ambitions towards "conspicuous consumption"

The above changes in ω agree with that implied by LES as $|\omega|$ falls with income in both cases. Although Frisch did not work within the LES framework, the combination of his conjecture with LES provides some interesting implications. Given ω and its change, the income change implied by Eq. (11.5) is $d(\log M) = \frac{d(\log|\omega|)}{1+\omega}$. For consumer groups g and $g + 1$, this difference can be evaluated as

$$\log \frac{M_{g+1}}{M_g} = \frac{\log(\omega_{g+1}/\omega_g)}{1+\overline{\omega}}, \tag{11.8}$$

where $\overline{\omega} = \frac{1}{2}(\omega_{g+1} + \omega_g)$. For the comparison of group $g + 1$ with g, the use of the average value of ω in the above equation seems natural.

Table 11.1 uses Eq. (11.8) to obtain the income associated with the values of ω suggested by Frisch. The final column of the table shows that income grows by 16 per cent in moving from the extremely poor to the slightly better-off, while those in the middle are 65 per cent more affluent than the extremely poor. These implications might seem not completely unreasonable and provide some support for using

Table 11.1 Frisch-LES implied income

Group g	Frisch parameter ω	Average ω $\frac{1}{2}(\omega_{g+1} + \omega_g)$	Difference in Frisch parameter $\log \frac{\omega_{g+1}}{\omega_g} \times 100$	Income: Difference $\log \frac{M_{g+1}}{M_g} \times 100$	Income: Level (Group $1 = 100$)
(1)	(2)	(3)	(4)	(5)	(6)
1. Extremely poor	−10	–			100
2. Slightly better-off	−4	−7	−92	15	116
3. Middle income.	−2	−3	−69	35	165
4. Better-off	**−0.7**				
5. Rich	**−0.1**				

Notes

1. The ω-values of column 2 are from the Frisch conjecture, as discussed in the text.
2. The income difference between groups $g + 1$ and g of column 5 is defined as in Eq. (11.8), viz., $\log(M_{g+1}/M_g) = (1+\overline{\omega})^{-1}\log(\omega_{g+1}/\omega_g)$, with $\overline{\omega} = (1/2)(\omega_{g+1} + \omega_g)$.
3. The income level of group $g + 1$ of column 6 is $M_{g+1} = M_g \exp\{\log(M_{g+1}/M_g)\}$, with $M_1 = 100$.
4. As $\omega < -1$ for groups 4 and 5, the LES condition in Eq. (11.4) is violated. As the corresponding income differences are no longer given by Eq. (11.8), the cells for the last two rows of columns 3-6 are left blank.

the Frisch conjecture as a guide to specifying ω. However, there are three problems. First, the middle-poor income gap appears to be too narrow. Second, Frisch's values of ω for the better-off and the rich violate the LES condition (11.4), which means that the approach breaks down for these groups. Third, the basis for Frisch's values in his conjecture is not clear-cut. That is not to say the Frisch conjecture is based on no evidence. The above quotation from Frisch follows immediately after his discussion of values of ω obtained by Johansen with Norwegian data from the 1950s. Frisch (1959, p. 189) gives three values of ω: -1.94 (derived from the demand elasticities for agricultural products), -2.13 (industrial foods and beverages), and -1.85 (land and air transport). Frisch comments enthusiastically (repeated from Chap. 3):

> It is truly remarkable that data taken from such different sources and giving such different budget proportions and Engel elasticities, give such consistent values of [ω]. A compromise value of about -2 for the money flexibility [ω] ought to be a reasonable estimate.

Thus, Frisch's value for the middle-income bracket of -2 is consistent with this evidence, but the source for his other values is not revealed. Relatedly, the range of his values could be questioned: In going from -10 to -0.1, these values differ by a factor of 100, which for an elasticity, is huge. It seems fair to conclude that, taken as a whole, the Frisch conjecture is more impressionistic than econometric.

11.4 The Lluch-Powell-Williams Book

A widely used source of values of the Frisch parameter ω, especially in CGE modelling, is the book by Lluch et al. (1977). This work is a landmark in applied demand analysis and has significant citations in the literature.

Lluch et al. (1977) estimated the extended linear expenditure system (ELES, Lluch 1973) with time-series data. In this model, $\omega = -\frac{M}{M - p'\gamma} < 0$, which is the same as for the linear expenditure system. For a given value of $\boldsymbol{p}'\boldsymbol{\gamma}$, ω falls absolutely as income (M) rises. But as Lluch et al. (1977) estimate ELES separately for each of a number of countries with time-series data, $\boldsymbol{p}'\boldsymbol{\gamma}$ and ω take their own values for each country, so that there is no *algebraic* relationship between the value of the Frisch parameter and income across countries. There is, however, an *empirical* relationship identified by Lluch et al. (1977). For 14 countries, they regressed their estimates of the logarithm of $-\omega$ on the logarithm of GDP per capita to give (p. 76)

$$-\omega = 36 \times \text{GDP}^{-0.36}. \tag{11.9}$$

Thus, ω declines in absolute value as income rises, which agrees with the Frisch conjecture. While the income elasticity is modest at -0.36, with a standard error is 0.10 it is highly significant. The estimates of ω used to obtain Eq. (11.9) are based on data from the 1950s and 60s. This equation can be used to give ω-values for a number of countries in more recent times. Lluch et al. (1977) measure GDP in terms of US dollars at 1970 prices. Starting with GDP in 2018 in US dollars of 2018, in order to apply Eq. (11.9), GDP is converted in 1970 prices; this obviously yields real GDP in 2018 expressed in 1970 prices. Some rough guesses have to be made for the appropriate US inflation rate. There are obvious uncertainties involved in this process. The GDPs in 2018 US dollars involve the conversion from domestic currency units into US dollars: It is not clear what exchange rate should be used—the market rate at mid-year, end-of-year, the average over the year, PPP, or any other of a host of alternatives. And even the choice of the nature of the inflation rate is not straightforward—what deflator should be used and does it adequately account for quality change, new goods and substitution of cheaper for more expensive goods?

Bearing in mind the above issues, Table 11.2 contains some illustrative applications of the approach. Several comments can be made about the projections of $-\omega$ in columns 5 and 6:

1. As expected, the results are sensitive to the underlying assumption regarding income. When inflation is taken to be higher, the associated income is lower and $-\omega$ is correspondingly higher: The column 6 values of $-\omega$ (based on inflation of 5 per cent p. a.) are more than 50 per cent larger than those of column 5 (2 per cent inflation).
2. The projections can be compared with those of the Frisch conjecture. As mentioned, the decline in $-\omega$ is consistent with Frisch. For the poorest country, Burundi, under the low-income assumption, $-\omega = 11.12$ (first entry of column 6). This is not far from Frisch's value of 10 for the extremely poor. Under the higher-income assumption, the value for the richest country (Monaco) is $-\omega = 0.64$, which seems some way away from Frisch for the rich of 0.1. However, these values refer to the extremes of the income distribution and by the nature of extremes, these are not representative of the population.
3. The values of $-\omega$ for the high-income countries of panel B of the table do not vary a great deal. The Frisch parameter for Singapore, the richest country in the panel, is only about 10 per cent less than that of Canada, the least rich. On a GDP-per-capita basis, Singapore is about 40 per cent richer than Canada (column 2). Thus, from Eq. (11.9), the ratio of the Frisch parameters for these two countries is about $1.4^{-0.36} = 0.9$, or Singapore's is about 10 per cent less, in accordance with the values of columns 5 and 6.
4. The column 5 values of $-\omega$ for the four richest countries are below 1, which is not consistent with the LES condition (11.4). The same problem occurs for Monaco (column 5, panel A).

There is much to admire in the Lluch et al. (1977) book. Its boldness of concept, breadth, and clarity make it easy to understand why it has been so influential. The book provides a valuable source for the Frisch parameter. But due to the issues noted above, the projections of ω are to be interpreted as only indicative of how the Lluch et al. results might be used in a contemporary setting. The above approach could be

Table 11.2 Frisch parameters, illustrative values

	GDP per capita in $US at			Frisch parameter, $-\omega$, with assumed US inflation (Per cent p. a.)	
		1970 prices, with assumed US inflation (Per cent p. a.)			
Summary of income distribution/country (1)	2018 prices (2)	2 (3)	5 (4)	2 (5)	5 (6)
A. *196 Countries from World Development Indicators*					
Poorest (Burundi)	272	105	26	6.74	11.12
25th percentile (≈ Solomon Is)	2142	828	206	3.20	5.29
Median (≈ Fiji)	6290	2431	605	2.17	3.59
75th percentile (≈ St Kitts)	19,214	7427	1847	1.45	2.40
Maximum (Monaco)	185,741	71,796	17,858	0.64	1.06
B. *Selected high-income countries*					
Canada	46,233	17,871	4445	1.06	1.75
Belgium	47,519	18,368	4569	1.05	1.73
Germany	47,603	18,400	4577	1.05	1.73
Hong Kong SAR, China	48,676	18,815	4680	1.04	1.72
Finland	50,152	19,386	4822	1.03	1.70
Austria	51,462	19,892	4948	1.02	1.68
Netherlands	53,024	20,496	5098	1.01	1.67
Sweden	54,608	21,108	5250	1.00	1.65
Australia	57,374	22,177	5516	0.98	1.62
Denmark	61,350	23,714	5898	0.96	1.58
United States	62,795	24,272	6037	0.95	1.57
Singapore	64,582	24,963	6209	0.94	1.55

Notes

1. Column 2 is from *World Development Indicators*, https://databank.worldbank.org/reports.aspx?source=world-development-indicators

2. Column 3 (4) converts GDP from 2018 prices (in column 2) to those of 1970 under the assumption of average US inflation of 2% p. a. (5% p. a.). That is, as there are 48 years between 1970 and 2018, (GDP in 1970 prices) = (GDP in 2018 prices) × $(1+\pi)^{-48}$, $\pi = 0.02, 0.05$.

3. Columns 5 and 6 contain values of (the negative of) the Frisch parameter derived from the equation estimated by Lluch et al. (1977, p. 76), viz., $-\omega = 36 \times$ (GDP in 1970 prices)$^{-0.36}$. Column 5 (6) assumes 2% (5%) inflation by using the GDP values of column 3 (4).

4. Since (GDP in 1970 prices) = (GDP in 2018 prices) × $(1+\pi)^{-48}$, $-\omega = 36 \times$ (GDP in 2018 prices)$^{-0.36} \times (1+\pi)^{48 \times 0.36}$. Thus, for $\pi = 0.02, 0.05$, column 6 (for 5% inflation) is a multiple $\left(\frac{1.05}{1.02}\right)^{48 \times 0.36} = 1.65$ of column 5 (2% inflation). When inflation is assumed to be higher, GDP in 1970 prices is lower, leading to larger values of $-\omega$.

5. The cross-country dispersion of GDP has risen substantially since 1970, the year used to derive Eq. (11.9) by Lluch et al. (1977). In 1970 the interquartile range of GDP was about 40 per cent more than the median. By 2018 this had risen to about 170 per cent. The 1970 gap of 40 per cent is itself considerable, so the increase to 170 per cent is indeed substantial. Thus, a qualification is required regarding the possible fragility of the extrapolations to a period of much more disparate incomes, extrapolations that might go beyond what could be reasonably considered the "relevant range" applicable to the original regression results.

used in future applications, but a more detailed consideration of the underlying income projections would be valuable.

11.5 Other Sources of Frisch

In view of the issues noted above, a case can be made for the simpler approach of taking ω to be constant and equal to -2. While this approach contradicts the range of values conjectured by Frisch, it agrees with his value for the "median part" of the population. This section briefly reviews previous studies and concludes that while the evidence in favour of $\omega = -2$ is not overwhelming, this is a reasonable value to use.

In the LES the Frisch "parameter" is not a constant parameter but a variable one, as noted previously. By contrast, in the Rotterdam model, due to Barten (1964) and Theil (1965), the reciprocal of Frisch parameter (denoted by ϕ) is parameterised as a constant. This parameter is known as the "income flexibility". Clements and Si (2017) estimate the Rotterdam model with time-series data for nine goods as a separate system for each of 37 OECD countries and Table 11.3 contains the ϕ-estimates. These seem to be more or less scattered randomly around the mean of -0.54. Using several tests, Clements and Si (2017) find that these estimates are unrelated to income. Clements and Si (2017, 2018) also apply a related approach to cross-country data for 176 countries from the International Comparison Program (World Bank 2015). This involves estimating ϕ via a cross-commodity regression for each pair of countries. As can be seen from and Table 11.3 the average ϕ-value is -0.52, with only the top income quartile (where $\phi = -0.22$) apparently substantially different. A histogram of the estimates is presented in Fig. 3.2. These findings indicate ϕ has a central value of about $-½$, or $\omega = \frac{1}{\phi} = -2$.

As discussed in Chap. 3 however, there is still some uncertainty surrounding the constancy or otherwise of the Frisch parameter. Nevertheless, if a single value is

Table 11.3 Income flexibility estimates, 176 ICP countries

	Income (US = 100)		Income flexibility ($\phi = \frac{1}{\omega}$)	
Income group of countries	Mean	SD	Mean	SD
Top quartile	68.5	13.9	−0.217	0.375
Quartile 3	35.3	7.5	−0.709	0.512
Quartile 2	16.2	4.6	−0.685	0.389
Quartile 1	4.1	1.9	−0.463	0.830
All countries	31.0	25.7	−0.518	0.592

required, $-\omega \approx 2$ would appear to be a reasonable choice, although one cannot be dogmatic. In terms of LES, $-\omega \approx 2$ implies that subsistence cost is about one-half of income based on Eq. (11.6), which again appears reasonable.

11.6 Empirical Application of LES

The previous chapter referred to the findings of Clements et al. (2022). This and the next two sections provide more details. LES is estimated using an up-to-date micro household data for Australia with 20 commodities separately distinguished. The LES parameters are estimated for five household types grouped according to income. The benefit of these quintile estimates is twofold: (1) it provides a better understanding of the heterogeneity of consumption behaviour across income levels, and (2) it provides a valuable input for CGE models with microsimulation capabilities.

The data used in the econometric estimation is the 2015–16 Household Expenditure Survey (HES) carried out by the Australian Bureau of Statistics. There are 10,046 households from the HES. The survey data provides spending on 693 disaggregated goods and services based on the Household Expenditure Classification. This was aggregated into 20 sectors based on the 1-digit commodity classification used in the national accounts. To put households of different size on more or less the same basis, equivalised expenditures are used for the estimation. The details of the sectoral mappings and other data transformations are set out in Clements et al. (2022).

Table 11.4 presents the descriptive statistics of expenditure across commodities and income groups. Overall, housing is the biggest single item among households contributing about a fifth of total expenditure (17.1 per cent), followed by insurance (10.6 per cent), food (9.9 per cent), and light goods manufactures (7.5 per cent). Regarding the patterns across household types, the budget shares of food, heavy goods manufactures, utilities, communications, and public administration decrease as income increases. In contrast, the budget shares increase with income for hotels and restaurants, private transport, finance, education, health, and other services. The shares of housing, insurance, and professional services appear to be more stable across income.

11.7 Homogeneous and Heterogeneous Consumers

Consider first the case in which all consumers are the same, the one-consumer case. System (11.2) can be estimated with n separate least-squares regressions of $p_i q_i$ on M. Columns 2 and 3 of Table 11.5 give the estimates for the $n = 20$ data described above. All coefficients are significant. The largest marginal share is for housing at 0.16, indicating that 16 cents of a one-dollar rise in income is spent on this good.

Table 11.4 Summary of expenditure data, Australia 2015–16

	All households H = 10,046			Lowest quintile H = 2009			Second quintile H = 2009			Third quintile H = 2009			Fourth quintile H = 2009			Highest quintile H = 2010		
Commodity group	Mean ($)	SD ($)	Share (%)	Mean ($)	SD ($)	Share (%)	Mean ($)	SD ($)	Share (%)	Mean ($)	SD ($)	Share (%)	Mean ($)	SD ($)	Share (%)	Mean ($)	SD ($)	Share (%)
1. Food	4559	2645	9.9	3008	1654	19.6	3948	1978	15.5	4462	2200	12.2	5233	2397	10.0	6142	3464	6.0
2. Beverages and tobacco	1477	2371	3.2	595	1141	3.9	1089	1823	4.3	1488	2114	4.1	1794	2522	3.4	2419	3280	2.4
3. Clothing and footwear	1430	2834	3.1	369	830	2.4	777	1333	3.1	1103	1710	3.0	1809	2586	3.5	3093	4849	3.0
4. Light goods manufactures	3448	6283	7.5	900	1176	5.9	1812	1968	7.1	2751	2947	7.5	3967	3875	7.6	7811	11,810	7.7
5. Heavy goods manufactures	2531	2227	5.5	1211	1063	7.9	1883	1306	7.4	2451	1772	6.7	3080	2138	5.9	4029	3088	4.0
6. Utilities	1867	1118	4.0	1529	857	10.0	1669	950	6.6	1810	994	5.0	1995	1060	3.8	2335	1453	2.3
7. Housing	7902	27,017	17.1	2432	3493	15.8	4393	4888	17.3	5676	5793	15.6	7789	7106	15.0	19,217	57,915	18.9
8. Hotels and restaurants	3012	4042	6.5	729	961	4.7	1486	1599	5.8	2412	2231	6.6	3788	3190	7.3	6642	6433	6.5
9. Private transportation	1738	7422	3.8	55	409	0.4	371	1631	1.5	941	3030	2.6	1938	4879	3.7	5385	14,866	5.3
10. Public transportation	1190	3321	2.6	278	753	1.8	567	1210	2.2	869	1548	2.4	1354	2267	2.6	2884	6430	2.8
11. Communications	1770	1343	3.8	1030	730	6.7	1428	916	5.6	1723	1053	4.7	2094	1336	4.0	2574	1829	2.5
12. Finance	2865	5577	6.2	267	957	1.7	855	2053	3.4	2148	3676	5.9	3814	4983	7.3	7237	8985	7.1
13. Insurance	4895	13,499	10.6	1445	1391	9.4	2058	1912	8.1	3156	3098	8.7	4740	4727	9.1	13,073	27,994	12.8
14. Professional services	561	3944	1.2	136	574	0.9	282	1051	1.1	403	1426	1.1	623	2173	1.2	1359	8287	1.3

15. Admin and support services	1016	4107	2.2	191	686	1.2	374	1324	1.5	757	2334	2.1	1202	3459	2.3	2556	7820	2.5
16. Public administration	491	1473	1.1	227	328	1.5	342	706	1.3	453	688	1.2	592	1032	1.1	841	2911	0.8
17. Education	1107	5679	2.4	95	420	0.6	289	913	1.1	633	1849	1.7	1323	3352	2.5	3194	11,802	3.1
18. Health	1147	6023	2.5	242	669	1.6	498	1125	2.0	971	2155	2.7	1324	2631	2.5	2700	12,822	2.7
19. Recreation	719	1991	1.6	194	553	1.3	369	830	1.5	615	1213	1.7	834	1564	1.6	1595	3706	1.6
20. Other services	2495	7902	5.4	430	992	2.8	959	1809	3.8	1637	2998	4.5	2793	4904	5.4	6654	15,817	6.5

Note: Dollar values are average annual equivalent household expenditures at 2015–16 prices; H is the number of households. Source of basic data is the Australian Bureau of Statistics

Table 11.5 LES estimates, consumption shares and elasticities, pooled data

	Coefficients (standard errors)				Subsistence budget share			Own-price elasticities	
Commodity group (1)	Intercept α_i (2)	Slope β_i (3)	Budget share (4)	Marginal share (5)	Proportion of income (6)	Proportion of total subsistence (7)	Income elasticity (8)	Marshallian (9)	Slutsky (10)
1. Food	1476 (29.24)	7.95 (0.13)	9.86	7.95	7.17	14.34	0.806	−0.408	−0.328
2. Beverages and tobacco	67 (23.03)	3.45 (0.10)	3.20	3.44	1.86	3.73	1.077	−0.498	−0.463
3. Clothing and footwear	−179 (19.12)	3.63 (0.09)	3.09	3.62	1.43	2.85	1.171	−0.576	−0.539
4. Light goods manufactures	−349 (30.38)	8.36 (0.13)	7.46	8.36	3.43	6.85	1.120	−0.587	−0.504
5. Heavy goods manufactures	295 (19.62)	5.48 (0.09)	5.48	5.47	3.37	6.74	0.999	−0.478	−0.423
6. Utilities	1252 (14.71)	1.51 (0.07)	4.04	1.51	3.46	6.92	0.373	−0.191	−0.176
7. Housing	−132 (67.93)	16.31 (0.29)	17.10	16.30	7.87	15.73	0.954	−0.589	−0.426
8. Hotels and restaurants	−352 (23.3)	7.47 (0.10)	6.52	7.47	2.97	5.94	1.146	−0.590	−0.515
9. Private transportation	−542 (31.14)	4.51 (0.14)	3.76	4.51	1.08	2.16	1.198	−0.690	−0.645
10. Public transportation	−152 (17.73)	2.89 (0.08)	2.58	2.89	1.12	2.23	1.122	−0.576	−0.548
11. Communications	531 (13.14)	3.05 (0.06)	3.83	3.04	2.67	5.34	0.795	−0.383	−0.352
12. Finance	−795 (33.31)	7.85 (0.15)	6.20	7.84	2.20	4.41	1.266	−0.668	−0.590
13. Insurance	−39 (38.83)	9.62 (0.17)	10.59	9.61	4.72	9.45	0.908	−0.552	−0.456
14. Professional services	−43 (15.6)	1.26 (0.07)	1.21	1.25	0.53	1.07	1.032	−0.545	−0.533
15. Admin and support services	−166 (22.64)	2.48 (0.10)	2.20	2.47	0.88	1.76	1.124	−0.595	−0.570
16. Public administration	90 (8.9)	0.93 (0.04)	1.06	0.93	0.66	1.31	0.871	−0.419	−0.410
17. Education	−275 (21.23)	2.72 (0.10)	2.39	2.71	0.76	1.52	1.133	−0.650	−0.623
18. Health	−154 (19.9)	2.77 (0.09)	2.48	2.76	1.05	2.10	1.114	−0.580	−0.553
19. Recreation	−79 (12.91)	1.81 (0.06)	1.56	1.80	0.73	1.46	1.154	−0.560	−0.542

20. Other services	−457 (31.99)	6.06 (0.14)	5.40	6.06	2.04	4.08	1.122	−0.622	−0.561
Sum	0	100	100	100	50	100	–	–	–

Note: Columns 3 to 7 are ×100. 2; column 5 = column 3; column 6 is $p_i\gamma_i/M = \alpha_i/M + \beta_i(1 + 1/\omega)$, with $\omega = -2$; elasticities are at sample means

The marginal shares are obtained directly from Eq. (11.2) but the subsistence parameters are not identified, as discussed previously. By combining Eqs. (11.6) and (11.7), the cost of subsistence can be obtained once the value of the Frisch parameter ω is known:

$$p_i\gamma_i = \alpha_i + \beta_i M\left(1 + \frac{1}{\omega}\right), \quad i = 1, \cdots, 20. \tag{11.10}$$

Here, α_i and β_i are the intercept and slope coefficients from system (11.2). The estimates of the coefficients, mean income (M), and Frisch parameter of $\omega = -2$ are used in Eq. (11.10). Column 6 of Table 11.5 contains the results in the form of the cost of subsistence as a proportion of income, $\frac{p_i\gamma_i}{M}$. Column 7 expresses subsistence cost of i as a fraction of the total cost of subsistence, $\frac{p_i\gamma_i}{\mathbf{p}'\boldsymbol{\gamma}}$ with $\mathbf{p}'\boldsymbol{\gamma} = \sum_{j=1}^{20} p_j\gamma_j$. For convenience, column 4 of this table reproduces the budget shares with an additional decimal place.

LES for good i can be expressed in share form as $w_i = s_i + \beta_i r = (1 - r) \times \frac{p_i\gamma_i}{\mathbf{p}'\boldsymbol{\gamma}} + r\beta_i$, where $s_i = \frac{p_i\gamma_i}{M}$ and $r = \frac{M - p'\gamma}{M}$ is the supernumerary ratio. When income rises, so does r, $dr = (1 - r)d(\log M) > 0$, and the change in the budget share of good i is

$$dw_i = \left(\beta_i - \frac{p_i\gamma_i}{\mathbf{p}'\boldsymbol{\gamma}}\right)(1 - r)d(\log M), \quad \sum_{i=1}^{20} dw_i = 0. \tag{11.11}$$

This shows that the budget share rises (falls) with income when the marginal share exceeds (is less than) the subsistence share. In this situation, the good is a luxury (necessity). Table 11.5 shows that food, utilities, and communications have a subsistence share substantially above their marginal share. Although Eq. (11.11) applies when price is constant, these results are consistent with the changes displayed in the plots of the budget shares contained in Clements et al. (2022). They are also consistent with the estimated income elasticities, discussed next.

The income elasticities are $\frac{\beta_i}{w_i}$, which we evaluate with means of the budget shares. As shown in column 8 of Table 11.5, food, utilities, and communication have the lowest elasticities. Those with higher elasticities are finance, private vehicles, apparel, recreation, and hotels and restaurants. Next, the Marshallian (or uncompensated) price elasticities are:

$$\eta_{ij} = \delta_{ij}\left(\frac{s_i}{w_i} - 1\right) - \frac{\beta_i}{w_i}s_j, \quad i,j = 1, \cdots, 20,$$

and Slutsky (compensated) counterparts are:

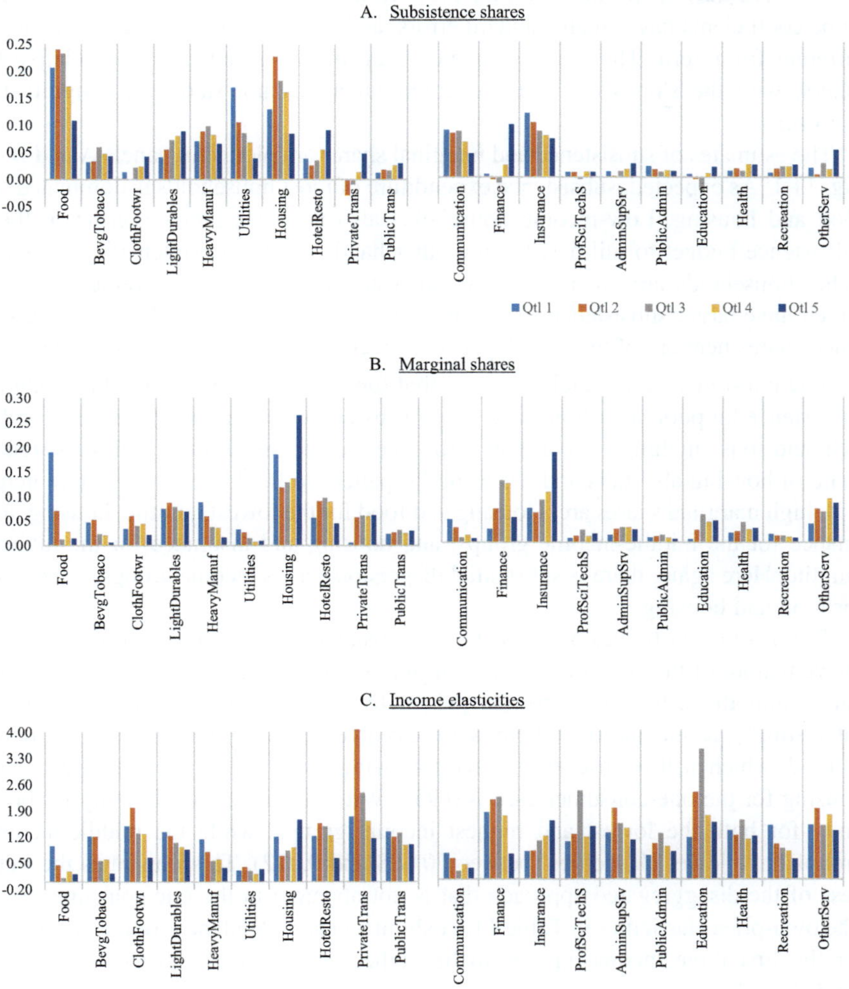

Fig. 11.1 Estimated shares and elasticities, quintiles

$$\eta_{ij}^{*} = \delta_{ij}\left(\frac{s_i}{w_i} - 1\right) + \frac{\beta_i}{w_i}\left(w_j - s_j\right), \quad i, j = 1, \cdots, 20,$$

where δ_{ij} is the Kronecker delta. Columns 9 and 10 of Table 11.5 give the own-price elasticities. As expected, these are all negative and less than one in absolute value with the Marshallian elasticities slightly larger than the Slutsky versions. For the full 20×20 matrices of price elasticities, see Clements et al. (2022).

Now consider the case of heterogeneous consumers, whereby the LES is estimated separately for each income quintile. The online appendices in Clements et al.

(2022) give the full results. Overall, these results reveal that the estimates of the slope coefficients have small standard errors, and most coefficients are significantly different from zero. The middle-income group performs rather poorly relative to others, with the slopes of food and communications not statistically significant from zero.

The estimates of subsistence and marginal shares are plotted in panels A and B of Fig. 11.1. As expected, subsistence expenditure of most households is dominated by food and housing. Low-income households also devote a larger portion of their subsistence budget to utilities. On the other hand, subsistence-intensive goods for richer households are finance, hotels and restaurants, and private vehicles (all of which have larger subsistence shares than those of poorer households). The subsistence shares here are of the form $\frac{p_i \gamma_i}{p' \gamma}, i = 1, \cdots, 20,$ which are treated as constants in the one-consumer case. Panel A reveals that food accounts for about 20 per cent of subsistence for poor households and this falls by about one-half to 10 per cent for the rich, and so is anything but constant across the income distribution. The subsistence share of housing also falls and has a similar pattern to food. Key expenditure items with high marginal shares are: Housing and food for the lowest quintile; housing and finance for the middle-income groups; and housing and insurance for the highest quintile. Here again, there is substantial dispersion across income groups, especially for food and housing.

The income elasticities of Table 11.6 and panel C of Fig. 11.1 simply reflect the above pattern of the subsistence and marginal shares. Food and housing are important commodities to consumers (as judged by their shares in total expenditure). Interestingly, as income rises there is a noticeable decrease in the income elasticity of food, which will be discussed in the following section. The income elasticity of housing for the one-consumer case is 0.954. With quintiles, this elasticity is above unity for both the lowest and highest income groups, while the middle-income groups have lower elasticities (between 0.688 and 0.922). This illustrates the richness of the disaggregated approach that is not apparent in the one-consumer case. The own-price elasticities in Table 11.6 exhibit a general tendency for the elasticities for the first three income groups to be higher relative to the pooled elasticities (of Table 11.5).

To summarise, disaggregation captures important heterogeneity of demand responses. Although the one-consumer case provides a general insight of the role of income and prices, there are certain characteristics of households significantly affecting demand responses that can be unveiled by allowing the parameters of LES to differ across the income distribution. The next section contains a further elaboration of the value-added of this type of disaggregation.

Table 11.6 Demand elasticities, quintiles

Commodity group	Income elasticity for quintile					Marshallian own-price elasticity for quintile					Slutsky own-price elasticity for quintile				
	1	2	3	4	5	1	2	3	4	5	1	2	3	4	5
1. Food	0.970	0.451	0.100	0.284	0.228	−0.578	−0.28	−0.062	−0.167	−0.125	−0.388	−0.21	−0.049	−0.138	−0.111
2. Beverages and tobacco	1.190	1.215	0.549	0.607	0.245	−0.612	−0.628	−0.291	−0.318	−0.127	−0.566	−0.576	−0.268	−0.297	−0.121
3. Clothing and footwear	1.406	1.967	1.287	1.288	0.701	−0.723	−0.984	−0.658	−0.66	−0.351	−0.689	−0.924	−0.619	−0.615	−0.33
4. Light goods manufactures	1.277	1.232	1.042	0.937	0.899	−0.674	−0.65	−0.559	−0.507	−0.478	−0.599	−0.562	−0.48	−0.435	−0.409
5. Heavy goods manufactures	1.120	0.804	0.546	0.609	0.407	−0.598	−0.438	−0.3	−0.329	−0.212	−0.51	−0.378	−0.263	−0.293	−0.196
6. Utilities	0.322	0.400	0.287	0.214	0.369	−0.186	−0.221	−0.156	−0.114	−0.189	−0.154	−0.195	−0.141	−0.106	−0.18
7. Housing	1.174	0.688	0.831	0.922	1.402	−0.666	−0.422	−0.491	−0.535	−0.824	−0.48	−0.303	−0.362	−0.397	−0.559
8. Hotels and restaurants	1.187	1.559	1.475	1.241	0.681	−0.621	−0.799	−0.763	−0.655	−0.36	−0.565	−0.708	−0.665	−0.564	−0.316
9. Private transport	1.577	3.921	2.340	1.625	1.177	−0.817	−1.907	−1.16	−0.824	−0.595	−0.812	−1.85	−1.099	−0.764	−0.533
10. Public transport	1.295	1.196	1.305	0.989	1.036	−0.661	−0.609	−0.663	−0.508	−0.515	−0.637	−0.582	−0.632	−0.482	−0.485
11. Communications	0.723	0.560	0.217	0.395	0.330	−0.391	−0.302	−0.118	−0.21	−0.169	−0.343	−0.271	−0.107	−0.194	−0.161
12. Finance	1.597	2.106	2.178	1.690	0.730	−0.843	−1.049	−1.078	−0.864	−0.384	−0.815	−0.979	−0.949	−0.74	−0.332
13. Insurance	0.758	0.760	1.026	1.161	1.451	−0.422	−0.418	−0.556	−0.625	−0.777	−0.351	−0.357	−0.467	−0.519	−0.591
14. Professional services	1.021	1.200	2.331	1.139	1.332	−0.511	−0.606	−1.162	−0.576	−0.673	−0.502	−0.592	−1.136	−0.563	−0.655
15. Admin support	1.214	1.886	1.486	1.365	1.052	−0.612	−0.945	−0.751	−0.692	−0.535	−0.597	−0.917	−0.72	−0.66	−0.509

(continued)

Table 11.6 (continued)

Commodity group	Income elasticity for quintile					Marshallian own-price elasticity for quintile					Slutsky own-price elasticity for quintile				
	1	2	3	4	5	1	2	3	4	5	1	2	3	4	5
16. Public administration	0.661	0.952	1.223	0.886	0.800	−0.336	−0.483	−0.617	−0.449	−0.39	−0.326	−0.47	−0.602	−0.439	−0.384
17. Education	1.072	2.296	3.382	1.704	1.445	−0.557	−1.145	−1.651	−0.858	−0.723	−0.55	−1.119	−1.593	−0.815	−0.678
18. Health	1.260	1.175	1.578	1.082	1.110	−0.644	−0.597	−0.798	−0.554	−0.578	−0.624	−0.574	−0.756	−0.526	−0.549
19. Recreation	1.385	0.948	0.825	0.764	0.596	−0.7	−0.481	−0.421	−0.39	−0.297	−0.683	−0.467	−0.407	−0.377	−0.288
20. Other services	1.377	1.877	1.437	1.724	1.267	−0.71	−0.943	−0.737	−0.875	−0.655	−0.671	−0.872	−0.672	−0.783	−0.572

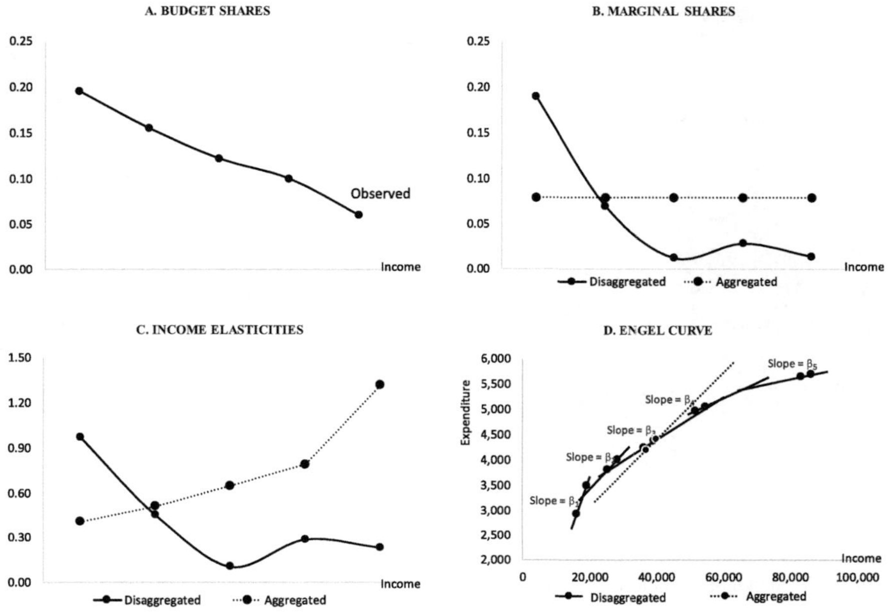

Fig. 11.2 Income and food

11.8 Further Implications of Disaggregating Consumers

In LES the marginal shares, β_i, are constant, so Engel curves are linear. It stretches credibility that affluent consumers would spend the same fraction of additional income on each good as would the poor. Moreover, as the income elasticity of good $\boldsymbol{i}$ is $\frac{\beta_i}{w_i}$, this elasticity is inversely proportional to the budget share, w_i. The budget share of a necessity falls with increased income, so its income elasticity must rise in LES. Thus, higher income causes the food income elasticity to move in the direction of unity—food is less of a necessity (or more of a luxury) for the rich, as compared to the poor. Is this unattractive implication of LES overcome by disaggregating consumers into quintiles?

Figure 11.2 contrasts the behaviour of the food income elasticity in two cases, (i) with the constant $\beta_i's$ obtained from the single-consumer estimates of LES and (ii) when quintiles are used. Panel A plots the budget share of food against income, while panel B contains the corresponding marginal shares—the horizontal curve for the single-consumer case and the (mostly) declining curve for quintiles. The budget share declines, but with quintiles the marginal share (mostly) falls faster leading to the corresponding income elasticity also falling, as shown in panel C. However, in the single-consumer case, the elasticity rises with income (the dotted line in panel C) so much so that it exceeds unity at the top quintile—food is a luxury for the rich! Evidently, the quintile case deals satisfactorily with the problematic behaviour of the

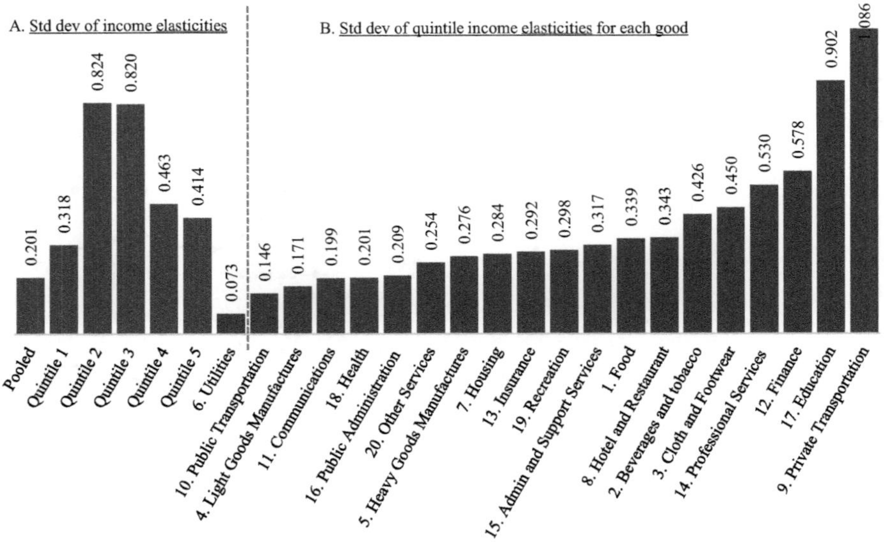

Fig. 11.3 Standard deviations of income elasticities

food income elasticity in LES. Panel D gives a further perspective on food by plotting the approximate Engel curve implied by the quintile estimates. This curve is clearly non-linear, with the slope declining as income rises in contrast to the one-consumer case, which is also shown in the figure (the dotted line).

The appropriateness of disaggregating consumers can also be analysed by examining the variability of the income elasticities across household and commodity types. Disaggregation would matter for the income elasticities if (i) the variance of income elasticities is higher for quintiles relative to the pooled estimate and (ii) the variances of the quintile elasticities for each commodity are large.

Figure 11.3 presents the standard deviations of the income elasticities. Panel A shows a substantially higher dispersion of income elasticities from the quintile estimates (std. dev. = [0.32–0.82]) relative to the pooled estimate (std. dev. = 0.20). Panel B also shows a large dispersion of the quintile elasticities across the 20 commodities with standard deviations ranging from 0.07 to 1.09. This higher dispersion implies that disaggregating LES estimates into more household types better captures the non-monotonic relationship between income and consumption. As emphasised by Ho et al. (2020), incorporating heterogeneous behaviour across household types is a necessary condition for achieving improvements in consumption modelling and for evaluating the distributional impact of policies or economic development.

11.9 An Input-Output Table

The previous chapter presented the econometric estimation of Mariano et al. (2024) on input substitution elasticities. This and the next section provide more detailed analysis of the results. Key input for estimating the substitution elasticities is a time series of input-output (IO) tables for Australia. IO tables record the flow of goods and services between producers and users and the flow associated with primary factor inputs. Suppose there are m industries that use intermediate inputs and there are n such inputs. Define $C_i = \sum_{j=1}^{n} p_{ij} q_{ij}$ as the total cost of intermediate inputs of using industry i, with p_{ij} the price of input j paid by i and q_{ij} the corresponding quantity. Then the cost of j as a share of $i's$ total cost of intermediates is

$$a_{ij} = \frac{p_{ij} q_{ij}}{C_i}, \quad 0 < a_{ij} < 1, \sum_{j=1}^{n} a_{ij} = 1.$$

Table 11.7 displays the evolution of the IO coefficients in Australia over 25 years by taking the log-changes of the shares from the first to the last year, $\log a_{ij,2019} - \log a_{ij,1995} = \log \frac{a_{ij,2019}}{a_{ij,1995}}$ for $i = 1, \cdots, 31$ users and $j = 1, \cdots, 12$ inputs. Note that these are pure numbers comparable across industries and inputs. The first 12 columns of the table contain the log-changes of the $a_{ij}'s$, while the final column summarises the picture with weighted averages $\sum_j a_{ij,1995} \log \frac{a_{ij,2019}}{a_{ij,1995}}$, which equals zero only when $a_{ij,2019} = a_{ij,1995}$ for each j, and is positive otherwise. This weighted average is a measure of the overall change in the structure of inputs. The mean over the 30 industries is 7.81 per cent (second last element of the last column), and the two largest are for textiles etc. and metal products (industries 5 and 8). This is understandable as over this period, these industries have experienced substantial import competition resulting from tariff reductions. Though there are some notable exceptions, larger changes in input structure tend to be concentrated among the primary sectors (industries at the top of the table), less so for services. Exceptions occur for accommodation and food services (industry 14) and healthcare services (26).

Divisia indexes can be used to give a compact understanding of the drivers of intermediate usage. The price and volume indexes are

$$DP_{it} = \sum_{j=1}^{12} \bar{a}_{ijt} Dp_{ijt}, \qquad DQ_{it} = \sum_{j=1}^{12} \bar{a}_{ijt} Dq_{ijt}. \tag{11.12}$$

Here $\bar{a}_{ijt} = \frac{1}{2}\left(a_{ijt} + a_{ij,t-1}\right)$ is the average of the input shares in years $t-1$ and t, and $Dx_t = \log x_t - \log x_{t-1}$, $x = p_{ijt}, q_{ijt}$ is the corresponding log-changes of prices and quantities. The corresponding dispersion measures are the variances of prices (Π_{it}) and quantities (K_{it}), and the associated covariance (Γ_{it}):

Table 11.7 Changes in input-output coefficients, Australia 1995–2019

	Users	Suppliers												Weighted average
		1 Elect	2 Petr etc.	3 Coal	4 OilGas	5 Minerals etc.	6 Agri etc.	7 Food etc.	8 Txt etc.	9 Durable Manuf	10 Non-durable Manuf	11 Trans	12 Servs	
1	Agriculture	− 41.54	− 119.19	26.72	− 110.11	92.12	16.79	77.24	66.74	20.61	30.08	− 5.11	− 22.72	6.44
2	ForFisAgSrv	− 43.02	− 105.46		− 9.62		− 21.02	98.23	70.71	28.01	70.65	42.06	1.52	10.50
3	EnrgyMinrl	7.45	− 26.33	61.82	94.48	− 16.80	− 19.32	65.06	9.74	1.88	51.36	− 20.16	− 31.37	9.12
4	FoodBevTob	− 75.65	− 49.51		− 48.23	42.21	− 16.88	35.17	14.36	27.92	65.57	− 17.17	− 35.86	4.99
5	TexCloFotwr	− 86.58	− 159.70		− 55.56		− 61.02	− 116.85	61.19	53.46	37.55	− 70.09	− 22.91	18.91
6	WoodPaper	− 111.48	56.55		− 127.54		− 52.66	120.51	24.06	16.89	70.76	− 29.27	− 33.07	13.30
7	ChemNonMet	− 92.77	7.84		− 178.03	− 38.10	− 73.28	32.78	− 18.64	33.38	56.55	− 31.09	− 29.32	14.40
8	MetProd	11.70	− 21.09	36.69	− 3.33	− 44.55	98.82	74.31	− 4.79	80.27	55.60	− 50.80	− 49.32	16.52
9	TrasEquip	− 110.82	− 74.75		− 50.62			31.79	− 37.52	37.40	9.05	− 57.67	− 67.70	10.95
10	MachEquip	− 107.04	− 37.75		− 62.91			62.09	− 3.85	9.47	46.81	− 20.37	− 29.02	2.59
11	FurnOthManuf	− 95.90	41.21		7.56	− 4.75	− 58.65	66.34	− 22.29	15.36	33.33	− 37.25	− 35.37	3.79
12	Construction	− 5.32	36.78		20.37	34.54	35.37	26.25	41.16	26.51	33.70	− 58.90	− 17.12	2.79
13	WholeReTrd	− 68.67	− 32.39		− 1.84	104.15	13.89	22.55	35.66	67.10	77.64	− 10.73	− 9.42	4.07
14	AcmFodSrv	− 49.66	− 45.99		− 41.88		− 20.02	47.31	34.83	− 3.55	43.78	− 40.81	− 62.61	12.82
15	TransServ	− 51.38	− 38.18		− 21.40		172.60	138.94	69.89	53.98	94.81	− 24.01	6.80	4.77
16	InfMedTelCom	− 16.67	11.05		− 115.68		77.14	89.05	25.01	− 15.61	116.23	− 14.89	− 6.05	4.60
17	FinInsSrv	− 51.88	− 199.38		− 8.01		285.11	240.20	152.94	57.88	167.36	− 16.17	− 2.82	5.15
18	RentHireSrv	− 73.77	− 68.89		− 89.19		38.03	124.64	85.99	− 10.88	106.86	− 21.64	1.64	4.14
19	DwellRelEst	− 7.26	77.47		20.50		179.29	167.99	170.49	160.15	136.63	25.91	− 5.01	4.50
20	ProfSciTech	− 13.14	− 46.67		− 1.83		108.47	138.27	107.87	66.76	200.83	55.99	− 11.32	7.98
21	AdmSuppSrv	17.91	67.81		15.03		137.32	111.75	89.94	39.22	141.11	29.75	− 13.04	7.12
22	PubAdmDefSec	26.36	27.68		− 33.00		107.73	81.26	35.78	− 9.75	113.97	26.63	− 15.43	5.97

23	PrimSecEdu	24.92	47.91		– 55.30		78.88	69.36	1.26	– 16.19	113.82	– 11.23	– 8.89	5.47
24	TertVocEdu	63.74	114.34		– 4.00		57.10	50.55	– 2.28	4.40	105.12	5.28	– 16.81	6.09
25	OtherEduc	38.90	75.89		– 47.32		75.89	127.60	52.36	37.41	143.51	– 13.43	– 17.87	9.76
26	HealthCare	24.66	88.88		– 1.11		– 60.64	– 7.24	55.23	– 20.54	138.57	– 11.66	– 28.84	15.81
27	HerCrePerArt	30.87	68.78		3.10		– 108.96	96.80	41.12	30.77	107.65	18.44	– 13.88	5.86
28	GambSporRec	– 0.69	31.69		– 104.96		– 1.64	71.86	90.66	29.35	– 13.75	13.31	– 19.03	4.95
29	RepairMaint	25.64	62.46		– 70.28		– 155.01	27.24	– 46.61	19.43	– 7.40	– 55.05	– 33.74	3.55
30	OthSrv	– 28.48	– 44.35		71.79		51.26	96.31	79.08	38.44	73.14	43.02	– 22.20	7.53
	Mean	– 28.65	– 8.44	41.74	– 33.63	21.10	31.59	75.58	42.67	29.32	80.70	– 11.90	– 21.69	7.81
31	National	– 34.38	– 30.53	29.56	11.47	– 28.39	29.44	63.90	92.76	34.99	83.71	– 3.19	– 23.61	6.73

Note: All elements are logarithmic changes ×100. The input-output coefficients a_{ij} used as weights in the weighted averages of the last column. Details of sources of underlying data are given in Mariano et al. (2024)

Table 11.8 Divisia indexes of intermediate inputs

	Using industry (1)	Price index $DP \times 100$ (2)	Quantity index $DQ \times 100$ (3)	Price variance $\Pi \times 100^2$ (4)	Quantity variance $\mathrm{K} \times 100^2$ (5)	Price-quantity covariance $\Gamma \times 100^2$ (6)	Elasticity of substitution $\sigma = -\Gamma/\Pi$ (7)
1	Agriculture	3.43	0.41	17.69	67.60	−9.23	0.522
2	ForFisAgSrv	3.04	−0.56	34.08	115.82	−18.48	0.542
3	EnrgyMinrl	4.23	3.37	93.30	84.48	−40.56	0.435
4	FoodBevTob	3.36	0.51	12.53	29.06	−3.72	0.297
5	TexCloFotwr	2.44	−6.21	13.65	136.18	−8.15	0.597
6	WoodPaper	2.39	−0.35	11.79	41.25	−4.24	0.360
7	ChemNonMet	2.62	0.16	29.13	68.20	−16.41	0.563
8	MetProd	2.96	1.16	40.57	118.34	−23.66	0.583
9	TrasEquip	1.68	−0.36	5.65	29.89	−0.41	0.072
10	MachEquip	2.06	0.40	5.93	18.32	−0.62	0.104
11	FurnOthManuf	2.22	−0.50	6.30	38.71	−1.68	0.267
12	Construction	2.98	3.72	11.33	19.82	−3.76	0.332
13	WholeReTrd	2.87	0.78	15.88	21.93	−10.91	0.687
14	AcmFodSrv	3.03	1.37	10.47	24.43	−5.71	0.545
15	TransServ	3.38	1.51	35.87	19.21	−10.35	0.289
16	InfMedTelCom	1.81	2.19	8.37	14.24	−3.87	0.463
17	FinInsSrv	4.17	2.20	3.29	17.06	−0.67	0.203
18	RentHireSrv	3.25	2.34	8.37	24.35	−1.45	0.174
19	DwellRelEst	4.01	1.82	2.38	15.41	−1.21	0.507
20	ProfSciTech	2.96	3.15	3.25	10.47	−0.67	0.206
21	AdmSuppSrv	2.92	1.86	4.03	17.81	−1.40	0.348
22	PubAdmDefSec	3.02	3.67	11.84	26.38	−4.97	0.419
23	PrimSecEdu	2.82	4.12	6.99	30.39	−1.53	0.219
24	TertVocEdu	2.81	5.62	11.05	34.34	−5.20	0.470

25	OtherEduc	2.69	5.69	5.76	49.27	−2.07	0.359
26	HealthCare	2.55	3.76	12.10	48.68	−3.83	0.317
27	HerCrePerArt	2.60	2.13	4.99	53.86	−2.24	0.449
28	GambSporRec	2.61	2.61	7.16	36.69	−5.01	0.700
29	RepairMaint	1.74	1.80	5.87	22.45	−3.50	0.595
30	OthSrv	3.18	2.04	11.19	25.55	−6.49	0.580
	Mean	2.86	1.68	15.03	42.01	−6.73	0.407
31	National	3.07	2.05	21.23	16.19	−8.48	0.399

Note: All elements are means of the annual transitions. Details of sources of underlying data are given in Mariano et al. (2024)

$$\begin{cases} \Pi_{it} = \sum_{j=1}^{12} \bar{a}_{ijt} \{Dp_{ijt} - DP_{jt}\}^2, \ \mathrm{K}_{it} = \sum_{j=1}^{12} \bar{a}_{ijt} \{Dq_{ijt} - DQ_{jt}\}^2 \\ \Gamma_{it} = \sum_{j=1}^{12} \bar{a}_{ijt} \{Dp_{ijt} - DP_{jt}\}\{Dq_{ijt} - DQ_{jt}\}. \end{cases} \quad (11.13)$$

The first 30 rows of columns 2–6 of Table 11.8 contain the results, averaged over years. On average, prices rise by 2.86 per cent p. a. and quantities by 1.68 per cent (second last row, columns 2 and 3). In most cases, quantities are more dispersed than prices, indicating sticky prices (columns 4 and 5). Take the means in the second last row as an example. Here, the standard deviation of prices is $\sqrt{\Pi} \times 100 = \sqrt{15.03} \approx 3.9$ per cent, while that of quantities is two-thirds larger at $\sqrt{42.01} \approx 6.5$ per cent. Column 6 reveals that for each using sector, prices and quantities are negatively correlated, suggesting price substitution. Column 7 of the table is discussed in the next section.

11.10 Estimates of Input Substitution

As demonstrated in Chap. 10, Selvanathan et al. (2024) introduced a convenient preliminary measure of the elasticity of substitution (σ) as the ratio of the weighted covariance to the price variance with the sign changed,

$$\sigma = -\frac{\Gamma}{\Pi}. \quad (11.14)$$

Column 7 of Table 11.8 contains the results. As can be seen, the average value of σ is 0.407, close to the national value of 0.399.

The CES framework can also be used to estimate σ with a system of demand equations for the n intermediate inputs. The log-differential of the CES cost-minimising demand for input i was previously presented in Eq. (10.18) of the previous chapter. For ease of reference, we reproduce this equation,

$$d \log q_i - d \log Q = -\sigma(d\log p_i - d \log P), \quad (11.15)$$

where $d \log Q = d \log C - d \log P$. To apply Eq. (11.15) infinitesimal changes are replaced with discrete changes and both sides of the equation are multiplied by the arithmetic average of the cost share of i, as before. This yields the system of n equations with $T - 1$ annual observations (the initial year is eliminated by the changes):

$$\bar{a}_{it}(Dq_{it} - DQ_t) = \gamma\{\bar{a}_{it}(Dp_{it} - DP_t)\} + \varepsilon_{it}, \quad i = 1, \cdots, n; t = 2, \cdots, T. \quad (11.16)$$

As before, $\bar{a}_{it} = \frac{1}{2}(a_{it} + a_{i,t-1})$; $Dq_{it} = \log q_{it} - \log q_{i,t-1}$ and $Dp_{it} = \log p_{it} - \log p_{i,t-1}$ are log-changes; $DQ_t = \sum_{i=1}^{n} \bar{a}_{it} Dq_{it}$ and $DP_t = \sum_{i=1}^{n} \bar{a}_{it} Dp_{it}$ are the

Table 11.9 Estimates of input demand equations

	Intercept for input i, θ_i					
Using industry	1 ElecGen	2 PetCoal	3 Coal	4 OilGas	5 MinrlExpMing	6 AgriForFish
1. Agriculture	0.015 (0.023)	0.182 (0.058)	−0.002 (0.002)	0.004 (0.004)	−0.001 (0.001)	−0.247 (0.155)
2. ForFisAgSrv	0.007 (0.014)	0.338 (0.186)		−0.001 (0.007)		0.235 (0.089)
3. EnrgyMinrl	−0.029 (0.186)	0.022 (0.1)	−0.087 (0.106)	−0.649 (0.22)	0.042 (0.214)	0.002 (0.004)
4. FoodBevTob	0.02 (0.021)	0.005 (0.009)		0.008 (0.024)	−0.002 (0.01)	0.082 (0.204)
5. TexCloFotwr	0.043 (0.069)	0.017 (0.017)		0.003 (0.008)		0.479 (0.157)
6. WoodPaper	0.053 (0.046)	−0.031 (0.017)		0.049 (0.062)		0.287 (0.005)
7. ChemNonMet	0.061 (0.044)	−0.055 (0.116)		0.314 (0.194)	0.068 (0.112)	0.039 (0.018)
8. MetProd	−0.021 (0.082)	0.018 (0.101)	−0.041 (0.137)	0.004 (0.067)	0.751 (0.66)	−0.001 (0.002)
9. TrasEquip	0.008 (0.022)	−0.018 (0.042)		−0.004 (0.013)		
10. MachEquip	0.015 (0.018)	−0.005 (0.008)		0.002 (0.006)		
11. FurnOthManuf	0.045 (0.053)	−0.011 (0.01)		−0.005 (0.009)	−0.001 (0.051)	0.009 (0.027)
12. Construction	−0.001 (0.004)	−0.084 (0.048)		−0.003 (0.004)	−0.015 (0.042)	−0.015 (0.002)
13. WholeReTrd	0.037 (0.032)	0.009 (0.017)		−0.015 (0.047)	−0.003 (0.003)	−0.022 (0.022)
14. AcmFodSrv	0.034 (0.033)	0.005 (0.006)		0.01 (0.031)		0.03 (0.241)
15. TransServ	0.011 (0.009)	0.053 (0.144)		−0.002 (0.015)		−0.007 (0.007)
16. InfMedTelCom	−0.006 (0.017)	−0.039 (0.043)		0.003 (0.003)		−0.008 (0.001)
17. FinInsSrv	0.008 (0.009)	0.035 (0.016)		0.001 (0.003)		−0.006 (0.017)
18. RentHireSrv	0.095 (0.065)	0.013 (0.015)		0.007 (0.009)		−0.021 (0.005)
19. DwellRelEst	0.003 (0.019)	−0.004 (0.006)		−0.001 (0.003)		−0.017 (0.003)
20. ProfSciTech	−0.002 (0.011)	0.002 (0.011)		−0.002 (0.003)		−0.008 (0.007)
21. AdmSuppSrv.	−0.006 (0.006)	−0.022 (0.01)		−0.004 (0.006)		−0.023 (0.013)
22. PubAdmDefSec	−0.097 (0.065)	−0.052 (0.037)		−0.001 (0.006)		−0.03 (0.024)
23. PrimSecEdu	−0.034 (0.026)	−0.022 (0.018)		0.001 (0.017)		−0.036 (0.053)
24. TertVocEdu	−0.041 (0.033)	−0.028 (0.023)		−0.008 (0.02)		−0.036 (0.054)

(continued)

Table 11.9 (continued)

Using industry	Intercept for input i, θ_i: 1 ElecGen	2 PetCoal	3 Coal	4 OilGas	5 MinrlExpMing	6 AgriForFish
25. OtherEduc	−0.037 (0.053)	−0.02 (0.019)		−0.001 (0.017)		−0.024 (0.052)
26. HealthCare	−0.03 (0.02)	−0.072 (0.036)		−0.015 (0.024)		0.007 (0.095)
27. HerCrePerArt	−0.012 (0.01)	−0.02 (0.019)		−0.002 (0.004)		0.018 (0.037)
28. GambSporRec	−0.002 (0.012)	−0.011 (0.019)		0.003 (0.003)		−0.003 (0.116)
29. RepairMaint	−0.01 (0.012)	−0.037 (0.023)		0.003 (0.004)		0.003 (0.007)
30. OthSrv	0.013 (0.019)	0.024 (0.026)		−0.018 (0.016)		−0.046 (0.03)
National	0.016 (0.022)	0.001 (0.023)	−0.011 (0.011)	−0.035 (0.024)	0.02 (0.05)	−0.075 (0.023)

Using industry	Intercept for input i, θ_i: 7 FoodBevTob	8 TxtLetCltFot	9 DurblManuf	10 NonDurManuf	11 Transport	12 Services	Price coefficient $\gamma = -\sigma$
1. Agriculture	−0.165 (0.155)	−0.006 (0.009)	−0.004 (0.06)	−0.061 (0.19)	0.04 (0.072)	0.245 (0.335)	−0.515 (0.052)
2. ForFisAgSrv	−0.157 (0.089)	−0.05 (0.063)	−0.1 (0.279)	−0.113 (0.203)	−0.095 (0.146)	−0.066 (0.301)	−0.579 (0.074)
3. EnrgyMinrl	−0.005 (0.004)	0.006 (0.015)	0.102 (0.143)	−0.019 (0.07)	0.128 (0.081)	0.489 (0.23)	−0.391 (0.051)
4. FoodBevTob	−0.281 (0.204)	0.009 (0.011)	−0.002 (0.053)	−0.068 (0.082)	0.063 (0.073)	0.168 (0.141)	−0.3 (0.08)
5. TexCloFotwr	0.24 (0.157)	−0.865 (0.579)	−0.027 (0.068)	−0.036 (0.073)	0.122 (0.11)	0.026 (0.258)	−0.556 (0.111)
6. WoodPaper	−0.01 (0.005)	−0.002 (0.023)	−0.096 (0.192)	−0.508 (0.155)	0.078 (0.076)	0.179 (0.215)	−0.357 (0.066)
7. ChemNonMet	−0.018 (0.018)	0.02 (0.018)	−0.149 (0.121)	−0.623 (0.249)	0.134 (0.093)	0.213 (0.172)	−0.587 (0.079)
8. MetProd	−0.002 (0.002)	0.002 (0.016)	−0.943 (0.559)	−0.03 (0.037)	0.092 (0.142)	0.171 (0.187)	−1.005 (0.081)
9. TrasEquip	−0.004 (0.004)	0.039 (0.028)	−0.423 (0.401)	−0.044 (0.069)	0.037 (0.056)	0.41 (0.335)	0.23 (0.146)
10. MachEquip	−0.007 (0.004)	0.011 (0.019)	−0.035 (0.291)	−0.096 (0.082)	0.018 (0.067)	0.099 (0.239)	−0.121 (0.106)
11. FurnOthManuf	−0.015 (0.027)	0.132 (0.138)	−0.212 (0.331)	−0.123 (0.119)	0.051 (0.098)	0.13 (0.183)	−0.377 (0.105)
12. Construction	−0.001 (0.002)	−0.001 (0.013)	−0.155 (0.226)	−0.032 (0.069)	0.034 (0.018)	0.27 (0.274)	−0.324 (0.061)
13. WholeReTrd	−0.022 (0.022)	−0.013 (0.019)	−0.087 (0.06)	−0.157 (0.069)	0.084 (0.085)	0.188 (0.113)	−0.724 (0.04)
14. AcmFodSrv	−0.918 (0.241)	−0.002 (0.011)	0.012 (0.035)	−0.013 (0.033)	0.01 (0.009)	0.835 (0.244)	−0.431 (0.056)
15. TransServ	−0.008 (0.007)	−0.007 (0.014)	−0.062 (0.126)	−0.047 (0.027)	0.374 (0.128)	−0.306 (0.184)	−0.283 (0.05)

16. InfMedTelCom	−0.002 (0.001)	−0.003 (0.006)	0.04 (0.086)	−0.178 (0.068)	−0.002 (0.04)	0.194 (0.108)	−0.463 (0.068)
17. FinInsSrv	−0.036 (0.017)	−0.003 (0.003)	−0.023 (0.051)	−0.073 (0.046)	0.026 (0.065)	0.071 (0.103)	−0.753 (0.1)
18. RentHireSrv	−0.008 (0.005)	−0.013 (0.017)	0.024 (0.048)	−0.078 (0.052)	0.053 (0.042)	−0.07 (0.135)	−0.176 (0.063)
19. DwellRelEst	−0.006 (0.003)	−0.007 (0.005)	−0.079 (0.049)	−0.069 (0.042)	−0.007 (0.012)	0.183 (0.102)	−0.893 (0.127)
20. ProfSciTech	−0.023 (0.007)	−0.011 (0.008)	−0.054 (0.057)	−0.116 (0.034)	−0.117 (0.061)	0.329 (0.095)	−0.383 (0.056)
21. AdmSuppSrv	−0.028 (0.013)	−0.021 (0.023)	−0.02 (0.057)	−0.16 (0.053)	−0.068 (0.085)	0.348 (0.103)	−0.35 (0.057)
22. PubAdmDefSec	−0.044 (0.024)	−0.005 (0.053)	0.061 (0.114)	−0.149 (0.07)	−0.044 (0.08)	0.356 (0.188)	−0.396 (0.046)
23. PrimSecEdu	−0.062 (0.053)	0.031 (0.053)	0.156 (0.186)	−0.109 (0.097)	0.037 (0.064)	0.037 (0.271)	−0.018 (0.092)
24. TertVocEdu	−0.06 (0.054)	0.038 (0.044)	0.092 (0.179)	−0.114 (0.091)	0.009 (0.081)	0.146 (0.282)	0.111 (0.131)
25. OtherEduc	−0.105 (0.052)	−0.011 (0.041)	−0.108 (0.224)	−0.195 (0.109)	0.037 (0.104)	0.463 (0.335)	−0.565 (0.111)
26. HealthCare	0.018 (0.095)	−0.094 (0.198)	0.417 (0.22)	−0.368 (0.164)	0.005 (0.05)	0.131 (0.285)	−0.04 (0.067)
27. HerCrePerArt	−0.093 (0.037)	−0.003 (0.046)	−0.094 (0.091)	−0.101 (0.087)	−0.026 (0.062)	0.33 (0.261)	−0.166 (0.109)
28.GambSporRec	−0.225 (0.116)	−0.057 (0.028)	−0.194 (0.272)	0.036 (0.077)	−0.016 (0.041)	0.467 (0.269)	−0.799 (0.071)
29. RepairMaint	−0.006 (0.007)	0.019 (0.015)	−0.345 (0.375)	0.013 (0.05)	0.051 (0.044)	0.31 (0.289)	−0.674 (0.062)
30. OthSrv	−0.06 (0.03)	−0.073 (0.062)	−0.074 (0.095)	−0.141 (0.078)	−0.097 (0.095)	0.469 (0.175)	−0.553 (0.056)
National	−0.095 (0.023)	−0.042 (0.022)	−0.081 (0.103)	−0.134 (0.045)	0.027 (0.049)	0.408 (0.102)	−0.402 (0.035)

Note: Standard errors are in parenthesis. Blank cells mean no input use

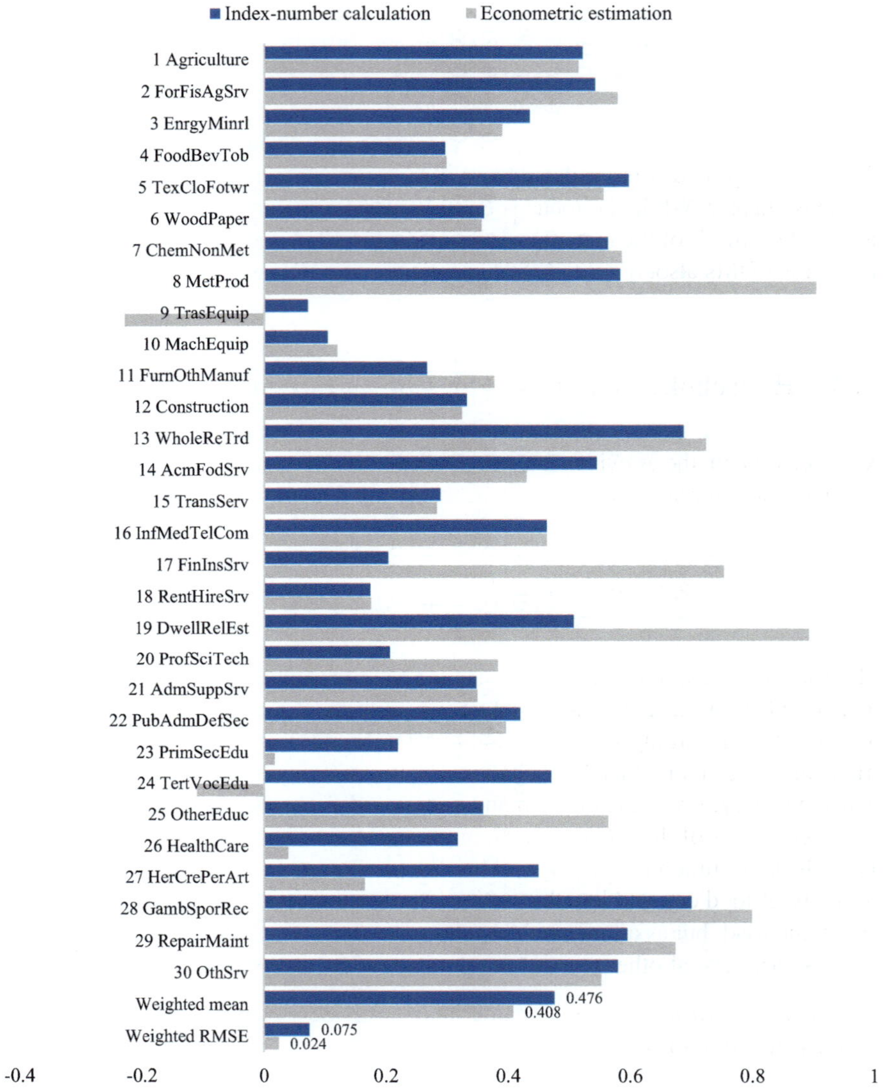

Fig. 11.4 Two sets of input substitution elasticities

indexes of Eq. (11.12); $\gamma = -\sigma$ is the elasticity of substitution with the sign changed; and ε_{it} is a disturbance term. Adding both sides of Eq. (11.16) over the n inputs yield $0 = 0 + \sum_{i=1}^{n} \varepsilon_{it}$, which shows that the disturbances have a zero sum, reflecting the allocation nature of the system.

Model (11.16) is estimated as a SURE system for each using industry with the input-output data described above with $T = 24$ years. To take account of any residual trend-like changes in the input mix, an intercept θ_i is added to each equation, with

$\sum_{i=1}^{n}\theta_i = 0$. Table 11.9 contains the results. There are about 350 estimates of intercepts, of which only about 10 per cent are highly significant. Additionally, there is no particular pattern among these estimates. We conclude residual trends do not appear to play a substantial role in driving intermediate input usage. The final column of the table gives the estimates of the price coefficient ($\gamma = -\sigma$) for each industry, and 24 of the 31 are significantly negative. There are two insignificant positive estimates.

There are now two sets of elasticity estimates, those just discussed and those based on the index-number approach (last column of Table 11.8). The two sets are summarised in Fig. 11.4. All are less than unity, and the weighted means are quite close: 0.476 for the elasticities from the index-number approach, and 0.408 for the econometric estimates. The econometric estimates have a weighted root-mean-square error (RMSE) of 0.024, which is considerably less than that of the other set of 0.075, suggesting more precision. Although there is not a substantial difference between the two sets of elasticities, the econometric estimates are possibly preferred because of their lower dispersion.

11.11 Domestic and Foreign Sources of Supply

For a certain good, suppose there are two varieties consumed, one produced domestically and the other produced abroad and imported into the home country. Let p^d be the price of the domestically produced variety and q^d the corresponding quantity, and p^f, q^f be the foreign counterparts. Then, total expenditure on the good is $p^d q^d + p^f q^f = M$ and the market shares of the two varieties are $w = \frac{p^d q^d}{M}$, $1 - w = \frac{p^f q^f}{M}$. Define Divisia price and volume indexes as:

$$d(\log P) = wd(\log p^d) + (1-w)d(\log p^f), \quad d(\log Q) = wd(\log q^d) + (1-w)d(\log q^f).$$

The change in total expenditure on the good is then:

$$d(\log M) = d(\log P) + d(\log Q). \tag{11.17}$$

Using Eq. (11.17), the change in the domestic share can be expressed as:

$$d(\log w) = d\left(\log \frac{p^d}{P}\right) + d\left(\log \frac{q^d}{Q}\right).$$

Thus, the change in the share is made up of the change in the relative price, $d\left(\log \frac{p^d}{P}\right)$, and the change in the relative quantity, $d\left(\log \frac{q^d}{Q}\right)$.

The changes in the relative price of domestic goods and the corresponding quantity can also be expressed as

$$d(\log\frac{p^d}{P}) = (1-w)\{d(\log p^d) - d(\log p^f)\},$$
$$d(\log\frac{q^d}{Q}) = (1-w)\{d(\log q^d) - d(\log q^f)\}.$$

Thus, the change in the share of the domestic variety becomes

$$d(\log w) = (1-w)\left\{d\left(\log\frac{p^d}{p^f}\right) + d\left(\log\frac{q^d}{q^f}\right)\right\}. \tag{11.18}$$

For discrete changes from year $t - s$ to t, define the log-change operator as $Dx_t = \log x_t - \log x_{t-s} = \log\frac{x_t}{x_{t-s}},\ x > 0, 0 < s < t$. A discrete approximation to Eq. (11.18) for the transition from year $t - s$ to t is

$$Dw_t \approx (1-\tilde{w})\left\{D\left(\frac{p_t^d}{p_t^f}\right) + D\left(\frac{q_t^d}{q_t^f}\right)\right\}, \tag{11.19}$$

where $\tilde{w}$ is a value of the share lying between $t - s$ and t.

Table 11.10 gives the means and standard deviations in the domestic shares of 20 commodities in Australia over the period 1995–2017. The domestic shares of agricultural-related products are higher compared to other commodities, with about 90 per cent of total consumption domestically produced. In particular, Australia imports only 4 per cent of the total demand for meat products (item 1 of Table 11.10), while less than 10 per cent of dairy and eggs (item 2) is imported. The import shares of other agri-forest products [e.g. fish (3), wood (11), paper (12), and furniture (13)] and mining products [non-metals (14), iron and steel (15), and non-ferrous metals (16)] are higher, roughly ranging between 10 per cent and 20 per cent. Australia does not manufacture its own cars but produces vehicle parts and transport equipment, so that there are high import shares for the relevant products (items 17–19). The import share of clothing and footwear (10) is also higher than most others at 29 per cent.

A scatter plot of relative quantity against relative price log-changes for all 20 goods combined is given in Fig. 11.5. It can be seen that while there is considerable variability, there is a distinct negative relation between quantity and price changes: The regression line is negatively sloped with a coefficient of −0.78. Thus, if we wished to combine all goods together, an initial rough-and-ready estimate of the common elasticity of substitution σ is 0.8. The quantity changes of commodity 16 (non-ferrous metal) and commodity 19 (transport equipment) are more dispersed relative to the others. All in all, there is preliminary evidence of substitution between domestic and foreign sources of supply.

The last four columns of Table 11.10 summarise the evolution of domestic market shares for the 20 commodities over the 23-year period. Over the last two decades, all 20 domestic shares have fallen (column 10). The most substantial fall is the

Table 11.10 Domestic and foreign sources of supply, Australia, 1995–2017

		Domestic sales shares		Relative prices (p^d/p^f) (Log-changes)		Relative quantities (q^d/q^f) (Log-changes)		Domestic share in		Change in share	Log-change in share
	Commodity	Mean	Std. Dev.	Mean	Std. Dev.	Mean	Std. Dev.	1995	2017	1995–2017	1995–2017
	(1)	(2)	(3)	(4)	(5)	(6)	(7)	(8)	(9)	(10)	(11)
1	Meat products	95.61	1.290	−0.126	13.541	−4.037	16.641	97.57	94.15	−3.43	−3.57
2	Dairy products and egg	92.70	1.523	−0.526	12.182	−2.370	15.079	93.63	88.59	−5.03	−5.52
3	Fish products	78.96	3.421	−1.361	10.938	−0.582	13.469	81.66	74.38	−7.28	−9.34
4	Other food products	85.72	4.013	−0.363	7.547	−3.988	6.901	90.59	78.70	−11.89	−14.06
5	Beverage and tobacco	93.06	2.527	3.002	5.365	−7.975	8.858	96.08	89.13	−6.95	−7.50
6	Coal, petroleum, and gas	74.16	8.420	0.257	26.578	−4.964	20.668	86.08	68.72	−17.37	−22.54
7	Basic chemicals	66.53	3.680	0.040	10.005	−1.988	8.852	68.05	58.11	−9.94	−15.79
8	Pharmaceutical products	60.76	5.762	1.739	4.091	−4.728	8.878	73.71	59.23	−14.48	−21.87
9	Textile and leather	69.12	3.129	0.917	8.889	−2.050	10.411	68.02	62.38	−5.64	−8.66
10	Clothing and footwear	71.00	7.076	−0.229	8.541	−5.185	9.143	82.50	58.89	−23.61	−33.71
11	Wood and products	88.82	1.143	−1.183	6.052	0.696	10.290	88.20	87.04	−1.16	−1.32
12	Paper products	83.98	2.561	0.761	8.218	−2.527	9.100	85.15	79.55	−5.61	−6.81
13	Furniture	80.72	7.413	−0.865	9.018	−6.343	10.111	92.02	70.25	−21.77	−27.00
14	Non-metals	79.34	2.325	0.608	9.212	−2.787	6.742	82.69	74.74	−7.96	−10.12
15	Iron steel	80.47	2.122	−2.188	10.566	0.672	10.049	82.59	77.26	−5.33	−6.67
16	Non-ferrous metals	80.84	5.732	−1.551	14.142	−4.217	30.868	90.77	73.44	−17.33	−21.19
17	Machinery equipment	49.08	3.902	0.275	7.620	−2.978	7.907	58.20	43.45	−14.75	−29.23
18	Motor vehicles and parts	56.94	8.719	0.501	3.422	−5.617	8.046	67.48	40.24	−27.24	−51.70
19	Transport equipment	55.00	6.146	−1.984	8.226	0.799	29.586	63.18	56.94	−6.24	−10.40
20	Other manufactures	66.94	5.920	2.259	9.502	−6.991	10.402	78.54	56.37	−22.16	−33.16
	Average	75.49	13.310	−0.001	1.356	−3.358	2.257	81.34	69.58	−11.76	−17.01

Note: All entries are ×100. The underlying data are from the Australian Bureau of Statistics' supply-use tables (SUT), the international trade statistics and the national accounts. Details are in Clements et al. (2021)

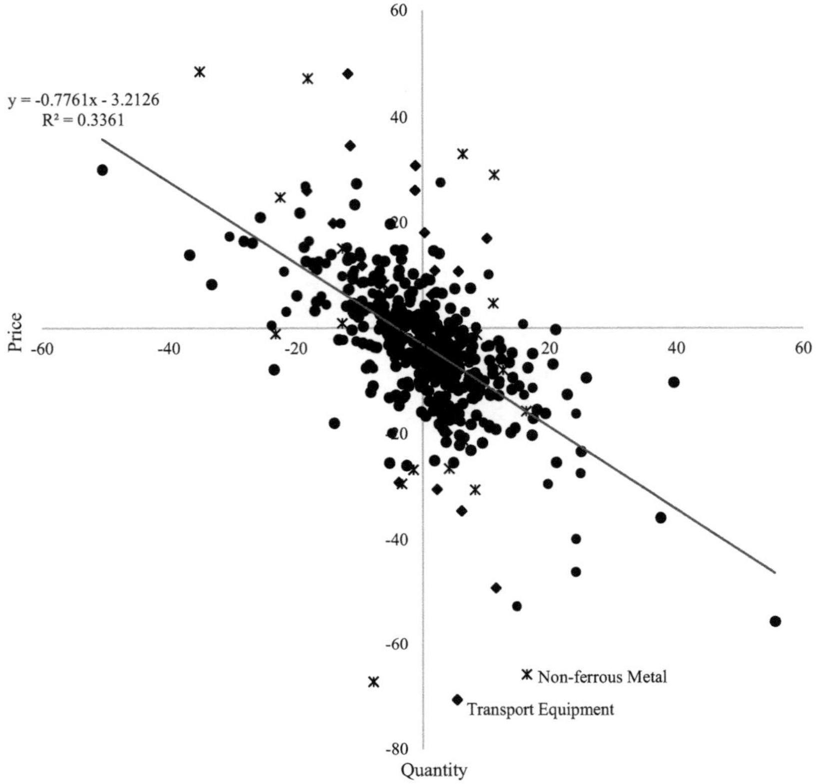

Fig. 11.5 Scatter plot of price-quantity log-changes (20 goods combined, Australia, 1995–2017). *Notes*: Quantity log-changes are on the vertical axis and price log-changes are on the horizontal axis. All entries are ×100

27 percentage points for motor vehicles (item 18). From column 11, the log-change (×100) of this share is −51.7, which implies a percentage change of $100(e^{-51.7/100} - 1) = -40$ per cent.

11.12 Import-Domestic Substitution

As described in the previous chapter, import-domestic substitution elasticities (the so-called "Armington elasticities") determine the degree of competitiveness in demand between similar products produced in different countries and are key parameters in a variety of numerical models of international trade. Armington (1969) introduced a manageable way to deal with the demand for goods distinguished by place of origin. In this framework, goods of the same type from different sources are imperfect substitutes. When foreign and domestic goods are perfect substitutes, the corresponding import demand is the excess demand, but when the two varieties are less-than-perfect substitutes, the conventional demand function for the foreign good is equivalent to the import demand function. This section sets out the Armington approach of CES aggregation over imported and domestic varieties of a particular good. This approach is an attractively simple way of reducing a large-scale problem to something more manageable, which accounts for its popularity.

Suppose that each of C countries supplies a different variety of each of the n goods to consumers in the country under consideration. One of the C countries is the domestic one. There are now n goods from each of C countries, so the total number consumed is $n \times C$. For example, if $n = 12$ goods and $C = 150$ countries, there is a total of $nC = 1800$ goods from all sources of supply. As it is not feasible to analyse a problem of this dimension in an unrestricted manner, substantial structuring of the analysis is needed in the form of restrictions on behaviour. It is natural to group goods of the same variety, that is, to place within the same group the varieties of same basic good supplied by the various countries (including goods produced at home). It could then be reasonably assumed that goods belonging to the same group are closer substitutes to each other than to goods from different groups. For example, French and Australian wines (members of the wine group) are likely to be closer substitutes than smart phones from China (the electronic group) and socks from Bangladesh (clothing).

The above discussion is consistent with the case of block-independent preferences whereby utility is additive in the n groups of goods, $u(\boldsymbol{q}_1, \cdots, \boldsymbol{q}_n) = \sum_{i=1}^{n} u_i(\boldsymbol{q}_i)$, where $u_i(\cdot)$ is the sub-utility function of group i and $\boldsymbol{q}_i$ is the vector of quantities belonging to group i. Within each group, goods can interact fully in a marginal utility sense, while there are no between-group effects. In other words, there is preference independence with respect to groups of goods. As presented in the previous chapter, when sub-utility $u_i(\cdot)$ is CES, as in Eq. (10.2), the conditional (or within-group) demands are given by Eqs. (10.3) and (10.4). With two varieties of good i, the relative demand function for the goods in log form is given by

$$\log\left(\frac{q_i^1}{q_i^2}\right) = \beta_i - \sigma_i \log\left(\frac{p_i^1}{p_i^2}\right), \tag{11.20}$$

where superscripts represent the domestic and imported varieties of the good; for variety k $(k = 1, 2)$, q_i^k is the quantity demanded and p_i^k is the price; and $\beta_i = \sigma_i \log\left(\frac{\alpha_i^1}{\alpha_i^2}\right)$ is an intercept. Clements et al. (2021) estimated the above equation for the 20 commodity groups using least-squares and panel approaches.

Three sets of estimates of model (11.20) were produced. The first set involves single-equation least-squares estimates for each of the 20 goods given in Table 11.11, columns 2–5. Most of the substitution elasticities are significant and positive, particularly for the change formulation, where they range from 0.14 for motor vehicles to 2.06 for transport equipment, and the majority of the significant estimates are either less than unity or close to it. There appears to be significant

Table 11.11 Estimates of substitution elasticities $\log\left(\frac{q_{it}^1}{q_{it}^2}\right) = \beta_i - \sigma_i \log\left(\frac{p_{it}^1}{p_{it}^2}\right) + \varepsilon_{it};\ i = 1, \ldots, 20, t = 1995, \ldots, 2017$

		Single-equation least-squares estimates				Panel estimates	
		Levels of logs		Log-changes		Levels of logs	Log-changes
	Commodity	Elasticity of substitution σ	Durbin-Watson	Elasticity of substitution σ	Durbin-Watson	Elasticity of substitution σ	Elasticity of substitution σ
	(1)	(2)	(3)	(4)	(5)	(6)	(7)
1	Meat products	2.181 (0.419)	0.426	1.000 (0.160)	2.675	1.632 (0.224)	1.133 (0.185)
2	Dairy products and egg	0.050 (0.234)	0.860	0.906 (0.189)	2.404	1.403 (0.230)	1.051 (0.203)
3	Fish products	0.073 (0.276)	0.574	0.608 (0.239)	2.407	1.215 (0.249)	0.839 (0.230)
4	Other food products	0.493 (0.967)	0.037	0.710 (0.129)	2.337	0.745 (0.461)	1.013 (0.331)
5	Beverage and tobacco	2.406 (0.100)	0.678	1.009 (0.292)	2.457	1.506 (0.127)	1.268 (0.462)
6	Coal, petroleum, and gas	−0.121 (0.415)	0.342	0.642 (0.098)	1.816	0.352 (0.158)	0.747 (0.093)
7	Basic chemicals	1.371 (0.358)	0.363	0.637 (0.137)	2.158	0.260 (0.349)	0.849 (0.251)
8	Pharmaceutical products	2.191 (0.432)	0.253	0.523 (0.471)	1.514	−0.046 (0.312)	0.730 (0.603)
9	Textile and leather	0.771 (0.298)	0.355	0.682 (0.213)	2.320	−0.820 (0.325)	1.004 (0.282)
10	Clothing and footwear	2.055 (0.531)	0.176	0.775 (0.165)	2.017	1.217 (0.254)	1.033 (0.295)
11	Wood and products	0.252 (0.217)	1.101	0.823 (0.333)	2.328	2.363 (0.369)	1.210 (0.413)
12	Paper products	1.765 (0.171)	0.515	0.858 (0.157)	1.926	0.510 (0.205)	1.009 (0.303)
13	Furniture	1.634 (0.886)	0.060	0.826 (0.170)	1.782	1.487 (0.268)	0.991 (0.279)
14	Non-metals	1.353 (0.191)	0.445	0.552 (0.107)	2.439	0.211 (0.229)	0.777 (0.273)
15	Iron steel	0.518 (0.088)	1.257	0.301 (0.202)	2.907	1.649 (0.160)	0.494 (0.235)
16	Non-ferrous metals	−0.144 (0.275)	1.095	1.002 (0.434)	2.528	0.648 (0.141)	1.048 (0.174)
17	Machinery equipment	1.256 (0.316)	0.212	0.742 (0.162)	1.736	−0.076 (0.317)	0.978 (0.330)

18	Motor vehicles and parts	4.864 (0.986)	0.425	0.143 (0.525)	2.258	1.580 (0.556)	0.355 (0.728)
19	Transport equipment	0.522 (0.425)	1.194	2.056 (0.660)	2.608	1.862 (0.265)	2.246 (0.306)
20	Other manufactures	1.767 (0.135)	0.518	0.742 (0.180)	2.214	0.983 (0.121)	0.905 (0.264)
	Test for common sigma Chi-square	Value (df) 360.652 (19)	Prob 0.000	Value (df) 20.305 (19)	Prob 0.376	Value (df) 172.279 (18)	Value (df) 31.405 (18)

Note: Standard errors in parentheses

autocorrelation when levels are used, with low Durbin-Watson statistics, but this is much less of a problem for changes. From the last row of the table, on the basis of a Wald test we fail to reject a common σ for changes (but not for levels).

The second set of estimates use a panel approach, which has two advantages. First, it allows for the easy incorporation of a time effect for each year that affects all goods simultaneously. A second advantage is that the panel approach facilitates the testing of hypotheses covering multiple sectors, as will be demonstrated. The last two columns of Table 11.11 contain the results. Now, the elasticities tend to be more significant than before; they are also larger, ranging from 0.355 to 2.246. The Wald test rejects a common σ for both levels and changes.

Next, we test if groups of commodities share the same elasticity, rather than it being the same for every commodity individually. If true, this could represent a considerable simplification. Table 11.12 presents the results for when the 20 commodities form seven broad groups. The results show that only within the "transport, machinery and equipment" group are the elasticities statistically different.

The third set of estimates are presented in Table 11.13 where the group-pattern restrictions are imposed. All the substitution elasticities are positive and are mostly significant. For changes, the average elasticity is 1.046.

A summary of the three sets of elasticities (for changes) is presented in Fig. 11.6, where the label "Panel I" ("Panel II") refers to the case in which 20 (9) sectors are distinguished. On average, the substitution elasticities in Panel II are the highest (mean elasticity of 1.05), closely followed by Panel I (0.98) and then OLS (0.78). At the same time, however, the panel estimates are not too different to the unrestricted OLS counterparts.

11.13 CGE Application I: LES Estimates

The preceding material dealt with three distinct types of demand elasticities, (i) the LES household demand elasticities, (ii) the CES input substitution elasticities, and (iii) the Armington elasticities for the demand for domestic and foreign varieties. This and the next two sections illustrate how these elasticities can be used in a CGE model. The CGE model used refers to Australia and is adopted from Verikios et al. (2021). Key theoretical features of the model include:

- Optimising behaviour by households and businesses in the context of competitive markets with explicit resource and budget constraints.
- The price mechanism operates to clear markets for goods and capital.
- The labour market operates with a degree of friction so that some labour is always unemployed, but the rate of unemployment is held constant in the long run.
- Marginal cost equals marginal revenue in all activities.

Disaggregated (or heterogeneous) consumer responses are a potentially important driver of long-term structural change. We investigate this by embedding the disaggregated estimates of the LES in the CGE model that has 10,046 actual

Table 11.12 Test for common sigma for seven commodity groups

	Group name	Commodities	Null hypothesis	Test statistic	Value	df	Probability
I	Food and agricultural commodities	1. Meat products 2. Dairy products and egg 3. Fish products 4. Other food products 5. Beverage and tobacco	$\sigma_i = \sigma_I$, $i = 1, \cdots, 5$	F-statistic Chi-square	0.341 1.362	(4, 379) 4	0.851 0.851
II	Energy and minerals	6. Coal, petroleum, and gas 14. Non-metals 15. Iron steel 16. Non-ferrous metal	$\sigma_i = \sigma_{II}$, $i = 6,14,15,16$	F-statistic Chi-square	1.344 4.031	(3, 379) 3	0.260 0.258
III	Chemical	7. Basic chemicals 8. Pharmaceutical products	$\sigma_i = \sigma_{III}$, $i = 7, 8$	F-statistic Chi-square	0.147 0.147	(1, 379) 1	0.702 0.702
IV	Textile, leather, clothing and footwear	9. Textile and leather 10. Clothing and footwear	$\sigma_i = \sigma_{IV}$, $i = 9, 10$	F-statistic Chi-square	0.005 0.005	(1, 379) 1	0.942 0.942
V	Wood and paper products	11. Wood and products 12. Paper products	$\sigma_i = \sigma_V$, $i = 11, 12$	F-statistic Chi-square	0.161 0.161	(1, 379) 1	0.688 0.688
VI	Miscellaneous Manufacture goods	13. Furniture 20. Other manufactures	$\sigma_i = \sigma_{VI}$, $i = 13, 20$	F-statistic Chi-square	0.054 0.054	(1, 379) 1	0.816 0.816
VII	Transport, machinery and equipment	17. Machinery equipment 18. Motor vehicles and parts 19. Transport equipment	$\sigma_i = \sigma_{VII}$, $i = 17,18,19$	F-statistic Chi-square	5.867 11.734	(2, 379) 2	0.003 0.003

Table 11.13 Panel estimates of sigma for nine-sector model

	Commodity group (1)	Levels of logs (2)	Log-changes (3)
1	Food and agricultural commodities	1.472 (0.098)	1.051 (0.114)
2	Energy and minerals	0.741 (0.09)	0.782 (0.075)
3	Chemicals and pharmaceuticals	0.257 (0.258)	0.848 (0.232)
4	Textile, leather, and wearing apparel	0.582 (0.226)	1.043 (0.214)
5	Wood and paper products	0.992 (0.193)	1.095 (0.247)
6	Miscellaneous manufactured goods	1.134 (0.121)	0.961 (0.196)
7	Machinery equipment	0.065 (0.345)	0.997 (0.327)
8	Motor vehicles and parts	1.881 (0.604)	0.374 (0.722)
9	Transport equipment	1.765 (0.290)	2.264 (0.302)
	Fixed effects R-squared Durbin Watson	Cross-section, time 0.97 0.49	Cross-section, time 0.47 2.52

Note: Standard errors in parentheses

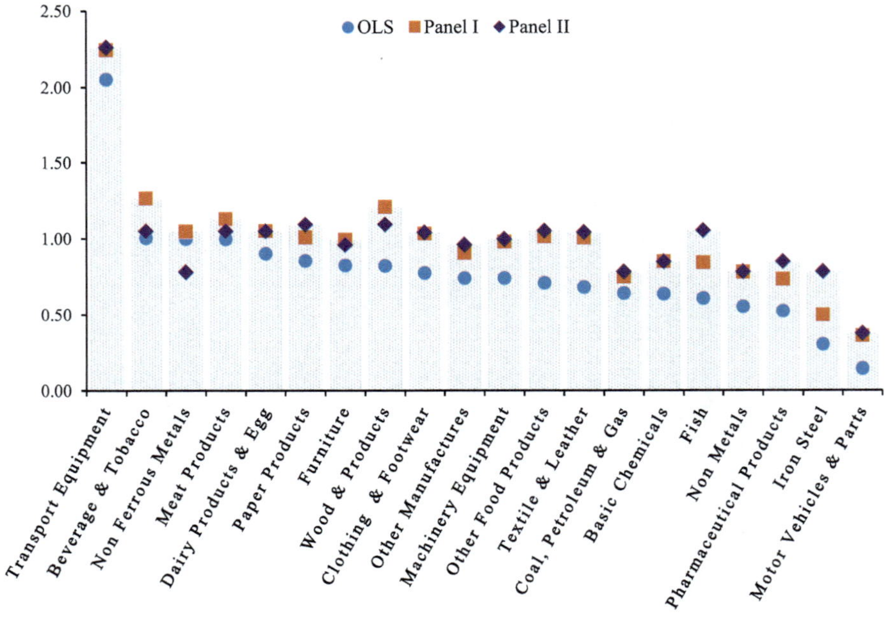

Fig. 11.6 Three sets of substitution elasticities

households. To identify the role played by disaggregation, stochastic simulations are employed with two sets of LES parameters—the pooled and quintile elasticities. Each simulation moves the Australian economy along a cyclically balanced growth path over a 30-year period beginning in 2020. The cyclicality derives from labour productivity growth with two components: a deterministic component of 0.70 per cent productivity growth p. a. and a stochastic component a_t generated by an AR1

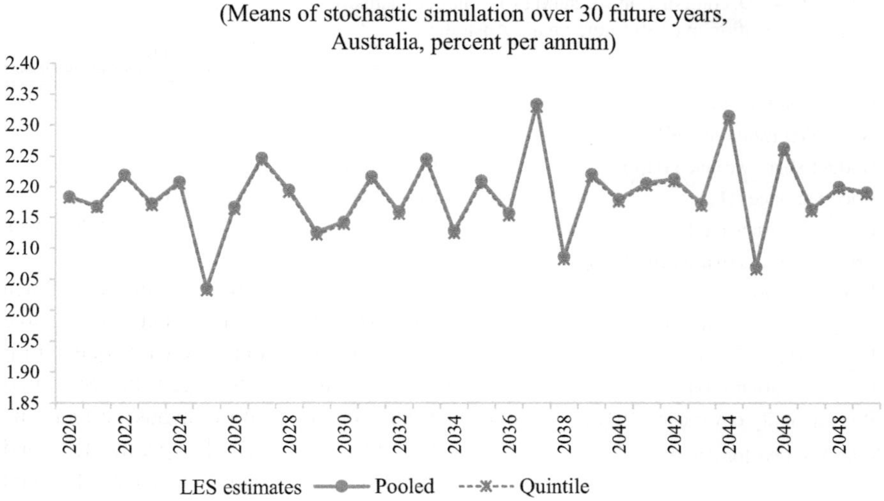

Fig. 11.7 Changes in real GDP (Means of stochastic simulation over 30 future years, Australia, per cent per annum)

process $a_t = \rho a_{t-1} + \varepsilon_t$, where $(\varepsilon_t)_{t=2020}^{t=2049}$ is a sequence of normal independent and identically distributed random variables with mean 0 and standard deviation of 0.0061 per cent per annum. The value of ρ is chosen so that the effect of ε_t on a_{t+2} is only 10 per cent of ε_t. All other annual shocks are deterministic and include 1.5 per cent growth in population/labour supply, 2.2 per cent growth in real government expenditure, export demand schedules, and land-based factors of production. Consumer prices also grow by 2 per cent annually.

Figure 11.7 shows that the forecast generates a cyclical growth path for real GDP. On average, the economy is projected to grow at 2.2 per cent per annum over the 30-year period, which is consistent with annual growth of 1.5 per cent in population and 0.7 per cent in labour productivity. As is to be expected, for GDP as a whole, there is almost no perceptible effect of household disaggregation as the two paths in Fig. 11.7 are almost identical. Nonetheless, as discussed in the previous chapter, there is substantial change in the structure of the economy over the 30-year period revealed by the significant changes in budget shares shown in Fig. 10.4. This structural change is larger when households are disaggregated.

Further insight into structural change is given by the distribution of expenditure as measured by the dispersion of the budget shares. For each of the 20 budget shares in each of the 30 years of the horizon, there are 50 trials, which we denote by $w_{it}^{(s)}, i = 1, \cdots, 20, t = 2020, \cdots, 2049, s = 1, \cdots, 50$. Consider the means over the 50 trials $\overline{w}_{it} = \frac{1}{50}\sum_{s=1}^{50} w_{it}^{(s)}, i = 1, \cdots, 20,$ with annual logarithmic changes $\Delta \log \overline{w}_{it} = \log \overline{w}_{it} - \log \overline{w}_{i,t-1}$. The cross-commodity variance of these changes in the shares is $\Pi_{wt} = \sum_{i=1}^{20} \overline{\overline{w}}_{it}(\Delta \log \overline{w}_{it} - \Delta \log W_t)^2$, with $\overline{\overline{w}}_{it} = \frac{1}{2}(w_{it} + w_{i,t-1})$ and

Table 11.14 Decomposition of changes in budget shares, with and without heterogeneous consumers (Simulation over 30 future years, Australia)

Dispersion measure	Year Start	Middle	End	Mean	Standard deviation
A. *Pooled estimates of LES*					
Budget-share variance (Π_{wt})	0.103	0.100	0.081	0.094	0.008
Price variance (Π_{pt})	0.088	0.134	0.128	0.117	0.023
Quantity variance (Π_{qt})	0.077	0.134	0.132	0.127	0.020
Price-quantity covariance ($2\Pi_{pqt}$)	−0.062	−0.167	−0.180	−0.149	0.042
B. *Quintile estimates of LES*					
Budget-share variance (Π_{wt})	0.150	0.146	0.119	0.141	0.012
Price variance (Π_{pt})	0.088	0.131	0.129	0.115	0.022
Quantity variance (Π_{qt})	0.106	0.174	0.168	0.167	0.024
Price-quantity covariance ($2\Pi_{pqt}$)	−0.044	−0.160	−0.178	−0.141	0.045

Note: See text for details

$\Delta \log W_t = \sum_{i=1}^{20} \overline{\overline{w}}_{it} \Delta \log \overline{w}_{it}$. This variance is budget-share weighted making it representative of the dispersion of the basket as a whole; it measures the change in the structure of expenditure patterns. The variance can be decomposed into more basic price and quantity contributions:

$$\Pi_{wt} = \Pi_{pt} + \Pi_{qt} + 2\Pi_{pqt}. \tag{11.21}$$

Here, $\Pi_{pt} = \sum_{i=1}^{20} \overline{\overline{w}}_{it} (\Delta \log p_{it} - \Delta \log P_t)^2$ is the cross-commodity variance of prices, with $\Delta \log P_t = \sum_{i=1}^{20} \overline{\overline{w}}_{it} \Delta \log p_{it}$; $\Pi_{qt} = \sum_{i=1}^{20} \overline{\overline{w}}_{it} (\Delta \log q_{it} - \Delta \log Q_t)^2$, the corresponding variance of quantities, with $\Delta \log Q_t = \sum_{i=1}^{20} \overline{\overline{w}}_{it} \Delta \log q_{it}$; and $\Pi_{pqt} = \sum_{i=1}^{20} \overline{\overline{w}}_{it} (\Delta \log p_{it} - \Delta \log P_t)(\Delta \log q_{it} - \Delta \log Q_t)$ is the price-quantity covariance.

Table 11.14 gives the decomposition in (11.21) for the start, middle, and end years of the simulation. Quantities tend to be more dispersed than prices, especially at the end of the period. Importantly, comparing panel B to A, when the quintile estimates of LES are used quantities are substantially more dispersed. From panel A, for the pooled estimates, the mean of the quantity variance (Π_{qt}) is 0.127, so the standard deviation is $\sqrt{0.127} = 0.356$, which is equivalent to $e^{0.356} - 1 = 42.8$ per cent. Contrast that with the corresponding value for the quintile case from panel B of $e^{\sqrt{0.167}} - 1 = 50.5$ per cent. This means that allowing for heterogeneity by disaggregation of the demand responses leads to a larger economy-wide quantity responses to shocks of about $\frac{51-43}{43} = 18.0$ per cent. In short, household heterogeneity is an important driver of structural change. This suggests including this feature with its added flexibility would possibly be a distinct advantage for CGE models of the future.

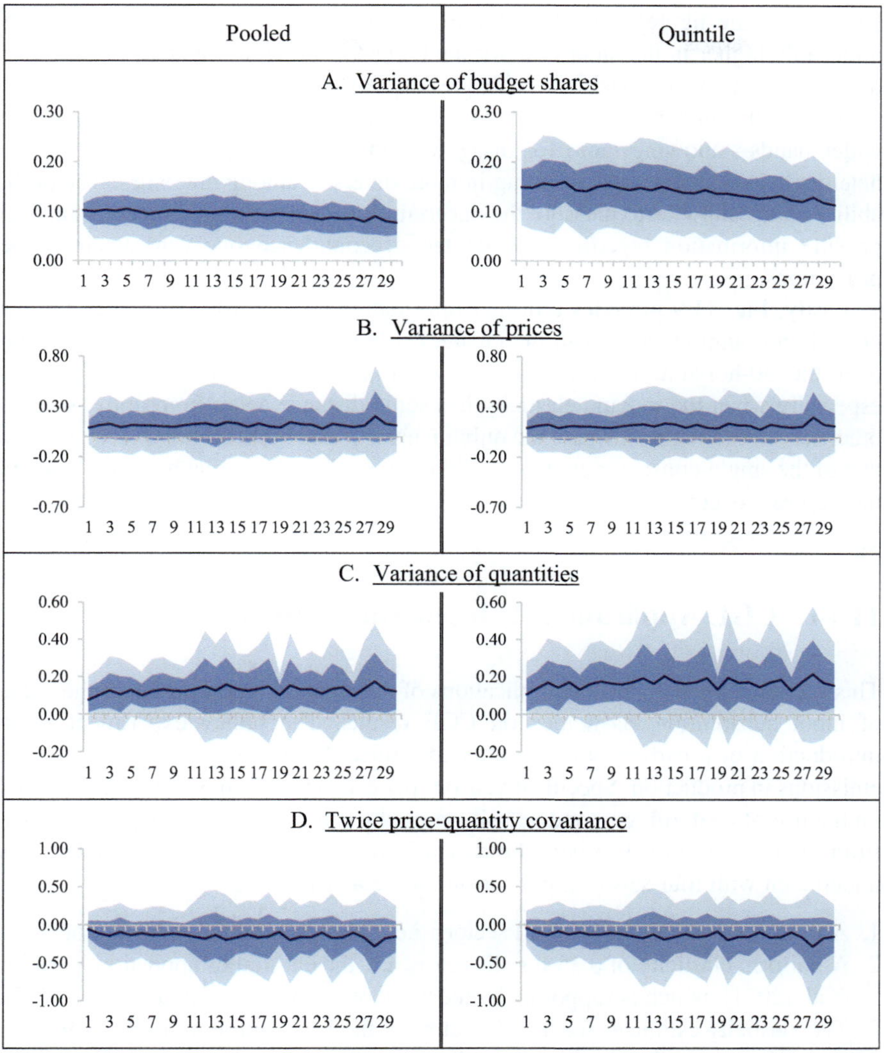

Fig. 11.8 Dispersion of budget shares and components. *Notes*: (1) Panel A uses the dispersion of budget share as a measure of structural change in a 30-year stochastic simulation of the CGE model. The solid lines are the means over replications and the shaded areas are ±1 and 2 standard deviations. (2) Panels B–D give the corresponding components of panel A. (3) The left- (right-) hand side of each panel uses the pooled (quintile) estimates of LES

The stochasticity of the simulations means there is a distribution of outcomes. Table 11.14 uses the mean outcomes (over the 50 trajectories) in each of the specified years. Figure 11.8 illustrates the nature of the underlying distributions with fan charts of the budget-share variance and its components. Here, the solid line is the mean and the shaded bands are ∓1 and 2 standard deviations of the 50 trajectories. A comparison of the results associated with the pooled estimates (given on the left side of the figure) with the quintile ones (on the right) reveals the mean is noticeably higher in the latter case for the budget share variance and the important quantity component, consistent with the above discussion of Table 11.14. Also notable is the higher dispersion among the quintile results as indicated by the wider bands—allowing more for disaggregated demand responses leads to more heterogeneity in behaviour, resulting in more diversity among outcomes. The probability bands allow us to measure the uncertainty associated with projections and so provide information regarding the degree of confidence one can attach to the projections.

Lastly, Fig. 11.9 provides a further information on the differences between the pooled and quintile cases with the changes in nominal consumption of each good over the 30-horizon. Disaggregation gives rise to some noticeable differences, especially when the income elasticity lies some distance away from unity, such as other services (a luxury), where the quintile growth (the broken line) clearly exceeds that of the single-consumer case (the solid line), and food (a strong necessity), where the opposite occurs.

11.14 CGE Application II: Input Substitution

This section demonstrates the implications of different assumptions about the value of input substitution elasticities on CGE results. The policy experiment is an introduction of a carbon price in order to reduce the intensity of greenhouse gas emissions in production. Specifically, a 100 per cent ad valorem sales tax is imposed on the use of coal, oil, gas, and petroleum products as a production input. Revenue from the tax is returned to households via lower income taxes. This simulation is undertaken with four sets of input substitution elasticities.

1. A uniform elasticity of 0 for all sectors, i.e. Leontief production technology.
2. A uniform elasticity of 0.25 for all sectors, i.e. the elasticities applied in Verikios et al. (2021), which is supported by the work of Bruno (1984) and Atalay (2017).
3. The elasticity estimates for the 30 sectors in the last column of Table 11.9.
4. A uniform elasticity of 1 for all sectors, i.e. Cobb-Douglas production technology.

All other parameters are held constant in the simulations.

Table 11.15 reports the detailed results of these simulations in which a long-run economic environment is assumed, i.e. (i) industry capital stocks expand or contract in order to maintain industry rates of return at their initial levels and (ii) there is a constant unemployment rate, but labour is able to move across industries while incurring some costs of adjustment. The carbon price raises the relative price of coal, oil, gas, and petroleum and provides an incentive for producers to switch to electricity generation, which is the only other energy commodity in the energy nest of the model. Note that although the model does not specify a range of electricity technologies (e.g. fossil fuel versus renewable), they are implicit in the

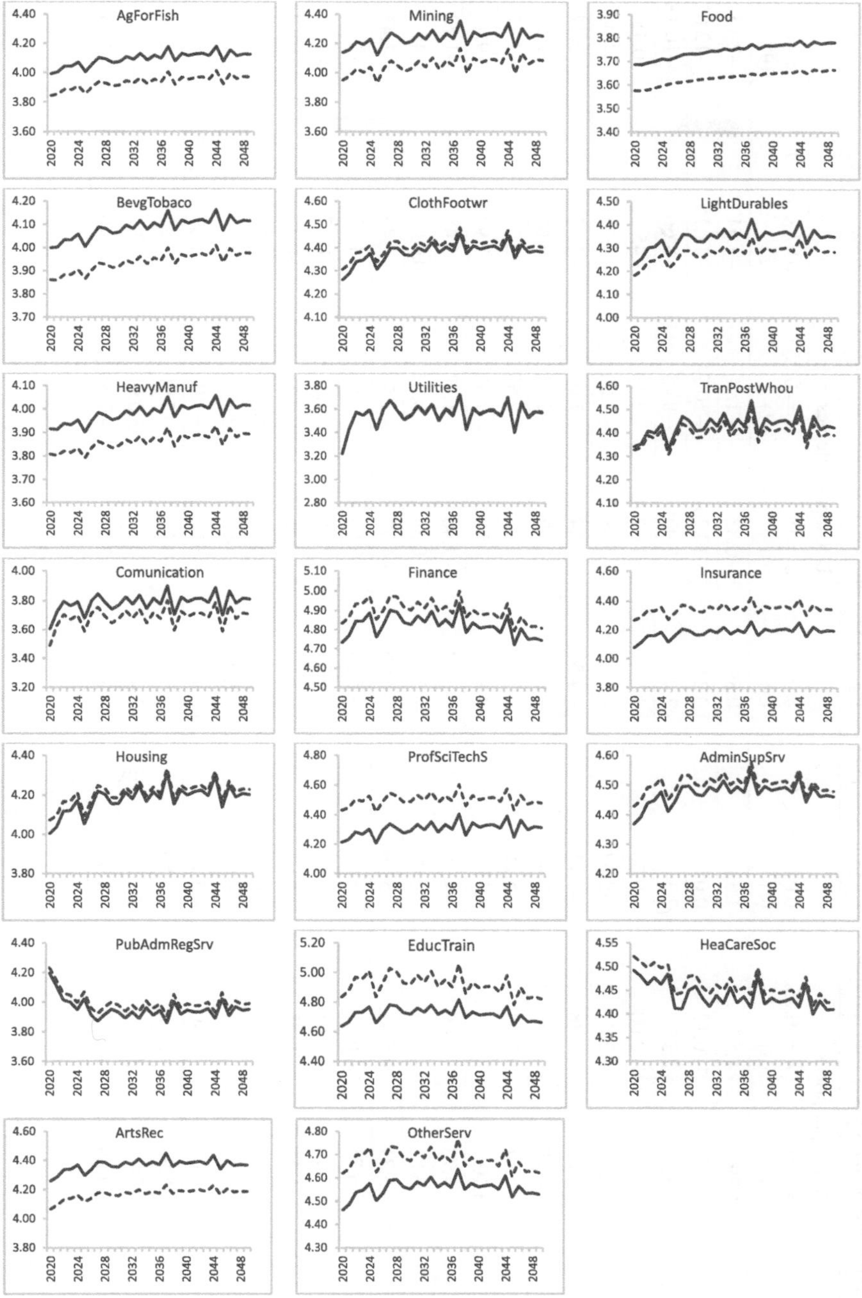

Fig. 11.9 Changes in consumption (Per cent per annum)

Table 11.15 Price and output effects with different values of σ (100 per cent tax on coal, oil, gas, and petroleum inputs; percentage changes)

	A. Output prices				B. Output volumes			
Industry (1)	$\sigma = 0$ (2)	$\sigma = 0.25$ (3)	$0.07 < \sigma < 1$ (4)	$\sigma = 1$ (5)	$\sigma = 0$ (6)	$\sigma = 0.25$ (7)	$0.07 < \sigma < 1$ (8)	$\sigma = 1$ (9)
AFF	1.79	1.53	1.33	0.89	−0.82	−1.20	−1.51	−2.13
Mining	−0.22	−0.12	0.05	0.23	−10.20	−10.74	−11.15	−12.62
Manufacturing	2.33	2.35	2.34	2.40	−7.90	−8.45	−8.66	−10.18
EGW	−3.49	−2.00	−0.50	4.39	−7.07	−2.40	1.45	10.45
Construction	−2.97	−2.81	−2.63	−2.39	−3.98	−4.00	−4.09	−4.06
WhlTrd	−4.05	−3.88	−3.75	−3.56	−0.54	−1.04	−1.42	−2.47
RetTrd	−6.89	−6.68	−6.47	−6.28	−1.99	−2.06	−2.09	−2.58
AccFood	−5.61	−5.44	−5.25	−5.06	−2.35	−2.55	−2.73	−3.37
TranStor	3.10	3.19	3.37	3.38	−6.73	−7.42	−7.92	−9.41
Comm	−4.73	−4.46	−4.20	−3.82	−1.40	−1.43	−1.48	−1.72
FinIns	−6.81	−6.44	−6.08	−5.54	−0.54	−0.24	0.08	0.45
PropServ	−5.71	−5.43	−5.16	−4.90	−1.72	−1.56	−1.43	−1.41
BusServ	−6.75	−6.39	−6.04	−5.54	−2.09	−1.66	−1.35	−0.65
Admin	−7.10	−6.81	−6.53	−6.21	−1.78	−1.17	−0.77	0.54
PubAdmin	−6.56	−6.25	−5.94	−5.53	−0.55	−0.45	−0.38	−0.17
Education	−7.33	−6.98	−6.64	−6.22	1.67	1.54	1.43	1.08
Health	−7.14	−6.84	−6.54	−6.23	0.48	0.41	0.34	0.12
ArtsRec	−5.62	−5.40	−5.19	−4.91	−1.00	−1.05	−1.07	−1.41
Other services	−5.98	−5.78	−5.59	−5.33	−3.01	−2.96	−2.85	−2.88
SD	3.34	3.25	3.22	3.47	3.03	3.03	3.29	4.75
Mean	−4.20	−3.93	−3.65	−3.17	−2.71	−2.55	−2.40	−2.23

CV	−0.80	−0.83	−0.88	−1.10	−1.12	−1.19	−1.37	−2.13

Notes

1. Industry key: AFF—agriculture, forestry, fishing; EGW—electricity, gas, water supply; WhlTrd—wholesale trade; RetTrd—retail trade; AccFood—accommodation, food services; TranStor—transport, storage; Comm—communication; FinIns—finance, insurance; PropServ—property services; BusServ—business services; Admin—administrative services; PubAdmin—public administration; ArtsRec—arts, recreation. This 19-industry classification used in this table is a broader aggregation of the 30-industry classification used for the econometric estimates of Table 11.9
2. The elasticities applied in columns 4 and 8 are from Table 11.9

inputs used by the electricity supply sector. Compared to fossil fuel technologies, renewable technologies generally use unpriced energy sources (e.g. solar, wind, geothermal) but are more capital intensive.

Under Leontief technology ($\sigma = 0$) higher prices of coal, oil, gas, and petroleum flow through to higher output prices as producers cannot substitute electricity for coal, oil, gas, and petroleum. The largest output price increases (or smallest decreases) occur in industries that are the most intensive users of these commodities: agriculture, manufacturing, and transport services. Thus, besides agriculture, these industries generally also experience the largest reductions in output. Mining is also an intensive user of fossil fuels, and it experiences the largest fall in output (-10.2 per cent). Note that the general effect of the carbon price is to reduce output prices (mean $= -4.2$ per cent, SD $= 3.3$ per cent, given in the second and third last entries of column 2) and output volumes (mean $= -2.7$ per cent, SD $= 3$ per cent). This implies that, while the first-round effect of the carbon price is to raise the price of coal, oil, gas, and petroleum and the industries using them, the general equilibrium (or total) effect will be to lower prices as the higher taxes will lead to a fall in total demand.

When $\sigma > 0$ a noticeable change occurs in the pattern of the effects. The output reductions are smaller: for $\sigma = 1$ the mean reduction in output is -2.2 per cent. More importantly, the standard deviation is much larger: 4.8 per cent vs 3.0 per cent. This reflects larger output contractions for most sectors and a large output expansion for the broader electricity, gas, and water supply (EGW) sector. As substitution possibilities increase, all industries are able to substitute electricity for other fuels to a greater extent. This increases the demand for electricity by all industries such that the EGW sector expands by 10.5 per cent with Cobb-Douglas technology compared to a contraction of 7.1 per cent with Leontief technology. Consistent with this change in the pattern of output effects is the change in the pattern of price effects. The price decreases are smaller: for $\sigma = 1$ the mean reduction in price is -3.2 per cent.

11.15 CGE Application III: Armington Elasticities

This section analyses the sensitivity of CGE results to foreign-domestic substitutability by using two sets of Armington elasticities. The policy simulation employed is the complete removal of tariffs on all imported goods. This is implemented over a 50-year horizon whereby tariff rates are reduced annually by 20 per cent of their initial value over the first 5 years. The tariff cut starts in year 2 of the simulation such that all imported commodities will be tariff-free at the beginning of year 7.

In conducting the sensitivity analysis, the effect of the policy shock is first simulated using older estimates of the Armington elasticities taken from Alaouze et al. (1977) (hereafter referred to as Simulation 1). Then, a similar simulation is run but using the new estimates in Table 11.11, column 7 (hereafter referred to as Simulation 2). The broader commodities in the econometric estimates are mapped into the more detailed commodity classification in the CGE model. Commodities

Table 11.16 Armington elasticities for simulations 1 and 2

Commodity	Armington elasticity in simulation 1	Armington elasticity in simulation 2	Commodity	Armington elasticity in simulation 1	Armington elasticity in simulation 2
Sheep, grains, beef, and dairy	1.10	1.10	Paper product	1.10	1.01
Poultry and other livestock	1.70	1.70	Printing	2.00	1.01
Other agriculture	2.00	2.00	Petroleum and coal	0.40	0.75
Aquaculture	0.50	0.50	Human pharmaceutical	2.00	0.73
Forestry and logging	2.00	2.00	Veterinary pharmaceutical	2.00	0.73
Fishing, hunt & trap	0.50	0.50	Basic chemical	2.01	0.85
Coal mining	0.50	0.50	Cleaning compounds	1.65	0.85
Oil and gas extraction	2.00	2.00	Polymer	1.75	0.78
Iron ore mining	0.50	0.50	Natural rubber	1.50	0.78
Non-ferrous metal ore mining	0.50	0.50	Glass and glass	1.20	0.78
Non-metallic mineral mining	2.00	2.00	Ceramic	1.20	0.78
Exploration & mining services	2.00	2.00	Cement, lime, & concrete	0.38	0.78
Meat and meat product	0.50	1.13	Plaster and concrete	1.10	0.78
Processed seafood	0.50	0.84	Other non-metallic mineral	1.20	0.78
Dairy product manufacturing	1.60	1.05	Iron and steel	0.82	0.49
Fruit and vegetable product	0.80	0.80	Basic non-ferrous metal	1.10	1.05
Oils and fats	1.70	1.70	Forged iron and steel	0.82	0.49
Grain mill and cereal product	2.10	2.10	Structural metal	1.50	1.05
Bakery product	1.10	1.10	Other sheet metal	1.50	1.05
Sugar and confectionery	1.25	1.25	Other fabricated metal	1.75	1.05
Other food product	0.50	1.01	Motor vehicles and parts	5.20	1.58
Soft drinks, cordials, and syrup	1.10	1.27	Ships and boat	0.50	2.25
Beer manufacturing	1.10	1.27	Railway rolling stock	0.50	2.25
Wine, spirits, and tobacco	3.40	1.27	Aircraft	0.50	2.25
Textile manufacturing	2.76	1.00	Prof. and scientific equipment	0.50	0.98
Leather product	2.00	1.00	Electrical equipment	1.37	0.98
Textile product	1.93	1.03	Domestic appliance	1.60	0.98
Knitted product	1.90	1.03	Specialised machinery	0.50	0.98
Clothing	2.80	1.03	Furniture	2.30	0.99
Footwear	6.80	1.03	Other manufactured	1.83	0.91
Sawmill product	2.30	1.21	Water, pipeline, other transport	2.00	2.00
Other wood product	1.45	1.21	Air passenger	2.00	2.00
Pulp, paper, and paperboard	1.10	1.01	Air freight	2.00	2.00

that belong to the same broader category are assigned with a similar elasticity based on their respective mapping. Table 11.16 gives the two sets of Armington elasticities. There are two things to note about these parameters. First, services are not assigned with any Armington elasticity since these non-merchandise goods are mostly complimentary rather than substitutable with imported services. Second, the Armington values from Alaouze et al. (1977) were adopted for commodities

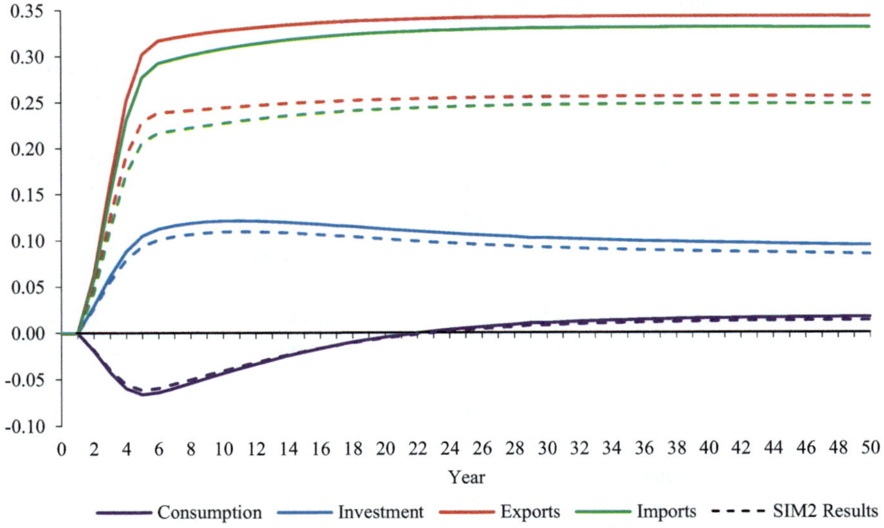

Fig. 11.10 GDP expenditure components (Simulation of tariff removal over 50 future years, Australia, percentage deviations from baseline)

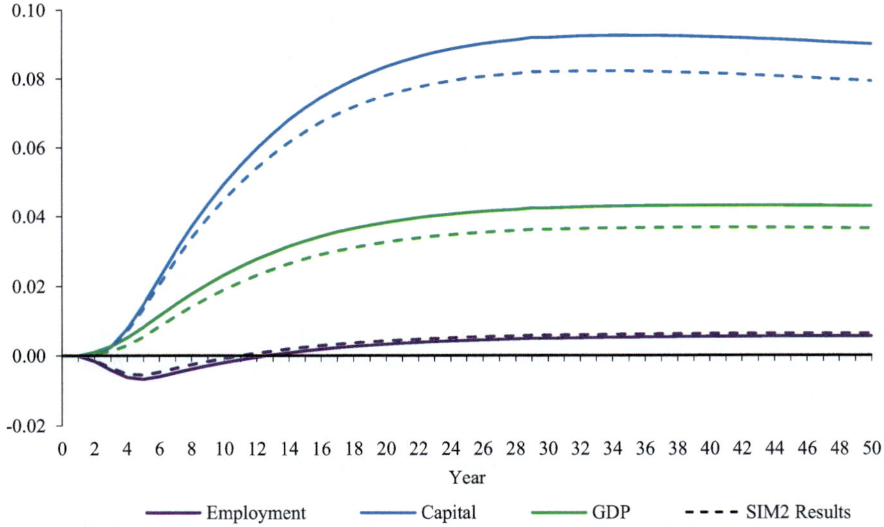

Fig. 11.11 GDP and income components (Percentage deviations from baseline)

where there are no new estimates due to lack of price and quantity data (e.g. primary agriculture such as livestock and raw minerals).

In presenting the results, we first explain the effects of the tariff removal using the results of Simulation 1 and then later compare these with the results of Simulation

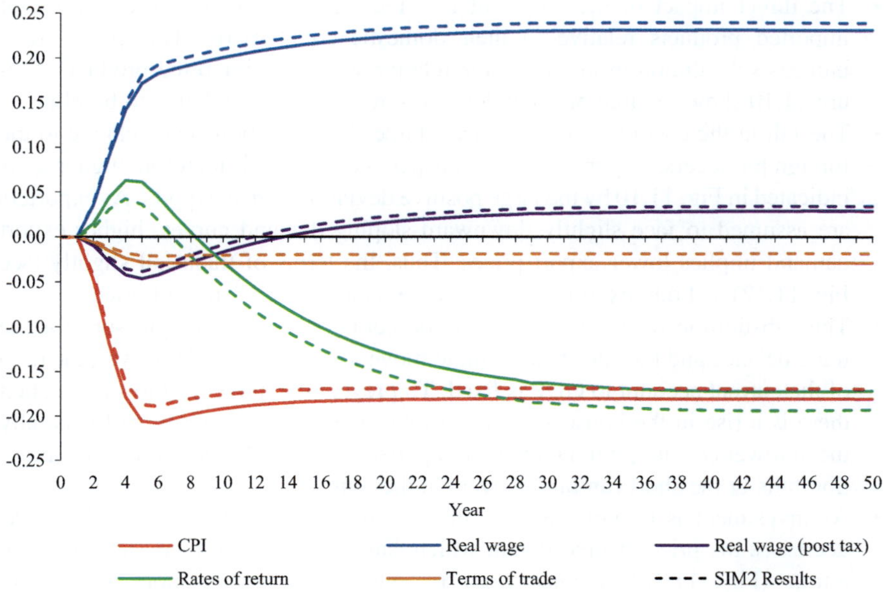

Fig. 11.12 Price indexes (Percentage deviations from baseline)

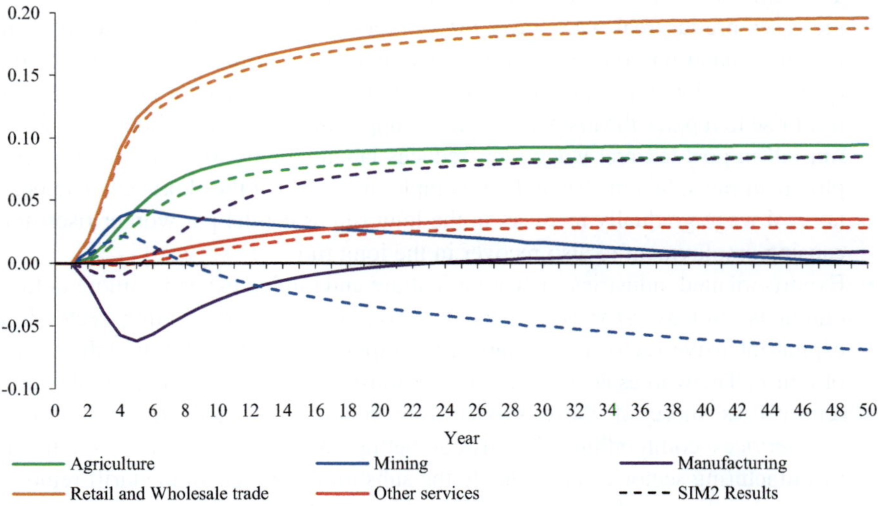

Fig. 11.13 Industry output (Percentage deviations from baseline)

2. Figures 11.10, 11.11, 11.12, and 11.13 show the macroeconomic and sectoral effects: The results of Simulation 1 are presented as solid lines in these figures.

Key results are as follows:

- The direct impact of the tariff cut is a reduction in the purchaser's price of imported products relative to their domestic counterparts. This price effect induces substitution in favour of the relatively cheaper imported products. Figure 11.10 shows a large positive deviation in real imports relative to baseline.
- The fall in the cost of imports reduces domestic production costs relative to the foreign producers. Exports are now cheaper and demand is therefore higher, as is indicated in Fig. 11.10 by the large positive deviation in real exports. As exporters are assumed to face slightly downward-sloping demand curves, higher export demand implies lower export prices. Thus, the terms of trade fall slightly (see Fig. 11.12) as f.o.b. export prices decrease relative to c.i.f. import prices.
- The substitution of imports for domestic commodities creates pressure for the trade balance and the current account to move towards deficit. However, the ratio of the current account to GDP is fixed. To prevent the movement towards deficit there is a rise in the household saving rate. A higher saving rate will generally mean lower consumption and higher exports. Figure 11.10 shows that consumption falls in the short run but recovers in the long run.
- As investment is import intensive in Australia, the fall in the cost of imports decreases the price of investment, which causes a short-run increase in rates of return (Fig. 11.12). Higher rates of return encourages more investment (Fig. 11.10) leading to a larger capital stock (Fig. 11.11). In the long run, investment growth stabilises as rates of return fall.
- The removal of tariffs causes a general reduction in consumer prices and this increases pre-tax real wage rates for workers (Fig. 11.12), leading to a fall in labour demand for some industries. Nevertheless, in the short run there is also a temporary reduction in post-tax real wage rates as the personal income tax rate must rise to replace the lost tariff revenue (approximately $3.7 billion). The short-run fall in post-tax real wage rates reduces labour supply and with fixed unemployment rates, labour demand, and employment fall in the short run. The post-tax real wage gradually recovers in the long run as capital per worker rises thus causing employment to also recover in the long run.
- Export-oriented industries such as agriculture and mining expand as more of their output is sold overseas (Fig. 11.13). Nevertheless, as the mining sector is a capital-intensive sector its expansion in output is dampened by the fall in rates of return. The wholesale and retail trade industry benefits strongly from the tariff removal as more of these services are required to facilitate the sales of non-services commodities. Import-competing industries such as those in the manufacturing sector contract due to the substitution effects of the tariff removal on merchandise goods.

The results of Simulation 2 (with the new Armington elasticities) are shown as dashed lines in Figs. 11.10, 11.11, 11.12, and 11.13. We see that the results are sensitive to the new elasticities. Although the pattern of effects is similar in both simulations, the magnitude of results is different. At the macro level, the absolute deviations in real variables are higher in Simulation 1 than in Simulation 2. As indicated above, there has been a strong decline in the domestic market share of

Australian import-competing goods over the last two decades. This change in market structure alters the way consumers respond to the relative price of domestic and imported products. The new estimates of Armington elasticities reveal that consumers are less responsive to recent changes in the relative price of domestic and imported goods as indicated by a lower average of the new elasticities (1.16) relative to the old (1.54). Consequently, this generates smaller responses in quantity variables in Simulation 2. At the sectoral level, a noticeable result is the output deviation for manufacturing. Simulation 1 has a bigger initial response to the tariff removal relative to Simulation 2. That is, the old elasticities generate a larger and longer reduction in output while the new elasticities generate a smaller and temporary fall in output. This reflects the lower substitution possibilities. There is also a substantial difference in the output of mining. In the short run, Simulation 1 shows a larger increase in its output relative to Simulation 2. In the long run, the output gain in Simulation 1 is enough to outweigh the dampening effect on output of lower rates of return, whereas this is not the case for Simulation 2 where mining contracts due to the larger long-run fall in the rate of return.

11.16 Sources

Much of the content in the first half of the chapter draw heavily on Clements et al. (2022). Sections 11.9–11.12 include material from Mariano et al. (2024) and Clements et al. (2021). Sections 11.13–11.15 draw together results from the above three papers.

References

Alaouze CM, Marsden JS, Zeitsch J (1977) Estimates of the elasticity of substitution between imported and domestically produced commodities at the four digit ASIC level. IMPACT project, Industries Assistance Commission, Working paper no. 0-11, Melbourne, January

Armington PS (1969) The geographic pattern of trade and the effects of price changes. IMF Staff Papers XVI, pp 176–199

Atalay E (2017) How important are sectoral shocks? Am Econ J Macroecon 9:254–280

Barten AP (1964) Consumer demand functions under conditions of almost additive preferences. Econometrica 32:1–38

Bruno M (1984) Raw materials, profits, and the productivity slowdown. Q J Econ 99:1–30

Clements KW, Mariano MJM, Verikios G (2021) Foreign-domestic substitution, import penetration, and CGE modelling. Appl Econ 53:209–231

Clements KW, Mariano MJM, Verikios G (2022) Expenditure patterns, heterogeneity and long-term structural change. Econ Model:113

Clements KW, Si J (2017) Notes on the pattern of OECD consumption. Unpublished working paper, UWA Business School

Clements KW, Si J (2018) Engel's law, diet diversity and the quality of food consumption. Am J Agric Econ 100:1–22

Frisch R (1959) A complete scheme for computing all direct and cross demand elasticities in a model with many sectors. Econometrica 27:177–196

Ho M, Britz W, Delzeit R, Leblanc F, Roson R, Schuenemann F, Weitzel M (2020) Modelling consumption and constructing long-term baselines in final demand. J Glob Econ Anal 5:63–108

Howe H (1975) Development of the extended linear expenditure system from simple saving assumptions. Eur Econ Rev 6:305–310

Lluch C (1973) The extended linear expenditure system. Eur Econ Rev 4:21–32

Lluch C, Powell AA, Williams RA (1977) Patterns in household demand and saving. Oxford University Press, Oxford

Mariano MJM, Verikios G, Clements KW (2024) Are input-output coefficients really fixed? Appl Econ:1–24

Pollak RA, Wales TJ (1978) Estimation of complete demand systems from household budget data: the linear and quadratic expenditure systems. Am Econ Rev 68:348–359

Powell AA (1973) Estimation of Lluch's extended linear expenditure system from cross-sectional data. Aust J Stat 15:111–117

Selvanathan EA, Selvanathan S, Clements KW (2024) Estimating the elasticity of substitution: an index number approach. J Int Trade Econ Dev. Forthcoming

Stone R (1954) Linear expenditure systems and demand analysis: an application to the pattern of British demand. Econ J 64:511–527

Theil H (1965) The information approach to demand analysis. Econometrica 33:67–87

Verikios G, Hanslow K, Mariano MJM, Clements KW (2021) Understanding the Australian economy: a computable general equilibrium model with updated data and parameters. Department of Accounting, Finance and Economics, Discussion Paper Series 2021-06, Griffith University

World Bank (2015) 2011 International comparison program results. Available online at https://www.worldbank.org/en/programs/icp/brief/reports#2017

GPSR Compliance

The European Union's (EU) General Product Safety Regulation (GPSR) is a set of rules that requires consumer products to be safe and our obligations to ensure this.

If you have any concerns about our products, you can contact us on ProductSafety@springernature.com

In case Publisher is established outside the EU, the EU authorized representative is:

Springer Nature Customer Service Center GmbH
Europaplatz 3
69115 Heidelberg, Germany

Batch number: 10703869

Printed by Printforce, the Netherlands